THE LIFE OF

Lady Mary Wortley Montagu

Lady Mary Pierrepont

From a painting by Charles Jervas [1710]

THE LIFE OF

Lady Mary Wortley Montagu

by

ROBERT HALSBAND *,1914 -*

OXFORD

At the Clarendon Press

1956

Oxford University Press, Amen House, London E.C.4

GLASGOW NEW YORK TORONTO MELBOURNE WELLINGTON
BOMBAY CALCUTTA MACRAS KARACHI
CAPE TOWN IBADAN NAIROBI ACCRA SINGAPORE

PRINTED IN GREAT BRITAIN

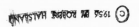

PREFACE

LADY MARY WORTLEY MONTAGU's name is sometimes confused with that of her young cousin-by-marriage, the blue-stocking Elizabeth Montagu. Although uncommonly learned, Lady Mary disdained such a reputation, thinking of herself as an aristocratic lady and a *bel esprit*; she began her literary career as the daughter of a duke, and ended it as the mother-in-law of a prime minister. But her many-faceted career was far from monotonous: she scribbled witty and scandalous verse, she bravely accompanied her husband on his embassy to Turkey, she brought back and popularized smallpox inoculation, she was first adored and then bitterly attacked by the greatest poet of the day, she patronized worthy writers and plain hacks, she published anonymous essays on feminist and political topics, and then, most enigmatically, she left England to spend the last two decades of her life on the Continent.

Her most substantial fame, however, came after her death, when her brilliant Turkish Embassy letters were published, and won the admiration of readers as diverse as Johnson, Gibbon, Walpole, and Voltaire. Still later, her reputation was strengthened by the publication of her private letters, particularly the ones to her sister Lady Mar, with their cynical picture of London high life, and the ones to her daughter Lady Bute, with their philosophical and literary ruminations. As a letter writer she easily took her place among other eighteenth-century masters of that form. Few anthologies of great letters omit specimens of her effortless art; and hardly any social history of her period fails to quote her pungent comments on manners and morals. Yet it is curious that so fascinating and omnipresent a figure should have received scant attention from scholars. Her letters have not been edited since W. Moy Thomas's incomplete 1861 edition; and the only thorough biography, by 'George Paston' [Emily Morse Symonds] in 1907, relies on superficial printed sources and the Wortley Manuscripts.

There have thus remained important gaps and unsolved mysteries in the record of Lady Mary's long, full life. Editors and biographers have tried in vain to explain why she retired to Italy at the age of fifty. Through a new series of her unpublished letters I have been able to reconstruct that episode in detail; it makes a story of oddly varied intrigues. Later in her retirement she maintained a baffling friendship for ten years with an Italian nobleman, which I have tried to clarify by means of her own affidavit. (This document first came to light one hundred years ago, but was 'mislaid' and never published.) In untangling the legal intricacies of her custody of Lady Mar, I have been fortunate enough to turn up new family letters and documents. The full history of Wortley's embassy to Turkey I have pieced together from dispatches and letters in diplomatic archives. In many other puzzling matters, including her marriage, her friendship with Pope, her literary entanglements, and her relations with her children, I have found new fragments to fill in the complicated mosaic of her life.

Any biographer must, consciously or not, take into account the current reputation of his subject. Lady Mary's reputation today is usually derived from the writings of Pope and Walpole, both of whom describe her most vividly as a dissolute and profligate woman. To what extent this is true can best be judged not by their evidence—particularly when we remember that Pope bent his genius to writing effective satire and that Walpole often relied on casual gossip—but by the documented facts. These can be read in the following pages. If the reader feels that I have not sufficiently 'interpreted' Lady Mary's character and personality, I can only plead that in the past she has so often been interpreted on insufficient, biased, or superficial grounds that it seemed to me most important to set down what facts I could discover; from these the reader can draw his own conclusions. A simple, consistent portrait would not represent her as she was—complex, versatile, and changeable, responding with bewildering energy to the constantly shifting pattern of her life.

A final, personal remark. During the years I have spent gathering material for this book I have almost without exception been welcomed and shown every courteous assistance. My very warm gratitude is inadequately expressed in the acknowledgements.

R. H.

Katonah, New York
June 1956

ACKNOWLEDGEMENTS

For the use of unpublished manuscript materials: Archives d'Avignon (Palais des Papes), Marquess of Bath, Henry W. and Albert A. Berg Collection of the New York Public Library, Jonkherr Frans Teding van Berkhout, Rev. P. B. G. Binnal, Bodleian Library, Theodora Marchioness of Bristol, Archivio di Stato (Brescia), British Museum, Marquess of Bute, Duke of Devonshire, Earl of Haddington, Major J. R. Hanbury, Earl of Harrowby, Henry E. Huntington Library, Mr. and Mrs. Donald F. Hyde, Mr. W. S. Lewis, Earl of Mar and Kellie, Ministère des Affaires Étrangères (Paris), Pierpont Morgan Library, Sir John Murray, National Library of Scotland, Northwestern University Library, University of Nottingham, Mr. James M. Osborn, Duke of Portland, Principal Probate Registry (Somerset House), Princeton University Library, Public Record Office (London), Royal Society, Royal College of Physicians, John Rylands Library, Society of Antiquaries, St. George's Church (Hanover Square), Duke of Sutherland, University of Sydney, Major-General Sir Eustace F. Tickell, Municipal Library of Treviso (Italy), Church of St. Mary the Virgin (Twickenham), Archivio di Stato (Venice), Elfreda Countess of Wharncliffe.

For the use of books and photographs: libraries listed above, Columbia University Library, Library of Congress, Harvard University Library, National Portrait Gallery, Newberry Library, New York Academy of Medicine, New York Public Library, Scottish National Portrait Gallery, Yale University Library, Victoria and Albert Museum.

For assistance of various kinds: Mr. G. K. Adams, Dott. Rolando Anzilotti, Miss Catherine Armet, Mr. R. L. Atkinson (Public Record Office), Miss Phyllis Biscoe (English Speaking Union), Professor Rae Blanchard, Mr. M. G. Brock, Professor John Butt, Major S. V. Christie-Miller, Mr. W. D. Clark, Mr. A. F. Clunie (J. C. Brodie, W.S.), Professor James L. Clifford, Miss Dorothy Coates, Miss W. D. Coates (National Register of Archives), Dr. J. C. Corson (University of Edinburgh Library), Professor T. M. Cranfill, Hon. David Erskine, Mr. G. E. Flack, Miss Margaret Franklin, Mrs. Ruth Graydon, Professor Allen T. Hazen, Mr. Rennie Hoare, Mr. M. J. C. Hodgart, Professor John C. Hodges,

Mr. R. G. Howarth, Mr. Bernhard Knollenberg, Dr. George L. Lam, Mr. J. P. Lamb (Sheffield City Libraries), Professor Louis Landa, Mr. William Le Fanu (Royal College of Surgeons), Sir Shane Leslie, Professor Kathleen M. Lynch, Mr. C. T. McInnis (General Register House, Edinburgh), Mr. D. Y. Miller (Twickenham Borough Library), Mr. John Grey Murray, Mr. Francis Needham, Duchess of Newcastle, Miss M. Moyca Newell, Professor Henry Pettit, Dr. J. H. Plumb, Professor Moody E. Prior, Miss Virginia Rice, Professor J. F. C. Richards, Professor R. W. Rogers, Mr. Romney Sedgwick, Professor George Sherburn, Professor D. Nichol Smith, Dr. Warren H. Smith, Dr. Peter Smithers, Professor W. T. Starr, Professor R. P. Stearns, Dr. F. Taylor, Professor Angelo Tursi, Mr. Richard Webster (British Council), Mrs. A. Frank van Westrienen, Sir Thomas A. W. White, Colonel C. H. Wilkinson, Sir Harold Williams, Mr. R. M. Wilson, Mr. David Woolley, Professor Bunker Wright.

For extraordinary and unflagging kindness: Lord Harrowby, custodian of the Harrowby Manuscripts; for permission to enjoy leaves of absence from my teaching duties at Hunter College: President George N. Shuster and the late Professor Marjorie Anderson; and for her help, encouragement, and patience: my wife, Dr. R. A. N. Weil, to whom I dedicate this book.

CONTENTS

LIST OF PLATES

NOTES

ALL dates in England before 1752 are given in Old Style (o.s.), and on the Continent in New Style (N.S.), eleven days later. After my first citation of a book, I give only author and short title. All references to Lady Mary's letters, essays, and verse, unless otherwise cited, come from her *Letters and Works*, ed. Lord Wharncliffe, 3rd ed. rev. by W. Moy Thomas (1861), and are given only by volume and page numbers. (Other main editions: 1803, ed. James Dallaway; 1837, ed. Lord Wharncliffe.) Quotations from manuscript are normalized in spelling, capitalization, and punctuation.

ABBREVIATIONS AND
COLLECTIONS

Ad:	Admiralty Records, Public Record Office, London.
Add. MS:	Additional Manuscripts, British Museum.
Bagshawe MS:	Bagshawe Muniments in the John Rylands Library, Manchester.
BM:	British Museum.
Bod. MS:	Bodleian Library, Oxford.
Bristol MS:	Ickworth Park, Suffolk; owned by Theodora, Marchioness of Bristol.
Bute MS:	Mount Stuart, Isle of Bute; owned by the Marquess of Bute.
CB:	MS Commonplace Book; formerly a Wortley MS; now in the Fisher Library, University of Sydney, Australia.
DNB:	*Dictionary of National Biography.*
Eg.:	Egerton Manuscripts, British Museum.
Finch MS:	On deposit at the Historical Manuscripts Commission; owned by Major J. R. Hanbury.
Harley MS:	On deposit in the British Museum; owned by the Duke of Portland.
Harrowby MS:	Sandon Hall, Stafford; owned by the Earl of Harrowby.
HMC:	Historical Manuscripts Commissions Reports.
Huntington Libr. MS:	The Henry E. Huntington Library, San Marino, California.
M:	Lady Mary (Pierrepont) Wortley Montagu.
Manvers MS:	Owned by the University of Nottingham.

Mar and Kellie MS: Alloa House, Clackmannanshire; owned by the Earl of Mar and Kellie.

Morgan Libr. MS: The Pierpont Morgan Library, New York City.

MS: Manuscript *or* Manuscripts.

Murray MS: Owned by Sir John Murray.

Paston: George Paston [Emily Morse Symonds], *Lady Mary Wortley Montagu and Her Times*, 2nd ed. (1907).

Pope

    Corr.:   *Correspondence*, ed. George Sherburn (1956).

    Elwin and Courthope: *Works*, ed. Whitwell Elwin and W. J. Courthope (1871–89).

    Twickenham: The Twickenham Edition of the Poems. II, *The Rape of the Lock*, ed. G. Tillotson (1940); III, ii, *Epistles to Several Persons*, ed. F. W. Bateson (1951); IV, *Imitations of Horace*, ed. John Butt (1946); V, *The Dunciad*, ed. J. Sutherland (1943); VI, *Minor Poems*, ed. N. Ault and J. Butt (1954).

PRO: Public Record Office, London.

SP: State Papers, Public Record Office.

Spence: Joseph Spence, *Anecdotes, Observations, and Characters, of Books and Men*, ed. S. W. Singer (1820).

Stuart: Lady Louisa Stuart, 'Introductory Anecdotes', in vol. i of M's *Letters and Works* (1861).

Tickell MS: Owned by Major-General Sir Eustace F. Tickell.

W: Wortley (or Edward Wortley Montagu).

W MS: Wortley Manuscripts (vols. i–viii are Harrowby MS vols. 74–81).

Walpole, *Corr.*: Horace Walpole's *Correspondence*, ed. W. S. Lewis and others (1937–).

Wharncliffe MS: Wharncliffe Muniments on deposit in the Sheffield Central Library; owned by the Earl of Wharncliffe.

I. *Childhood and Maiden Days*

(1689–1708)

TODAY Covent Garden is the fragrant centre of London's wholesale fruit and vegetable market, though the Piazza and St. Paul's Church (designed by Inigo Jones) remain to hint its former elegance. At the end of the seventeenth century, when it was a fashionable living quarter, a christening was entered in the church registry under the date of 26 May 1689: 'Mary daughter of Evelyn Peirpont Esq. by the Lady Mary his wife.'[1] The young parents, who had been married for two years, probably rented lodgings in the parish. The same year his first child was born, Evelyn Pierrepont (as his name was properly spelled) was elected to Parliament for East Retford in Nottinghamshire, and took his seat with the Whigs.

Although born the youngest son of Elizabeth Pierrepont, he looked forward to inheriting a substantial estate from her. His grandfather Sir John Evelyn had died in 1684 leaving his Wiltshire estates to his daughter with instructions that she pass them on to her youngest son should he prove obedient and dutiful.[2] His father, Robert Pierrepont, grandson of the first Earl of Kingston, died in 1669, and so the earldom passed to the eldest of the three Pierrepont sons. With the death of the eldest at an early age in 1682, it passed to the second son. When he too died, in 1690, Evelyn Pierrepont unexpectedly found himself Earl of Kingston.[3] His infant daughter was henceforth entitled to be called Lady Mary Pierrepont.

On her mother's side she was descended from another aristocratic family. Lady Mary Fielding was the only daughter of the

---

[1] *Reg. of St. Paul's Church, Covent Garden*, ed. W. R. Hunt (1906), i. 79.
[2] R. C. Hoare, *Hist. of Mod. Wiltshire* (1837), 23. Date corrected from tombstone in Chantry Chapel, West Dean.
[3] G. E. Cokayne and V. Gibbs, *Complete Peerage* (1910–40), *sub* Kingston.

third Earl of Denbigh. She was twenty-one when she bore her daughter Mary, and three other children followed: two girls, Frances and Evelyn, and finally a son William in 1692. Almost nothing else is known of her brief life; even the year of her death, 1693, is not definitely recorded.[1] In 1697 her remains were buried in the vault of her husband's family at Holme Pierrepont, near Nottingham.[2]

As a girl Lady Mary described her feelings toward her mother and father in an untitled 'autobiography', highly coloured after the fashion of French romances. 'I am going to write a history so uncommon', she began, 'that in how plain a manner so ever I relate it, it will have the air of a romance, though there shall not be a syllable feigned in it except that of the names, which I cannot resolve to set down at length.' Then, writing of herself in the third person, she continued: 'Her first misfortune happened in a time of life when she could not be sensible of it, though she was sufficiently so in the course of it; I mean the death of a noble Mother, whose virtue and good sense might have supported and instructed her youth, which was left to the care of a young Father, who, tho' naturally an honest man, was abandoned to his pleasures, and (like most of those of his quality) did not think himself obliged to be very attentive to his children's education.'[3] This self-pity remained vivid in her mind; as an old lady she sobbed over Samuel Richardson's novel, finding in his picture of the handsome, self-indulgent Sir Thomas Grandison and his virtuous, mistreated Lady what she had heard of her mother and seen of her father.[4] To a more impartial observer than Lady Mary, her father was merely 'a very fine Gentleman, of good Sense, well bred, and a Lover of the Ladies'.[5]

His children spent their early years under the care of his mother Elizabeth Pierrepont on the manor of West Dean, near Salisbury. The large, square Jacobean manor house stood in a

---

[1] Lady Louisa Stuart to Walter Scott, 4 Dec. 1820, Nat. Libr. of Scotl., MS 867, f. 94; Stuart, 51.

[2] *DNB* (*sub* Pierrepont, Evelyn); Cokayne (*sub* Kingston).

[3] W MS, vii. 196. She probably wrote it in 1711. Most of it is printed in Paston, 4 ff.

[4] To Lady Bute, 22 Sept. 1755, ii. 285; *Sir Charles Grandison*, Letter XVII.

[5] *Mem. of the Secret Services of John Macky* [1705], Roxburgh Club Pub. (1895).

grove of elm trees with a succession of terraces dropping away into formal gardens facing west. Its park was well timbered, and in the Dutch manner cut by canals fed from a large fish pond over which hung a bank of dark yew.[1] In this setting Lady Mary passed the first eight years of her life.

One activity of her childhood stayed in her memory until the end of her days: her 'childish desire of catching the setting sun, which I can remember running very hard to do: a fine thing truly if it could be caught; but experience soon shows it to be impossible'.[2] With the advantage of hindsight, one may read great significance in the picture of the child running across the meadow to catch hold of the great golden ball of fire sinking on the horizon. The pursuit of the unattainable and the realization of its impossibility was one of the recurring patterns of her long, varied life.

The grandmother with whom she lived stands out as an energetic, forceful woman. She impressed her cousin John Evelyn the diarist with her 'prodigious memory' and her qualities as 'a most excellent and prudent lady'.[3] In taking care of her grandchildren she was assisted by her daughter, who was married to Viscount Cheyne, and by two nurses and a Mrs. Dupont (probably a French governess)—to whom she left bequests. Her will, drawn up in 1698 (a half year before her death), displays her attitude toward the nine-year-old Lady Mary. She appointed Lord Kingston main legatee, and did not mention his son, presumably because he would inherit the father's estates and title. Of her three granddaughters, she left the great sum of £12,000 to Evelyn, the youngest, and £1,000 to Frances; but nothing to Mary. (If Evelyn were to die before marriage, her legacy was to be divided between the other two girls if they married with their father's and aunt's permission.)[4] Why Lady Mary was thus cut off by her grandmother remains unaccountable. Her relations with her maternal grandmother are less mysterious. From her earliest age she wrote to the Dowager Lady Denbigh (actually her step-grandmother), and retained a warm recollection of her.[5]

---

[1] Edith Olivier, *Wiltshire* (1951), 254–5.
[2] To Lady Bute, 7 July 1757, ii. 309.
[3] *Diary and Corr.* ed. W. Bray (1898), i. 260; ii. 364.
[4] Copy of her will, 2 Aug. 1698, MS Eg. 3517, ff. 153–65.
[5] To Lady Bute, Sept. 1748, 6 Mar. 1753, ii. 171, 231.

In spite of her complaints of her father's neglect, Lady Mary later loved to relate how proudly he had exhibited her wit and beauty when she was not yet eight years old. He belonged to the newly formed Kit-Cat Club, a group of fashionable men devoted to the Whig cause and Hanoverian Succession. At one of their meetings when they wished to elect a beauty as their toast for the year, Lord Kingston nominated Lady Mary; and when the other Club members objected to judging a candidate they had never seen, he ordered the girl to be finely dressed and brought to the tavern. There she was unanimously voted the reigning beauty. In this company 'she went from the lap of one poet, or patriot, or statesman, to the arms of another, was feasted with sweetmeats, overwhelmed with caresses, and, what perhaps already pleased her better than either, heard her wit and beauty loudly extolled on every side. Pleasure, she said, was too poor a word to express her sensations; they amounted to ecstasy: never again, throughout her whole future life, did she pass so happy a day.'[1] If this charming episode is true, it illuminates her remark some years later: 'I came young into the hurry of the world.'[2]

Her childhood was not always filled with such rapture. By turns she was neglected and pampered by her father. With her brother and her sister Frances—her sister Evelyn lived with Lady Cheyne—she was left to the care of servants in her father's house on Arlington Street off Piccadilly or at Thoresby, the Pierrepont seat in Nottinghamshire. This imposing country house had been designed by William Talman in the Palladian style, with an entrance portico flanked by two columns and an ornamental balustrade along the top of the third story. Its design formed her taste for classical architecture. The grounds around the house were as splendidly laid out—with a canal three-quarters of a mile long, a lake covering 65 acres, and fountains and formal gardens in a vast pattern. Beyond these lay the deer park, and then Sherwood Forest with its venerable oaks.[3]

Within the house the actual rooms where she spent most of

---

[1] Related by Stuart (52–53), who often told the same anecdote to her friends (*Letters of Lady Louisa Stuart to Miss Louisa Clinton*, ed. James A. Home [1901], i. 254).

[2] M to W, 9 Apr. 1711, i. 186.

[3] Plans of house and park in Colin Campbell, *Vitruvius Britannicus* (1717–25).

her time can be reconstructed. The children's nursery had three bedsteads covered with 'blue printed stuff', a colour repeated in the window curtains. The spacious library was furnished with two large walnut tables lined with green cloth, twelve morocco leather chairs, and a step-ladder to reach the high shelves. When she looked up from her reading she could see hanging on the wall framed prints and two 'very fine pictures of philosophers' heads'.[1]

Her education was left to a governess who (in her later opinion) gave her 'one of the worst in the world' by filling her head with superstitious tales and false notions; but she supplied her own antidote with her 'passion for learning'.[2] In her father's well-furnished libraries she could read as much as she wished. By the time she was fourteen she had read a great number of books, as can be seen in the lists of titles and characters she jotted into a notebook. They include the plays of Beaumont and Fletcher, Dryden, Rowe, Lee, Otway, Congreve, Molière, Corneille; and stout romances in French and English, among them the *Grand Cyrus*, *Pharimond*, *Almahide*, and *Parthenissa*, the sort of books recommended by Jonathan Swift in his satirical directions for the education of young ladies 'to soften their nature, and make them tender-hearted, &c.'[3] So tender-hearted did she become that at fourteen she was utterly charmed with Prior's ballad of Henry and Emma, about an heiress eloping with a bandit-lover.[4]

Along with reading she began her writing career at an early age. In 1703 she copied her pieces into an album entitled 'Poems, Songs &c. Dedicated to the Fair Hands of the Beauteous Hermensilde by her most obedient Strephon', and composed a preface.

I Question not but here is very manny faults but if any reasonable Person considers 3 things they wou'd forgive them
    1 I am a Woman
    2 without any advantage of Education
    3 all these was writ at the age of 14.[5]

---

[1] Inventory of Thoresby, 1726, Manvers MS 4883.
[2] To Lady Bute, 6 Mar., 28 Jan. 1753, ii. 227, 229.
[3] 'Directions to Servants', ch. xvi.
[4] To Lady Bute, 23 Aug. 1755, ii. 281.
[5] W MS (Harrowby, vol. 250).

An ambitious, bookish girl is reflected in the collection. Stimulated by reading the popular epistolary romance *The Adventures of Lindamira*, which had been published in 1702, she imitated it in a series of five epistles (from Lindamira's friend Indamora), and added: 'I desire the reader would compare the two lives.' Her conventional romance of love, misunderstanding, and final reunion is remarkably skilful. The verse which follows, though imitative and clumsy, displays her varied attempts: Cavalier love lyrics, complimentary verse, several poems in praise of the country, and (inevitably) a poem on death as the great leveller.

Another collection of her juvenilia, compiled a year or two later and pompously entitled 'The Entire Works of Clarinda', reveals more of her developing mind and talent.[1] She copied in more polished form the verse and romance from her earlier album. One new piece is a prose allegory mixed with verse telling of Strephon's adventures in quest of true love. First he finds a castle called Marriage, where Discord, Strife, and Uneasiness live together. 'Love and marriage are irreconcilable enemies', declares the youthful author, who had obviously learned from Restoration comedy. Strephon finds the palace of True Love ruined and uninhabited. Resolved to shun Love, he dallies in the Wood of Coquetry with two nymphs. They discover his duplicity and ask him to choose between them; but since he cannot bear to give up either he gives up both and leaves. That is how Lady Mary ends her tale, a curious mixture of romantic emotionalism and cynical rationalism—the two contrasting sides of her own nature.

The collection contains a new group of her poems, imitations of Latin poets—several of Ovid's epistles, an episode from his *Metamorphoses* (the death of Adonis), and an imitation of Virgil's tenth eclogue. She could have gathered these from English or French translations, but she had by now probably begun to read Latin, and thus advanced into studies which would later enable her to collaborate and compete with men of letters. In her 'autobiography' she told how 'without considering the toilsome task she undertook, she began to learn herself the Latin grammar, and with the help of an uncommon memory and indefatigable labour, made herself so far mistress

[1] W MS (Harrowby, vol. 251).

of that language as to be able to understand almost any author....
Her Father, though no scholar himself, was flattered with a
pleasure in the progress she made. . . .'[1] Many years later she
more specifically explained that her admiration for the *Metamorphoses* had induced her to study Latin.[2] Evading her
governess, she secretly got hold of a Latin dictionary and grammar, and hid in the library every morning from ten to two and
every afternoon from four to eight. By this assiduous study for
two years, from the age of thirteen, she learned the language as
well as most men.[3] She tended to be a blue-stocking proud of
her erudition, though she later regarded a reputation of learning
as a misfortune in a woman. Her studious disposition, she
thought, distinguished her from other girls her age. At fifteen
one of her great desires was to found an English monastery for
ladies; and had she possessed an independent fortune she would
have carried out the project and elected herself lady abbess.[4] In
this idea she was probably influenced by the feminist writings
of Mary Astell and Daniel Defoe.

As she grew out of her teens she applied herself to polite
studies more suited to her sex and social position. Her father
arranged for her to study Italian; and he engaged a master to
teach her drawing, but she practised it so eagerly that it
weakened her eyes, and the master was dismissed.[5] After the
season in town, when she moved to Thoresby, she could spend
more time reading and writing in the library. She had household
duties as well, for she did the honours of the house for her
widowed father, who in 1706 had been elevated in the peerage
to Marquess of Dorchester. As a leading Whig politician he
maintained a hospitable table, and to Lady Mary fell the task
of meat-carving, an art requiring skill, strength, and tact in
those days of great dinners and prodigious meat-joints. In order
to learn it she took lessons three times a week from a carving
master. Then on the days when she presided over the table she
ate her own dinner earlier in order to perform without distraction.[6]

---

[1] Paston, 4.   [2] Spence, 232.
[3] Spence to his mother, 25 Feb. 1741 (based on his conversations with Lady
Mary), MS Eg. 2234, f. 247.
[4] To Sir James Steuart, 19 July 1759, ii. 363; to Lady Bute, 20 Oct. 1755,
ii. 291.   [5] To Lady Bute, 28 Jan. 1753, ii. 228.
[6] Stuart, 56.

Her father's friends whom she frequently met included Joseph Addison, Richard Steele, William Congreve, already retired as a playwright, and Dr. Samuel Garth, the physician and wit.[1] They encouraged her precocious learning, directly or by their example; Congreve in particular proved useful after he discovered she studied Latin.[2] In these men literature and politics were joined. 'I was educated in the principles of Old Whiggism', she remarked many years later, adding that many of the Kit-Cat Club members were 'dupes to their leaders'—who included her own father.[3] She herself always remained firmly attached to the Whig principles she had learned from him and his friends.

In London during the winter season she was busy with the customary round of social activities. One of her friends was Anne Wortley, daughter of the Honourable Sidney Wortley. (He was the second son of Admiral Montagu, first Earl of Sandwich, and had taken the name of Wortley on marrying an heiress of that name, who was the ward of his father.)[4] The friendship between the two girls somehow led to Lady Mary's meeting Anne's brother Edward Wortley. In her 'autobiography' Lady Mary sketched their meeting as part of a romantic intrigue: at a card party she wins his interest away from a young heiress by discoursing brilliantly about a new play, and then when the conversation turns to poetry she astonishes him further by revealing herself well read in the classics too.[5] Or perhaps, according to her family tradition, when he met her one day among his sister's friends he was charmed by her witty intelligence, and especially by her solid understanding of Latin. On her saying that she had not read Quintus Curtius (the historian of Alexander's campaign in Asia Minor), he sent her a superb edition with a flattering inscription in verse.[6] In either case, the sombre Mr. Wortley found himself attracted to the pretty girl who unexpectedly showed an intellectual bent.

---

[1] Spence, 232.   [2] Spence on p. 7, n. 3 above.
[3] CB MS, f. 9 (entry probably written in the 1750's).
[4] Joseph Hunter, *South Yorkshire* (1831), ii. 319. Hence his son Edward was called Wortley or Montagu or Wortley Montagu.   [5] Paston, 7–8.
[6] Stuart, 60. The verse survives as copied by Lady Mary into one of her albums (Harrowby, vol. 255). She told Spence that Wortley had first given her the idea of studying Latin (p. 7, n. 3 above), but this seems unlikely.

He was a severely handsome man, eleven years older than she, and by the time they met he could boast of an impressive career. After passing through Westminster School under the famous Dr. Busby, he had matriculated at Trinity College, Cambridge, though he did not stay for a degree. Instead he entered the Middle Temple to study law, and was called to the bar in 1699.[1] From 1700 to 1703 he travelled on the Continent, part of the time with Addison, who became his intimate friend. In 1705 he was elected to Parliament for the Borough of Huntingdon, a seat controlled by his cousin Lord Sandwich.[2] He distinguished himself with a 'fine speech' in February 1708 in favour of a bill to naturalize French Protestants, and a month later spoke so 'incomparably well' on another bill that he was put into the Speaker's chair.[3] His friend Steele lavishly praised his learning, and Addison valued his conversation more than any other man's.[4] As a student of the classics, a friend of prominent literary men, and a rising Member of Parliament, Wortley easily impressed Lady Mary. Their friendship remained formal, with his sister as intermediary. In her 'autobiography' Lady Mary claimed to have found pleasure in his company only when he directed her in choosing books or explained a passage in Virgil or Horace. She still planned a life of retirement and study, and pretended to look on marriage as a form of servitude.[5]

For the winter season of 1708, when she was nineteen, she again came up to London. Her father generously allowed her £200 a year, and occasionally bought fans as presents for her and her sisters.[6] Although she was a pretty girl of prominent family she did not attract the attention of poets who celebrated the young town beauties, as her friend Anne Wortley did.[7] If she made no impression on flattering versifiers, she at least made her mark on Wortley.

[1] H. A. C. Sturgess, *Reg. of Admissions to the Middle Temple* (1949), i. 233.
[2] Edward Porritt, *Unreformed House of Commons* (1909), i. 320.
[3] Richard Chandler, *Hist. and Proceedings of the House of Commons*, iv. (1742), 113; Addison to Lord Manchester, 12 Mar. 1708, *Letters*, ed. Walter Graham (1941), 101.
[4] Dedication to the *Tatler*, vol. ii (1710); Addison to Wortley, 1 May 1708, *Letters*, 112.
[5] Paston, 21.
[6] 1 Feb., 17 Apr. 1712, Dorchester's account book, Manvers MS 4265.
[7] *The British Court: A Poem* (1707), 10–11: *The Mall: or, The Reigning Beauties* (1709), 12; *St. James's Park: A Satyr* (1709), 14.

II. *The Courtship*

(1709–12)

THE earliest correspondence between Lady Mary and Wortley, like their friendship, came through his younger sister Anne. In London the two girls frequently met at social functions and exchanged visits, Lord Dorchester's house in St. James's being close to the Wortley lodgings on Great Queen Street. In the country, where they were separated by thirty miles of muddy roads, they visited each other only rarely, though at least once Anne was accompanied to Thoresby by her brother.[1] Their letters, filled with trivial gossip and effusive compliments, served to bridge the distance. Before long Lady Mary knew that someone else directed her friend's pen. When she boasted of studying only dictionaries and grammars, Anne replied that she had read the letter to a Cambridge doctor, and he insisted that her fresh wit was the better for not being encumbered with pedantic learning. 'Take back the beauty and wit you bestow upon me', protested Lady Mary; all she desired, besides a comfortable mediocrity, were sincerity, constancy, and plain dealing.[2] At the beginning of September 1709, when Anne urged her to send Latin queries because she would soon be alone, Lady Mary sent instead her objection to the hint that she had favoured another man at the Nottingham races: 'To be capable of preferring the despicable wretch you mention to Mr. Wortley, is as ridiculous, if not as criminal, as forsaking the Deity to worship a calf.'[3] Knowing that Wortley himself would read this, she was obviously not discouraging him.

By November she was again at her father's house on Arlington Street.[4] Her friend Anne's sudden death distressed her, but

---

[1] From Anne Wortley, 20 Aug. 1709, i. 164.
[2] 21 Aug. 1709, i. 167.
[3] i. 170–1; 5 Sept. 1709, i. 171.   [4] To Mrs. Hewet, Nov. 1709, i. 147–8.

she often met Wortley at Court and at friends' houses, and conversed with him. She could speak out more resolutely in writing, and on 28 March 1710 she sent him the very first letter she had ever addressed to a man. He had sent her several issues of the *Tatler*, one of them satirizing women's vanities, and she challenged such wrong notions. As to her own tastes, she insisted that she preferred a life of simplicity to one of great wealth and rank. 'If I am your wife', a phrase in her letter, clearly announces the topic of their thoughts and conversations.[1]

She continued to write to him without her father's permission. It became more difficult when her family moved to their villa at Acton, at that time a pleasant suburban village famous for its mineral springs. It was a hateful house to Lady Mary and her sister, 'dull and disagreeable', without even a library.[2] A few weeks later when she fell ill of the measles she asked her maid to write Wortley to tell him of it. A flurry of misunderstanding ensued. The frightened lover hurried to Acton, and left his name. Then he sent her a distraught note revealing his jealous love. 'I should be overjoyed to hear your Beauty is very much impaired, could I be pleased with anything that would give you displeasure, for it would lessen the number of Admirers.'[3] Not at all grateful, she scolded him for his indiscretion, which had put her in a 'pretty pickle'; and she dismissed him with: 'Forgive and forget me.' In his patient reply he defended himself, and cautiously hinted that he would deal with her father if he were sure they could be happy together.[4] His tentative proposal made her forget her irritation and launch into a full recital of her attitude toward marriage.

A courtship is frequently like other kinds of negotiations; the dealer will adjust his terms to the prevailing market. Lady Mary's terms may have been sincere, but they clearly encouraged Wortley. She denied that she was guided by emotions, which were too transitory: 'I can esteem, I can be a friend, but I don't know whether I can love.' After setting forth all her terms—including her deference to his superior sense—she warned him: 'Make no answer to this, if you can like me on my

[1] i. 172-3.
[2] Kingston to Dorchester, June 1710, Paston, 58; 'autobiog.', Paston, 28.
[3] 17 Apr. 1710, Paston, 39-40 (date from MS).
[4] Paston, 41-43. Her romanticized version in her 'autobiog.', Paston, 28-29.

own terms.' Her own terms were clearly the same as his. But his proposals must not be made to her, she again reminded him. He refused to be taken in by her modesty and boldness; her letter deferring to his sense proved that her own had no superior, and her terms displayed only her self-interest.[1] Before she received his defence, she again upbraided him for his indiscretion. She was to be sent 'into a frightful solitude instead of repairing to London, where my family is now persuaded I have behaved myself very ill. . . . Either think of me no more, or think in the way you ought.'[2]

Their correspondence endangered him as well. In one note endorsed: 'her being better in 1710, the consequence of its being known that I write to her', he warned her that if gossip of it reached one of his near relations he would not receive a 'conveyance' about to be made over to him.[3] Still, their notes continued to pass between Acton and London until, in the early summer of 1710, the suitor's reluctance was overcome. As described in Lady Mary's 'autobiography', a servant in her house found his letter, and carried it to her father. It put him 'in the utmost rage'. Wortley, however, flattered himself that she had given the letter to her father as 'an artifice to bring the affair to a proper conclusion'. The next day he called on her father with a formal proposal, and lawyers for both sides were appointed.[4] Whether this version is fiction or fact (it is probably a mixture), by some means Wortley made a formal proposal; and Lord Dorchester, not wishing his daughter to meddle, sent her away, not to Thoresby, which was too near Wharncliffe, but to West Dean in Wiltshire, where she had not been since her childhood.

Marriage at that time dealt more with finance than romance. It was 'a social and economic contract, designed to protect private property and male inheritance'.[5] Wortley was an eligible enough suitor, as heir to his father's ample estate and to the Earldom of Sandwich if his cousin Viscount Hinchingbroke

[1] M to W, 25 Apr., i. 174-5; W to M, 5 May 1710, Paston, 45-47.
[2] Paston, 43-44.
[3] W MS, i. 78-79. Perhaps meaning his uncle Charles Montagu's, who altered his will in Oct. 1709 to leave him £500 (W MS, vii. 120).
[4] Paston, 29-30.
[5] Rae Blanchard, 'Richard Steele and the Status of Women', *Studies in Philology*, xxvi (1929), 343.

had no sons. But Lord Dorchester firmly insisted on one condition in the marriage contract: that Wortley's estate be entailed on the first son born to him. This he refused to do, having calculated that £10,000 would be required immediately—a crushing burden on his estate, he carefully explained to Lady Mary.[1] For stubbornness he found his match in Lord Dorchester, who insisted he would not allow his grandson to be a beggar.[2]

To bolster his suit Wortley thought of publishing his views on marriage contracts in the *Tatler*. In the second volume of the paper, dedicated to Wortley, Steele praised his classical learning and delightful conversation, and added: 'I am very proud that there are some Things in these Papers which I know you will pardon'—a hint that Wortley occasionally gave him ideas for his essays. A week later, in the issue of 18 July, a specimen appeared. In this eloquent argument against mercenary marriages, one of the specific abuses is the bridegroom's assigning his estate without knowing whether he will be succeeded by a sot or a man of merit. As for the woman, she is set up as though at auction:

> Her first lover has ten to one against him. The very hour after he has opened his heart and his rent rolls he is made no other use of but to raise her price. . . . While the poor lover very innocently waits, till the plenipotentiaries at the inns of court have debated about the alliance, all the partisans of the lady throw difficulties in the way, till other offers come in; and the man who came first is not put in possession, until she has been refused by half the town.

These arguments did not persuade Lady Mary's proud father.

While she remained secluded at West Dean, her suitor found a way of maintaining their correspondence. On 28 July, when his negotiations had reached a definite impasse, he told her that because of his indisposition—mainly a loss of appetite—he would go to the Spa, the popular watering-place in Belgium. He refused to be moved by her warning that another suitor now dealt with her father.[3] The next day he dined with Steele. That uxorious husband apologized to his Dear Prue for not returning home because he had 'businesse of Consequence with

[1] 10 Aug. 1710, Paston, 62–64. W's notes and calculations on marriage settlements in W MS, vii. 258–65.

[2] Stuart, 61–62.

[3] Paston, 61–62 (date from MS).

Mr. Montague who goes out of Town tomorrow in order to take a Voyage'.[1] After a leisurely journey to Harwich, Wortley waited until his last day ashore to write to Lady Mary, lest her answer make him alter his plans. In his long turgid letter, lightened by some empty flattery, he asked her to write him in his absence.[2] He then sailed for the resort where he hoped to forget his tangled courtship and restore his appetite.

In the meantime she tried to accustom herself to dull country life in Wiltshire. She had expected 'quite a new world'; instead it was not at all agreeable, and only a few of her neighbours were tolerable. She spent most of her time with her books. Reading Italian poetry she tried to fill her imagination with romantic swains from Tasso and to forget the boorish country squires occupied with hunting and drinking.[3] For more serious study she translated Epictetus's *Enchiridion*, a handbook of stoic advice by the Greek philosopher. Using a Latin text she performed the task in one week, and sent it with a letter to Bishop Burnet, the Whig politician, who lived in Salisbury, close to West Dean. 'You have already forgiven me greater impertinences', she told him, 'and condescended yet further in giving me instructions, and bestowing some of your minutes in teaching me.' More interesting than her capable translation is her long letter on feminism. Women should be allowed an education beyond the superficial smattering which encourages vanity and impertinence. Then, lest she seem presumptuous, she assured the Bishop: 'I am not now arguing for an equality of the two sexes. I do not doubt God and nature have thrown us into an inferior rank; we are a lower part of the creation, we owe obedience and submission to the superior sex, and any woman who suffers her vanity and folly to deny this, rebels against the law of the Creator, and indisputable order of nature.'[4] Her suitor would have been pleased but not convinced by her pious sentiments.

Although he had instructed her how to direct her letters (to Steele or to his bookseller Godwin), he neither claimed them nor wrote to her. With ample time to brood she sent him six

---

[1] *Corr.* ed. Rae Blanchard (1941), 263.
[2] 10 Aug. 1710, Paston, 62–64.
[3] To Mrs. Hewet, 1710, i. 148, 149–51.
[4] 20 July 1710, ii. 2–4; to Lady Bute, 14 July 1758, ii. 325. Her translation with Burnet's corrections is a W MS [Harrowby, vol. 252].

letters during his two months abroad. 'I am torn with [a] variety of imaginations, and not one pleasing one', she confessed. 'I conjure you to write, I beg it of you, and promise to tease you no longer upon the least intimation of being troublesome. 'Tis impossible to express the pain I write in, when I neither know whether you'll receive my letter nor into whose hands it may fall.' Although unaware of her anxiety and humility (until his return), he himself had thought deeply about their vexing courtship, and endorsed his eventual reply: 'After travelling and seeing into her heart.'[1]

Before leaving London he had given Steele some pages of notes, and later endorsed them: 'This Tatler writ for the benefit of my fair benefactors.'[2] Steele issued this matrimonial propaganda in his essay of 12 September 1710, where Isaac Bickerstaff discusses mercenary marriages. To prove the absurdity of entailing estates, he ironically sets forth the typical marriage settlement: the suitor declares that 'in full and perfect health of body, and a sound mind, not knowing which of my children will prove better or worse, I give to my first-born, be he perverse, ungrateful, impious, or cruel, the lump and bulk of my estate ... hereby further confessing and covenanting, that I am from henceforth married, and dead in law'. As before, Lady Mary's father remained unpersuaded, even by such gracefully expounded arguments.

London during the summer of 1710 was being agitated by more important issues than the evils of marriage contracts. In the spring Henry Sacheverell, a High Church clergyman in favour of the Jacobite cause, had been tried for preaching a seditious sermon, and had been virtually acquitted. It was a sign that the Whig prosperity was about to ebb. The remaining Whig ministers were dismissed in September and Parliament dissolved. In the new election the Whigs were crushingly defeated. But the absent Wortley, again put up for Huntingdon, was re-elected on 5 October. He hurried home, and reached London by the 20th, when he spent the evening over a bottle of wine with Addison and Swift, both of whom were deeply involved in the political turmoil.[3] A month later the new Tory Parliament

---

[1] W MS, i. 232–3, 46–47.
[2] W MS, vii. 130–4.
[3] Swift, *Journal to Stella*, ed. Harold Williams (1948), 65.

met for its opening session. Wortley now had to fight on two
fronts—political and marital.

On 24 October he sat down to read four of Lady Mary's
letters kept for him by Steele. (The two others were delayed or
lost.) He read her familiar protestations—that she was obedient
to her father, modest in her requirements, and perfectly sincere
—and replied with a long ungracious answer before leaving for
Wharncliffe Lodge.[1] She waited a full week before answering
his tirade. In the exchange of monotonous, bickering letters that
followed, a new theme emerged. Wortley tried to discover her
father's exact financial terms, especially the size of her dowry.
She denied knowing it: 'People in my way are sold like slaves;
and I cannot tell what price my master will put on me.' Like a
cautious business man Wortley did not wish to commit himself
until he knew the price, and he again asked her.[2] He even calculated for her how her father and brother could raise her dowry
to £25,000, but then fearfully wondered whether his impertinence might raise the settlement demanded of himself.[3] It was
more than she could bear. 'I begin to be tired of my humility. . . .
You say you are not yet determined: let me determine for you,
and save you the trouble of writing again. Adieu for ever! make
no answer.'[4] Like a prima donna she made her farewells too
frequently to be convincing.

However equivocal his courtship, Wortley pursued his parliamentary activities among the Whig minority with admirable
vigour. On 12 December 1710 his Place Bill was put forward
for a second reading. It forbade any Member to accept a pension
from the Ministry—a political practise tantamount to bribery,
since the party in power could thus hold and augment its
adherents. To block action, the Tories introduced another bill,
to Wortley's disgust.[5] His bill passed the Commons but was
defeated in the House of Lords.[6] As a law it would have purified
much of the parliamentary corruption.

Always a staunch Whig herself, Lady Mary could not witness
her suitor's activity; she had been sent to Thoresby for the

[1] Paston, 69–72.
[2] M to W, 14 Nov., i. 178; W to M, 21 Nov. 1710, Paston, 77.
[3] W MS, i. 37–38.
[4] Nov. 1710, i. 178–9.
[5] Dunbar to J. Erskine, HMC *Mar and Kellie MSS* (1904), 485–6.
[6] G. N. Clark, *Later Stuarts. 1660–1714* (1949), 243, n. 2.

PLATE 2

Edward Wortley Montagu

From a painting by an unknown artist

Christmas holidays. While heavy frosts and snow kept her from
visiting her country friends she consoled herself with her studies
and writing. She sent letters in Italian and English to her friend
Miss Banks, who lived at Scofton on the other side of Sherwood
Forest, and in return received verses and the latest London
pamphlets.[1] When she returned to town in January (1711) she
wrote to her old nurse, addressed as 'Dear Nanny', to describe
how even women's dress was infected with politics.

'Tis divided into parties. All the High Church ladies affect to
wear heads in the imitation of steeples, and on their muffs roses. . . .
The Low Party (of which I declare my self) wear little low heads
and long ribands to their muffs. This [is] a full account of that
important business, dress, which is at present much talked of
against the birth night where everybody is endeavoring to out-
shine the other. The town is very full, and diversion more followed
than ever I knew it. I am invited to a ball tonight. . . .'[2]

In all the giddy freedom of London she could deal with her
rejected but persistent suitor.

''Tis so very dangerous for me to write to you,' she admitted,
'I tremble every time I do it.'[3] Safe channels for his letters were
her trusted servant Mrs. Dupont or a friend who lived at Lord
Loudoun's house on Pall Mall.[4] They also managed to meet
where their social life centred: at the Court Drawing-Room, the
theatre and opera, and the houses of aristocratic and political
families. On Sunday afternoons, after service at St. James's
Chapel, he sometimes led her downstairs, and snatched a few
words alone with her. He suggested other, less respectable
places—Colman's toyshop or Corticelli's warehouse.[5] But she
cautiously refused, fearing gossip would reach her father.

The safest rendezvous, friends' houses, raised complications.
Several ladies whom Wortley knew were not acquainted with
her; and several she knew, not with him. Of those whom both
knew, a few received her visits so rarely that her calling at
the same time as Wortley would arouse their suspicion. The
harassed lovers finally agreed to use the house of Lady Jekyll,

[1] Miss Banks to M [n.d.], Paston, 78.
[2] M to Mrs. Anne Justice [n.d.], Morgan Libr. MS.
[3] W MS, i. 205-6.
[4] 21 Mar., W MS, i. 201-2; Paston, 81-82 (MS end. 10 Feb.).
[5] Paston, 85-87.

wife of the Whig politician and sister of Lord Somers. At
Wortley's suggestion she called on Lady Jekyll, and found her
pleasant, and the house convenient and safe. But they still had
to be on guard lest their hostess become suspicious.[1] The other
lady at whose house they could frequently meet was an intimate
friend of Wortley's, and more tolerant if less fashionable. At
Mrs. Steele's on Bury Street, St. James's,[2] they could be completely free. She was not only a woman of high principles,
Wortley assured Lady Mary, but also 'simple' enough to be in
love with her husband. As each difficulty was smoothed, another
arose.[3] Which had precedence: Lady Mary's rank or Mrs.
Steele's age? Lady Mary submitted, and in the evening of 22
February made the first call. It embarrassed her, and on the
way home in their coach her sister Frances scolded her for mis-
conduct; but she continued to call on Mrs. Steele and to meet
Wortley, who had full liberty of the house while the Steeles
were out.[4]

Their meetings seemed only to sharpen their discords. As a
pretty girl of high spirits going about in society Lady Mary
easily indulged in friendships and flirtations with other men.
Wortley was deeply jealous, and fearful that flirtation was a
habit she would continue after marriage. He once accused her
of being acquainted with 'every man of fashion in town and
with several of 'em too much'; and another time, of having gone
somewhere against his orders and flirting with two men. She
sometimes tried to placate him: 'I obeyed your commands and
stayed at home yesterday. If I pleased you, it is giving myself
more pleasure than the opera could have done.'[5] He answered
with shrill accusations: 'Is it possible for you to remove the
strong suspicions which you know I have entertained with so
much reason? Can you convince me I shall have no more of
them? It is pretty clear to me you cannot.'[6] His specific accusations centred on a Mr. K., whom he had seen press close to her
in the Drawing-Room; and who had escorted her to the park,
operas, and assemblies, and had been among the small group
who serenaded her at Acton and then went to dance at a

[1] M to W, Paston, 81–82; Paston, 86 (date from MS); W MS, i. 205–6.
[2] Steele, *Corr.* 272.   [3] Paston, 87, 89.
[4] M to W, Paston, 91; W to M, 3 Mar. 1711, i. 182.
[5] W MS, i. 65–66, 94–95 (21 Mar. 1711), 201–2.
[6] 22 Mar., W MS, i. 39.

duchess's ball.[1] She bluntly denied having any affection for the attentive Mr. K., and tried to disarm his suspicions with a confession. 'Perhaps I have been indiscreet; I came young into the hurry of the world; a great innocence and an undesigning gaiety may possibly have been construed coquetry and a desire of being followed, though never meant by me.'[2] But she also had a native shrewdness that told her 'the best way to make [sure of] an old lover is certainly to engage to a new one'.[3]

In traditional fashion her admirers sent her their poetical effusions. Her wide reading in the English poets enabled her to recognize some of them as plagiaries.[4] A few of her favourites she copied into an album. Lord Castlecomer, a young Irish peer in Parliament on the Whig side of the House, sent her some verse to describe his suffering, and concluded with:

> It nought avails to treat me with disdain,
> I have a secret pleasure in my pain;
> I must adore, persist, and still pursue,
> It is my destiny, it is her due.

Another poetical admirer begged 'the Nymph that presides over the Medicinal Waters of Acton' to influence Lady Mary:

> Bid her some noble youth's just suit allow,
> Soft to his prayer, propitious to his vow.
> Then shall succeed with her own glorious frame
> A phœnix race from chaste connubial flame;
> Then beaming will a young Maria rise,
> Whose spring of beauty shall with fresh supplies
> Maintain the empire of her mother's eyes.[5]

These innocent compliments were a balm against Wortley's harsh wrangling.

Once she was surprised by admirers of a far different sort, friends of her father's. In her diary, as recalled by her granddaughter, Lady Mary told of an afternoon spent with Dolly

---

[1] Paston, 105–6.

[2] 17 Apr., Paston, 107; 9 Apr. 1711, i. 186.

[3] To Mrs. Justice, Morgan Libr. MS. In 1740 Horace Walpole—who was born in 1719—set down some gossip about Lady Mary's amours, but it cannot be substantiated (*Corr.* xiv, 243, 246).

[4] To Lady Bute, 28 Jan. 1753, ii. 226.

[5] W MS (Harrowby, vol. 255). The second was from E. Vernon—almost certainly Edward Vernon, son of a Whig politician, and famous later as a naval commander.

Walpole at Acton where her 'father was giving a great men-dinner. After tea the two girls, thinking his company engaged with their wine, strolled into the garden: but Lord Wharton and Lord Carlisle, spying them from the dining-room windows, agreed to steal out and surprise them: which they did; and a noble game of high romps followed.' The young naïve Dorothy had been brought from the country by her brother Robert Walpole; and Lady Mary, in spite of the high romps, thought of herself as the girl's 'protecting genius'.[1]

At the beginning of 1711 her father turned from the problem of her marriage to that of her docile brother. On 20 February he introduced into the House of Lords the 'Marquis of Dorchester Estate Act' on the intended marriage of Lord Kingston, his eighteen-year-old son ('an infant'), to Rachel Baynton. It provided that he settle his estates on his son and raise £8,000 for his daughters, and that the estate of one John Hall be settled on Lord Kingston.[2] On 16 May the amended bill received the Royal Assent, a short time after the marriage of the boy to the sixteen-year-old bride, Hall's illegitimate daughter, who displaced his legitimate heirs at his death (in September).[3] To Lady Mary it was a frightful view of mercenary marriages. She blamed her father for having destroyed her brother's happiness and peace of mind by marrying him to a silly, childish girl for the sake of her fortune.[4] It may have hardened her resolution not to submit to such a marriage herself.

At the end of March her father determined to end her persistent friendship with Wortley. He summoned her to a conference, and after forcing her to promise not to write, hustled her off to West Dean. She broke her promise to tell Wortley at length of her rights and his duty: 'Had you had any real Affection for me, you would have long ago applied yourself to him, from whose hand only you can receive me.'[5] His final decision on 2 May, after a speedy exchange of further disagreements, was that since she did not love him, their friendship must end. 'Adieu, Dearest L[ady] M[ary]. This once be assur'd you will

[1] Lady Louisa Stuart to Wharncliffe, *c.* 1838, Wharncliffe MS 439; Stuart, 68–69.
[2] HMC *House of Lords MSS*, ix. N.S., 1710–12, ed. M. F. Bond (1949), 95.
[3] Joseph Foster, *Collectenea Genealogica* (1883), i. 17–19.
[4] Stuart, 68.
[5] M to W, W MS, i. 182–3; 2 Apr. 1711, Paston, 105.

not deceive me. I expect no answer.'[1] Unbelievable though it
seems, she apparently sent none for the rest of the summer. A
truce between the lovers had been achieved.

Wortley, then in Yorkshire, began to plan a new scheme of
life as a bachelor. When his friend Addison proposed spending
a month with him, he extolled life in the country, and invited
Addison to stay with him, and then in the autumn to accompany him to Newcastle.[2] He repeated his invitation more solicitously; and then again in October, when he found a suitable
house for them to stay in until January or perhaps longer.[3] His
lengthy residence in the country would prevent his meeting
Lady Mary, who customarily returned to London in the
autumn.

In October he received a short note from her—probably the
first since the suspension of hostilities—telling him she had
delayed returning to town because smallpox had broken out in
the house next to her father's in Arlington Street. In his ill-
natured reply he brought up a new point: that if he married her
without her father's consent he would lose a £20,000 dowry
and incur his own father's anger. She generously set him free of
all obligations toward her, and smugly added: 'without affectation I wish who ever you choose may make you too happy to
think of me'.[4] Renunciation was a pose she favoured. On her
journey from West Dean up to London she rehearsed his unjust
accusations and her modest ambition, and cautioning him not
to think of her any more, postured still another farewell: 'You
are unjust and I am unhappy—'tis past—I will never think of
you more—never.'[5]

From Addison came a less emotional gesture. After a month's
holiday in Bath, he had returned to London to put his 'hand to
the plow'. He urged Wortley to give up his plan of staying in
the country and instead to attend Parliament, where an important treaty was to be discussed, the Tory-sponsored Treaty
of Utrecht with France. Addison proposed to rent a house in

[1] W MS, i. 8–9 (frag. in Paston, 111).
[2] Addison to W, 21 July, *Letters* (1941), 263–4; W to Addison, 28 July 1711,
Cat. of the Morrison Coll. iv (1890), 285.
[3] 25 Aug., *Addisoniana* [1803], i. 238–9; 8 Oct. 1711, *Morrison Coll.* iv. 285.
[4] M to W, Paston, 122 (corrected from MS); Paston, 123 (MS end. '20 Oct.
from Dean'); W MS, i. 253–4.
[5] Paston, 113–15.

Kensington, hire a good cook, and take him in as his lodger. Wortley agreed, with the expectation of reaching London in the middle of December.[1] And so again, at the end of 1711, when both he and Lady Mary were in London their estrangement seemed actual. Perhaps when they met at friends' houses or at the opera or Drawing-Room they exchanged small talk or glances. But no letters passed between them to irritate and titillate the curious love they bore for each other.[2]

In London early in 1712 Lady Mary led a more peaceful life than before, freed from the double oppression of a disapproving family and a cantankerous lover. At the beginning of March she received a letter in a too familiar hand, begging for a meeting.[3] 'I was never more surpris'd in my life than at seeing a letter from you', she answered; 'I am willing to believe only curiosity made me weak enough to receive it.' And thus they resumed, for the last time, their correspondence and courtship. She suggested Sir Godfrey Kneller's house for their meeting, but when she arrived there late and missed him, she asked him to come that afternoon to Colman's toyshop. The reason she overcame her scruples against such a scandalous place was clear from what she told him: 'I did not ask you to write, nor desire to see you; as circumstances are, I know no use it can be to me. . . . My Family is resolved to dispose of me where I hate. I have made all the opposition in my power.' Her news did not surprise him, since he had 'for some time been grieved to hear you was to be confined to one you did not like, and in another country'.[4] He had resumed his courtship because, with a rival ready to take her, he realized that perhaps he wanted her for himself.

Other acquiescent suitors had applied to her father. He assured one of them, an unidentified peer, 'that having had lately occasion to talk seriously to my daughter of marriage, I find she is in very good earnest when she declares against it, which I am very sorry for . . .'.[5] This may have been Lord Dorchester's own tactful refusal. For when he did accept a suitor, he disregarded her feelings. The successful one was the

[1] 13 Oct., *Letters*, 265–6; 1 Nov. 1711, *Addisoniana*, i. 241–2.
[2] Paston, 123, prints a letter of 13 Nov., an error for 13 Mar. (W MS, i. 251–2); and W's answer (Paston, 124) probably belongs to the early spring of 1711.
[3] 3 Mar. 1712, Paston, 127.
[4] W MS, i. 242–3; Paston, 127–9, 137.
[5] N.d., MS owned by Mr. James M. Osborn.

same Mr. K. who had been so attentive to her the season before; and his identity has only recently become known. He was the Honourable Clotworthy Skeffington, about eight years her senior, the son and heir of the Irish Viscount Massereene.[1] His marriage contract contained very liberal provisions for her, an allowance of £500 a year as 'pin-money', and £1,200 a year if he died. If he lived, she pathetically added (for Wortley's sympathy): 'I shall enjoy every pleasure of Life, those of Love excepted.'[2] The problem of entailment, which had wrecked Wortley's suit, did not arise because the future Lord Massereene would automatically be succeeded by his eldest son.

She emphasized the benefits of her marriage contract to impress Wortley. She had once protested against his suffering by taking her without a dowry; now she put it somewhat differently: 'I have neither folly nor vanity enough to suppose you would think of running away with me.'[3] An elopement conjures up a romantic vision of impetuous love; in this one, however, the lovers boasted of how much each was about to sacrifice. Wortley faced the loss of her dowry with great reluctance; and up to the very end, while her family prepared for her marriage to Skeffington, he thought of coming to terms with her father. Or even of coming to terms after an elopement! But she clearly and firmly discarded both these suppositions.[4] Her honesty was admirable, for she could have cajoled him with empty promises. Her sacrifices were greater than his. Besides the generous terms from her suitor, she would forfeit £8,000 raised by her father on her brother's marriage. (Her sister Evelyn, on marrying Lord Gower in March, had taken possession of the £12,000 under their grandmother's will, thus depriving her of ever getting half of it.) Beyond these financial losses her elopement would alienate her family, and she therefore begged Wortley only to make some provision for her if she were left a widow. In the lovers' contest as to who gave up more by elopement she held the trump card: that she threw herself entirely on his generosity without the safeguards of a contracted marriage. As she wrote, with more flourish than accuracy, she

[1] James Brydges to Anthony Hammond, 29 Aug. 1712, *The Times Lit. Suppl.* 4 Sept. 1937.
[2] Paston, 149, 131.
[3] 20 Oct. 1711, spring 1712, Paston, 123, 125.
[4] Aug. 1712, i. 193.

was ready to abandon all for him—Fame, Family, and Settlement![1]

They seemed to agree on their own terms of marriage. Love, solitude, and economy were the main articles of their private settlement. With Wortley's small income, his father still being alive, they would have to live modestly, and she did not want to allow her family the satisfaction of gloating over her rash act. Hence she proposed that they live in Italy, a pleasant and economical exile; and Wortley agreed.[2] They agreed with surprising frequency, even to the proposition that they loved each other.

As the date for her marriage approached she appealed to her father once again, asking to remain single rather than be forced to marry a man she could not love. She could make her own decision, he answered, but he would not permit her to marry anyone else, and would bequeath her only £400 a year. As he requested, she consulted her relations. To her protest that she did not love her Irish suitor, they said she merely had to live with him; and as to loving him, that was an imprudent, romantic notion: very few women were in love with their husbands, and yet many of them were happy. When she told her father that she could not overcome her aversion but would obey him, he took it as her tacit consent. She sent this account of her family conferences to Wortley.[3] Its implication was that she could be forced into the marriage.

Before the end of July she was sent to her father's villa at Acton, where her brother and his family lived, to remain until her wedding. It was to be very elaborate, her father having already laid out £400 for her wedding clothes.[4] 'Lady Mary Pierrepont is not yet married', one of her friends gossiped (on 19 July), 'but is to be very soon. . . .'[5] By a fortunate accident, however, it was discovered that the marriage contract was faulty, and would have to be sent to Ireland to be signed again.

---

[1] M to W, Aug. 1712, i. 190; Paston, 132, 145, 139, 131. Although Wortley usually cried poverty, he boasted of a greater income and better reversions than her Irish suitor (Paston, 148). But without the safeguard of a marriage contract, his superior resources (if true) were valueless to her.

[2] Paston, 132, 145, 147–8.

[3] 4 July 1712, i. 187–9.

[4] M to W, i. 190.

[5] Mrs. Hewet to the Duchess of Newcastle, Portland MS (Longleat), xiv. 8. Owned by the Marquess of Bath.

The delay allowed the lovers more time to plan their elopement.
Then, on Monday, 11 August, her father appeared at Acton and
ordered her to leave for West Dean in a week's time, to stay
there until the wedding. She proceeded to outline a course of
action for Wortley: he was to come to Acton the following
Sunday (17 August) at ten o'clock after dark, and wait for her
on the road near the garden; they would begin their journey
immediately—to Naples, she specified. More modestly, she
offered him the choice of changing his mind altogether or
waiting until she returned from West Dean: 'Let us both be at
Liberty till the Parson puts an end to it.'[1] Her modesty succeeded. With transports of love he thanked her for fixing the
day. 'I shall go to meet you with more joy than I should to take
possession of riches, honour, or power . . .'; and he even conceded that since no one could match her intelligence, he would
never contend with it.[2]

Yet during the final week of their unwedded life they could
not stop wrangling. She had to assure him that it was useless to
think of dealing with her father, and that she was completely
sincere, her principal concern being to make their love eternal.[3]
He could express his fervor in long turgid compliments: 'I shall
wish to dye with you rather than to live without you in the
highest circumstances of Fortune.' Yet as late as Friday, two
days before their planned elopement, he warned her: 'If you are
likely to think of cuckoldom you are mad if you marry me.' She
had already renounced gallantry; and now she did so again,
even forgiving him his coarse expression.[4]

On Friday it seemed as though both were certain of their
decision. 'All I can say is that in two days more you are mistress
of yourself and me', he ended his nagging letter. 'I tremble for
what we are doing', she answered. 'Are you sure you will love
me for ever? Shall we never repent?' A moment later she added:
'My resolution is taken. Love me and use me well.' The next
morning she had to tell him again that her father was beyond
negotiating, and that he could not hope for any financial benefits. 'Reflect now for the last time in what manner you must

---

[1] Paston, 145–6. The dates of the final week's letters are now worked out for
the first time. [2] W MS, i. 160–1.
[3] i. 193–4 [Tuesday, 12 Aug.].
[4] Paston, 152, 148 (where 'cuckoldom' is bowdlerized to 'gallantry'); i. 195,
192.

take me. I shall come to you with only a night-gown and petti-coat, and that is all you will get with me.' She suggested a change in their plans, that he should be at her door with a coach on Monday morning to start on their journey.[1]

Wortley needed a special marriage licence so that the posting of banns for three days could be waived, and he waited until Sunday the 17th to procure it. The formal document begins: 'Thomas Providen[tia] Divina Cantuarien[sis] Archiepiscopus totius Angliae Primas et Metropolitanus[2] Dilectis Vobis in Christo Eduardo Mountague parochiae Sanctae Margarettae Westminsteri in Comitatu Middlesexiae caelibi et Mariae Pierre-pointae parochiae Sancti Dunstani in Occidente London solutae —*Salutem* et gratiam. . . .'[3] Early that morning she received a disturbing note from Wortley, probably news of the wedding licence. 'If my F[ather] knows of it, tis past. I shall be sent to Dean early tomorrow morning, and hindered tonight. He comes to-day. I am coward enough to apprehend his rage to a degree of being ready to swoon. I know he may make me do what he will.'[4] Her angry father did come that day, and after telling her that he knew of her clandestine correspondence, he ordered her to leave for West Dean the next morning under her brother's care. For the rest of the day she waited in vain for an answer from Wortley. At six o'clock the next morning, still hoping that he would come up with a coach, she stole out to the balcony and waited until seven. 'But heaven was not so kind to bring you', she wrote him that night—from an inn on the road to West Dean.[5]

The final hours of their courtship were confused, and even comical. Accompanied by a servant Wortley set off on horse-back to pursue her. Her party stopped at an inn, and she retired early. A short time later Wortley and his servant arrived at the same inn and spent the night without either of the lovers know-ing the other was there. Some people in the inn suspected that he was a highwayman—perhaps because of his mysterious, dis-traught hurry.[6] On Tuesday morning (the 19th) the pursuit

---

[1] Paston, 148; i. 196, 191.
[2] Archbishop Tenison, a friend of the Banks family of Scofton, knew and admired Lady Mary. He had sent a message to her that spring (Paston, 79, 134).
[3] Licence among W MS. The date is now for the first time given correctly.
[4] W MS, i. 162–3.   [5] W MS, i. 172–3 (frag. in Paston, 159–60).
[6] Paston, 160 and 161 (combined in MS).

continued, Lady Mary somehow managing to scribble short notes to her pursuer. In the last one she vowed: 'I would not see a relation after 'tis over.'[1] These were the last written thoughts of Lady Mary Pierrepont.

Henceforth she was Lady Mary Wortley Montagu. The exact time and place of her marriage are not known. On Thursday, 21 August, Wortley dined in London with his friend Steele.[2] Since he pursued his bride on Tuesday, he probably married her on Wednesday the 20th, their licence being valid anywhere in London or the country. For their wedding night, as Lady Mary had suggested, they must have gone to his lodgings.[3] A week later James Brydges (later Duke of Chandos) wrote to a friend that Lady Mary, instead of marrying her contracted suitor 'everything being agreed on, and the day appointed, has marryed herself privately to worthy Montagu'.[4] As the daughter of a peer she continued to bear her title (an irrevocable gift), while her husband remained plain Mr. Wortley.

In retrospect she regarded her courtship in a somewhat different way. When she met Joseph Spence in Rome thirty years later, she told him that for a month before her marriage she scarcely slept one night because she had such a vast number of offers, 'and the thing that kept her awake was, who to fix upon. Most part of the month she was determined but as to two points; which were, to be married to somebody, and not to be married to the man her father . . . advis'd her to. The last night of the month she determined; and in the morning left the man her father had fixed upon, buying a wedding-ring for her; and scuttled away, and married Mr. Wortley.'[5] How much truth is there in this later version? Her granddaughter, though calling it 'mere rattle', conceded that likely enough 'she more than once wavered between Mr. Wortley and others, though unwilling ever to lose her hold of him entirely. It is pretty plain that he suspected this.'[6]

---

[1] W MS, i. 301 (frag. in Paston, 162).   [2] Steele, *Corr.* 278.
[3] i. 191. One tradition has them eloping from West Dean (*Greville Mem. 1814-1860*, ed. L. Strachey and R. Fulford [1938], iv. 95).
[4] Brydges to Hammond, 29 Aug. 1712.
[5] Spence to his mother, 25 Feb. 1741, MS Eg. 2234, ff. 247-8.
[6] Lady Louisa Stuart to the Rev. Stuart Corbett, 7 Sept. 1834, Wharncliffe MS 439.

Her courtship, for all its oddity, did have a typical quality. In Samuel Richardson's novel *Clarissa Harlowe*, published thirty-five years later, Clarissa's stern father tries to force her to marry the rich, ugly Solmes, who will give her a very generous allowance. She is forbidden Lovelace, whom she loves, on account of his libertine past. One of her dearest friends advises her: 'Marry first, and love will come after.'[1] Instead Clarissa elopes with Lovelace from a country house. Thus they begin their long tragic history. When Lady Mary read it, she wrote to her daughter: 'This Richardson is a strange fellow. I heartily despise him, and eagerly read him, nay, sob over his works in a most scandalous manner. The two first tomes of Clarissa touched me, as being very resembling to my maiden days.'[2] She was then an old woman living in lonely retirement in Italy, and the novel poignantly evoked her own courtship. But the aftermath of her elopement did not match Clarissa's. Wortley was no Lovelace; he lacked his charms as well as his vices.

[1] Letter XXXII.
[2] To Lady Bute, 22 Sept. 1755, ii. 285.

III. 'A Proper Matrimonial Style'

(1712–14)

DESPITE their plan of fleeing to the proud, economical exile of Naples, Lady Mary and Wortley stayed in England. Two months after their marriage they travelled up to Wharncliffe Lodge to receive the blessings of Wortley's father. He was a large, rough-looking man who talked loudly and swore at the servants in his crowded household, which included his daughter Katherine, his brother the gentle Dean of Durham Cathedral, and the Dean's chaplain. (His mistress lived in another house nearby.) Lady Mary was so struck by the surrounding landscape that she entered her impressions of it in her diary. In contrast to the placid Wiltshire downs and the Nottingham plains and forests which she knew, the Lodge hung like an eagle's nest over a wild and rugged prospect of craggy mountains. It was a rude, sequestered spot, she noted in her diary, yet she admitted not disliking it, odd though her fancy might be.[1]

Their visit completed, Wortley continued alone by horseback to Durham, to look after his family's business interests. At the same time Lady Mary journeyed with her maid by coach to visit Wallingwells, near Worksop in Nottinghamshire, about twenty miles to the east. Her host there was Thomas White, M.P. for the nearby town of Retford, most of which he owned. A portly, good-natured squire of forty-five, he was surrounded by his noisy flourishing family of a young wife and five children ranging in age from two to thirteen.[2] Although he was her father's second cousin, he did not disapprove of her elopement, but greeted her when she arrived on the night of 20 October.

---

[1] Stuart, 66. In 1743 she remembered this view as a 'most beautiful land-prospect' (to W, ii. 122).
[2] *Mem. of the House of White of Wallingwells* (1886), 22.

Two days later she sent Wortley her very first letter as his wife. 'I don't know very well how to begin', she wrote; 'I am perfectly unacquainted with a proper matrimonial style. After all, I think 'tis best to write as if we were not married at all.' Then she artfully sketched the felicities of family life at Wallingwells (including the squalling of children), which struck her imagination as an agreeable picture of their future life together when 'the noise of a nursery may have more charms for us than the music of an opera'. She always remembered him in the daily family prayers, and in her private ones thanked Heaven for making her his wife.[1] As she told him of her love, and of her grief at their separation, she expressed the sentiments of a sincerely affectionate wife. The cynicism in her previous feeling had apparently been dissolved by her marriage. But Wortley's insensitivity, shown so often during his courtship, had not been lessened. On the contrary, now that he possessed her, he became casual or neglectful. At least, that is suggested by their letters during the first years of their marriage.

Quite normally, the young wife worried whether he had arrived safely at Durham, ninety miles away. Allowing time for his arrival, she wrote to him several times, without any answer from him. Her imagination was filled with the fears of a woman and a lover. 'Pray, my dear, write to me', she said in one of the letters, 'or I shall be very mad.' Before she finally heard from him she had lain ill in bed for four days with a prodigiously swollen face, which had to be lanced, and she had been in the utmost need of money.[2] Marriage, she could see, was not a completely blissful state. At the beginning of December Wortley returned to accompany her to Hinchingbroke, Lord Sandwich's seat in Huntingdon, about fifteen miles from Cambridge; he then continued to London alone to look after business affairs. His main reason for leaving her in the country must have been that he had no place in London where they could stay together. Her visit was lonely and cheerless—none of the family was there—but she could at least console herself with the thought that if Lord Sandwich's son had no male heir the great stone house might some day be Wortley's. For the time being she was only a poor relation.

[1] i. 197-8.   [2] i. 198-9.

She remained there at least a month, moody and unhappy. When she reported that while walking on the terrace she had been accompanied by a good-natured robin redbreast almost all afternoon, Wortley replied crossly that the reason she did not write more often was that she had better company than the robin. His jealousy, in this instance, had no basis. During her first week there she did not speak to a single person until some young ladies from Huntingdon came to visit.[1] Their gossip was only a temporary distraction. She would have read, but the library at Hinchingbroke offered nothing, until she discovered a trunk of old papers, the letters of Wortley's grandparents. She still complained to him of her monotonous life: 'But idleness is the root of all evil: I write and read till I can't see, and then I walk; sleep succeeds; and thus my whole time is divided.' Her idleness made her melancholy, which she feared not so much for her own sake, she told him, 'but in the condition I am, I believe it may be of very ill consequence.' Her pregnancy deepened her depression, but her love did not diminish. 'Adieu!' she ended one letter, 'je suis à vous de tout mon cœur.' Before her elopement she had envisioned 'romantic scenes' to herself of 'Love and Solitude'.[2] But it was solitude à deux she had meant, and not cheerless life alone in a country house.

In London Wortley looked after more than his own business. For in spite of all Lady Mary's high-flown protestations that she would never again see her family, she now agreed to attempt a reconciliation with her father. Her antagonist in the family was her father's sister, Lady Cheyne, who had supervised the motherless family; but another important relation favoured them, Lord Pierrepont, her father's uncle, who was rich, old, and childless, and hence influential in the family's affairs. She advised Wortley to call on him to thank him for his advocacy. Another influential champion was Lord Halifax, the prominent Whig politician, who respected her and esteemed Wortley, to whom he was related. Her old friend Bishop Burnet also stood by her. She encouraged Wortley to gain their favour. As Christmas approached, although anxious to see him, she cautioned him that if he came up for the holidays he would have to do a great deal of expensive entertaining.[3]

---

[1] M to W, 6 Dec. 1712, i. 200; Paston, 168; 9 or 11 Dec. 1712, i. 203.
[2] i. 200–4; Paston, 132, 140.   [3] i. 202, 204, 201.

During these doldrum months, at the end of 1712 or early in 1713, Wortley thought of a way of distracting her. His friend Addison had written four acts of a tragedy on the death of Cato of Utica, the stoic hero famous for his opposition to Julius Caesar's tyranny. The Whig party had been out of power for almost three years, and Addison's friends saw that his play could be rousing propaganda for their side, with the virtuous Cato as a Whig patriot opposing the tyrannical Tory rule. Addison then wrote a fifth act to complete his blank verse tragedy. Wortley procured a copy of it, and sent it to Lady Mary, requesting her to write a critique of it.[1]

She went about her task with thoroughness, comparing the tragedy to one by Shakespeare and one by Racine, and judging it by the critical precepts of Aristotle and Horace. She praised what she could, especially the characters and their pathetic situations, and found Cato's suicide especially touching, though she suggested that Addison should expand the soliloquy on the immortality of the soul. She even tried to improve the diction of such a careful stylist as Addison by correcting the 'low' words and expressions in his elevated tragedy. She ended her critique with wifely modesty: that she had undertaken what was far beyond her skill only because Wortley had commanded it. Addison followed most of her suggestions, including one that each act be ended with rhymed couplets. But he suffered from extreme sensitivity to public criticism; perhaps that is why she headed her critique: 'Wrote at the desire of Mr. Wortley; suppressed at the desire of Mr. Addison.' Its respectful tone bears out her private opinion that Addison was 'the best company in the world'.[2] Whether she intended it to be printed, or merely circulated among her friends, the neatly written paper lay unpublished among her manuscripts until the present century.

Like Addison's other friends, she urged him to present the play on the stage because she thought it might 'renew in the minds of the audience the lost love of liberty and contempt of servitude'. On 14 April 1713—five days after the stormy Parliament had opened—it was staged at the Drury Lane Theatre. It

---

[1] The section here on *Cato* is abstracted from my article in *Publ. of the Mod. Lang. Assoc.* lxv (1950), 1122–9. See also Peter Smithers, *Life of Addison* (1954), 250–6.
[2] Spence, 232.

was an immediate, spectacular success, mainly because of its
political propaganda. But the Tory patriots, who accused the
Duke of Marlborough of being a Caesar, claimed it for their
side. To avoid the appearance of immoderate partisanship,
Addison had asked Alexander Pope, the Catholic poet whose
sympathies were thought to be Tory, to write the prologue, and
Dr. Garth, a prominent Whig, to write the epilogue; and both
pieces were spoken from the stage. Lady Mary also wrote an
epilogue, which, in the customary style of such pieces, was
witty at the expense of the play's noble purpose:

> You see in ancient Rome what folly reign'd;
> A folly British men would have disdain'd.
> Here's none so weak to pity Cato's case,
> Who might have liv'd, and had a handsome place;
> But rashly vain, and insolently great,
> He perish'd by his fault—and not his fate.
> Thank Heav'n! our patriots better ends pursue,
> With something more than glory in their view.
> Poets write morals—priests for martyrs preach—
> Neither such fools to practise what they teach. . . .

Her cynical epilogue, however, remained unspoken and unpublished.[1]

By this time she had come to London herself to await her
confinement; and she undoubtedly went to see the popular play
in which she had to a slight extent collaborated. She took part
in another Whig celebration when her name was printed as a
toast of the Hanover Club, a group of thirty-one ardent Whigs
who looked to the 'reigning Fair' to inspire them.[2] She must
have been nominated by Wortley, who in his more significant
Parliamentary activity delivered a glorious speech on 14 May
to defeat a bill for French free-trade.[3]

On 16 May Lady Mary gave birth to a son, who was proudly
christened Edward Wortley Montagu, Junior. As custom de-
creed she remained in her house a whole month to regain her

---

[1] ii. 453 (first printed 1803). During this period of her literary activity, she
may have written the three-act comedy 'Simplicity', which is preserved in her
autograph (W MS, vii. 160–87), an ingenious comedy of intrigue and sentiment dealing with a romantic courtship.
[2] Robert J. Allen, *Clubs of Augustan London* (1933), 55.
[3] William Cobbett, ed., *Parl. Hist. of Engl.* vi (1810), 1211–12; M to W [23
July 1713], W MS, ii. 270–1.

strength. On 23 June Wortley left her for a week's visit to Hinchingbroke; and a few hours after his departure she wrote him a letter (which she sent off the next day). It contained her first mention of their six-weeks-old child: 'Your little Boy is very well, and would present his duty to you, if he could speak.'[1] During the child's early years she never failed to mention him with the greatest solicitude.

In the same letter she also revealed her feelings toward her husband, and something of his toward her. She confessed that she could not keep her thoughts from dwelling on him

in a Manner you would call Affectation, if I should repeat it to you. That Reflection brings me back to remember I should not write my thoughts to you. You will accuse me of deceit when I own opening my heart to you, and the Plainness of expressing it would appear Artificial. I am sorry to remember this, and cheque the Inclination that I have to give a loose to my tenderness, and tell you how melancholy all things seem to me in your Absence.

How clearly this shows the disparity of their temperaments! Despite a hard, unemotional exterior, her personality did have a capacity for tender feelings. What would have happened, one wonders, if her husband had been responsive? He was not cruel or mean, but he seemed dour and humourless, without any genuine tenderness to match hers.

Once during the first year of her marriage, while with friends —who were perhaps discussing marital fidelity—she improvised some verse on the subject, and inscribed it with a sharp diamond on a window glass. Women always have a 'thirst of power and desire of fame', and encourage men to pursue them to the brink of virtue; but the young wife resolves to follow a different course:

> Let this sure maxim be my virtue's guide,
> In part to blame she is, who has been tried;
> Too near he has approached, who is denied.[2]

It shows not only Lady Mary's facility in versifying, but her resolution to sustain her marriage with discretion and idealism.

---

[1] Paston, 174-5.
[2] W MS album [Harrowby, vol. 256], entitled: 'Written ex tempore in company in a glass window the first year I was married.' As 'The Lady's Resolve' it was printed in *The Plain Dealer* of 27 Apr. 1724. The conclusion is similar to a stanza in Thomas Overbury's *The Wife* (1614), repr. 1936, 106.

In her first letter to Wortley after he left London, besides their infant son's 'duty', she sent ominous news. Her brother had fallen ill of smallpox, one of the most dreaded diseases of the time. On Tuesday, 24 June, she heard the report; on Thursday Dr. Garth, who attended him, feared that the pocks were dangerously full; and on the following Wednesday he was dead. Although not yet twenty-one he left a widow and two children. Lady Mary was stricken with grief for the loss of her family champion. A few days later, when she went to Acton to console the family, her father refused to see her; he was so affected, her sister told her, that he did not intend to go to the country that summer, and 'he had not seen her nor nobody, nor spoke of any kind of business'.[1] Lady Mary probably attended the burial at Holme Pierrepont on 9 July, for she was then on her way north to Wharncliffe Lodge with her child.

She arrived there safely, as she informed Wortley on 12 July, in a letter signed 'with the greatest tenderness, faithfully yours'.[2] Still depressed by melancholy memories, she was overjoyed when his first letter reached her a few days later. After a short stay at the Lodge, which was too small and crowded for long visits, she accepted her friends' invitation to Wallingwells, but left her son with his nurse.[3] Wortley could not join her because of his political activity for the approaching parliamentary elections. Instead of being a candidate for Huntingdon Borough, as before, he was displaced by his father (who had himself been displaced in Peterborough). He travelled up to the Yorkshire town of Boroughbridge; and he stayed there during the summer of 1713.

Because of his 'very disagreeable and fatiguing' business there, Lady Mary assumed the task of renting a house for their little family. She had begun dealing with it before leaving London, and now continued with tenacity and shrewdness: she interviewed land agents and house owners, worried about house-fittings, plate, and furniture, and even considered the price of food in the various localities. Her prudent economy demonstrated her sincerity, so often repeated during their courtship, that she could flourish in a modest station of life. After having

[1] Paston, 175; i. 205; W MS, ii. 264-5.
[2] W MS, ii. 329-30 (frag. in Paston, 176).
[3] W MS, ii. 264-5, 270-1; i. 205-6.

dickered over one rental, she assured him: 'There is no inconvenience so great as the possibility of your being uneasy, and there is nothing upon earth so dear to me as your quiet; and if I can any way convince you of my love I am happy.'[1]

But she still complained of his neglect, not so much for herself as for their son, whose improved health she was especially pleased to report. Once she tartly reminded him: 'You have forgot, I suppose, that you have a little boy.'[2] She probably looked forward to seeing the end of his neglect when they were all settled under one roof.

By mid-summer she found a suitable house in the village of Middlethorpe near York. In taking it she displayed a curious economy. She favoured that village because its proximity to York would allow their friends in the city to come for short afternoon visits instead of dinner. And Wortley cunningly instructed her to pretend they were on bad terms with his sister (Katherine) to persuade their landlord she would not stay with them. In September Lady Mary arranged to move their belongings there, even packing Wortley's papers (which she promised not to read); and she chose to ship everything by water, the cheapest method. Indeed, she practised the most stringent economy.[3] She suggested meeting him at Doncaster to travel north together. At last, at the end of their first year of marriage, they would be together in their own small family.

Until the following summer Wortley was able to remain with his wife and child, for his expenditure of a large sum of money had not won him a seat in Parliament. In Lady Mary's opinion, he had been unwise even to stand for election.[4] But like other Whigs he regarded his defeat as a temporary setback, and took part in whatever political activity he could. When Steele was expelled from the House for his seditious pamphlet *The Crisis* he applied to Wortley for advice. And as in the previous year, Wortley nominated Lady Mary a toast of the Hanover Club.[5]

---

[1] To W, [July 1713], 3 Aug. [1713], both addressed to Boroughbridge, W MS, ii. 270–1, 341–2, 321–2 [n.d.].
[2] 28 Aug., W MS, ii. 357–8; ibid. 309–10.
[3] W MS, ii. 337–8; Paston, 180; M to W Junior, 3 Mar. 1762, Paston, 529 (date corrected from MS).
[4] Sept. [1714], W MS, ii. 272–3; 17 Sept. 1714, i. 214.
[5] Steele to Hanmer, 21 Mar. 1714, *Corr.* 93; broadside among Tonson Papers, Nat. Port. Gall.

In the early summer of 1714 she returned to London, leaving her child in the country; and once again she put her pen at Addison's service. He had resumed publication of the *Spectator* on 18 June, after a lapse of one-and-a-half years. The issue of 30 June (No. 561) contained his satiric letter about a club of nine widows headed by Mrs. President, a redoubtable dame about to take her seventh husband. Four weeks later an answer appeared in No. 573 from Mrs. President herself; and it was Lady Mary who held her pen. 'Smart Sir,' she began, 'You are pleased to be very merry, as you imagine, with us widows; and you seem to ground your satire on our receiving consolation so soon after the death of our dears, and the number we are pleased to admit for our companions; but you never reflect what husbands we have buried, and how short a sorrow the loss of them was capable of occasioning.' Then, to justify her brief periods of mourning, she describes the foibles of her six husbands. Her seventh suitor, who has pursued her and her fortune ever since the death of her first husband, is named the Honourable Edward Waitfort—surely a glance at a husband whose courtship had been long and querulous. She called the physician in the essay Dr. Gruel, perhaps a jibe at her old friend Dr. Garth. Altogether it is a spirited essay, and still another sample of Lady Mary's ready wit.

Addison's friend Thomas Tickell, with others, later took over the periodical, and when he prepared a preface for the collected edition of the eighth volume, he listed the various contributors. After starting with Addison, he wrote: 'I wish I had leave to name the Author of No. 573.' By her sex and rank Lady Mary was entitled to follow the master himself— and a contemporary hand jotted her name in this place on Tickell's manuscript.[1] When published, the preface merely stated: 'I have not been able to prevail upon the several gentlemen who were concerned in this work to let me acquaint the world with their names.' Perhaps Lady Mary hoped to be allowed to write some additional essays for the paper, as implied in the last sentence of Mrs. President's letter: 'If the other ladies you name would thus give in their husbands' pictures at length, you would see they have had as little reason as myself to lose

[1] Tickell MS. Discussed by M. J. C. Hodgart in *Rev. of Eng. Stud.* v (1954), 372-4.

their hours in weeping and wailing.' But it was apparently her only contribution to the *Spectator*, and her first published essay.

Before it appeared in print she had left London (in the middle of July) to return to Middlethorpe. Wortley remained for the express purpose of speaking to her father.[1] If she had not been estranged from him she would have remained in London to attend the marriage of her sister Frances to John Erskine, Earl of Mar, on 20 July. The thirty-seven-year-old Earl, a widower, stood high in the Tory ministry as Secretary of State for Scotland. It was odd that a staunch Whig like Lord Dorchester should allow his daughter to marry a Tory politician, and other Whigs remarked on it. Thomas Burnet, the Bishop's son, wrote to a friend, 'My Lord Marr is marry'd to my Lady Frances Pierpoint, so that there is a good Whig *marr'd* by taking a Scotch Jacobite for her Husband.'[2] The match, arranged by Lady Cheyne, greatly displeased Lady Mary, for she detested Lord Mar and his politics, and foresaw an unhappy future for her sister.[3]

Then Lord Dorchester, after consenting to deal with Wortley, 'flew off' without warning. As Lady Mary had long suspected, he harboured matrimonial ambitions for himself.[4] Two weeks after disposing of his last daughter, he married Lady Isabella Bentinck, youngest daughter of the Dutch-born Earl of Portland, a woman only one year older than Lady Mary. The Fair Isabella, as Lady Mary called her stepmother, had long been pursued by the rich, elderly Marquess, but had held him at bay, insisting that he wait until all his daughters were married off.[5] Possibly he had allowed a Jacobite to take his last one in order to speed his own match.

Lady Mary's part in the strategy of reconciliation was to win over Lord Pierrepont. On her way north from London she heard that he was at Hanslope, his seat in Buckinghamshire, and she stopped to visit him. When she reached Nottingham, she urged Wortley to hire a footman and pay him a visit because he was well disposed toward them. From Middlethorpe, where

---

[1] M to W, 4 Aug. 1714, i. 208.
[2] *Letters of Burnet to Duckett 1712–1722*, ed. D. N. Smith (1914), 69.
[3] M to W, Paston, 186; Stuart, 67.
[4] M to W, Paston, 185; Aug. 1712, i. 190.
[5] Stuart, 78; Walpole, *Corr.* xiv. 243.

she was beset with domestic worries and her child's ill health, she did not forget to advise him again to visit Lord Pierrepont; and she cynically remarked that while it would be easy to win the old man's favour, he would still live a long time. However uncharitable she felt, it was for the sake of her own little family; as she told Wortley: 'I have set my heart upon you and my boy.'[1]

A few days later, on 1 August 1714, an event took place in London with momentous consequences on European politics; it also changed the future of the young ambitious pair. Queen Anne, the last reigning Stuart, died; and the Elector of Hanover, whom the Whigs had so strenuously supported, was immediately proclaimed King. The Tory ascendency was definitely ended, and Wortley, along with his party, could now expect rewards for supporting the Protestant succession. In Middlethorpe Lady Mary did not hear the fateful news for several days. A week later she went to York in triumph and heard the King proclaimed. The Archbishop walked attended by the mayor, gentry, and crowds of people. She afterwards saw an effigy of the Pretender dragged through the streets and burned, while bells rang and bonfires blazed. But the local zeal for the new king frightened her too, since Jacobites loyal to the Pretender were expected to raise a rebellion in Scotland (where he subsequently landed and rallied his forces), and the city of York, so far north and conspicuously Hanoverian, would be endangered. So would nearby Middlethorpe, where she and her child lived. About fifteen miles north of York stood the massive Castle Howard, the seat of Lord Carlisle, then in London as a Lord Justice awaiting the King's arrival. His three daughters, who were friends of Lady Mary, remained safe within the stout walls of the house; and when they invited her to come there with her child she gladly accepted, assuring Wortley that ''tis the same thing as pensioning in a nunnery, for no mortal man ever enters the doors in the absence of their father'.[2] At the beginning of September, when political stability seemed secure, she left her refuge to return to Middlethorpe.

A week after the Queen's death, on hearing that Parliament would be dismissed in six months and a new election held, she

---

[1] 20, 27 July [1714], W MS, ii. 286–7, 323–4; i. 207–8.
[2] 9 Aug. 1714, i. 209–10.

began to plan a great political career for her husband—becoming, as it were, his unofficial campaign manager. At the expense of her pleasure in having him with her, she advised him to stay in London to see the King on his arrival from Hanover. Instead of a modest country retirement, which had satisfied her earlier, she now projected a vision of splendid wealth and rank. The Whigs had been out of office at the time of her courtship and marriage, and so she had adjusted her ambition to Wortley's meagre opportunities; now she wished him to take the fullest advantage of his party's ascendency. She still extolled the joy of poverty in a garret if it would serve his country; but that was merely rhetoric to persuade him that he owed it to himself and to the world to shine in a high position.[1] She prodded him with a vivid picture of how quickly aggressive men advanced:

The Ministry is like a play at Court; there's a little door to get in, and a great crowd without, shoving and thrusting who shall be foremost; people who knock others with their elbows, disregard a little kick of the shins, and still thrust heartily forwards, are sure of a good place. Your modest man stands behind in the crowd, is shoved about by every body, his cloaths tore, almost squeezed to death, and sees a thousand get in before him, that don't make so good a figure as himself.[2]

She even sent him advice on the practical side of his career, on his running for Parliament. It was difficult for her to work out an exact pre-election campaign in the autumn of 1714, for she could only depend on local country gossip and Wortley's laconic letters. The safest constituency for him would have been Huntingdon, but his father insisted on standing there again—which she thought 'surprising' and 'prodigious'. The desirable seats for large, important towns like Newark and York had already been assigned. Of the remaining few safe pocket boroughs the seats controlled by Lord Pelham (at Aldborough and Boroughbridge) went to other claimants. As a last resort Lady Mary advised Wortley to deposit a sum of money in a friend's hands in order to 'buy some little Cornish borough'.[3] It is surprising that she knew so much about the intricacies of election politics. She must have acquired her knowledge from the Whig politicians she had met at her father's house, and later

[1] Paston, 187; i. 214–15. [2] i. 215.
[3] i. 210–14; Paston, 187–92; Sept. [1714], W MS, ii. 365–7, 343–4, 272–3, 268–9.

from Wortley and his friends. Her own ambition, deprived of an outlet, was projected into her husband's career. He finally won the seat for the City of Westminster at the beginning of the next year, when he was high in his party's councils.

At her house in Middlethorpe, where she returned from Castle Howard on 3 September, Lady Mary resumed her multiple role as housekeeper, mother, political adviser, and family mediator. The winning of her grand-uncle's favour and her father's forgiveness were still important goals. She urged Wortley to visit Lord Pierrepont in town or to dine with him in the country if invited, and she even set down for him the exact words to say during their meeting.[1] Lord Pierrepont was now being courted for his own sake rather than for his influence on her father, for Lord Dorchester had at last consented to see his estranged son-in-law. When Wortley called on him for the second time, she sent a message whose dramatic force lies in its casual tone: 'My duty to Papa.'[2] Their long campaign to win him had apparently succeeded. No belated dowry or settlement came from him; victory brought only the moral advantage of family unity. But Wortley, like his father-in-law, could look forward to rich rewards for his adherence to the Hanoverian Whigs.

The Elector had landed in England on 18 September, and proceeded to London where his coronation took place a month later. At the beginning of October Lord Halifax was appointed First Lord of the Treasury; and he offered his young relation an appointment as Junior Commissioner. But Wortley was reluctant to accept a non-cabinet post. He did not think any offer below that of Secretary of State worth accepting.[3] Lady Mary thought otherwise, and tried to convince him. The post would enhance his reputation and facilitate his forthcoming election to Parliament, she argued; and after his election his power among the Whigs and his interest among the Tories would surely carry him to the Speaker's chair in the House. She embellished these arguments with a patriotic tag: 'being chose by your country is more honourable than holding *any* place from *any* king'.[4] On 13 October he agreed to accept the post.

[1] Paston, 190, 191, 192.　　[2] M to W, 1 Oct. [1714], W MS, ii. 288–9.
[3] Lady Mary's 'Account of the Court of George the First at His Accession', i. 123.　　[4] 6, 9 Oct. 1714, i. 215–16.

He had not been persuaded by Lady Mary, but (as she later explained) by 'a rich old uncle of mine, Lord Pierrepont, whose fondness for me gave him expectations of a large legacy'.[1] The ambitious young couple looked for future rewards from both their families. On his side there was still an earldom. Rather anxiously Lady Mary reported to him in October that Lord Sandwich's daughter-in-law was with child.[2] When the birth took place she made a brief entry in her journal: 'Lady Hinchinbroke has a dead daughter—it were unchristian not to be sorry for my cousin's misfortune; but if she has no live son, Mr. Wortley is heir—so there's comfort for a Christian.'[3]

Because of their newly gained rewards (besides the potential ones) they decided that Lady Mary would end her economical exile in the country and move to London in time for the opening of Parliament at the beginning of January.[4] Before her lay the dazzling prospect of life at Court where her reconciled family and her husband would raise her to a prominent place. That still distant prospect sharpened her unhappy loneliness in the country. She missed the pageantry of the King's entry into St. James's and the solemn ceremonial of the Coronation. She accepted the deprivation of these pleasures and of Wortley's company, for she wanted him to stay in London to press his political advantages; but she could not accept his coldness and neglect. She tried gentle chiding: 'I wish you would learn of Mr. Steele to write to your wife.' Then in November she sent him the most forthright of her many complaining letters. His busy political career explained the infrequency of his letters, and even his disregard of their child, she conceded; but she resented his utter indifference to her, and the absence of any expression of regret for being separated from her for more than four months. If he no longer loved her, she begged him to confess it and put her mind at ease. As a warm-hearted young woman, she required some affection from him, and he could not for some reason respond.[5]

[1] 'Account', i. 123. Corroborated by W to Addison, 18 July 1717 O.S., Tickell MS.   [2] 20 Oct. [1714], W MS, ii. 276–7.
[3] Stuart, 65.   [4] M to Mrs. Hewet, Nov. 1714, i. 155–6.
[5] 27 Oct., 24 Nov. 1714, i. 217–18. In her old age she stated that in 1714 Wortley had 'that sort of passion for me, that would have made me invisible to all but himself, had it been in his power' ('Account', i. 123). But this must refer *only* to his jealousy.

In the formal aspects of marriage they continued to conduct their domestic arrangements with propriety and a fair amount of agreement. Since he was in London, the job of house-hunting fell to him. She did her share: by worrying about the domestic facilities of the houses he inspected, by arranging to move their belongings, and by deciding whether to take their child on the long mid-winter journey. During December 1714 all these matters, along with political advice, filled her frequent letters. The house Wortley chose was in Duke Street, Westminster, close to St. James's Palace and to Parliament. Its location on the east side of St. James's Park made her fear that it was damp or unsound. After Wortley assured her that it would not fall down on their heads, she had other misgivings. Some years before, the wife and child of the house's owner had died of smallpox, and she feared that the infection remained. If it was the same house, then the bedding must be changed. She also inquired whether the house had necessary linens (sheets and table-cloths) and a nursery. Then a new difficulty arose; its present tenant had promised to move by Christmas, but was apparently delaying. Finally, on 21 December, she agreed that what she knew of the house satisfied her.

A more important question to be decided was whether to take her son to London with her. In the week-long journey he would have to face the hazards of travelling in the cold and the possible accident of overturning on the icy roads. He was in such good health that she did not want to risk these dangers. Since his nurse refused to live in London a new one had to be tried, which would take time. Repeatedly she asked Wortley to help her in a decision.[1] His answer revealed his dour attitude: 'As to the child, if you do wrong about him, you will have no reason to blame me, for I desire it may be as you like best.'[2] Her final decision was to leave him with his nurse in York where friends would look after him.

She had been ready to depart by 15 September, but the tenant's obstinacy and her new nurse's training held her back. Whether to obtain horses from York or have them sent up from London was the final matter to be settled. Instead of either plan, a team was sent over from Wharncliffe Lodge—probably

---

[1] Paston, 196–9; 11, 15, 20 Dec., W MS, ii. 317–18, 311–12, 339–40.
[2] 9 Dec., W MS, i. 150–1.

because that was cheapest. A week later, with all arrangements completed, she was ready for the journey. 'I love travelling', she assured her husband, and set the day of her departure for Monday after New Year's Day, when the light of the new moon would allow her to make faster progress.[1] On 3 January 1715 her coach rattled out of York bound for London.

[1] M to W, 21 Dec. [1714], W MS, ii. 345–6.

IV. *Courtiers and Couplets*

(1715–16)

LADY MARY returned in triumph to London in January 1715 in time to see the Whigs win a sweeping victory in the Parliamentary elections. She settled down to a busy social routine: on Mondays the Drawing-Room, Wednesdays the opera, and Thursdays the playhouse. On the other evenings of the week she visited ladies, and was served tea, cards, and gossip. In general it was 'a perpetual round of hearing the same scandal, and seeing the same follies acted over and over'.[1] Although she may occasionally have been bored, she was undoubtedly pleased and stimulated by living near the Court of St. James, instead of in a country village.

Under George I the Court had greatly changed. He came to the throne in his fifty-fifth year, a stolid German settled in tastes and habits, having reluctantly left his palaces in Hanover to ascend an alien throne which he regarded only as useful for the foreign policy of his Electorate. His character was very keenly observed and analysed by Lady Mary. 'In private life he would have been called an honest blockhead; and Fortune, that made him a king, added nothing to his happiness, only prejudiced his honesty and shortened his days. . . . He could speak no English, and was past the age of learning it. Our customs and laws were all mysteries to him, which he neither tried to understand, nor was capable of understanding if he had endeavoured it. He was passively good-natured, and wished all mankind enjoyed quiet, if they would let him do so.'[2] However unappealing, the King was still the source of power for her and her husband. At his dull evening parties he preferred his German suite, and did not invite many English. Lady Mary attended, and tried to ingratiate herself with him and his favourites. One of her friends who

---

[1] M to Pope, 17 June 1717, i. 332. [2] 'Account', i. 126–7.

observed her there was the Countess of Loudoun, a young, agreeably naïve woman. While Lord Loudoun was with the army in Scotland, she tried to amuse him by sending him news of the town; and in one of her letters (on 5 March 1715) she described the ambitious young wife: 'Lady Mary Wortley learns German to make her court to the King.' Then she added: 'But that won't do, for he can't like anybody so little, let their mind be as large as it will.'[1] The small and vivacious Lady Mary could not, her friend thought, appeal to a king who preferred women of more ample charms.

He already possessed three mistresses of varied ages, temperaments, and functions. (His wife, divorced for being detected in a *liaison*, was imprisoned in Germany.) Two of them had come to England with him, and Lady Mary also cultivated their friendship; for apart from their personal merit, they exercised considerable power, or pretended to, through the King and his German advisers. She preferred the Baroness Kielmannsegge, of whom she wrote: 'She had a greater vivacity in conversation than ever I knew in a German of either sex. She loved reading, and had a taste of all polite learning. Her humour was easy and sociable. Her constitution inclined her to gallantry. She was well bred and amusing in company. She knew how both to please and be pleased, and had experience enough to know it was hard to do either without money.' The other Royal mistress in England was the Baroness von Schulenburg, whose temperament was closer to the King's. In Lady Mary's opinion, 'She was duller than himself, and consequently did not find out that he was so.' Still, her friendship was valuable, and Lady Mary was no doubt glad to receive scribbled, affectionate notes in French from the Baroness asking her to call.[2] The King's third and favourite mistress, the Countess von Platen, remained in Hanover, where she received his frequent visits.

Soon after his accession he had been followed to England by his only son Prince George and his son's wife, the Princess Caroline. Father and son were on bad terms, but ambitious courtiers could seek favour with each separately. Lady Mary thought the Prince a man whose every look and gesture showed his fiery temper. Unhappily his limited intelligence could not

[1] Huntington Libr. MS.
[2] 'Account', i. 127–8; Mlle von Schulenburg to M, W MS, iv. 240–1.

control his inordinate pride: 'he looked on all the men and women he saw as creatures he might kick or kiss for his diversion.' Although she considered the Princess a woman of low cunning, inclined to cheat everybody she conversed with, Lady Mary must have found her intellectually sympathetic.[1] The Princess patronized men of letters, science, and philosophy, and encouraged an intellectual atmosphere at her court.

While Lady Mary attempted to win social favour at Court, Wortley applied himself to political advancement. The King usually spoke French in transacting business, and since Wortley was the only man on the Treasury Board (except perhaps Lord Halifax) who spoke the language, it was thought that he would thus gain considerable influence. But to his disappointment the King dealt with the Treasury through his ministers instead of in person. Wortley's luck continued unfavourable. In May 1715 Lord Halifax died; and when Robert Walpole was appointed Lord of the Treasury in October, Wortley correctly assumed that he would be turned out in favour of one of Walpole's appointees.[2] He later claimed that Walpole proposed to compensate him with an appointment for life worth about £3,000 a year, and that the King agreed, with the remark: 'J'en suis bien aise.'[3] But instead he was soon to be offered something else.

Rewards from another source had failed to come to him and Lady Mary. At Lord Pierrepont's death in May 1715 it was found that his will, drawn up in 1682, had never been changed. His estate went to Lady Mary's father,[4] who was soon elevated by the King to the Dukedom of Kingston-upon-Hull, and the following year appointed Lord Privy Seal.

While her father's fortunes rose, her favourite sister's fell. Lady Mar, who with her husband lived in a house in the Privy Gardens of Whitehall Palace, had anticipated a prosperous future for him at the new Court, but Lord Mar was realistic enough to admit his discouragement.[5] When it was clear to him that he could not hope for any favour, he joined the Jacobite

---

[1] 'Account', i. 133–4.
[2] Wortley, 'On the State of Affairs when the King Entered', printed with M's letters, i. 140.
[3] W to Addison, 18 July 1717 o.s., Tickell MS.
[4] Copy of will in Somerset House; *Post Boy*, 21–23 June 1715.
[5] M to W, [20 Aug. 1714], W MS, i. 228–9; Mar to J. Erskine, 7, 16 Aug. 1714, HMC *Mar and Kellie MSS* (1904), 505, 506.

faction plotting to raise a rebellion. On 1 August 1715 he kissed the King's hand at St. James's, and the next day departed for Scotland to lead the rebels. By the end of the year his army was defeated, and in February (1716) he fled to France. But Lady Mar continued to live at Whitehall, and go about as before, though she was occasionally molested by overzealous patriots.[1] Her exiled husband asserted that she never meddled in his politics nor had even known of his flight to lead the rebels.[2] Her family was so prominently and unimpeachably Whig that she did not suffer personally for her husband's disgrace; nor did she ever forfeit the devotion of her favourite sister.

During her first year in London Lady Mary began to cultivate literary men whom she had not previously known. In Court circles she met the Abbé Antonio Conti, Italian savant, philosopher, and poet. He had come to London in April 1715 to observe the eclipse of the sun, and had been received by Princess Caroline and, with particular favour, by the King.[3] Lady Mary was greatly stimulated by his cosmopolitan culture, as she showed by addressing to him a French essay and later some letters. Perhaps through Congreve, she met other wits in London—the poet John Gay, the physician and satirist Dr. John Arbuthnot, the painter Charles Jervas, and Pope, with whom she began the most important literary friendship of her life.

Pope was then preparing to issue the first volume of his *Iliad* translation, the work which earned him his fortune. Possibly Lady Mary had long ago (in 1704) read his *Pastorals*, which, he noted, 'passed through the hands' of Lord Dorchester.[4] In his portraits the feverishly bright eyes tell of a high-strung nature, the result in part of his physical deformity and ill health. Since early boyhood he had been afflicted with curvature of the spine, and never grew beyond four-and-a-half feet. His life, as he wrote, was a 'long Disease'. Emotionally, he was excessively sensitive, equally capable of warmly affectionate friendships and bitterly vindictive enmities. By the summer of 1715 he and

---

[1] *News Letter*, 21 Jan. 1716; 2 Mar. 1716, *Cal. of Treasury Papers 1714–1719*, ed. J. Redington (1883), 197.
[2] 'The Earl of Mar's Legacies to Scotland' (1726), *Publ. of the Scotch Hist. Soc.* xxvi (1896), 176–7.
[3] Conti, *Prose e Poesie*, ii (1756), 23, 39.
[4] George Sherburn, *Early Career of Pope* (1934), 52–53.

Lady Mary were active correspondents. While visiting his
parents in Windsor Forest he depended on her to relay the
news from London, which was then agitated by political
changes and the Jacobite uprising.[1] In the autumn, when she
again met him, they were joined by Gay in a literary scheme
whose outcome they could not have foreseen.

Gay had devised a new genre by cleverly adapting Virgil's
pastoral eclogues into satiric town eclogues in which shepherds
and shepherdesses are transformed into London beaux and belles
who also suffer from love and vanity.[2] At the meetings of the
poetical triumvirate, three town eclogues were at first composed. 'The Toilet', written mostly by Gay, is the lament of
Lydia, a superannuated beauty neglected by her lover Damon;
finally she is restored by her maid's flattery, and hurries off to
the playhouse. Under the pseudonyms of Lydia and Damon
the eclogue satirized specific persons—Mrs. Coke and Lord
Berkeley.[3] In coffee houses and Court circles such malicious
gossip was relished, but this stock situation was relatively
mild.

The other two eclogues were much sharper, and were
written by Lady Mary, with some help from Pope and Gay.
'The Basset Table' tells of Cardelia's passion for cards and
Smilinda's for a faithless lover named Sharper. Each lady insists
she has cause for stronger grief, but Betty Loveit, who judges
their contest, calls it a draw. Lady Mary had intended Cardelia
to stand for Lady Bristol, who was notoriously addicted to
cards; and Smilinda and Sharper to be herself and Lord Stair.
As Smilinda tells of Sharper's effect on her, she is most per-
suasive:

> Then when he trembles, when his blushes rise,
> When awful Love seems melting in his eyes!
> With eager beats his Mechlin cravat moves:
> He loves, I whisper to myself, He loves!
> Such unfeign'd passion in his look appears,
> I lose all mem'ry of my former fears;

[1] Pope to Teresa and Martha Blount, [23 July 1715], *Corr.* i. 309.
[2] The following sections dealing with the town eclogues come from my
article in *Publ. of the Mod. Lang. Assoc.* lxviii (1953), 237–50.
[3] In 1740 Lady Mary told Horace Walpole the identity of the characters in
the eclogues, and he later noted the names in his copy of the 1747 edition of
her poems, now owned by Mr. W. S. Lewis.

My panting heart confesses all his charms;
I yield at once, and sink into his arms.
Think of that moment, you who Prudence boast!
For such a moment, Prudence well were lost.[1]

It is tempting to read this as an autobiographical reference to
Lady Mary, especially since Horace Walpole elsewhere called
Lord Stair her first 'gallant' after her marriage.[2] But more probably, as in the other eclogues, her versatile skill and empathy
enabled her to express any point of view.

Her satire in the third eclogue, 'The Drawing-Room', dealt
with the far more serious subject of Princess Caroline. Here
Roxana complains of how she has sacrificed her modest pastimes
to attend the Princess at frivolous, worldly ones; yet the Princess has given the post of Lady of the Bedchamber not to her
but to the undeserving Coquetilla.

Ah! worthy choice! not one of all your train
Whom censure blasts not, and dishonours stain. . . .
A greater miracle is daily view'd,
A virtuous Princess with a court so lewd.
  I know thee, Court! with all thy treach'rous wiles,
Thy false caresses and undoing smiles!
Ah! Princess, learn'd in all the courtly arts
To cheat our hopes, and yet to gain our hearts.[3]

Unlike the other eclogues, 'The Drawing-Room' definitely hit
at several ladies, for the Princess had appointed the Duchess of
Shrewsbury as Lady of the Bedchamber, while the Duchess
of Roxburgh (Roxana) remained without a post.[4] It was daring,
if not dangerous, for Lady Mary to criticize the Princess of
Wales's court as immoral.

What could Lady Mary and her fellow poets do with the
eclogues, particularly the dangerous one? Among their circle,
manuscript copies were only lent to friends who could be
trusted. 'It was not the business of a man of quality to turn

---

[1] *Six Town Eclogues with some other Poems* (1747), 25–26. This text is
a copy (by Walpole) of Lady Mary's own autograph of the eclogues
(Harrowby, vol. 256).
[2] James Prior, *Life of Malone* (1860), 150; 'before her marriage' in Walpole's
'Anecdotes of Lady Mary Wortley Montagu and Lady Pomfret' [1740],
Corr. xiv. 243.   [3] *Six Town Eclogues* (1747), 7–8.
[4] Besides Walpole's notes, these identifications are given in a transcript
owned by the 2nd Earl of Oxford (BM MS Lansd. 852, ff. 184–5).

author', she contended many years later; 'he should confine himself to the applause of his friends.'[1] This custom was very neatly described in *The School for Scandal* when Lady Sneerwell says, 'I wonder, Sir Benjamin, you never publish any thing', and Sir Benjamin Backbite answers, 'To say truth, ma'am, 'tis very vulgar to print; and as my little productions are mostly satires and lampoons on particular people, I find they circulate more by giving copies in confidence to the friends of the parties.'[2] In similar fashion Lady Mary's town eclogues were passed about, presumably to discreet friends.

In the middle of December 1715 she was suddenly struck by smallpox.[3] The disease which had killed her brother now filled her with the greatest terror, for she expected either death or disfigurement. Two of the most eminent medical men in England attended her, Hans Sloane and Dr. Garth. Unable to cure the disease, Dr. Garth tried to quiet her fears, but in vain. She described her feelings in verse written soon after her recovery.

> In tears, surrounded by my friends I lay,
> Mask'd o'er and trembling at the sight of day;
> [Sloane] Mirmillo came my fortune to deplore,
> (A golden headed cane well carv'd he bore)
> Cordials, he cried, my spirits must restore:
> Beauty is fled, and spirit is no more!
> Galen, the grave; officious Squirt, was there,
> With fruitless grief and unavailing care:
> [Garth] Machaon too, the great Machaon, known
> By his red cloak and his superior frown;
> And why, he cry'd, this grief and this despair?
> You shall again be well, again be fair;
> Believe my oath; (with that an oath he swore)
> False was his oath; my beauty is no more![4]

Only half of Dr. Garth's oath proved true, for her beauty was marred. She was left without eyelashes, and with a deeply pitted skin.

---

[1] To Lady Bute, 23 July 1753, ii. 238.   [2] (1777) I. i.
[3] The material on Lady Mary's connexion with smallpox is drawn from my article in the *Journal of the Hist. of Medicine*, viii (1953), 390-405.
[4] Stuart, 88; *Six Town Eclogues* (1747), 35-36. The identification of Sloane and Garth comes from Walpole's annotated copy; and 'trembling' in line 2 (instead of 'trembled') comes from Lady Mary's autograph.

Her friends were curious as to the effects of her illness. The kind Lady Loudoun thought that her 'good eyes' would counteract the damage to her skin; other ladies who knew that she had exceedingly full pocks and would be severely marked devised the pun that she was very full and yet not pitted [pitied]. It was repeated by James Brydges, who predicted that she would live to be revenged on some of her sex.[1] Her tongue, like her pen, had apparently been put to sharp use before.

Politics and literature were also involved in her illness. She had fallen ill, according to Brydges, 'just as it began (to her great joy) to be known she was in favour with one whom every one, who looks on, cannot but love. Her Husband too is inconsolable for the disappointment this gives him in the [career] he had chalkt out of his fortunes.'[2] In the eyes of politicians like Brydges, Lady Mary's favour with the King was considered an important asset to her husband's career. Now her clever eclogue criticizing the Princess threatened to wreck another important friendship at Court. The strange story of how it began to be circulated was told by Lady Loudoun to her husband at the beginning of January 1716.

'Lady Mary is now very well. I do not think she ever was in danger, but the town said she would die two days together, upon which a friend of hers (I do not know who it was) showed a poem she had entrusted them with writ upon the Court. I have not yet seen it, but I'm told it is very pretty and not a little wicked. I'm promised it in a day or two. The Princess has seen it. Poor Lady Mary will not know how to come to Court again. This would put a body with a good assurance out of countenance. How will her modesty go through with it?'

A few days later Lady Loudoun sent her husband the poem, which was still a secret; but she thought the whole town would have it in a day or so. Brydges, who found it 'very entertaining', sent copies to at least two friends.[3] It helped spread Lady Mary's reputation for witty malice.

[1] Lady Loudoun, 22 Dec. 1715, Huntington Libr. MS; Brydges to Col. Bladen, 28 Dec, 1715, 26 Jan. 1716, quoted in Sherburn, *Early Career*, 208 n., 204.   [2] Ibid. 208 n.
[3] Lady Loudoun, 3, 7 Jan. 1716; Sherburn, *Early Career*, 204.

Recovered from her illness, she resumed her attendance at Court, where her position had apparently not been affected. The Princess herself was a clever woman, and pride in her own intellectual *esprit* may have blunted her resentment. On a womanly plane, she may have thought a wicked satire trivial in comparison to Lady Mary's close escape from death. As though to celebrate her return to health and activity, in March Pope gracefully complimented her by name in his 'Epistle to Jervas' as a beauty whose eyes other beauties shall envy.[1] But her reputation henceforth was mainly that of a wit.

Her two town eclogues, along with Gay's single one, had been circulated so widely that they had fallen into the hands of Edmund Curll, the piratical printer. The Unspeakable Curll, as he has been called, was a literary scavenger who made a speciality of obscene and scandalous publications. On 26 March he issued the three eclogues in a pamphlet entitled *Court Poems*. On his title-page he asserted that the poems had been found in a pocket book at Westminster Hall on the last day of Lord Winton's trial—which had ended ten days earlier with a verdict of death for the Jacobite rebel. Not content with that bid for publicity on the title-page (dated 1706), he attached a preface to tease the reader with conjectures as to the author of the poems: that at the St. James's Coffee House they were attributed to a 'lady of quality'; at Button's to Mr. Gay, whose previous poetry was similar; and that a gentleman near Chelsea [Addison] pronounced them to be by the judicious translator of Homer [Pope]. The London coffee-house critics had something to ponder.

If Curll intended to confuse, he succeeded. But Pope stated the case accurately in a pamphlet attacking the printer; that by attributing the poems to a 'lady of quality' Curll escaped one revenge—since that designation was so general as to be anonymous; but that by naming Gay and Pope (whose second volume of Homer had been issued only four days earlier) he still had two revenges in reserve. Pope took both revenges in his own hands, and in a strangely ribald way. He invited Curll to join him and Lintot, his friend and printer, for a drink in a tavern. There, in the course of a fruitless argument as to whether or

---

[1] Pub. 20 Mar. (*London Gazette*, 17–20 Mar. 1716); Elwin and Courthope, iii. 213.

not the satires should have been published, he secretly added a
strong emetic to Curll's wine; and then they parted. The aftermath can be imagined. Or it can be read, with disgusting detail,
in Pope's prose narrative of his revenge, issued a few days later
as *A Full and True Account of a Horrid and Barbarous Revenge
by Poison, on the Body of Mr. Edmund Curll, Bookseller*. Curll
took more gentle revenge himself by printing the eclogues
thereafter without any teasing preface about their authorship;
they were, his title-page announced, by Mr. Pope.

But how does all this concern Lady Mary? It is usually
assumed that Pope took revenge on her behalf, but there is no
proof of this gallant interpretation. He may have been trying
to shield Gay, who was soliciting a place from the Princess
Caroline and could not afford to satirize her Court in print; and
he was certainly taking revenge on his own behalf: as he wrote
to a friend, Curll had 'printed some satirical pieces on the Court
under my name. I contrived to save a fellow a beating by giving
him a vomit . . .'.[1] Two of the poems were Lady Mary's, to be
sure, but her friends (and enemies) at Court had known that for
several months, and so she needed no protection and suffered
no punishment there. And to the general public she was merely
a Court beauty, celebrated for her fine eyes.

She could not hope that Curll would allow her satiric gift to
remain private. Only two months later he issued in his *State
Poems* some verse by a 'lady of quality'. 'The Ramble between
Belinda a Demy-Prude, and Cloe a Court Coquette' tells how
when two ladies go out on a ramble, the coquettish one steals
off to meet the other's husband. Curll republished it several
times in various makeshift collections; and in the following
year, 1717, added a footnote that the best lines were taken from
Fontaine and that 'a fam'd Female *Wit*, (the Lady *W—y
M—gue*,) assisted in the Translation'. It is very doubtful that
she wrote the crude, inept verse, since Curll's label carries no
authority.

In the spring of 1716, after recovering from her illness, she
composed three additional town eclogues: the 'St. James's
Coffee House', where two town beaux compare their con-
quests, with rather indelicate details; 'The Tête-à-Tête', where
Dacinda reproves Strephon for pursuing her, and then warns

[1] To Caryll, 20 Apr., *Corr.* i. 339.

him to escape down the backstairs as her husband returns home. Since each eclogue was named for a day of the week, she completed the set with 'Saturday, or The Small Pox', in which Flavia utters an elaborate farewell because the disease has ruined her beauty. Her illness probably served Lady Mary as the occasion for still another literary exercise, a brief French essay 'Carabosse'.[1] In this adaptation of Perrault's fairy tale of the sleeping beauty, the good fairies award the infant princess a series of blessings which the wicked Carabosse nullifies. 'Je la doue d'une beauté noble et touchante', decrees the first good fairy; and Carabosse cries out, 'Je veux que cette fille chérie perde cette beauté admirable par la petite vérole dans l'âge qu'elle commence à sentir ses avantages.' The superlative virtues of intellect shall attract enemies and make her the prey of fools; the riches of her father and husband shall not be at her disposal; her excellent health shall make her undertake dangerous enterprises; and, finally, her freedom from vice, misfortune, envy, and avarice shall be cancelled by a great fund of tenderness. In a sense Lady Mary was sketching her own portrait to show, in addition to a forgivable egotism, the subtlety and cynicism which were hers in real life.

During the untidy aftermath of Curll's publication, she had more to think of than literary squabbles, for it was announced on 7 April that Wortley was appointed Ambassador Extraordinary to the Court of Turkey, in place of Sir Robert Sutton.[2] He would also represent the Levant Company, which held the charter to trade in the Near East. At first he had refused the post because its emoluments fell far short of the £3,000 a year proposed by Walpole, but he was persuaded to accept it after he was promised great rewards at the termination of his Embassy.[3] The Levant Company thereupon informed Sutton of his replacement, and instructed their treasurer in Constantinople to pay Wortley £500 for travelling expenses and to provide him with the customary presents.[4] Because of the expense of replacing appointees, ambassadors entered into articles of agreement with the Company to stay at least five years.[5] Wortley's

[1] ii. 419–20; discussed in my article in *Comp. Lit.* iii (1951), 174–7.
[2] *Eve. Post*, 5–7 Apr. 1716, and other newspapers.
[3] W to Addison, 18 July 1717 o.s., Tickell MS.
[4] 10 May, 11 July 1716, SP 105/116.
[5] Levant Co. to Onslow, 8 Oct. 1717, ibid.

immediate predecessors, Sutton and Lord Paget, had served fifteen and ten years each.

None of the newspaper reports or official documents mentioned the Ambassador's wife, yet her part in his Embassy was to make her famous throughout Europe, and her journey to the East would be remembered long after his mission was forgotten. Constantinople had always seemed to her an impossibly remote place.[1] She later told Spence how she had felt at the news of her husband's appointment. 'Lady Mary, who had always delighted in romances and books of travels, was charmed with the thoughts of going into the East, though those embassies are generally an affair of twenty years, and so 'twas a sort of dying to her friends and country. But 'twas travelling; 'twas going farther than most other people go; 'twas wandering; 'twas all whimsical, and charming; and so she set out with all the pleasure imaginable.'[2]

But she first had to prepare for the journey. Soon after his appointment Wortley went alone to Wharncliffe Lodge, and Lady Mary informed him of the political situation in London. On 18 April, while visiting Lady Jekyll, she wrote him that 'the place bill' was not being mentioned. It would affect him, she explained the next day, because some people questioned his right to membership in Parliament while holding a government appointment.[3] The bill was defeated, however, and so he could simultaneously occupy a Parliamentary seat and an ambassadorial post a thousand miles apart. Lady Mary also took care of such chores as selecting a chaplain—a Reverend Mr. Crosse was engaged—and ordering twenty suits of livery for their servants.[4] She invited Sarah Chiswell, a childhood friend from Nottingham, to be her companion, but the lady's fearful relatives kept her from accepting. Lady Mary was of braver mettle. Having decided to take along her precious son, she ordered the sister of her servant Matthew Northall to be sent down from Yorkshire to be trained as the boy's nurse.[5] The surgeon Charles

[1] M to W, 23 Aug. 1714, Paston, 188.
[2] Spence to his mother, 25 Feb. 1741, MS Eg. 2234, f. 248.
[3] M to W, 18 Apr., W MS, ii. 266–7; Paston, 227.
[4] Levant Co. to Stanyan, 27 Nov. 1717, SP 105/116; M to W, Apr. 1716, i. 219–20.
[5] M to Sarah Chiswell, 13 Aug. 1716, i. 228; M to W, [19 Apr.], W MS, ii. 359–60 (frag. in Paston, 227).

Maitland was also engaged to look after the health of the party on their long, dangerous journey.

The diplomatic task which now confronted Wortley was extremely delicate and consequential. The European balance of power, so important to England's policy, was in danger. Turkey had been at war with the Venetian Republic since 1714; and the Austrian Emperor, who was committed by treaty to come to Venice's assistance, threatened to enter the conflict; if he did so, his army could not be depended on to offset Spanish power in the Mediterranean.[1] England had to mediate between Austria and Turkey, and prevent their going to war. As the summer drew on, the diplomatic tension increased. In mid-June the Emperor's army prepared to leave for Hungary, but he detained the English messenger in Vienna because, it was thought, he wished to postpone any mediation until his army had gone into action, since he could then demand better truce terms. There was no doubt that he was making vigorous preparations for war. The situation was so serious at the end of June that James Stanhope, Secretary of State, was rumoured as going to Constantinople; actually he went only to Hanover to be with the King.[2]

Since Wortley grumbled about his expenses, Stanhope offered him the opportunity of profiting from his travel allowance by going via Marseilles or directly to Constantinople by boat. Instead he determined to go by way of Vienna in order to carry a letter from the King to the Emperor—which he thought would expedite his mediation and treaty.[3] His credentials were signed on 2 July 1716.[4] During the rest of the month, the newspapers carried notices of his imminent departure.

Among those to whom Lady Mary bid farewell was Pope. Their friendship had developed a debonair informality, as can be seen in the note Jervas sent to him: 'Lady Mary W—y orderd me by an Express this Wensday Morning, sedente Gayo, et ridente Fortescuvio, to send you a Letter or some other proper Notice to come to her on Thursday about 5 a Clock which I suppose she meant in the Evening.'[5] It would

---

[1] Wolfgang Michael, *England under George I* (transl. 1936, 1939), i. 359–60.
[2] *Daily Courant*, 20 Apr., 15 May, 19 June; *Flying Post*, 10 May; *Eve. Post*, 28–30 June 1716.   [3] W to Addison, 18 July 1717 o.s., Tickell MS.
[4] W MS, vii. 123.   [5] Pope to M, *Corr.* i. 340–1.

be a tragic deprivation to him when she left England; and he confessed as much to her a short time before her departure: '. . . indeed I find I begin to behave my self worse to you than to any other Woman, as I value you more. And yet if I thought I shou'd not see you again, I would say some things here, which I could not to your Person. For I would not have you dye deceivd in me, that is, go to Constantinople without knowing, that I am to some degree of Extravagance, as well as with the utmost Reason, Madam. . . .'[1] His epistolary homage to her, then and later, owed much to his reading of the French masters of the art. As a more substantial token of his extravagant friendship, he had copied in his 'fairest hand' her five town eclogues into an album richly bound in red Turkey leather, and presented it to her. She left it in his custody for her sojourn abroad.[2] Two days before she left, he came to town from his house in nearby Chiswick; and perhaps on that day she gave him some of her 'last Moments'.[3]

At last the Ambassador, Lady Mary, their child, and a numerous entourage set forth. They were not encumbered with heavy baggage, which had been sent by boat to Leghorn.[4] (From there it could be shipped to Turkey.) Still they travelled in great pomp with twenty servants; and, to her friends' amusement, Lady Mary dignified herself by wearing a black full-bottomed wig.[5] They left London on Wednesday, 1 August, and the next day at Gravesend embarked on a yacht bound for Holland.[6]

---

[1] Pope to M, *Corr.* i. 345.
[2] Pope to M, autumn 1717, ibid. 441. Now in the Arents Coll. of the N.Y. Public Library.
[3] Pope to Parnell, 29 July; to M, 18 Aug. 1716, ibid. 348, 355.
[4] Methuen to Cotterel, 17 July 1716, *Cal. of Treasury Papers 1714-1719*, 21.
[5] Pope to M, 10 Nov. 1716, *Corr.* i. 368, 369.
[6] HMC *Polwarth MSS*, i (1911), 49, 52; *Weekly Journal or Br. Gaz.* 4 Aug. 1716.

v. Journey to Constantinople

(1716)

SINCE Lady Mary accompanied an official embassy, her journey can be outlined from diplomatic dispatches and newspaper reports, but for its substance we must rely on her own writings. She recorded her observations and experiences in a journal, which no longer exists.[1] The journal served her as a literary storehouse from which she drew material for letters to her friends (only a few of these survive) and for a series of fifty-two letters, compiled within a few years after her return to England. These Embassy Letters are the fullest record we have of her thoughts, activities, and observations.[2] Their dates, even if sometimes inaccurate, are usually close to the actual ones; and the names she put at the heads of the letters are a few of the many friends to whom she sent actual letters.[3] Although their form is partially fiction, the Embassy Letters tell the substance of her life abroad.

After leaving Gravesend the Ambassador's yacht was becalmed for two days. On the third night a storm arose, so fierce it threw the sailors off their feet. Although the captain appeared to be frightened, Lady Mary (as she boasted in her first Embassy Letter) felt neither fear nor sea-sickness. The party disembarked at Helvoetsluys to begin their overland journey. She liked everything about Holland; its neatness, cleanliness, and industriousness; and its countryside, geometrically patterned with canals and rows of trees, like a large neat garden. The central square in The Hague, where people of quality walked or rode in coaches, seemed to her a combination of Hyde Park

---

[1] It was burned by her daughter after her death (Stuart, 65, 80).

[2] Printed in i. 225–403. Unless other sources are cited, these letters are used to document M's two years abroad.

[3] The 'Heads of Letters', her memorandum of actual letters from 1 Apr. 1717 to 1 Mar. 1718, is printed in i. 17–19.

and the Mall in St. James's Park. The town of Nijmegen, she wrote Sarah Chiswell, was very much like Nottingham. She often used such comparisons during her journey, not out of any narrow insularity but rather to convert the strange into the familiar for the readers of both her actual and compiled letters. With hired horses the party hurried south toward Vienna, where Wortley was to begin his mediation, and after unexpected delays reached Cologne. In her sightseeing Lady Mary was very much shocked and amused by a Jesuit church. Although she had scoffed at the Calvinist church service (in Nijmegen), she directed her most pointed ridicule at the Catholic churches she saw in Germany and Austria. As a moderately sceptical and professing Anglican she felt that religion, except for simple externals, was a private affair to be accepted without too intense an inquiry into its basis; and for people in general it was a socially useful institution. She was equally against atheistic 'free-thinking', over-zealous 'enthusiasm', and—what she now observed in Germany—'superstitious' Catholicism. In Nuremberg she bestowed her sarcasm impartially on the religious relics of a Lutheran church and on the decoration of a modest Catholic one—where to provide finery 'they have dressed up an image of our Saviour over the altar in a fair full-bottomed wig very well powdered'. Then, to convince her correspondent, she gave assurances, often repeated in other letters, that she would not take advantage of the usual privilege of travellers to exaggerate or lie.

The party next stopped at Ratisbon, seat of the German Imperial Diet; and because she had caught cold she remained there a few days, enough time to observe the turmoil of its court and diplomatic corps. Everybody quarrelled and formed social cabals, but she refused to be drawn into any: 'I know that my peaceable disposition already gives me a very ill-figure, and that it is *publicly* whispered, as a piece of impertinent pride in me, that I have hitherto been saucily civil to everybody, as if I thought nobody good enough to quarrel with.' She was saved from further disgrace by her departure. The party embarked on a comfortably furnished houseboat rowed by twelve men, and made swift progress down the Danube. Along its shores Lady Mary saw a new kind of landscape: 'romantic solitudes... charmingly diversified with woods, rocks, mountains covered with vines, fields of corn, large cities, and ruins of ancient castles.' It was a relaxing prelude to the rigours of the Imperial Court in Vienna.

The political crisis there had greatly changed, for on 5 August the Imperial army under Prince Eugene had defeated a Turkish army twice its size at Peterwardein, and had driven back the remnants as far as Belgrade. Wortley reached Vienna on 14 September, and the next day was received by the Emperor Charles VI.[1] It was generally thought, the English Ambassador to Vienna reported, that the war could be ended without the fall of Belgrade if the already frightened Turks could be persuaded that the Emperor intended to continue his campaign; and that Wortley would be able to initiate a peace treaty before leaving.[2] He remained in Vienna over two months for that purpose.

To Lady Mary the Dutch and German cities must have seemed provincial compared to the rococo splendour of Vienna. She could not be presented at Court until a dress of the prescribed style was made for her. 'I was squeezed up in a gown', she wrote, 'and adorned with a gorget and the other implements thereunto belonging: a dress very inconvenient, but which certainly shews the neck and shape to great advantage.' She first had a half hour's private audience with the Empress Elizabeth, a creature of unbelievable perfection; then the other ladies of the Court entered to play cards while she sat at the Empress's right and watched. When the Emperor came in he spoke to her 'in a very obliging manner'; and that evening she met the Dowager Empress Amelia with her two daughters. Her impression of royalty was almost reverent except for that of the old Dowager Empress Eleanore: 'a princess of great virtue and goodness, but who piques herself so much on a violent devotion, she is perpetually performing extraordinary acts of penance, without having ever done anything to deserve them'.

She also entertained herself with ordinary sightseeing and visits. In the city itself she was most impressed by the towering buildings magnificently furnished within. On her excursions to the suburbs she inspected treasure-collections in villas and the

---

[1] *Daily Courant*, 25 Sept.; *Weekly Journal*, 29 Sept. 1716.
[2] Schaub to Townshend, 16 Sept. 1716, SP 80/33.

beautiful gardens of Schönbrunn. She was invited to many dinners, and taken to elaborate theatrical productions, among them an opera about Alcina and a comedy about Amphitryon. Although the comedy was played in German, she understood most of it. Yet a few months later, when visiting the Duchess of Blankenburg, she excused herself from attending church because (she protested) she did not understand the language well enough to pay her devotions in it.

She found the gay side of social life more attractive, and took stock of its varied patterns. Youthfulness was considered of such slight importance that a woman could continue in favour long after her first bloom. And custom did not encourage a woman to be so prudish as to pretend fidelity to her own husband; and the husband usually deputized for someone else's. Thus, Lady Mary wrote, "'tis the established custom for every lady to have two husbands, one that bears the name, and another that performs the duties'. Once, at a party, a young gentleman volunteered to be her gallant, or if he did not please her to help find one who did. Although shocked, she gravely thanked him, knowing he meant only to be courteous. 'Thus you see, my dear,' she concluded her explanation to her English friend, 'gallantry and good-breeding are as different, in different climates, as morality and religion. Who have the rightest notions of both, we shall never know till the day of judgment.' She continued to apply this attitude of comparative morality to other institutions she observed in her travels.

Her personal interest in gallantry led her to study it; and she knew that her observations would amuse many of her correspondents, court ladies like Lady Rich and Lady Bristol, and genial wits like the Abbé Conti and Congreve. She kept her English friendships in repair by means of her amusing letters. But none of her friends' letters to her survive for this period except Pope's, and they outline a curious friendship.

His admiration for her, fervent enough when she left England, increased as their 'unhappy Distance' lengthened. In his first letter, two weeks after her departure, he assured her: 'You may easily imagine how desirous I must be of a Correspondence with a person, who had taught me long ago that it was as possible to Esteem at first sight, as to Love: and who has since ruin'd me for all the Conversation of one Sex, and almost all the Friendship of the other.'[1] Under his verbal extravagance appears a sincere anxiety, unmatched in any of his letters to other women, that she should take him seriously. 'It would be the most vexatious of all Tyranny', he told her, 'if you should pretend to take for Raillery, what is the meer disguise of a discontented heart that is unwilling to make you as melancholy as itself; and for Wit, what is really only the natural Overflowing and Warmth of the same Heart, as it is improved and awakend by an Esteem for you.'[2] It was not long before his admiration took an erotic turn. The distance between them, he wrote on 18 August, removed punctilious restrictions and decorums; and in successive letters he continued to remove them. 'Let us be like modest people, who when they are close together keep all decorums, but if they step a little aside, or get to the other end of a room, can untye garters or take off Shifts without scruple.' The prospect of her journey to the sensual courts of the East —where he imagined she would abandon herself 'to extreme Effeminacy, Laziness, and Lewdness of life'—encouraged him to be so outspoken a rake; and so he described her destination as 'the Land of Jealousy, where the unhappy Women converse with none but Eunuchs, and where the very Cucumbers are brought to them Cutt'. In the same vein he could wryly confess that he was aware of his own deformity: 'I am capable myself of following one I lov'd, not only to Constantinople, but to those parts of India, where they tell us the Women best like the Ugliest fellows, as the most admirable productions of nature, and look upon Deformities as the Signatures of divine Favour.' If sufficiently encouraged, he persisted, he would meet her in Lombardy, 'the Scene of those celebrated Amours between the fair Princess and her Dwarf'.[3]

Lady Mary's attitude toward his elaborate compliments and innuendoes can be seen in the Embassy Letters which she addressed to him. Since these are 'compiled', they are less accurate a record than those letters he sent. In hers, she apparently encouraged him but did not commit herself, thus allowing him to advance without cutting off his retreat. Although she could accept his expressions merely as witty gallantry, she told him, she was disposed to believe them

---

[1] 18 Aug., *Corr.* i. 353–4.   [2] 1716–17, ibid. 383.
[3] Ibid. 354, 384, 406, 368, 364–5.

sincere. But her (compiled) letters to him are almost impersonal; as she ended one of them, devoted mostly to Oriental learning: 'I wish my studies may give me an occasion of entertaining your curiosity, which will be the utmost advantage hoped for from it by, &c.' She sent him the varied programme of her travels, observations, and studious pursuits. That she did not reciprocate his effusive adoration in her actual letters seems clear from his gratitude for one or two expressions in one of them 'too generous ever to be forgotten by me'.[1] She had nothing to lose by such generosity; it brought her flattery from the leading poet in London.

Wortley, who played no part in these affairs of heart and pen, was busy with his own grim business. By November the Turkish Sultan Achmet III, usually addressed as the Grand Seignior, had expressed a willingness to allow the English to mediate; and the Pasha of Belgrade had sent back Wortley's courier (on 4 November) to advise him to hasten into Turkey. Prince Eugene was expected in Vienna at the beginning of December for a meeting of the Imperial War Council.[2] During the lull in military activity Wortley could have begun his mediation. Yet on 24 November he left for Hanover with Lady Mary. This was reported by the English Ambassador to Vienna, who commented that although Wortley proposed to hasten his return as much as he could, it would have been preferred there if he had left for Constantinople, above all by those who were for peace.[3] But the detour had not been Wortley's plan; he had been ordered by Stanhope to secure further credentials from the King.[4]

On their northward journey Wortley and Lady Mary rode for three days and nights without stopping, until they reached Prague; then again for twenty-four hours, entering Saxony at night on a terribly dangerous road high above the Elbe.[5] When Lady Mary, who could never sleep in a coach, looked out of the window, she saw by moonlight how dangerous the road was. Wortley innocently dozed by her side. When the pos-

[1] *Corr.* i. 407.
[2] *Weekly Journal*, 10 Nov.; *Daily Courant*, 13 Nov. 1716.
[3] Schaub to Townshend, 25 Nov. 1716, SP 80/33.
[4] W to Addison, 18 July 1717 o.s., Tickell MS.
[5] In 1777 Nathaniel Wraxall found Lady Mary's description 'literally verified' (Elizabeth Montagu, *Letters 1762–1800*, ed. Reginald Blunt [1923], ii. 40).

tilions began to nod with sleep on their galloping horses, she shouted to them, and awakened Wortley as well. In Leipzig, where they stopped briefly, she bought pages' liveries, cheaper there than in Vienna, and some cloth for herself. Then, after pausing at Brunswick, they arrived in Hanover at the beginning of December.

They found many English friends who had accompanied the King there. As the Ambassador and his lady they had rooms in the palace, and could easily attend the festive court. The King's company of French comedians played every night, and he himself frequently dined and supped in public. Lady Mary's startling success with him was witnessed by an Englishman (who proudly sent a description to his daughter Lady Cowper): 'Mr. *Wortley Montague* and his Lady . . . were so very impatient to see His *Majesty* that they travelled Night and Day from *Vienna* here. Her *Ladyship* is mighty gay and airy, and occasions a great deal of Discourse. Since her Arrival the *King* has took but little Notice of any other Lady, not even of Madame *Kielmansegg*, which the Ladies of *Hanover* don't relish very well; for my Part, I can't help rejoicing to see His *Majesty* prefer us to the Germans.'[1] But even the King's intimate adviser Baron Bothmer had foreseen that Lady Mary's vivacity would lend a carnival spirit to Hanover.[2]

As a curious traveller she explored wherever she could. In the King's palace one night she was quite astonished to find that in spite of the cold December weather she was served oranges, lemons, and pineapples. The Germans had devised plain stoves for the plant-houses, and handsomely painted and gilt ones for their dwellings. How obstinate of the English to shiver with cold six months a year when they could use stoves, she exclaimed to her sister (in an Embassy Letter): 'If ever I return, in defiance to the fashion, you shall certainly see one in [my] chamber.' She apparently never imported a stove; but she remained receptive to new ideas on her travels.

Wortley stayed with her in Hanover for several weeks, and received his 'Additional Instructions' from the King. At the suggestion of Abraham Stanyan, the newly appointed English

[1] J. Clavering, 15 Dec. 1716, *Diary of Mary Countess Cowper 1714–1720*, ed. S. Cowper (2nd ed., 1865), 195.

[2] To Robethon, London, 7/18 Dec. 1716, BM MS Stowe 229, ff. 329–30.

Ambassador to Vienna, he was instructed to share his powers as mediator with the Dutch envoy to Turkey.[1] After leaving, he and Lady Mary made a long detour to Blankenburg near the Rhine, arriving in Vienna on 7 January 1717. He talked of setting out for Belgrade in a short time, but did not fix the day of his departure. 'In the mean time', Stanyan wrote to Lord Stair, then English Ambassador in Paris, 'Lady Mary is pretty much the subject of conversation here. She sticks to her English modes and manners, which exposes her a little to the railleries of the Vienna ladies. She replies with a good deal of wit, and is engaged in a sort of petty war; but they all own she is a witty woman, if not a well-dressed one.'[2] Her new importance as a diplomat's wife was recognized in Paris by Lord Mar, who wondered whether if he sent his compliments to her through the Jacobite agent in Vienna she would receive them; he also inquired whether her beauty had been ruined by smallpox.[3] If it had, her wit remained unimpaired.

The carnival season in Vienna had begun, and she enjoyed its diversions before setting out on her journey across the frozen plains of Hungary. On every side she was warned of the dangers: 'I am threatened at the same time, with being frozen to death, buried in the snow, and taken by the Tartars, who ravage that part of Hungary I am to pass.' Prince Eugene, whom she saw often, tried to persuade her to wait until the Danube was thawed, when she could sail down by boat. She was fearful not so much for her own safety as for her child's: 'when I think of the fatigue my poor infant must suffer, I have all a mother's fondness in my eyes, and all her tender passions in my heart.' Their departure was again postponed until the arrival of Wortley's passport from the Prime Vizier.[4] He still conferred, meanwhile, with the Emperor and his ministers, who carefully instructed him as to their terms of mediation.[5] At last, on 27 January, after three weeks in the Austrian capital, he set out with his party for Peterwardein en route to Belgrade.[6]

[1] W MS, vii. 121-2 (Paston, 242-3); Stanyan to Townshend, 9 Dec. 1716, SP 80/34.

[2] Ibid. 9 Jan. 1717; Stanyan to Stair, 9 Jan. 1717, *Annals and Corr. of the Earls of Stair*, ed. J. M. Graham (1875), ii. 35-36.

[3] Mar to Walkingshaw, 24 Dec. 1716, HMC *Stuart Papers*, iii (1907), 353.

[4] *Weekly Journal*, 2 Feb. 1717.   [5] W to Methuen, 13 Jan. 1717, SP 97/24.

[6] Stanyan to Methuen, 27 Jan. 1717, SP 80/34.

Lady Mary's dismal anticipation of their journey proved wrong. They were blessed with fine weather, and by fixing their coaches on sleighs they travelled swiftly over the deep snow, stopping only briefly at small villages. On 1 February they reached Buda, a place still devastated from the previous war between Turkey and Austria.[1] They crossed the frozen Danube and went over very deep snow to Essek, travelling with nineteen horses besides four extra carriages (with hired horses) for the baggage and some of the servants. After sending ahead a message to the Pasha, they resumed their journey for three more days until they arrived at Peterwardein, the last Imperial outpost.[2] They were lodged in the best apartment of the governor's house, and entertained in a very splendid manner. Now that Wortley was about to enter Turkish territory the diplomatic protocol became more elaborate. After some confusion his party departed with an Imperial escort of 100 musketeers, 50 grenadiers, and 50 hussars as far as Betsko. At this border his party was met by a Turkish guard of 130 horsemen as escort to Belgrade.[3] They arrived in the Turkish city on 16 February 1717.

In Belgrade Lady Mary had her first view of two contrasting sides of Turkish life—despotic barbarism and opulent culture. The city, officially ruled by a pasha, was actually controlled by fierce janissary troops. A whole chamber of them guarded the Ambassador's party in the house where he lodged while awaiting a summons from the Sultan in Adrianople. His host was a learned and cultivated *effendi*, Achmet Bey, who supped with Lady Mary every evening, and undertook to educate her in the literature and institutions of his country. He read and explained Arabian poetry to her; and when she understood its musical measures, she thought the love poetry 'very passionate and lively'. On the subject of religion she found the *effendi*'s ideas very sympathetic. Educated and enlightened Turks believed in deism, he explained, for like the Christians the Mohammedans had put superstition and revelation into their theology only to

---

[1] *London Gazette*, 12–16 Feb. 1717.
[2] W to Stanyan, 5 Feb. 1717, SP 80/34; W to Stanhope, quoted in M's letters i. 276 n.
[3] *London Gazette*, 5–9 Mar.; *Post Boy*, 26–28 Mar.; *Daily Courant*, 7 Mar. 1717. According to Lady Mary, the Turks sent an escort of 100 men more than the Austrians (i. 278).

win the credence of the ignorant; and the Alcoran itself contained only the purest morality. She could not help being pleased by her first glimpse into Islam when so much of it conformed to her own ideas.

About 8 March 1717, after three weeks in Belgrade, Wortley and his party continued on their way to Adrianople. He wished to go down the Danube by boat, a quicker and more convenient method than lying in the miserable houses along the road, but the Pasha refused to give him a special escort. Although he had been informed that their land-route was free of the plague, he was distressed to discover one of his servants stricken.[1] A doctor was left to look after the ill man, and the party travelled on. Lady Mary was unaware of the danger, having been told the servant suffered from a great cold; and she did not discover the truth until after his recovery.

At Sophia, where the party stopped, she visited the famous hot baths. Dressed in a riding habit, her usual travelling costume, she went incognito in a Turkish coach. In her Embassy Letters she painted a ravishing picture of the beautiful bathers, who when they saw her corset believed she had been locked in it by her jealous husband. She related this delightful anecdote to Spence in a less formal version:

> The first time she was at one of these baths, the ladies invited her to undress, and to bathe with them; and on her not making any haste, one of the prettiest run to her to undress her. You can't imagine her surprise upon lifting my lady's gown, and seeing her stays go all round her. She run back quite frightened, and told her companion, 'That the husbands in England were much worse than in the East, for that they tied up their wives in little boxes, of the shape of their bodies.' She carried 'em to see it. They all agreed that 'twas one of the greatest barbarities of the world, and pitied the poor women for being such slaves in Europe.[2]

From this experience she began to develop the paradox of Turkish women's liberty and English women's slavery.

The day after her adventure the Ambassador's party left Sophia and passed through Phillippopolis and the rich flourishing countryside of Adrianople, then serving as capital of the Turkish Empire. After two centuries of seclusion within the

---

[1] W to [?], 10 Apr. 1717, SP 97/24.
[2] MS Eg. 2234, f. 250. Cf. Spence, 230–1.

Grand Seraglio of Constantinople, the Sultans had transferred their court to the freer atmosphere of the city in the north, with its game preserves and lovely gardens and villas along the river banks. The reigning Sultan's passion for amusement, especially of the field and garden, kept him there with his government.[1] At that particular moment, when he prepared to intensify his war against the Austrians, the time was ripe for a mediator.

Wortley made his entry on 24 March 1717, but was not officially received by the Grand Vizier until almost three weeks later, nor by the Sultan until 18 April. From that date his daily allowance of £10, which had been paid by the Treasury, was charged to the Levant Company and continued until his return to England.[2] His official reception may have been delayed because his servants' liveries had not yet arrived, and new ones were being made in Adrianople.[3] Or, the French Ambassador surmised, he was ashamed of the meanness of his suite (ten or twelve people) and his household.

The French Ambassador, who looked forward with great curiosity to the newest member of the diplomatic corps, was the Marquis Jean-Louis de Bonac. As described by the Duc de Saint-Simon, acidulous chronicler of French court life, Bonac was a man of *esprit* who had shown great ability in his career. The delicate and extremely lucrative appointment to Turkey had come to him both as a reward for his services and as a dowry for his wife, eldest daughter of the Maréchal de Biron.[4] When he observed the English Ambassador and Lady Mary, he described them in his dispatch to Paris.

C'est un homme d'esprit qui a été employé dans les affaires de son pays, et qui est uniquement attaché aux maximes du gouvernement présent. Il amène Madame sa femme avec lui, et un petit enfant de trois ans. Elle est encore jeune. Elle a joué un rôle en Angleterre par son esprit, par son savoir, et par la beauté. La petite vérole lui a fait quelque tort, et je crois qu'il y a autant de dépit que de courage dans le parti qu'elle a pris de suivre son mari. Je ne sais si elle trouvera dans Virgile et dans Horace, qu'elle sait par cœur, de quoi se consoler de la diminution de sa beauté et du changement du Roi d'Angleterre à son égard. L'envie que le mari

---

[1] Barnette Miller, *Beyond the Sublime Porte* (1931), 115–20.
[2] *London Gazette*, 4–8 June 1717; *Cal. of Treasury Papers 1714–1719*, 413.
[3] [?] to [? Stanhope], Pera of Constantinople, Mar. 1717, SP 97/24.
[4] *Mémoires Complets et Authentiques* (1840), xxvi. 45.

et la femme ont de faire leurs affaires en ce pays et l'application qu'ils y donneront les dédommagera en quelque manière de leur éloignement.

Bonac was so impressed by Lady Mary's (damaged) beauty and knowledge of Latin that he discussed them again in another dispatch ten days later. He also found her so full of good maxims about her duties that he hoped his own wife, married only two years before, would learn from her.[1]

In Adrianople Lady Mary lived in a palace where the Sultan had set aside lodgings for the Ambassador and his suite. From her chamber window she admired the handsome gardens laid out along the river; and in the simple life of the people she saw revived the idyllic pastimes of Theocritus and the noble customs of Homer (which she was reading in Pope's translation). Her study of Turkish had advanced sufficiently for her to send Pope discourses on Turkish poetry and samples of her translations. 'You see', she told him, 'I am pretty far gone in Oriental learning; and, to say truth, I study very hard.' Proof of her boast can be seen in her vocabulary lists in Turkish and Italian (probably the *effendi*'s Western language) and in her drafts of translations.[2]

Outside her palace she rambled everywhere, alone or with the French Ambassadress. But since the Frenchwoman preferred tiresome forms and ceremonies, she often went on solitary excursions dressed in a Turkish costume of a heavy veil and loose full robes, which made for ease and concealment. In this disguise she could see more of the city than most Europeans did. Her sex and her social rank allowed her a great privilege not given to most travel-writers—that of visiting Turkish court ladies in their harems. She was invited to dinner by the Grand Vizier's lady, and attended in her elaborate Viennese court dress; but she found little diversion in the long ceremony presided over by the sedate Sultana. Her guide then persuaded her to visit the lady of the Vizier's lieutenant; and here she entered a world closer to the Arabian Nights. Her young hostess Fatima was enchantingly beautiful, and lived in the most dazzling opulence. When Lady Mary left she could not help imagining she had been in Mahomet's paradise.

[1] 30 Mar., 13, 23 Apr. 1717, Ministère des Affaires Étrangères, Constantinople, vol. 57, ff. 123, 151, 153.
[2] W MS, vii. 270–83; CB MS, ff. 18–20.

In the western European courts she was able to impress diplo-
mats and courtiers because women mixed freely with them; but
at the Ottoman Court, where women were confined to the
harem, they played no part in politics or formal court life. In
Vienna she had been honoured by the Emperor's personal
attention; in Adrianople she observed the Sultan only from a
distance. It was enough for her to detect a paradox behind the
magnificent pageantry of his pomp and wealth: that he was so
entirely governed by the army that he trembled at a janissary's
frown, and was as much a slave as any of his subjects.

Her comments on statecraft and politics were probably
limited by her own ignorance as well as the indifference of her
correspondents. Her favourite theme instead was the freedom
of Turkish women. The *effendi* had pointed out that in spite
of their confined existence Mohammedan wives could easily
betray their husbands. In their costumes, Lady Mary observed
for herself, they were in a perpetual masquerade, unrecognized
by their husbands (should they meet) and sometimes unidentified by their lovers. 'You may easily imagine', she told her sister,
'the number of faithful wives very small in a country where
they have nothing to fear from a lover's indiscretion, since we
see so many that have the courage to expose themselves to that
in this world, and all the threatened punishment of the next,
which is never preached to the Turkish damsels. . . . Upon the
whole, I look upon the Turkish women as the only free people
in the empire.' The realization that the Sultan was a slave and
every veiled woman a queen was a step in Lady Mary's education.

A more revolutionary idea struck her when she observed the
practice of smallpox inoculation there. (She had apparently not
read descriptions of it in the 1714 and 1716 *Transactions of the
Royal Society*.) She was so convinced of the operation's efficacy
and safety that she determined to have it done to her 'dear little
son' when she could. Her determination was more than selfish,
as she explained (in a letter addressed to Sarah Chiswell):

I am patriot enough to take pains to bring this useful invention
into fashion in England; and I should not fail to write to some of
our doctors very particularly about it, if I knew any one of them
that I thought had virtue enough to destroy such a considerable
branch of their revenue for the good of mankind. . . . Perhaps,

if I live to return, I may, however, have courage to war with them. Upon this occasion admire the heroism in the heart of your friend.

Her bravado was no empty flourish, but a promise of enlightened heroism in the future. During these months in the spring of 1717, Wortley was occupied with his diplomatic mission. In London the secretaries of state had been replaced by Lord Sunderland and Addison, and so he sent his reports to his old friend. But the great distance between them did not allow rapid consultations; nor could he confer with Sutton, who had sailed from Constantinople at the end of March.[1] After more than a month's negotiations with the Grand Vizier, Wortley emerged with definite terms for a truce: the Turks would cease fighting if Temeswar were restored to them. (It had been captured by the Austrians the previous November.) He sent the terms to Prince Eugene and the Emperor's minister, as well as to London (through Stanyan); and he urged the settlement for two reasons: the terms might be changed by a different Turkish ministry, and the Sultan might use his great wealth to prolong the war. He was most optimistic that peace could be won.[2]

But in Vienna his proposals were considered so absurd that the ministry thought them undeserving of a reply. Prince Eugene's plan to besiege Belgrade had terrorized the Turks because their troops from Asia had not yet arrived.[3] Wortley's illogical strategy puzzled the Imperial ministers, for he had made the Turks think the Emperor very desirous of peace, when he had been instructed to talk 'in a quite contrary style'. This report, which Stanyan transmitted to Lord Stair in Paris, continued: 'And I know one of the ministers here said t'other day, that Lady Mary came hither with a design of making conquest of Prince Eugene; but they now begin to suspect the Grand Signor's favourite was the handsomer man, and had got her over to the Turkish interest.'[4] Behind the joke about Lady Mary lay what Bonac also had observed, that she took an active part in her husband's diplomatic mission. Wortley himself told Addison that the 'men of consideration among the Turks appear

---

[1] Sutton to [? Stanhope], 29 Mar. 1717, SP 97/24.
[2] W to [? Sunderland], 21 May 1717 o.s. (2 letters), SP 97/24.
[3] de Busi to Paterson, 23, 26 June, HMC *Stuart Papers*, iv. 383, 386; *Daily Courant*, 1 July 1717.   [4] 23 June 1717, *Annals of Stair*, ii. 36.

in their conversation as much civilized as any I have met with in Italy'.[1] Possibly he favoured the Turks in his negotiations because he and his aggressive wife held them in very high regard.

Now that he had submitted his mediation terms he had no further reason to remain in Adrianople. Lady Mary had her last glimpse of the Sultan as he departed at the head of his army to defend Belgrade, for she arose at six in the morning to watch (for eight hours) his ceremonious procession. Then, at the end of May 1717, the Ambassador and his entourage set out for Constantinople, furnished by the Sultan with thirty wagons for their baggage and five coaches for women attendants. Lady Mary rode in a berlin, a four-wheeled carriage on which the footmen sat in the back. On the three-day journey their road led through fields smelling of flowers and herbs, and then for most of the way through 'fine painted meadows' along the Sea of Marmora. It was a suitable approach to the magical city.

[1] 22 Aug. 1717, Tickell MS.

VI. *The Turkish Embassy*

(1717–18)

IN Constantinople the Ambassador rented a palace in Pera, the
hill that looks down on the Golden Horn from the north. He
estimated its furnishings would cost £250, and requested that
sum along with an allowance for other expenditures.[1] The
elaborate household to be maintained there included a secretary, treasurer, resident chaplain, three dragomen or inter-
preters, a Turkish scribe, and a guard of janissaries to protect
the family in public against fanatical Moslems. The palace itself
was staffed by a large retinue of attendants, servants, and
grooms, most of them Greeks and Armenians hired in Constantinople and dressed in the Ambassador's liveries.[2] This was the
household of which Lady Mary found herself mistress.

When she looked out of her window in the palace, she saw
'the port, the city, and the seraglio, and the distant hills of Asia;
perhaps, all together, the most beautiful prospect in the world'.
In one of her Embassy Letters she sketched her impression of
the skyline configuration of trees, domes, and minarets:

The unequal heights make it seem as large again as it is (though
one of the largest cities in the world), shewing an agreeable mixture of gardens, pine and cypress-trees, palaces, mosques, and
public buildings, raised one above another, with as much beauty
and appearance of symmetry as your ladyship ever saw in a cabinet
adorned by the most skilful hands, jars shewing themselves above
jars, mixed with canisters, babies,[3] and candlesticks. This is a very
odd comparison; but it gives me an exact image of the thing.

Because of the rising summer heat she soon moved to Belgrade
Village, close to the Black Sea and surrounded by woods. 'We

---

[1] 21 May 1717 o.s. [3rd letter], SP 97/24.
[2] A. C. Wood in *Eng. Hist. Rev.* xl (1925), 538–41.
[3] A small bowl used as a mark in that game.

pass our time chiefly at a country house ten miles from Constantinople,' Wortley wrote to Addison, 'this being the plague season, though there is little of it this year.' Then he added a compliment to Addison's wife: 'Lady Mary presents her humble service to my Lady Warwick and hopes she has by this time a little Mr. Addison to play with.'[1] In the village, where other rich Christian families stayed, she led a peaceful, simple life. Her week's activities, as she outlined them to Pope, were: 'Monday, setting of partridges—Tuesday, reading English—Wednesday, studying the Turkish language (in which, by the way, I am already very learned)—Thursday, classical authors —Friday, spent in writing—Saturday, at my needle—and Sunday, admitting of visits, and hearing music.'

Her life seemed so calm and remote from the world, she told Pope, that she could imagine herself deceased and inhabiting the Elysian fields. Playfully developing the elegiac theme, she reminded him that she desired to live in the remembrance of only a few friends, him among them, 'though dead to all the world beside'. The theme was not new to Pope, who two weeks after her departure had passed her London house 'with the same Sort of Melancholy that we feel upon Seeing the Tomb of a Friend'. Her symbolic death had served him to some extent as poetic inspiration. In June 1717 he wrote her that he was sending the newly issued third volume of his *Iliad* with some other things. 'Among the rest, you have all I am worth, that is, my Workes: There are few things in them but what you have already seen, except the Epistle of Eloisa to Abelard; in which you will find one passage, that I can't tell whether to wish you should understand, or not?'[2] Actually there were two poems in the handsome quarto volume which are related to her absence, and display a deep strain of pathetic emotion. The 'Verses to the Memory of an Unfortunate Lady' mourns the death abroad of a lady who was prevented from marrying the man she loved. Like Lady Mary, Pope's lady had 'beauty, titles, wealth, and fame'.[3] He even used the epithet 'love-darting eyes', his favourite compliment to her.

[1] 18 July 1717 o.s., Tickell MS.
[2] *Corr.* i. 354, 407. She thanked him for his works on 8 Jan. 1718, according to her memorandum (i. 19).
[3] Lady Mary's connexion with the 'Verses' is fully treated by Geoffrey

But 'Eloisa to Abelard', as he had hinted, was the poem directed to her. It is the Ovidian lament of Eloisa recollecting her love for Abelard many years after their separation. Pope probably did not refer to the couplet:

> Still on that breast enamour'd let me lie,
> Still drink delicious poison from thy eye....

but when Lady Mary read it she put a cross next to the word *eye*, and at the bottom of the page wrote: *mine*.[1] The concluding lines plainly pointed to her:

> And sure if fate some future Bard shall join
> In sad similitude of griefs to mine,
> Condemn'd whole years in absence to deplore,
> And image charms he must behold no more,
> Such if there be, who loves so long, so well;
> Let him our sad, our tender story tell;
> The well-sung woes will sooth my pensive ghost;
> He best can paint 'em, who shall feel 'em most.[2]

Although Pope had closely followed a translation of Abelard's letters, he seems to have infused his lines with some of his hopeless, impassioned love for Lady Mary. As he confessed, he had painted the woes of a disappointed lover because he had felt them himself. By the time his volume reached her, she had left her summer Elysium to return to Constantinople. There she saw her husband's embassy enter its most crucial phase.

While Wortley patiently waited for the Emperor's reply to his mediation terms, Stanyan in Vienna connived to supplant him both as ambassador and mediator. (Wortley knew of his animosity, but could not account for it.)[3] In July Stanyan had informed Lord Sunderland that the Emperor deliberately refused to deal with Wortley about the terms or anything else.[4] The Emperor could afford to wait; for as Wortley knew, Belgrade was besieged by an Austrian army.[5] On 16 August they launched a sudden attack, totally defeating the Turks; and six days later the city capitulated. Stanyan acted quickly: he

---

Tillotson in the *Rev. of Eng. Stud.* xii (1936), 401 ff. and (with revisions) in Twickenham, ii. 331–6.

[1] In M's copy, owned by Lord Harrowby.
[2] Twickenham, ii. 309, 327.
[3] W to Addison, 19 July 1717, Tickell MS.
[4] 3, 14, 28 July 1717, SP 80/34.
[5] W to Addison, 2 Aug. 1717, SP 97/24.

informed Lord Sunderland that the moment was favourable for
making peace, and he offered his services as mediator 'in case
Mr. Wortley be recalled'.[1]

Although he must have known of the Turks' defeat, Wortley
advised Addison (on 2 September) that they still demanded the
return of Temeswar.[2] Three weeks later he left Constantinople
for the Turkish camp near Philippopolis, a journey of twelve
to fifteen days, in order to be near the Sultan.[3] He went without
Lady Mary, who was expecting another child. In Vienna his
courier was dismissed by the Emperor without an answer to the
ridiculous terms, but Stanyan detained the man until (he wrote
to Lord Sunderland) he knew 'how his Majesty will please to
determine about the Turkish Embassy'.[4] The King had not
been slow in determining.

On 13/24 September 1717 Addison informed the Levant
Company that Wortley was recalled, and that Stanyan was to
be the ambassador and the co-mediator with Sutton in negotiating a peace treaty.[5] (Sutton, who was then in Paris on his way
home, hurried instead to Vienna.)[6] Stanyan's presence in Vienna
had been of great advantage. As early as 24 June, for example,
Wortley had sent him a long dispatch urging peace terms; and
although he must have received it within a week or two, he kept
it three months, and then forwarded it to London with the
comment that it was no longer applicable.[7] More definite proof
of his intrigue lies in Sutton's explanation (to Addison): 'It is
my duty to acquaint you (without any partiality or regard to
myself, it being indifferent to me to be colleague with Mr.
Wortley or Mr. Stanyan) that Monsieur de St. Saphorin, who
is one of the King's Ministers here for the affairs of the Empire
and I suppose is known to you, upon certain views of his own,
put Mr. Stanyan upon suing for the Embassy in Turkey and
being joined in the Commission for the mediation.'[8] Unaware
of the change Wortley continued on his way to the Sultan's
camp to continue his fruitless negotiations. Stanyan was so
impatient to supplant him that he asked Lord Sunderland

---

[1] 21 Aug. 1717, SP 80/35.   [2] 22 Aug. 1717 o.s., SP 97/24.
[3] Bonac to the Regent, 21 Sept. 1717, Ministère des Affaires Étrangères,
Const., vol. 58, ff. 55-56.   [4] 22 Sept. 1717, SP 80/35.
[5] Addison to Onslow, Paston, 270-1.   [6] Daily Courant, 30 Sept. 1717.
[7] Stanyan to Sunderland, 29 Sept. 1717, SP 80/35.
[8] 20 Oct. 1717, SP 97/24.

whether he should start alone immediately or wait for Sutton to join him.[1]

In London the diplomatic change had caused a flurry in the affairs of the Levant Company. They were much disturbed because the King had broken the precedent that they approve his choice beforehand; and they appealed to him to retain Wortley at his post.[2] When their appeal failed, they agreed that special circumstances had forced the new appointment; and they asked £4,000 as compensation for the change.[3] In due form Lord Onslow, Governor of the Company, waited on the King to announce that they had chosen Stanyan ambassador; and on that occasion all six members of the Company were presented to His Majesty and awarded the honour of knighthood.[4]

Having signed his friend's official recall, Addison sent him a private letter with tactful consolation and the promise of a new post—that of an auditor of the imprest.[5] Stanyan had been chosen because of his high favour in Vienna, Addison explained; and Wortley's return would bring him near the King, who thought very highly of him.[6] Some time elapsed, however, before Wortley received either his official recall or its consolations. Distance as well as Stanyan continued to be to his disadvantage. He vigorously proceeded with his attempts to mediate. At the beginning of October he arrived at the Grand Vizier's camp near Sophia, and made an impressive entrance.[7] 'The retinue and pomp with which I am bound to appear in Turkish camps', he wrote to Addison, 'are greater and more expensive than I have known used by ambassadors in other courts.' As before, he asked for additional money, explaining, 'What I have is little more than can be thought sufficient for the family I leave behind me.' At the same time he asked Addison (in a private letter) to use his influence to have the Dutch Ambassador removed as co-mediator; the Turks, he explained, trusted

---

[1] 3 Oct. 1717, SP 80/35.

[2] Sir John Williams to W, 5 Sept., 3 Oct. 1717, W MS, v. 51–54.

[3] Levant Co. to Onslow, 8 Oct. 1717, SP 105/116. The King paid them exactly that amount in Dec. (*Cal. of Treasury Papers 1714–1719*, 413).

[4] *Post Boy*, 29–31 Oct. 1717.

[5] The grant for the office was passed in November (*Weekly Journal*, 30 Nov. 1717).

[6] 28 Sept. 1717, Addison, *Letters*, 376–7.

[7] Hefferman to Tickell, 30 Nov. 1717, SP 97/24.

neither the Dutchman, because he was in the pay of the Czar, nor the Frenchman, because he was a liar; but they had the greatest respect for him!¹ In his attempt to shoulder out the Dutch Ambassador, he had asked the Turks to send for him alone, but had been turned down.² By then, Stanyan's credentials as mediator were on their way to Vienna.³

When the Levant Company informed Wortley of his recall, at the beginning of November, they instructed their treasurer in Constantinople not to pay any part of his requested £2,500 for his expenses at Belgrade; but they later allowed him £1,200 for his return to England.⁴ The Admiralty had already been ordered to send a ship to carry him and his family either directly home or to land them at any port in France or Italy. The *Preston*, a man-of-war commanded by Captain Robert Johnson, was commissioned to sail to Constantinople for that purpose.⁵ In the meantime Wortley persisted with astonishing *naïveté* and pertinacity. In his answer to Addison's private letter (on 23 December) he acknowledged Sutton and Stanyan as mediators, but insisted that his favour with the Turks made him their best mediator. He acted with the energy and folly of desperation, for if he could negotiate a peace before his successors arrived he would win all the glory and rewards. How else can his next move be interpreted? He wrote to Prince Eugene— who he knew did not favour him—and asked him to intercede with the King to have him retained in the negotiations. The reply he received was icy: that the Emperor had to leave it to His Britannic Majesty how he chose to employ his Ministers.⁶ In spite of rebuffs and replacements, he continued to work with the Dutch envoy on treaty terms.⁷ Stanyan finally left Vienna on 15 March 1718, while Sutton remained there to deal with the Emperor's ministers.⁸ Obviously their chances of success were greater than Wortley's, who had been pro-Turkish and stationed at that court when it was the losing side.⁹

¹ 7 Oct. 1717 o.s. (both received 9 Dec.), SP 97/24.
² Sutton to Addison, 4 Dec. 1717, SP 97/24.   ³ Addison, *Letters*, 456.
⁴ Levant Co. to Barker, 7, 15 Nov., 17 Dec. 1717, SP 105/116.
⁵ Addison to Lords of the Admiralty, 2 Nov. 1717, *Letters*, 386–7; *Weekly Journal*, 30 Nov., 7 Dec. 1717.
⁶ Michael, *England under George I*, i. 363.
⁷ *Daily Courant*, 7 Mar.; *Original Weekly Journal*, 22–29 Mar. 1718.
⁸ *Daily Courant*, 25 Mar. 1718.
⁹ For a summary of W's failure, see Smithers's *Addison*, 389.

He could not have been a very happy man at the beginning of May in Adrianople when he met Stanyan in order to present him to the Grand Vizier. At that very moment the Vizier was violently replaced by a new one, who explained the change as caused by the Turks' desire for peace; and he instructed Stanyan to tell the Emperor so.[1] It was now clear beyond a doubt which side was ready to submit. His last official duty done, Wortley prepared to set out for Constantinople.

Lady Mary had remained there without him since the previous autumn. She undoubtedly carried on her usual activities, including her writing. In January (1718), as she sat in her garden pavilion gazing out at the city in the sunlight, she was moved by its beauty to voice her serene happiness in a long introspective poem.[2] Enchanted as she was by the 'prospects all profusely gay', she was much more so by being in her retreat 'secure from humankind'. She struck an attitude of noble detachment from the world's follies and fears, and looked upon herself as one 'Who dares have virtue in a vicious age'.

Her introspective temper was heightened, probably, by the fact that she was in the last months of pregnancy. In the middle of February she gave birth to a daughter, who was christened Mary Wortley. Excellent medical attention was available in Maitland, the Embassy surgeon, and Dr. Emanuel Timoni, the most eminent physician in Constantinople, whom Wortley had engaged to attend his family.[3] It was Dr. Timoni, a Fellow of the Royal Society, whose description of smallpox inoculation had been published in the 1714 transactions. Lady Mary had observed the operation herself in Adrianople; and perhaps encouraged by him, she had it performed on her son on Tuesday, 19 March o.s. It was later described by Maitland:

The Ambassador's ingenious Lady, who had been at some Pains to satisfy her Curiosity in this Matter, and had made some useful Observations on the Practice, was so thoroughly convinced of the Safety of it, that *She* resolv'd to submit *her* only Son to it, a very hopeful Boy of about Six Years of Age: She first of all order'd me to find out a fit Subject to take the Matter from; and then sent for an old *Greek* Woman, who had practis'd this Way a great many

---

[1] *London Gazette*, 3–7 June 1718.
[2] 'Verses Written in the Chiosk of the British Palace', ii. 449–51 (correct date from MS).   [3] W to Addison, 26 Aug. 1717, SP 97/24.

PLATE 3

Lady Mary Wortley Montagu and her Son

From a painting by an unknown artist [1718]

Years: After a good deal of Trouble and Pains, I found a proper Subject, and then the good Woman went to work; but so awkwardly by the shaking of her Hand, and put the Child to so much Torture with her blunt and rusty Needle, that I pitied his Cries, who had ever been of such Spirit and Courage, that hardly any Thing of Pain could make him cry before; and therefore Inoculated the other Arm with my own Instrument, and with so little Pain to him, that he did not in the least complain of it.

The boy's arms swelled and after the third day bright spots appeared on his face. Between the seventh and eighth days he became feverish and thirsty for a few hours; and then about one hundred pustules appeared, but they crusted and dropped off without leaving any scars.[1] Only the needle scars on his arms remained as evidence of the operation.

Lady Mary took this daring step on her own initiative, while Wortley was at the Grand Vizier's camp near Sophia. She waited five days before telling him: 'The boy was engrafted last Tuesday, and is at this time singing and playing, and very impatient for his supper. I pray God my next [letter] may give as good an account of him. . . . I can not engraft the girl; her nurse has not had the smallpox.' A week later she was able to send a favourable report: 'Your son is as well as can be expected, and I hope past all manner of danger.' But Wortley did not seem as concerned over their child as the fond mother thought he should be. 'Your son is very well', she wrote him again (on 9 April); 'I cannot forbear telling you so, tho' you do not so much as ask after him.'[2] Her reprimand, as in the early days of their marriage, suggests the disparity of their temperaments.

And as before, she shrewdly advised him on his affairs. She told him to send a civil letter to her father, and date it as though on the occasion of their daughter's birth. While she transmitted diplomatic gossip to him, she pretended to others that she knew nothing of his business. Yet she directed him on the occasion of his replacement: 'I suppose you know the allowance the King has made the Company on this occasion. I think you may with more justice insist on your extraordinaries, which has never yet been refused neither Sir R. Sutton nor no other ambassador.'

---

[1] Maitland, *Account of Inoc. the Small Pox* (1722), (2nd ed., 1723), 7–8.
[2] Sunday, 23 Mar. [o.s.], Wharncliffe MS 507; 1 Apr. 1718, W MS, i. 309–10; Paston, 275–6 (date from MS).

She also looked after her own financial affairs. Through her uncle William Fielding she had been given the sum of £2,000, and when it was delivered to her in gold pieces she had to decide whether to convert it back into pounds. She suggested to Wortley that it might be used, instead, to purchase goods—if he would be allowed to bring them home free of duty.[1]

While she remained in the capital during the spring of 1718, beset as she was with children, operations, and business matters, she continued her study of Turkish and its poetry, learning the language so well (she boasted with mock seriousness) that she was in danger of forgetting English. Her curiosity was, as she called it, a powerful passion. She rambled every day, and wearing a native costume crossed the Golden Horn to inspect the monuments, buildings, and bazaars in the old quarter. When she looked through the late Grand Vizier's huge palace, the guardian assured her that it had eight hundred rooms. 'I will not answer for that number, since I did not count them', she artfully told her correspondent. But of the Sultan's seraglio, the most tantalizing building in the city, she saw only what she could from a distance; even she did not succeed in the virtually impossible.

One of the most impressive sights was the great Byzantine church of Saint Sophia, then (as now) a mosque. Unlike ordinary mosques it was forbidden to Christians. Many years later, Lady Mary told Spence a fantastic story of visiting it, and he immediately wrote down her account.

She had a vast curiosity to see the great church of St. Sophia. She had demanded a permission, and could not get it; but the curiosity of a lady is not so easily to be balked. There was then at Constantinople the Princess of Transylvania, a Christian (as much, at least, as herself) though of the Greek Church. They were equally desirous of seeing this fine sight, and consulted together what was to be done. They at last resolved to dress themselves up in men's clothes, and to run the risk of it together. They got in without being suspected, and were forced to leave their men's slippers at the door, for the place is too sacred to be trod on by anything but naked feet. This embarrassed Lady Mary extremely. As she had been used to walk with high heels she tottered, and was ready to tumble down every moment. In short she was forced to return to

[1] 23 Mar., 1 Apr 1718.

the corner where she had left her slippers, and to steal'em on again. The men wear long robes in Asia, and she had so long an one that she contrived to hide her feet so well with it that they ventured on again into the church with them. The Princess went before her, and she walked slow, and with all the care and concealment she could, after her. When they came into the finest part of the church, the Princess of Transylvania could not help bursting into tears. She was struck with seeing all those riches which had belonged formerly to the Christians in the hands of the infidels;[1] and besides it put her strongly in mind of the Greek emperors who formerly reigned in that city, till they were drove out by the Turks. She was herself descended from one of those emperors, and when she thought of that the tears flowed down in spite of all her resolution. Lady Mary did all she could to stop her. 'Do you consider where you are?' says she to the Princess, as softly as she could, 'and what a discovery in this place would cost you? I indeed might escape under the character of Mr. Wortley as ambassador now here, but if you are discovered, you know what a cruel death must be the consequence. Methinks I see the flames already lighted! For God's sake, leave off blubbering! Why will you be your own destruction?' The Princess, on so just advice, restrained her grief, wiped her eyes in private, and went on as well as she could. After this they had no other particular danger. They took a view of all the beauties of the place, and returned home undiscovered and in safety.[2]

Lady Mary's amusing story, told to the enraptured Spence, has its counterpart in the Embassy Letters. Since the Turks were 'more delicate' in allowing Christians to visit this mosque she was forced to send three requests to the governor of the city, who assembled his learned men and religious leaders to confer on her request. She insisted so strongly that at last permission was granted. Which version of her visit is true? Neither can be substantiated, but the sober one in her Embassy Letters seems more credible. Perhaps her visit was actually as decorous as an ambassadress's; but in retrospect she preferred to convert it into an adventure in an oriental romance.

In her social visits to Turkish palaces, she called on the late Sultan's favourite, a lady who had remained faithful to his memory. Like the Sultana in Adrianople, she offered costly and dull entertainment, though her sad devotion pleased Lady

---

[1] In her verses from Pera, Lady Mary describes Saint Sophia in similar terms (ii. 450).   [2] MS Eg. 2234, f. 249.

Mary's taste for the sentimental. In a contrasting visit she spent an afternoon in the magnificent palace of Fatima, her young acquaintance, who looked even more beautiful than before. Fatima greeted her with an angelic smile, and said: 'You Christian ladies have the reputation of inconstancy, and I did not expect, whatever goodness you expressed for me at Adrianople, that I should ever see you again. But I am now convinced that I have really the happiness of pleasing you; and, if you knew how I speak of you amongst our ladies, you would be assured that you do me justice if you think me your friend.'

Thus began their battle of compliments. Lady Mary did well enough: she assured Fatima that if all the Turkish ladies were like her, it was absolutely necessary to confine them from public view, for the repose of mankind; and then told her 'what a noise such a face as hers would make in London or Paris'.

'I can't believe you', she replied; 'if beauty was so much valued in your country as you say, they would never have suffered you to leave it.' Lady Mary repeated the compliment not out of vanity—or so she protested—but as proof of Fatima's spirit and wit.

In another conversation with an amiable lady of high station (perhaps Fatima again), the subject of feminism arose. 'Que vous êtes libertines', she said to Lady Mary, 'vous autres dames Chrétiennes! il vous est permis de recevoir les visites d'autant d'hommes que vous voulez, et vos loix vous permettent sans bornes l'usage de l'amour et du vin.' Lady Mary assured her that she was badly informed; that the visits which Christian ladies receive were full of respect and formality, and that it was a crime to be heard speaking of love, or of loving anyone except one's husband. The Turkish lady laughed, and answered: 'Vos maris sont bien bons de se contenter d'une fidélité si bornée: vos yeux, vos mains, votre conversation est pour le public, et que prétendez-vous réserver pour eux? Pardonnez-moi, ma belle Sultane, j'ai toute l'inclination possible de croire tout ce que vous me dites, mais vous voulez m'imposer des impossibilités. Je sçai les saletés des infidelles; je voye que vous en avez honte, et je ne vous en parlerai plus.'[1]

Lady Mary's idealized view of Turkish women's status

---

[1] 'Sur la Maxime de M. de Rochefoucault', ii. 427. The last part is repeated in Spence, 230.

suffered from one blemish; she was embarrassed by the abomin-
able belief that 'women are treated in Turkey as something
between beasts and men', and possess an inferior order of souls.[1]
In an Embassy Letter she looked at the distinction more favourably: although the women's souls may be inferior to the men's,
after death they enter a paradise of eternal bliss (apart from the
men's). Except for this minor reservation she found Islamic
ideas and institutions sympathetic, and often stimulating. She
was not at all horrified by the practice of slavery, finding that
slaves were treated so well they were no worse off than free
servants. Her initial concept of the Mohammedan religion was
confirmed by her observations: that the religion of enlightened
Moslems was no different from the deism of sensible Christians.

She used these paradoxical comparisons and 'singularities' to
embellish the more sober factual accounts in her travel letters,
particularly those she sent to a *bel esprit* like the Abbé Conti.
In the early spring of 1718, when he was in Paris, she sent him
a full letter. It began modestly:

Je suis charmée de votre obligeante Lettre, Monsieur; et vous
voyez par ce grand papier, que j'ay dessein de repondre exacte-
ment à toutes vos questions, du moins si mon François me le permet.
Car comme c'est une langue que je ne sçai pas à fonds, je crains
fort que je seray obligée de finir bientot, faute d'expressions.
Souvenez vous donc, que j'ecris dans une langue qui m'est etran-
gere, et croyez bonnement que toutes les impertinences et les
fadaizes, qui partiront de ma plume, ne viennent que de mon in-
capacité à pouvoir exprimer ce que je pense, mais nullement de
stupidité ou d'une legereté naturelle.

She then launched into a brilliant and elaborate discourse on
the women, religion, and mixed races in Constantinople.[2] The
Abbé was so impressed that he showed the letter to his friend
Toussaint Rémond de Saint-Mard, a *littérateur* of varied tastes.

Rémond, who was thirty-six years old, had published some
prose *Dialogues des Dieux* and a dull poem entitled *La Sagesse*.
The Duc de Saint-Simon, in dissecting him in his *Mémoires*,
thought that he was an intriguing fool; and that although he
had a great deal of *esprit*, he had even more impudence, conceit,

---

[1] Spence, MS Eg. 2234, f. 248.
[2] Its appearance in print in 1719 is discussed on p. 100 below.

and contempt for others. 'Il se piquait de tout savoir, prose, poésie, philosophie, histoire, même galanterie; ce qui lui procura force ridicules aventures et brocards. Ce qu'il sut le mieux fut de tâcher de faire fortune, pour quoi tous moyens lui furent bons.'[1] When Rémond read Lady Mary's letter he was ravished; and to such a degree that he was impelled to tell her so. While she prepared for her journey home, a letter came to her in a stranger's hand, dated Paris, 20 April 1718. It began abruptly:

Si vous aimez les choses extraordinaires, cette lettre ne vous déplaira pas. Je n'ai jamais eu l'honneur de vous voir et vraisem-blablement je ne l'aurai jamais. . . . Jugez ma vanité: sur cette seule lettre j'ai cru connaitre la singularité de votre caractère et les agréments infinis de votre esprit. Depuis ce jour là je ne puis parler aux femmes les plus spirituelles de cette cour. . . . Je n'écoute plus votre ami sur Monsieur Newton; je ne lui parle que de M. M. et je n'aime moins Sharper [Lord Stair], avec qui j'étais tendre-ment uni depuis qu'il est en ce pays. Si j'étais beau et aimable je crois que je serais allé m'embarquer à Marseille, et vous auriez été bien surprise de voir un disciple de Socrate venir. . . . J'ai tou-jours suivi mes sentiments plutôt que ma raison, et jusqu'à cette heure je ne m'en suis jamais mal trouvé. Voici la plus forte preuve que j'en donnerai de ma vie. Vous allez me croire le plus grand fou du monde. Je veux bien en courir le risque si vous êtes aussi aimable que votre lettre.

Her curiosity and interest were sufficiently piqued for her to answer him; and what she wrote is clear from his reply, hastily sent to reach her before her departure: she told him of her gratitude for his flattering letter, of Plato (whom she called 'ce tendre philosophe'), and of her apprehension about meeting him. 'Ne vous effrayez donc point du voyage que vous ferez içi', he reassured her; but although he promised friendship rather than love, his amorous frenzy showed no diminution, his last words being: 'Adieu, pensez quelquefois à moi, et soyez assurée qu'aucune femme n'a jamais été aimée autant que je vous aime!'[2]

She still received Pope's epistolary gallantry; and the pros-pect of her homecoming excited his ardour too. 'I can't express how I long to see you, face to face', he exclaimed. 'If ever you come again I shall never be able to behave with decency, I shall

---

[1] *Mémoires Complets et Authentiques*, xxxii. 266.
[2] W MS, iv. 212–13, 223–4.

walk, look, and talk at such a rate that all the Town must know
I have seen something more than human—Come for God's
sake, come Lady Mary, come quickly!'[1] He offered to travel
to Italy to accompany her home—just as he had several times
proposed to visit with her in Italy should she stay there on her
way to Turkey. But his impetuous proposals and exclamations
were probably intended, and believed, to be only verbal extravagances.

Lady Mary was undoubtedly saddened to have to leave
Turkey. 'You need not apprehend my expressing any great joy
for our return', she told Wortley gloomily. 'I hope 'tis less
shocking to you than to me, who have really suffered in my
health by the uneasiness it has given me, tho' I take care to conceal it here as much as I can.'[2] She did not conceal her disappointment in an Embassy Letter where she regretted, though
gracefully, that her 'rambling destiny' was sending her home
when she had become used to the climate, learnt the language;
and much as she loved travelling, she trembled at 'so great a
journey with a numerous family, and a little infant hanging at
the breast'. Wortley expressed his disappointment privately in
another form. He wrote out drafts for two essays. In one
entitled 'Fame' he argued that fame was vain and profitless;
and in the other, 'Losses', he consoled himself with convenient
stoicism.[3] The dismissed Ambassador thus tried to rationalize
his failure.

In the meantime the *Preston*, assigned to carry him home,
had sailed on 10 January 1718.[4] She was one of a large number
of new ships built by England as a warning to Spain—a two-
deck medium-sized vessel carrying fifty guns and a crew of
240.[5] On 19 June she reached Constantinople, and moored in
the Golden Horn near the Seraglio Point. The captain immediately began to stock her with fresh provisions. On 24 June
Wortley came aboard to inspect her, and was greeted with a
salute of fifteen guns and twenty-one on going ashore. The

---

[1] *Corr.* i. 469–70.   [2] [9 Apr.], Paston, 276.
[3] End. 1718, W MS, vii. 126–9.
[4] Unless otherwise stated, all facts about the *Preston*'s voyage come from
the captain's and the master's logs, Ad 51/4296, Ad 52/254; and all dates are
Old Style.
[5] W. L. Clowes, *Royal Navy* (1898), iii. 8–9, 30, 120 n.; Treasurer's Pay
Book, Ad 33/310.

next day part of his baggage was taken aboard, and on 2 July four of his horses. On 4 July the remaining baggage was put aboard, including Lady Mary's Turkish costumes.[1]

The following day, Wortley and his retinue, which included nineteen servants victualled with the crew, went aboard at 3 p.m., and a half hour later the ship moved off. At noon on Saturday the *Preston* passed through the western opening of the Sea of Marmora and into the Straits of the Dardanelles. From there she sailed through the Hellespont into the Aegean Sea, and on the 8th anchored in Troy Bay within sight of Mount Ida. The Ambassador, no doubt accompanied by Lady Mary, went ashore to view the ruins of Troy. Then after skirting around the southern end of the Greek Morea, the ship passed Cape Matapan on 13 July and Cape Sapientza on the 14th, and then across a wide stretch of sea to Cape Stilo, at the foot of Italy. The voyagers had been lucky in having fair weather, with moderate strong winds. On 21 July, a day of fresh gales and fair weather, they saw to the north-west Mount Etna, the volcano of Sicily. At half past eleven that morning a more dangerous sight appeared—a Spanish squadron, which fired several shots and was answered by the ship's guns. From a passing English transport the captain learned that the Spanish fleet was at Messina, on the north-east tip of Sicily, which had declared itself on the Spanish side. The *Preston*, fortunately, was headed south. With fair weather prevailing she reached the Bay of Carthage on 1 August. The next day the captain ordered thirteen guns fired at one o'clock: 'being his Majesty's happy accession to the throne'. His next port was Leghorn, where he anchored on 11 August, and stayed for two days. Wortley was at this moment undecided exactly where to disembark. On the 15th the *Preston* reached Genoa and cast anchor. Although by now he intended to go on to Toulon, the steady calm persuaded him to land at Genoa with Lady Mary 'and parts of his Family' —servants, probably.[2] On the 17th at 7 p.m., saluted by fifteen guns, he left the ship.

This colourless but securely definite record of dates and places hardly indicated the effect of the journey on Lady Mary's imagination and sensibility. She displayed its effect in

---

[1] In 1740 W shipped them to her in Italy (W MS, i. 117-18).
[2] Johnson to Burchett, 21 Aug. 1718 o.s., Ad 1/1982.

an extraordinarily long Embassy Letter, addressed to the Abbé
Conti. It was a voyage of discovery for her, especially exciting
because she saw the terrain of the Classics she knew so well and
felt with such immediacy. In the Hellespont, where the castles
of Sestos and Abydos were pointed out, she was infected by the
poetical air, and broke into verse:

> The swimming lover, and the nightly bride,
> How Hero loved, and how Leander died.

In the country near Troy, which invoked Helen and Menelaus,
she held her copy of Homer before her, admiring his exact
geography and annotating the landscape. She arose at two in
the morning 'to view coolly' the ruins that remained; and she
copied inscriptions, and even tried to transport some ancient
stone monuments, but they were too heavy. The places asso-
ciated with Virgil were so numerous that she reeled them off,
but then stopped herself:

> I will pass by all the other islands with this general reflection,
> that 'tis impossible to imagine any thing more agreeable than this
> journey would have been between two or three thousand years
> since, when, after drinking a dish of tea with Sappho, I might have
> gone the same evening to visit the temple of Homer in Chios, and
> have passed this voyage in taking plans of magnificent temples,
> delineating the miracles of statuaries, and conversing with the most
> polite and most gay of human kind. Alas! art is extinct here; the
> wonders of nature alone remain.

At Carthage, where she and the Ambassador were met by the
English consul to Tunis, she rode in his chaise to see the ruins
on a moonlit night, and again in the early morning, though she
was soon broiled by the sun. She was an energetic tourist, determined to see all the remaining wonders of nature, though she
could not drink a dish of tea with Sappho.

When she and Wortley disembarked to complete their
journey more speedily by land, they left their 'Son and Part of
the Family'—their infant daughter and several servants—to
continue home on the *Preston*.[1] The children were spared an
arduous land journey, but on an English ship sailing around the
Iberian peninsula they ran the danger of attack or capture. Lady
Mary somehow stifled her maternal tenderness and parted from

---

[1] *Daily Courant*, 23, 27 Sept. 1718.

them. As the *Preston* sailed on, the captain chased Spanish ships
several times, prepared all his guns and carriages, and took on
stocks of powder along with provisions. The children were also
threatened with illness which sent twenty-eight of the crew to
the hospital. In spite of war and disease they arrived home safely
the following January.

In Genoa Lady Mary and her husband had to stay in quarantine for ten days.[1] They passed the time very agreeably as guests
of Henry Davenant, the consul, at his Palladian villa in a suburb
of the city. Lady Mary was allowed to receive visitors, but a
noble Genoese kept watch to see that they did not touch
her. She observed 'the custom of cecisbeos'—gentlemen who
devoted themselves to the service of married ladies. (She had
seen a similar custom in Vienna.) With her characteristic un-
moral judgement, she thought it a great social benefit: it prevented family feuds, occupied the young men, and brought
peace and good spirits to everybody. Her sojourn in Genoa was
so pleasant that she could have been happy there for the rest of
her life, but she was 'not destined to so much tranquillity'.
After a two-day journey she arrived in Turin, where she was
presented to the queen-duchess, like most royalty an exceedingly sweet and affable lady. Ahead of her lay the fearful
Alpine pass of Mount Cenis, the most frequently used in her
time; and as she crossed it, carried on the backs of porters, she
was thrilled by its magnificent scenery. 'The prodigious prospect of mountains covered with eternal snow, clouds hanging
far below our feet, and the vast cascades tumbling down the
rocks with a confused roaring, would have been solemnly
entertaining to me, if I had suffered less from the extreme cold
that reigns here.' As a result, she became ill of a swollen sore
throat, and tarried in Lyons to recover, though she could not
resist going out to inspect its antiquities.

She arrived in Paris with her husband on 18 September o.s.
1718.[2] It was her first visit there, and she eagerly surveyed the
opera and theatre, the ladies, the palace of Fontainbleau, and
the young King. Except for him—'tall and well-shaped'—she
found Paris not at all to her liking: the opera and theatre coarse,
the women absurdly dressed and painted, and Fontainbleau too

[1] P. 88 above, n. 2.
[2] Stair to William Stanhope, 29 Sept. [N.S.] 1718, SP 78/162.

irregular. But she once again saw her friend the Abbé Conti; and she met for the first time the gallant Rémond. If her impression of him was the same as the Duc de Saint-Simon's, she saw a small man, looking unfinished like a faulty biscuit, and with a large nose, big bulging eyes, gross ugly features, and a hoarse voice like that of a man suddenly awakened in the middle of the night. Although so ugly, he exerted his great talent for ingratiating himself, and won Lady Mary's friendship. In a note to her while she was still in Paris he made a curious request (along with amorous flummery): 'Toute la commission que je vous donne est d'examiner la petite bague pour voir si vous la trouvez jolie et de me permettre ensuite de la porter tant que je vivrai.'[1] But she could not have seen much of him altogether, for much to her surprise she found in Paris her favourite sister, Lady Mar, who had arrived with her small daughter only one day earlier. She had been given permission by the King to leave England and join her husband, then in Italy with the Pretender's court.[2] Overjoyed at meeting, the sisters bombarded each other with questions, answers, exclamations, and compliments, and then passed almost all their time together visiting and sightseeing. Their reunion did not last very long, for Lady Mary and her husband stayed in Paris less than two weeks.

In crossing from Calais they sailed through dangerously rough waters. This may have affected her first thought on English soil: that Old England held all the comfort and serenity a human could wish for. While her party stayed at a Dover inn to regulate their 'march to London, bag and baggage', she read a letter which had been forwarded from Paris.

It was from Pope, and in his customary style contained a compliment to her fine eyes and dimpled cheeks, and a naughty innuendo: 'Without offence to your modesty be it spoken, I have a burning desire to see your Soul stark naked, for I am confident 'tis the prettiest kind of white Soul, in the universe.' Then he related a somewhat irrelevant tale of pathetic love: at Stanton Harcourt near Oxford, where he was staying, a pair of country lovers who had sought shelter from a storm were found

[1] W MS, iv. 222.
[2] *Post Boy*, 6–9 Sept. 1718; HMC *Stuart Papers*, vii (1923), 332, 351. Before leaving England she had seen his 'cipher' people (ibid. 287), which proves that she took some part in his political activities.

struck dead by lightning, and in a position showing that the man
had tenderly tried to shield the girl. The pair were buried in one
grave, and Pope submitted to Lady Mary the two epitaphs he
had composed for their monument. The first, which opened by
calling the pair 'Eastern Lovers' feeding the funeral fire, concluded:

> Hearts so sincere, th'Almighty saw well-pleas'd,
> Sent his own Lightning, and the Victims seiz'd.

His other epitaph, preferred by his friends as more godly, had a
similar conclusion:

> Virtue unmov'd, can hear the Call,
> And face the Flash that melts the Ball.

But the perfect monument for the two lovers, Pope gracefully
assured her, would be 'a Tear from the finest eyes in the
world. I know you have Tenderness; you must have it: It is the
very Emanation of Good Sense and virtue: The finest minds
like the finest metals, dissolve the easiest.'[1] Were Lady Mary in
England, he added, she could have written a better epitaph.

But Lady Mary did not dissolve easily—at least not in such
a situation. Her answer, whether or not she actually sent it,
survives in an Embassy Letter. After applauding Pope's good
nature in supposing that the lovers would have lived on with
joy and happiness, she continued :

I see no reason to imagine that John Hughes and Sarah Drew
were either wiser or more virtuous than their neighbours. That a
well-set man of twenty-five should have a fancy to marry a brown
woman of eighteen, is nothing marvellous; and I cannot help thinking, that, had they married, their lives would have passed in the
common track with their fellow parishioners. His endeavouring to
shield her from the storm, was a natural action, and what he would
have certainly done for his horse, if he had been in the same situation. Neither am I of opinion, that their sudden death was a reward
of their mutual virtue. . . . Time and chance happen to all men.

She then accepted his challenge, and composed an epitaph,
which compared to his she considered as 'perhaps more just,
though not so poetical'. After a cynical résumé of the accident,
she finished with:

---

[1] *Corr.* i. 493–6. He also sent the pathetic tale and epitaphs to several other
friends.

Who knows if 'twas not kindly done?
For had they seen the next year's sun,
A beaten wife and cuckold swain
Had jointly curs'd the marriage chain;
Now they are happy in their doom,
For P. has wrote upon their tomb.

The author of this jaundiced view of marriage then joined her husband to complete their journey.

They arrived in London on 2 October 1718.[1] Two days later a notice from Hampton Court announced: 'Mr. Wortley Montague being returned from his Embassy at the Ottoman Porte, this Day waited on His Majesty.'[2] While he had been on his way home, the Austrians and Turks had signed the Treaty of Passarowitz, mediated by Sutton and the Dutch envoy; and the Emperor had joined the Quadruple Alliance proposed by England. The failure of Wortley's diplomatic mission was thus mitigated. But its great success lay in another direction; it had enabled Lady Mary to travel through the varied courts of Europe, into the provocative culture of Islam, and along the suggestive shores of the Mediterranean.

---

[1] *Weekly Journal or Br. Gaz.*, 11 Oct.; *St. James's Eve. Post*, 2–4 Oct. 1718.
[2] *London Gazette*, 7–11 Oct. 1718; *Cal. of Treasury Papers 1714–1719*, 413.

VII. *'The Second Eve'*

(1718–22)

ALTHOUGH Wortley was reputed to have returned home very rich, he applied to the Treasury for the sum of almost £9,000 as reimbursement for his embassy expenses.[1] In a memorandum he drew up about twenty years later, he wrote that he was offered £10,000 in discharge of his debt and possession of the place for life promised him on leaving the Treasury, but only on condition that he support the Peerage Bill, which he refused to do. He was then paid £5,000, and lost the balance of the debt as well as the place for life (both of them diverted by Walpole to his own use).[2] But still a Member of Parliament, he resumed his seat; and with the exception of the Peerage Bill, he usually voted on the government side. For the rest of his life he remained in Parliament, elected from his family seats of Huntingdon in 1722 and Peterborough in 1734, but he never again held a government post. He blamed his disfavour on his 'refusing to oblige Lord S[underland] in the Peerage Bill, and after to declare himself a friend to Sir R[obert] W[alpole]'.[3] Lady Mary had attempted to help him during his earlier Parliamentary years and on his embassy, but henceforth she seems to have detached herself from his career.

During her two-year absence she had tried to maintain her friendships at Court, sending letters to Princess Caroline, Mademoiselle von Schulenburg, and Madame Kielmannsegge. She was especially persistent in writing to the influential Count Bothmar, to whom she once complained that he had not

---

[1] Bacon to Montagu, Paston, 289; *Cal. of Treasury Papers 1714–1719*, 413.
[2] W's memorandum, drawn up about 1747 (MS in my possession). For some reason, on 28 Mar. 1720 he surrendered the post of auditor granted to him Nov. 1717 (*Cal. of Treasury Books and Papers 1735–1738*, ed. W. A. Shaw [1900], 394).   [3] W's MS memorandum of 1747.

answered her previous three letters.[1] In London she resumed
her life at Court—or, more properly, at the two Courts, for
since the beginning of 1718 the King and the Prince of Wales
had been estranged. Driven from St. James's, the Prince had
gathered a rival Court at Leicester House. The schism brought
social complications, as Pope had warned Lady Mary: 'Our
Gallantry and Gayety have been great Sufferers by the rupture
of the two Courts here. Scarce any Ball, Assembly, Basset table,
or any place where two or three are gathered together.'[2] But
soon, under the clever Princess, Leicester House became popular with the livelier part of Court society; and as it became a
centre of political opposition, those who attended it were forbidden entry at St. James's. Lady Mary was enterprising enough
to attend both.

She never held any of the posts awarded to ladies for their
family or beauty; and in her old age declared that she 'could
never endure with tolerable patience the austerities of a court
life'. On the Embassy she had learned how 'the glance of the
monarch is watched, and every smile waited for with impatience, and envied by those who cannot obtain it'.[3] In her
own encounters with the King at Hanover she had witnessed
as well as shared the nervous waiting, and had been rewarded
by his attention. At St. James's she again attended his dull
parties. Among the other English there was young James
Craggs, a secretary of state, who owed his advancement to his
favour with Madame von Platen. In Lady Mary's opinion, he
possessed great vivacity, a happy memory, and flowing elocu-
tion, as well as bravery, generosity, and a universal good will,
but 'there appeared a heat and want of judgment in all his words
and actions'.[4] She herself was the victim of his impetuosity at
one of the King's parties. Wishing to be dismissed early she
explained her reasons to the Duchess of Kendal (formerly
Mademoiselle von Schulenburg). When the Duchess informed
the King, he acquiesced, after flattering Lady Mary and teasing
her to stay. On her way out she met Craggs at the foot of the
stairs, and in answer to his question boasted of the King's atten-
tions. Without a word he snatched her in his arms, carried her
upstairs, deposited her in the antechamber, and fled; whereupon

---

[1] 'Heads of Letters', i. 17–19.   [2] *Corr.* i. 470.   [4] 'Account', i. 131.
[3] To Lady F. Steuart, 4 Sept. 1758, ii. 331; to Lady Mar, i. 346.

the startled page boys opened the doors, and she stood again in the King's presence. 'Ah! la re-voilà!' he and the Duchess exclaimed, and thanked her for changing her mind. Taken off guard, she related what had happened. A moment later the door opened and Craggs entered, cool and composed. 'Mais comment donc, Monsieur Craggs,' the King said, 'est-ce que c'est l'usage de ce pays de porter des belles dames comme un sac de froment?' Bewildered for a moment by the rebuke, Craggs regained his poise, and with a bow answered, 'There is nothing I would not do for your majesty's satisfaction.' As soon as the King turned away, Craggs bitterly reproached her for talebearing. When she recorded the incident in her journal, she acknowledged her mistake in forgetting that discretion was a prime virtue at Court.[1]

The King's parties were ordinarily stolidly formal; at Leicester House the Princess welcomed her to a gayer place. At one of the card parties there, according to Lady Mary's journal, the Prince openly admired her, and called out to his wife to see how becomingly she was dressed. 'Lady Mary always dresses well', she replied drily. But not long after, when the Prince heard that Lady Mary had attended one of his father's select parties, he accused her of having deserted to the enemy. After that she dressed with care, but he took no notice of her. The Princess tried to make amends by being especially gracious.[2] On one occasion, probably in the summer of 1720, she sent a message to Lady Mary that she hoped to see her at Richmond, where her Court passed the summer.[3]

Again at home in England, Lady Mary remained involved in a correspondence with Rémond. But she did not regard him with sufficient ardour (as he complained): 'Votre écrit est très spirituel mais ce n'est pas une lettre. Je suis fort baissé auprès de vous. La singularité de l'impression que vous avez faite sur mon âme ne vous amuse plus, et vous êtes déjà rebutée d'un commerce de quelques mois qui sont des siècles pour vous. Il faut donc faire taire l'amant et que le pédant réponde à votre dissertation.' True to his threat, he then delivered a pedantic disquisition on English language and literature, on Greek and Roman concepts of dramatic rules, and then on love, slyly inserting one sentence in English: 'I love you, My Lady, at all

---

[1] Stuart, 76–77.   [2] Stuart, 74–75.   [3] Lady Stafford to M, W MS, iv. 248.

PLATE 4

Covent Garden Market

From a painting by Franz de Paula Ferg (1689–1740)

my heart.'[1] Pope, from whom she had received epistolary gallantry too, remained fairly restrained when she returned to the land of the living. He had retired to Stanton Harcourt to finish his *Iliad*, but he begged her to let him know of her arrival through Jervas's servants in London. He may have come up to London to see her, but he returned to the country immediately to stay until almost the middle of October.[2]

Soon after their return from the Embassy, the Wortley Montagus rented a large house in the Piazza of Covent Garden, paying an annual rent of £125.[3] This served them as their town residence; and in the late spring of 1719 they began to look for a suitable country house at Twickenham. There Lady Mary could have the setting, when she wished it, for the Horatian solitude she had extolled in her verses from the Turkish kiosk: 'Give me, great God, a little farm. . . .' Pope, who had moved to the village in March, may have persuaded them to settle there; at least he exerted himself to help them find a house. Their friend Sir Godfrey Kneller owned one which seemed suitable, and Wortley entered into negotiations to rent it. When he and Lady Mary went to Twickenham to inspect it, Pope invited them to stay with him—an invitation Wortley accepted.[4] When he had finished his inspection, however, he asked for only a short lease because he considered the house unsound. Still using Pope as his friendly agent Kneller strongly objected: his surveyor judged the house to be strong, requiring only minor repairs; and he insisted on a long lease or a sale.[5] Evidently some agreement was reached, for on 16 June 1719 Kneller informed Pope of the alterations being made in the house and stables. He did not omit sending his 'humble respects' to Lady Mary.[6] (She may have been Pope's guest again, or occupying another house in the vicinity.) In 1722, ultimately, Wortley purchased the house, a medium-sized one near the Twickenham heath about a third of a mile from Pope's modest Thames-side villa.[7]

[1] W MS, iv. 214.
[2] To M; to Burlington, 11 Oct. ('I went to Town a Fortnight since . . .'); to Dancastle, 25 Oct. 1718, *Corr.* i. 505, 517, 518.   [3] Wharncliffe MS 508.
[4] W to Pope, *Corr.* ii. 6.   [5] Pope to W, ibid. 12.   [6] Ibid. 6–7.
[7] Its size can be gauged from the fact that in 1722 Wortley paid a poor-rate of 15 shillings, and Pope 10; while seventeen other householders paid more than a pound (parish records, Church of St. Mary the Virgin, Twickenham).

Pope and Lady Mary were the hub of a steady whirl of friends. Congreve, visiting Ashley Park, sent his 'humble service' to her, asking Pope to explain why he could not visit her.[1] A more direct sample of Pope's friendship with her appears in a letter sent to him by Arbuthnot in August 1719: 'I am as glad you are turnd such a Bon Vivant. but you have so good a ham over against you, I wonder you want any other. This is the manner of your Conversation with Lady Mary for which you are so often reprimanded, and never reformd; may I take the freedom to give her ladyship my most humble respects. Ile tell you freely when I go to Twitenham it is to pay my respects to her ladyship, and not to see you. for you never stay a moment with me.'[2] Their close friendship impressed others in their circle. When Pope completed the last volume of his *Iliad*, Gay welcomed his return from Homeric Greece with some light verse. Pope stepping ashore is greeted by Lady Mary, the first of the 'goodly dames':

> What lady's that, to whom he gently bends?
> Who knows not her? ah! those are Wortley's eyes:
> How art thou honour'd, number'd with her friends?
> For she distinguishes the good and wise.[3]

To signalize his romantic admiration for her, Pope decided at about that time to have her portrait painted for himself. Quite logically he commissioned Kneller, who had already painted her twice before, in 1710 and 1715.[4] In her new portrait she was to wear a Turkish costume. The aged Kneller painted very little at this time, and his undertaking the new commission was probably a favour to both patron and sitter.[5] He went about it in a way extremely flattering to Lady Mary. First he called at her home in Twickenham to sketch her face with crayons; then, to save her the bother of posing, he transferred his drawing on to canvas in his own studio—a manner, Pope explained, 'in which they seldom draw any but Crown'd Heads; and I observe it with a secret pride and pleasure'.[6] At another sitting,

---

[1] *Corr.* ii. 13.   [2] Ibid. 9-10.
[3] *Additions to the Works of Pope* (1776), i. 97. In Gay's autograph, 'Howard' is substituted for 'Wortley', a change no doubt made at a later date (Add. MS 6419, f. 54).
[4] J. P. Richter, *Cat. of Paintings Lent by Marquis of Bute* (1883), 59-60.
[5] Lord Killanin, *Kneller and His Times* (1948), 49.
[6] Cf. R. H. Wilenski, *English Painting* (1933), 57.

Kneller sketched her in her dress.[1] The finished portrait, dated 1720, shows Lady Mary seated in a half-reclining position of affected indolence, her right hand held up as though supporting her head. Across her shoulders lies an ermine cloak over a blue dress with a low-cut bodice to display her handsome bosom. On her head she wears a loosely arranged Turkish head-dress secured by a single heavy jewel, and from her ear hangs a large tear-drop pearl. But her face is the focus of the composition— with rounded dimpled chin, full shapely lips, small nose, and large, dark, piercing eyes. Presumably Kneller was paid about twenty guineas for the picture, that being his usual fee for a head with one hand shown.[2] Pope was so pleased with it that he wrote some 'extemporaneous verses' praising

> The Equal Lustre of the Heavenly mind
> Where every grace with every Virtue's join'd,
> Learning not vain, and wisdom not severe
> With Greatness easy, and with wit sincere.[3]

He gave the poetic tribute to her, but hung the lovely portrait in his best room fronting the Thames, and there it remained for the rest of his life.[4]

In endowing her with 'wit sincere' he echoed his praise in a *jeu d'esprit*, written when she was abroad, that her brains were as good as any man's.[5] A far more elaborate compliment to her intellect began to circulate in February 1719 when Thomas Burnet enlivened his correspondence with 'a Copy of Verses that came very lately from my Parnassus . . . made upon a Lady that is famous for Reading'. It begins:

> In Beauty or wit
> No Mortal as yet
>   To question your Empire has dar'd;
> But men of discerning
> Have thought that in Learning
>   To yield to a Lady, was hard.

It goes on to say that if the first woman of creation received hard doom for tasting one apple, what punishment must be

---

[1] Pope to M, *Corr.* ii. 22, 22–23.   [2] Killanin, *Kneller*, 33.
[3] Twickenham, vi. 212.
[4] *Notes & Queries*, 6 S. v (1882), 364. She had Jonathan Richardson paint her full figure with Turkish dress (picture now owned by Lord Harrowby).
[5] 'Sandys's Ghost' (printed in 1727), Twickenham, vi. 173.

found for the lady who has tasted and robbed the whole tree![1]
A copy of the poem fell into the hands of Curll, who (in March
1720) printed it as 'The Second Eve' by Pope. Thereafter,
although it was reprinted under his name, Pope never disclaimed it.[2] In her growing public reputation Lady Mary's
name was synonymous with a witty woman.[3] Her fame was
fortified by the publication of a print showing her wearing a
Turkish dress and holding a book. Entitled 'Lady M-y
W-r-t-l-y M-nt-g-e The Female Traveller', it paid homage in
four lines of doggerel:

> Let Men who glory in their better sense,
> Read, hear, and learn Humility from hence;
> No more let them Superior Wisdom boast,
> They can but equal M-nt-g-e at most.[4]

She was thus being put forward in the rising feminist movement
as an extraordinary intellectual woman.

The publication of her own writings gave visible proof of
her powers. Her brilliant letter from Constantinople to the
Abbé Conti was printed (without her authority), its title-page
calling her 'an English Lady, who was lately in *Turkey*, and
who is no less distinguish'd by her Wit than by her Quality'.[5]
Then a miscellany (in May 1720) printed her 'Verses' written
in the kiosk. She had sent the poem to her uncle William
Fielding, but it had been 'by his (well intended) indiscretion
shown about, copies taken, and at length miserably printed'.[6]
She now saw her name blazoned on a title-page with the names
of Pope, Prior, Hughes, and the disreputable Mrs. Manley. She
was sufficiently proud of the poem to copy it into the red album
containing Pope's transcript of her eclogues, which she had
reclaimed from him on her return from the Embassy.

[1] Burnet to Duckett, 5 Feb. 1719, Burnet, *Letters*, 163–5; Burnet's *Verses* (1777), 9–11. In an album of verses (Harrowby, vol. 255) Lady Mary assigned the authorship to 'Judge [i.e. Thomas] Burnet'.

[2] Sherburn, 'Notes on Canon of Pope's Works, 1714–20', *Manly Anniv. Stud. in Lang. and Lit.*' (1923), 174; Twickenham, vi. 423.

[3] Specimen in *HMC 12 Rep.* ix (1891), 188.

[4] Copy in Princeton Univ. Library.

[5] *The Genuine Copy of a Letter written from Constantinople by an English Lady ... To a Venetian Nobleman ...* , London, J. Roberts and A. Dodd. With a new title-page it was reissued the same year as a 'Second Edition'.

[6] *A New Miscellany of Original Poems*, ed. A. H. [Anthony Hammond] (1720), 95–101; to Lady F. Steuart, 4 Sept. 1758, ii. 332.

PLATE 5

Lady Mary Wortley Montagu
From a painting by Godfrey Kneller [1720]

Her friendship with Rémond, or at least his letters, had taken a new turn in February 1720. Love and literary tags played only a small part; he mainly discussed politics, commerce, and finance. Soon after, in another letter, he thanked her for 'ces conseils que vous me donnez pour assurer ma petite fortune chancelante. . . . Si j'étais le maître de ma destinée, ne croyez pas que je puisse imaginer autre chose que de passer ma vie auprès de vous, à ne voir et à n'adorer que Mil. M. Oui, je préférerais d'être l'été à Thuydenham [*sic*] et l'hiver à Kinsington, sans connaître ni la ville ni la cour, à être Régent de France sans vous.'

Perhaps his hints of coming closer made her draw back; in any event she ceased writing to him, and he chided her in terms that barely concealed a threat:

Je suis étonné, madame, de votre long silence. Est-ce la cour ou la philosophie qui vous détourne? Peut-être que mes lettres vous importunent pendant que les vôtres font un des grands plaisirs de ma vie. . . . Si j'étais aussi indiscret que l'abbé Conti je gagnerai autant à faire imprimer vos lettres que j'ai gagné aux actions du Missisipi, et rien ne flatterait tant ma pédanterie qu'un commerce si délicieux avec une personne aussi distinguée que vous. . . . Je souhaite quelquefois d'être en Angleterre parceque vous daignez prendre soin de mon pauvre esprit. Nous lirions Homère avec M. Poppe, et vous nous y feriez remarquer des beautés qui lui échapent à lui même. . . .

He hoped some time to be in England, he said at the end.[1] The combination of Pope's friendship, Rémond's promises, and financial speculation were to have some strange results for her.

In the spring of 1720 the South Sea Company, using the Mississippi scheme as a model, took over the national debt, and expanded its stock holdings.[2] In April its shares stood at £325, in May they went to £500, and continued to rise. Men and women of every class speculated in the hope of making quick profits. Although the Mississippi stock had begun to fall in May, the English public continued to inflate the South Sea Bubble. At the end of June a third public subscription was opened, and immediately sold out. Like others at Court, young Craggs had been specially favoured by the directors with presents and influence. As a friend and Twickenham neighbour

---

[1] W MS, iv. 218–19, 220, 225–6.
[2] L. Melville, *The South Sea Bubble* (1921), *passim*.

Lady Mary appealed to him more than once to have her name
entered in the lists. On 18 July she sent him a note: 'When
I have so much reason to return you thanks for your last
favour, I am ashamed to trouble you for another. You are so
often importuned in this manner I hope you know how to
forgive it, though to say truth I do think it very impertinent in
me to desire you to put my name in your next list of subscribers
to the South Sea stock, for what sum you please.'[1] Craggs, who
suffered from the importunities of many such applicants,
replied to her somewhat formally: although he would recommend her, he could not be sure that the directors would accept
another subscriber.[2] In anticipation of the list's opening, the
stock continued to rise above £900 as August drew on.

Meanwhile Rémond, inspired by the rising market, arrived
in England in the early summer. During his first fifteen days in
London he saw Lady Mary only once, at a supper party, and
she did not say one word to him. He complained of this to a
friend in London, adding: 'Dîtes, je vous prie, à Mil. M. qu'elle
n'aime que les absents. . . . J'ai resolu de réparer le temps perdu
et dès aujourd'hui je la chercherai par tout.' His pressing purpose was far from love: he wanted her advice on how to use his
letter of credit to purchase stock. But Lady Mary resisted his
attempts to force an interview, and he had to send her a note;
in it he begged for an appointment, and for her advice on
whether to sell his £2,000 worth of stock at a 'mediocre' profit
or risk it for a much greater one.[3] Lady Mary's account of their
dealings corresponds to his. He had brought over his modest
capital, she told Lady Mar, and immediately laid it out on South
Sea stock. On her advice he sold it for a modest profit. Then,
when she urged him to leave, he reluctantly agreed (in the
middle of August), but asked her to invest his money for him.
At first she refused; but he won her consent by his debonair
assurance that he was willing to lose or double such a small sum.
Since it was generally believed that South Sea stock would continue to rise, she bought some with his money.[4]

He was not the only one for whom she speculated. On behalf

[1] Tickell MS.
[2] Craggs to George Clarke, 30 June 1720, MS Eg. 2618, ff. 221–2; to M,
25 July 1720, M's letters, ii. 9.
[3] Rémond to Alvarez, Rémond to M, W MS, iv. 227, 216.
[4] i. 450–1.

of Lady Gower, her sister's mother-in-law, she used her influence with a director of the Company to set aside £5,000
worth of stock for a down payment of £500.[1] Pope had also
caught the universal fever, and on 22 August sent her an urgent
note to advise her that the stock would certainly rise in the next
few weeks, and that buying would bring certain gain.[2] Two
days later the fourth subscription was opened and immediately
sold out. Lady Mary was presumably lucky enough to be
admitted to the list. On that occasion a versifying friend sent
her a poem, which she copied into an album, prophesying that
her fearful tongue and eyes would raise the shares to a veritable
Mississippi South Sea![3] Almost immediately the stock dropped
to £820, a week later to £700, then to £400; and by the beginning of October to £240. The widespread bankruptcy and distress shook the government; and public credit was not restored
until the following spring.

Lady Mary's investment for Rémond, according to her own
explanation, had taken an unhappy turn. After a slight gain, she
had ordered his stock to be sold through a firm of goldsmiths,
but they absconded, leaving it in her ownership—just as the
slump reduced its value to £400.[4] Rémond, who knew nothing
of this, sent her a long letter from Paris on 4 September, in
which he told her:

Je ne regrette point le climat ni la société d'Angleterre, mais bien
la conversation de quelques personnes surtout la vôtre, dont je n'ai
joui que rarement et que je mets au dessus de toutes les autres pour la
vertu des sentiments aussi bien que pour la délicatesse de l'esprit. Je
comptais que nous aurions un commerce plus vif et plus assidu, mais
le mouvement des actions et le goût de la campagne vous occupent
uniquement. . . . Si vous venez jamais en France (en vérité c'est un
beau pays) vous serez plus contente de moi que je n'ai du être
content de vous. Tout ce là n'est pas pour me plaindre. Je sais que
les dames Anglaises sont incapable d'amitié et d'amour. . . .

Then after some chitchat, he innocently remarked that wise
heads in Paris did not have much faith in the success of the
South Sea Company.[5] As soon as possible she explained how his

---

[1] M to [Katherine] Lady Gower [n.d.], MS owned by the Duke of Sutherland.   [2] *Corr.* ii. 52.   [3] W MS, viii.
[4] Cox and Cleeve, the goldsmiths named by Lady Mary (i. 451), declared
themselves bankrupt in 1721 (Ambrose Heal, *London Goldsmiths 1200–1800*
[1935], 132).   [5] W MS, iv. 229–30.

investment had declined, and asked him what he would like done with his remaining assets. But he disregarded her repeated question until, at the beginning of January 1721, he accused her of dishonest trickery; he was convinced that she had kept his money untouched, and he threatened that unless she returned it he would inform her husband of their transactions and print all her letters. For almost a year she remained terrorized by his threats.

A far different calamity loomed on the horizon in the early spring of 1721—a smallpox epidemic. Its fatality among children was especially high.[1] Taking advantage of public interest, a London physician issued a pamphlet in March describing inoculation. Lady Mary, who had seen it performed on her son, needed no instruction. In April she sent for Maitland, retired in the country since his return from the Embassy, and told him she was resolved to have her daughter inoculated. As he recalled the events the following year, he requested that they wait until better weather and that two other physicians be present as witnesses. At first Lady Mary refused, because (he surmised) she either wanted it kept secret or feared it would be unsuccessful; but then she consented. He ingrafted both arms of the child, who 'was neither blooded nor purg'd before, nor indeed was it necessary, considering the clean Habit of Body, and the very cool, regular Diet she had ever been kept to from her Infancy'. All went well. Three 'learned Physicians of the College were admitted, one after another, to visit the young Lady . . . and will on all Occasions declare, as they have hitherto done, that they saw *Miss Wortley* playing about the Room, chearful and well, with the Small Pox rais'd upon her . . .'. Other visitors— Lady Mary's friends, probably—also witnessed the medical miracle.

Another physician regarded the operation of signal importance because printed descriptions of it 'were regarded as *Virtuoso*-Amusements' until Lady Mary had the operation performed on her own daughter. Dr. Keith, one of the observers, was sufficiently impressed to have his surviving son inoculated in May. Popular interest soon followed. In June one of the weekly newspapers printed a description of inoculation;

[1] This and the subsequent sections on inoculation are drawn from my article in the *Journ. of the Hist. of Medicine*, viii (1953), 390–405.

and another paper reprinted it, but apologized a week later for the description 'inserted by way of amusement', calling it a 'visionary experiment'. Lady Mary had undertaken to make the experiment a practical success.

Rémond persisted with his threats through the spring. Although she begged him to appoint a lawyer to examine her accounts, he refused; and demanded £2,000 for his stock, which she valued at £500. In June he actually addressed a letter to her husband through an English friend who was considerate enough to give it instead to Lady Mary. Since she spent so much of her time in Twickenham she was in constant terror that Rémond would succeed in reaching Wortley in London. His tactics, as she described them, were simply those of a blackmailer: he would return her letters to her if she paid him the sum he demanded. Frantically she appealed to her sister in Paris to deal with him, and to Lady Stafford, who was a mutual friend; she even thought of asking Lord Mar to help her. To protect herself from the monster, the madman, the desperate wretch (as she called him) she thought of every kind of retaliation; 'if he dares to give me further trouble', she told Lady Mar, 'I shall take care to have him rewarded in a stronger manner. . . .'[1]

Lady Mar was not having an easy time herself. In Rome she had been regarded with suspicion by rabid Jacobites as a spy sent by the King and her father. She had suffered actual persecution from James Murray, her husband's political rival, who inflicted 'incivilities beyond measure'.[2] Then her husband, after being imprisoned in Geneva, had resigned his post, and they lived in Paris, supported by her jointure and an irregular pension from the English government. Except for occasional visits to England, one in the summer of 1720, she shared her husband's exile and struggled with an insecure income and mental depression.

Lady Mary was more resilient. Her house at Twickenham was a refuge from all sorts of nuisances, including persistent visitors. In London the recently married John Hervey and Mary Lepell had imposed on her with their 'ardent affection',

---

[1] i. 458.
[2] T. Bruce to Mar, 15 Nov. 1718, HMC *Stuart Papers*, vii (1923), 547; 'A Narrative by Lord Pitsligo', *Jacobite Court at Rome in 1719*, ed. H. Taylor (1938), 54, 63, 83–84, 114.

visiting her several times a day and 'perpetually cooing' in her rooms. She was glad to flee to Twickenham to pass her time 'in great indolence and sweetness'.[1] Since one of her favourite pastimes was music, she 'melted away' her time there 'in almost perpetual concerts'. During that summer (1721) Buononcini the composer, Mrs. Robinson the singer, and Senesino the great *castrato*, all lodged in Twickenham and performed at concerts. Lady Mary enjoyed the company of another friend at this time, while her husband was in Yorkshire. 'My fair companion', she told her sister, 'puts me oft in mind of our Thoresby conversations; we read and walk together, and I am more happy in her than any thing else could make me except your conversation.' Her friend, whose identity remains a mystery, stayed with her: 'I have taken my little thread satin beauty into the house with me', she told her sister; 'she is allowed by Bononcini to have the finest voice he ever heard in England.'[2] Perhaps at one of these concerts Lady Mary composed her 'Impromptu to a Young Lady Singing':

> Sing, gentle maid, reform my breast,
>   And soften all my care;
> Thus I can be some moments blest,
>   And easy in despair.
> The power of Orpheus lives in you;
> The raging passions of my soul subdue,
> And tame the lions and the tigers there.[3]

These sentiments were particularly applicable to her at this time when she felt both despair and bliss.

In the autumn her London and Twickenham circle were shocked by a crime involving Mrs. Griselda Murray. She was a friend of Lady Mary's, close enough to be placed at her side in Gay's welcome to Pope on returning from Homeric Greece; and Lady Mary dined at her house, and trusted her to receive her sister's letters about Rémond.[4] On 14 October Mrs. Murray, who was separated from her husband and lived in her father's house, was roused from her sleep at four in the morning by Arthur Gray, a young footman employed in the house. Armed

---

[1] To Lady Mar, July 1721, i. 456–7. [2] Ibid. 457, 459.
[3] W MS [Harrowby, vol. 255]. A slightly different version in ii. 499.
[4] Lady Grisell Baillie, *Household Book 1692–1733*, ed. R. Scott-Moncrieff (1911), 290; M to Lady Mar, i. 452.

with a sword and a pistol he approached her bed and threatened
to kill her if she made any outcry. She succeeded in wrenching
the pistol from him, and rang the bell to awaken the household.
Gray fled, but was captured a few hours later, and when taken
before a justice signed a confession.[1] The weekly newspapers
added embellishments to their reports. In one, Mrs. Murray
springs at the footman, throws him to the floor, and stands on
his chest: 'The Lady observ'd, that the Fellow who was always
esteemed the most stupid Wretch in the World, pleaded his
amorous Cause with all imaginable Eloquence. . . . A certain
great foreign Lady of Quality, upon hearing this Tale, said, she
pitied the poor young Man, since he was so much in Love.' This
hint could easily have inspired a versifier. Another weekly
paper added to its news report a dozen lines of verse praising
the brave heroine, and comparing her to Lucrece.[2]

At his trial the footman was found guilty of burglary and
felony, and sentenced to be hanged; but at the eleventh hour
Mrs. Murray's family interceded, and he was instead trans-
ported to New England.[3] Lady Mary drew a lesson from the
case. Writing to her sister about Rémond's threats, she moral-
ized: 'I am too well acquainted with the world (of which poor
Mrs. Murray's affair is a fatal instance), not to know that the
most groundless accusation is always of ill consequence to a
woman.'[4] One of the ill consequences was a ballad, printed on
a single broadsheet, entitled 'Virtue in Danger: or Arthur
Gray's last Farewell to the World'. In mock-heroic strain, its
twenty-four vigorous stanzas relate Mrs. Murray's ordeal, with
an obscene detail here and there; and its last stanza praises her:

> This Ladies Fame, shall ever last,
> And live in *British* Song,
> For she was like *Lucretia* Chaste,
> And eke was much more Strong.[5]

Such an ephemeral, topical ballad must have been written and
printed soon after the event. Its author was effectively hidden
by: 'Written by a Gentleman at St. James's.' The same ballad

---

[1] *Select Trials . . . in the Old-Bailey* (1742), i. 97–105.
[2] *Weekly Journal or Sat. Post*; *Weekly Journal or Br. Gaz.*, both 21 Oct.
1721.
[3] *Weekly Journal or Br. Gaz.*, 6 Jan. 1722.   [4] i. 460–1.
[5] Unique copy in Huntington Library.

with some slight changes was later published as 'Written by a Lady'.[1]

Who indeed was the author of _Virtue in Danger_? Mrs. Murray suspected Lady Mary, and thereafter regarded her with the most intense hatred. When Lady Mary later 'defied her to have any one single proof', she merely answered that she knew it.[2] One indication that the ballad was not of Lady Mary's authorship is that it does not appear in any of her poetry albums, where she usually copied her verse. But the same episode evoked from her the 'Epistle from Arthur Gray to Mrs. Murray', a far more serious and polished poem, opening with:

> Read, lovely nymph, and tremble not to read,
> I have no more to wish, nor you to dread:
> I ask not life, for life to me were vain,
> And death a refuge from severer pain.
> My only hope in these last lines I try;
> I wou'd be pitied, and I then wou'd die.

He tells of his fatal infatuation, and still in the pathetic vein pleads for the love his social position forbids. When Walpole printed the poem (from a copy in Lady Mary's album) he repeated a friend's opinion that 'scarce any woman could have written it, and no man; for a man who had had experience enough to paint such sentiments so well, would not have had warmth enough left'.[3] At the time of the scandal, perhaps gossip about Lady Mary's 'Epistle' had attached itself to the notorious, anonymous ballad.

Her own potentially scandalous friendship with Rémond came to an end at about this time, for she ceased complaining of his persecution. She had somehow placated him. Since his letters to her remained among her papers, endorsed by her husband, she probably confessed her rash speculation to him. The letters prove two unequivocal facts: that Rémond was never her lover, and that her explanation of their financial transaction was fairly accurate. He was notoriously experienced, according to Saint-Simon, in extracting pecuniary benefits from friends, and used any means he could. Why, then, was

---

[1] _Select Trials_, loc. cit.; reprinted as M's in _Additions to Pope_ (1776), i. 176, and endorsed as hers by Horace Walpole in his copy.

[2] M to Lady Mar, 1725, i. 482–3.

[3] _Six Town Eclogues_ (1747), 39–43; to Mann, 24 Nov. 1747, _Corr._ xix. 450.

Lady Mary so terrorized by his threats to expose her? She feared Wortley's anger; he was both strict and economical in regard to money matters. She also feared, perhaps more, the ridicule of her scandalmongering friends. Her attempt to suppress Rémond's persecution helped to spread it; and, ironically, it was later immortalized by Pope, who had so solicitously advised her to buy South Sea stock.

During this period her friendship with Pope seems to have been fitful. In the summer of 1721 he showed her a flattering letter from William Broome, his collaborator in translation, who planned to honour her with a poem on inoculation. When he went off to visit Lord Bathurst at the end of the summer, he was pleased that she walked about in his garden; and he invited her to hold concerts in his gallery during his absence, and to use his harpsichord there.[1] But the following spring they hardly ever met. 'I pass my time in a small snug set of dear intimates', she told her sister, 'and go very little into the *grand monde*, which has always had my hearty contempt. I see sometimes Mr. Congreve, and very seldom Mr. Pope, who continues to embellish his house at Twickenham. He has made a subterranean grotto, which he has furnished with looking-glass, and they tell me it has a very good effect.'[2] Yet that same summer, when Mrs. Murray had retired to Castle Howard to sit out the aftermath of her scandal, her mother informed her of Lady Mary's continued malice (in conversation), and of her own refusal to dine with her at Twickenham: 'She and Pope keeps so close yonder that they are a talk to the whole town. No lady else almost there goes near her, as I'm told. There is a thousand things said of her just now, but let not us introduce scandal; we have had enough of it ourselves. They say a great many things of her using Mr. Wortley like a dog. Indeed we owe her spite, but God keep us from revenge against the worst of our enemies.'[3] Upper-class society, from any point of view, was a school for scandal.

In contrast to these relatively trivial friendships and scandals, Lady Mary took part in the momentous development of inoculation. Princess Caroline, probably impressed by its success on

[1] Pope to Broome, 16 July 1721, *Corr.* ii. 77; to M, 15 Sept. 1721, ibid. 82–83.
[2] [April or May 1722], i. 461.
[3] 14 July 1722, MS owned by the Earl of Haddington.

Lady Mary's children, determined to test it. In the summer of 1721 six condemned criminals in Newgate were allowed to volunteer for the operation, with freedom as their reward should they survive; and Maitland was persuaded to act as surgeon. Many witnesses watched—physicians, surgeons, the apothecaries to the Prince and Princess, and members of the Royal Society. After the operation, Maitland confidently boasted of his success in Child's Coffee House. His optimism was justified, for five of the patients caught a mild attack of the disease, and the sixth, who had already had it, showed no change; all six then won their freedom. But the Princess wished to experiment further, and in the spring of 1722 had it performed on the orphan children of St. James's Parish, again with success. It was so much argued and discussed that Maitland published his account, dedicating it to the Prince and Princess. In April, exactly one year after Lady Mary's daughter had been inoculated, the operation was successfully performed on two of the Princess's daughters.

Just as royalty set the fashion in other things, so they did in this. Lady Mary told her sister: 'I suppose the . . . faithful historians give you regular accounts of the growth and spreading of the inoculation of the small-pox, which is become almost a general practice, attended with great success.' Lord Bathurst, at this time her friend, had all of his six children successfully inoculated. But then two patients died after the operation: a young servant in Lord Bathurst's household and the two-and-a-half year old son of the Earl of Sunderland. These cases of failure, as well as the Royal sponsorship, led to the controversy's most violent phase in the summer of 1722—when Lady Mary herself took a public part.

The opposition came from two camps, clergy and medical men. In July Edmund Massey, a clergyman, preached against it as a defiance of God's will, and was refuted by an anonymous, witty pamphlet. Maitland then issued a second edition of his *Account* to defend himself; and Massey in turn published a vindication of his sermon. Some theological opposition continued, but it was confined to high-church clergy. And in Boston, Massachusetts, where the smallpox epidemic and controversy raged, six clergymen publicly supported inoculation. Among eminent medical men, it won the support of Arbuthnot,

Sloane, James Jurin, and Richard Mead. The objections generally raised by physicians cited its risks to patients, the uncer-
tainty of its protective power, and the danger of its spreading
the disease. A typical argument was set forth in a pamphlet by
William Wagstaffe urging physicians not to allow their profession to be usurped by amateurs. 'Posterity', he concluded,
'perhaps will scarcely be brought to believe, that an Experiment
practiced only by a few *Ignorant Women*, amongst an illiterate
and unthinking People, shou'd on a sudden, and upon slender
Experience, so far obtain in one of the Politest Nations in the
World, as to be receiv'd into the *Royal Palace*.' A physician in
Portsmouth quickly stepped forward to refute Wagstaffe on
medical grounds and Massey on religious ones. Controversialists
came from all sides.

It may have been Wagstaffe's attack on the practice of
'ignorant women' that angered Lady Mary into taking up her
pen to defend inoculation publicly with an essay entitled 'A
Plain Account of the Inoculating of the Small Pox by a Turkey
Merchant'.[1]

> Out of compassion to the numbers abused and deluded by the
> knavery and ignorance of physicians [she began] I am determined
> to give a true account of the manner of inoculating the smallpox as
> it is practised at Constantinople with constant success, and without
> any ill consequence whatever. I shall sell no drugs, nor take no fees,
> could I persuade people of the safety and reasonableness of this easy
> operation. 'Tis no way my interest (according to the common
> acceptation of that word) to convince the world of their errors;
> that is, I shall get nothing by it but the private satisfaction of having
> done good to mankind, and I know no body that reckons that satis-
> faction any part of their interest.

She then described the correct method of inoculation, and con-
trasted it with the foolish and dangerous practice of English
physicians. 'After some few more sacrifices of this kind', she
sarcastically commented, 'it may be hoped this terrible design
against the revenue of the College may be entirely defeated,
and those worthy members receive two guineas a day as before,
of the wretches that send for them in that distemper.'

She submitted her essay to *The Flying-Post: or, Post-Master*,

---

[1] Wortley MS, vii. 201–3. Printed in full, with variant readings, in the
Journ. of the Hist. of Medicine, viii. 401–2.

a popular London newspaper, and it was published in the issue of 11–13 September 1722—with no author designated except the anonymous Turkey Merchant. The editor did not merely tinker with her style; he also eliminated her bitter criticism, her sarcasms against physicians and their College, and in general blunted her passionately indignant tone. In her public role she used a prose style of strident vigour, in contrast to the glittering wit of her letters and verse couplets, for she was performing in a different arena of literary expression. Less than two weeks after her essay appeared in print, a new antagonist sprang up. Isaac Massey, apothecary at Christ's Hospital (the boys' school), attacked the growing popularity of inoculation, insisting that sufficient time must pass before the cure be accepted as safe and certain. One of the advocates whom he refuted was the writer of 'a Sham Turkey Merchant's letter' in the *Flying-Post*. He had recognized the literary hoax, but apparently without discovering the actual writer. She remained effectively hidden for over two hundred years.

VIII. *Degrees of Friendship*

(1722–8)

In Twickenham during the summer of 1722 Lady Mary attended to the alterations in the buildings and garden of her newly purchased house; that and the education of her daughter were her two 'chief amusements'.[1] She had others, too, one being the companionship of the young Duke of Wharton, who leased a house there that year. She later told a friend that when she first became intimately acquainted with the Duke, Pope grew jealous.[2] Yet in July, reported Mrs. Murray's mother, Lady Mary and Pope kept so close that they were the talk of the whole town. Did anything happen to thrust them apart and thus begin the estrangement that led to their enmity? The cause suggested by Lady Mary could have occurred at this time: that Pope made a passionate declaration of love, and that she answered him with a fit of laughter.[3] As she had written in 'The Lady's Resolve': 'Too near he has approached, who is denied.'

Some corroboration that Pope was repulsed by her in the summer of 1722 may lie in the fact that by the end of September a new admirable lady, Judith Cowper, appeared on his horizon, and he began to lavish on her the kind of gallant epistles he had formerly sent to Lady Mary. 'Tho sprightly Sappho force our Love and Praise', he told Miss Cowper, he preferred her mild moon-like serenity, while 'the glaring Sun declines'. He immediately underlined his celestial allegory: 'The brightest Wit in the world, without the better qualities of the heart, must meet with this fate. . . .'[4] He did not withdraw his friendship from Lady Mary immediately; and as neighbours in Twickenham

---

[1] To Lady Mar, i. 462, 468.   [2] Spence, 235 n.
[3] Stuart, 92; repeated by her in Scott's *Letters 1819–21* (1934), 312 n.
[4] 18 Oct. 1722, *Corr.* ii. 139. The complaint is repeated in Lord Peterborough's 'Verses on Mrs. Howard 1723', probably in Pope's autograph, Morgan Libr. MS.

they resumed their neighbourly favours. About a year later
Lady Mary sent a servant to his house with a note: 'As I carefully returned your *Arcadia* without damage, I hope you will
trust me with a volume of Shakespeare's plays, which I shall
take the same care to restore.'[1] Her tone implies that she wished
to borrow more than he wished to lend; and she thus added still
another irritant to their sensitive relationship.

While she remained a private partisan of inoculation, she
could not escape her fame as its popularizer. The number of
patients steadily increased after the spring of 1723, when Dr.
Jurin's published statistics proved its success. Since the whole
town was taking to it, she wrote to her sister, 'I am so much
pulled about, and solicited to visit people, that I am forced to
run into the country to hide myself'. When she agreed to advise
her friends, she took along her daughter as proof of the operation's success. Her advice must have been this: 'I know nobody
that has hitherto repented the operation: though it has been
very troublesome to some fools, who had rather be sick by the
doctor's prescriptions, than in health in rebellion to the college.'[2]

She was both a medical saviour and an incomparably witty
woman. These two aspects were publicly joined in the summer
of 1724 in the pages of *The Plain Dealer* when Aaron Hill, who
had printed and praised 'The Lady's Resolve' in April, awarded
her the double empire of 'Protecting Beauty, and inspiring
Wit'.[3] Then Hill went on to quote from 'The Second Eve'—
which he assumed was by Pope—and to chide the poet for
treating the great lady with such levity. 'Praise', he declaimed,
'ought always to be *serious*, when it is address'd to the *Person
prais'd*, and where the *Subject* is of Weight, and Dignity.' This
public criticism could not have sweetened Pope's feeling for
the lady. A few months later, when Lord Bathurst in the
country asked him for news of her, Pope replied that he could
say little, but would try for his friend's sake to know more.[4]
For his own sake he apparently stayed away from her.

---

[1] Add. MS 4809, f. 85 (printed in my article in *Philological Quart.* xxix.
[1950], 350). Dated summer 1723 in Pope's *Corr.* ii. 194.
[2] To Lady Mar, i. 468, 471; Stuart, 90.   [3] 27 Apr., 3 July 1724.
[4] 17 Sept. 1724, *Corr.* ii. 258. An unconvincing anecdote about Pope and M
told by Bathurst (in 1775) in C. H. Parry's *Memoir of the Rev. Joshua Parry*
(1872), 124–5.

She exercised her wit not only in her letters and verse but in her conversation as well. In mixed society she remained rather silent unless the conversation took an interesting turn. Then she spoke gaily or forcefully; and though not ill natured would make cutting repartee, for she had very little patience with folly, and less with any kind of affectation.[1] Her friend the giddy Lady Rich, by this time a decayed beauty, affected a girlish simplicity unsuited to her mature years. Once in company someone mentioned the Master of the Rolls, who everybody knew had long been Sir Joseph Jekyll; but Lady Rich pretended a naïve ignorance. 'Pray who is Master of the Rolls?' she asked. Lady Mary chose offhand the most unlikely name that came to her mind. It disconcerted Lady Rich, and made the company laugh. 'Well! I am vastly ashamed of being so prodigiously ignorant', she went on. 'I dare say I ask a mighty silly question; but pray now, what is it to be Master of the Rolls? What does he do? for I really don't know.' 'Why, madam', Lady Mary replied, 'he superintends all the French rolls that are baked in London; and without him you would have no bread-and-butter for your breakfast.' This was too much for Lady Rich, and she admitted that Lady Mary's wit was more than she could cope with. 'Nay', Lady Mary answered, 'but look you, my dear madam, I grant it a very fine thing to continue always fifteen—*that* everybody must approve of; it is quite fair: but, indeed, indeed, one need not be five years old.'[2]

On occasion she put her tongue to work on more serious matters. When Walpole appointed the Duke of Newcastle Secretary of State, somebody wondered at his taking so insignificant an associate. 'Oh', said Lady Mary, 'I can account for it. If I was a country gentlewoman and came suddenly to a great fortune and set up my coach, I should like to show it to the neighbouring village, but I could not carry you with me, for people might doubt whether it was your coach or mine. But if you would let me carry your cat with me, I would; for nobody would think it was the cat's coach.'[3]

[1] Lady Louisa Stuart (1826), Add. MS 24483, f. 182.
[2] Stuart, 100–1. Master of the Rolls is the third member of the supreme judicature in charge of legal records.
[3] Told to Horace Walpole by Lord John Cavendish [*c.* 1780], in Walpole's

With her talent for repartee and couplets she found the Duke of Wharton a sympathetic companion, and joined him in writing squibs and ballads. Although this led to their quarrelling, she remained attracted by his bravado and impudence, and so they patched up their differences, and then quarrelled again.[1] He presented her with a copy of *Paradise Lost*, and she wrote some verse on the fly-leaf:

> This pair a certain happiness might prove,
> Confin'd to constancy and mutual love.
> Heaven to one object limited his vows,
> The only safety faithless nature knows. . . .[2]

While applicable to the book and to its donor, the lines express her own ideas on marriage, a topic which took up much of her observation and thinking during the 1720's.

Another of her changeable friends, Henrietta the junior Duchess of Marlborough, could serve as an example of an odd marriage partner. Although married to Lord Godolphin, she made no attempt to hide her love for Congreve, and bore him a daughter.[3] When Lady Mary invited her to a party, the Duchess replied: 'I am sure you won't dislike to have Mr. Congreve tomorrow if you can get him, for he is like all good things hard to come at. And though I shan't add to the company I have wit enough not to spoil it, which you must allow is being tolerable. What hour would you have me come?'[4] It was probably a concert, for the Duchess had an unquenchable taste for music. She patronized Buononcini with an annuity of £500 for life, and in return he entertained her with concerts twice a week.[5] 'She and I are not in that degree of friendship to have *me* often invited', Lady Mary told her sister: 'we continue to see one another like two people who are resolved to hate with civility.'[6] Congreve advised Lady Mary to hide her temper; it may have been when she was with the Duchess.[7] And so they

MS Book of Materials, p. 73 (now owned by Mr. W. S. Lewis). Newcastle was appointed in 1724.
[1] M to Lady Mar, i. 477, 479, 481, 484, 493.
[2] Volume now owned by Mr. Lewis. Another version of the poem in ii. 503.
[3] Kathleen M. Lynch, *A Congreve Gallery* (1951), 59–89.
[4] W MS, iv. 185 (Paston, 310).
[5] *Daily Courant*, 30 June 1731.
[6] i. 483–4.
[7] CB MS, f. 22.

continued to be civil to each other, and to attend each other's concerts harmoniously.[1]

Lady Mary succeeded in enjoying a more solid and comfortable friendship with Sarah the Dowager Duchess, a fierce woman famous for her quarrels. She quarrelled bitterly not only with Henrietta but with her younger daughter, the Duchess of Montagu, but Lady Mary was able to remain on intimate terms with both of them.[2] The Dowager Duchess knew how incisive her friend's tongue could be. Once when Lady Mary visited her, Lady Sundon came to call, wearing a pair of diamond ear-rings she had received as a bribe for securing a place at Court for a nobleman. As soon as she left, the Duchess turned to Lady Mary: 'How can that woman have the impudence to go about in that bribe?' 'Madame,' answered Lady Mary, 'how would you have people know where wine is to be sold, unless there is a sign hung out?'[3]

All the various people Lady Mary knew reflected various facets of her mind. Her interest in an important social problem made her a friend of Mary Astell, the founder of the feminist movement. Miss Astell, who was almost twenty years her senior, had written several pamphlets on religion and feminism. In her most important one, *A Serious Proposal to the Ladies, For the Advancement of their True and Greatest Interest* (1694), she advocated an institution for women's religious retirement, a project similar to Lady Mary's girlhood ambition. After they became acquainted, Miss Astell presented a copy of her *Serious Proposal* to Lady Mary, and inscribed it to her in a broad bold hand.[4] When Miss Astell inquired about her travels in the East, Lady Mary let her peruse the manuscript of her compiled Embassy Letters. The feminist was enthusiastic about their 'beauties and excellencies', and begged Lady Mary to let them be published, but she had resolved against it during her lifetime. Miss Astell stated this in the fulsome preface she inscribed on Lady Mary's copy, praising her noble friend as an outstanding woman who could compete intellectually with men.[5] At their frequent meetings the two ladies discussed

---

[1] To Lady Mar, i. 485; Henrietta to M, 8 Oct. [1726], W MS, iv. 187. A less friendly note (W MS, iv. 189) dates from before 1726.
[2] Sarah to M, in M's letters, ii. 9–10 (1722), 20 (1731); M to W, 17 July 1748, ii. 168.　　　　[3] Walpole to Mann, 7 Jan. 1742, *Corr.* xvii. 276–7.
[4] Now in the BM.　　　　[5] i. 221–4 (W MS [Harrowby, vol. 254]).

religious topics, and a few weeks before her death (in 1731) Miss Astell promised to revisit her friend as proof of her religious faith. No doubt Lady Mary had maintained the sceptic's view; and she was not disappointed, for the apparition never appeared to her.[1] Such visions were different from what Lady Mary's sharp eyes and sceptical mind ordinarily revealed to her.

Her intimate friends were of a different kind. John Hervey, who at his brother's death in 1723 became Lord Hervey, developed into one of her staunchest comrades in wit. They even exercised their wit on each other, as when he sent his brother some verse which (he said) had been stolen by Lady Mary and was as incomprehensible as herself. Lady Mary's comment about him is classic—that there were three sexes: men, women, and Herveys.[2] The French-born Lady Stafford, widow of the Earl, shared their intimacy, contributing her wit, humour, and entertainment.[3] When in a serious mood, Lady Mary found that her worldly-wise shrewdness was a respite from the gaiety of her frivolous companions.[4] When they were apart, Lady Stafford sent her letters filled with cynical commentary and debonair affection.[5] They met often enough at Twickenham, where, Lady Mary told her sister: 'I see everybody, but converse with nobody but *des amies choisies*; in the first rank of these are Lady Stafford, and dear Molly Skerritt, both of which have now the additional merit of being old acquaintances, and never having given me any reason to complain of either of 'em.' Maria Skerrett, her young friend with whom she could laugh and be gay, was the daughter of a London merchant, very pretty, agreeable, and intelligent.[6] They had been acquainted since 1720, and then became such close friends that in 1725 she stayed in Lady Mary's Twickenham house during the summer and then accompanied her into town in the autumn.[7] Together they visited Duncan Campbell,

---

[1] Stuart, 86.

[2] To Carr Lord Hervey, 27 Jan. 1722, Bristol MS; Walpole, *Corr.* xvii. 274, n. 31.

[3] Hervey, *Some Materials Towards Memoirs of the Reign of King George II*, ed. Romney Sedgwick (1931), 551.   [4] To Lady Mar, i. 468.

[5] W MS, iv. 242–57 (8 letters, 1720–33).

[6] 1725, i. 480, 486; Hervey, *Memoirs*, 86 and n.

[7] Lady Louisa Stuart, 'Supplement to the Anecdotes', Wharncliffe MS 439; M to Lady Mar, i. 486, 493.

the famous deaf and dumb fortune-teller, and he guessed their names.[1] He might have divined something far more intriguing.

In the early 1720's, probably, Maria Skerrett had become Walpole's mistress, and bore him a daughter in 1725. Lady X Mary may have helped arrange this left-hand liaison—Horace Walpole called Miss Skerrett her *élève*—but its beginnings are vague.[2] According to Lord Hervey, Walpole gave his mistress '(besides an annual allowance) £5,000 by way of entrance-money', and later maintained her in a 'bower of bliss' in Richmond Park.[3] It was easily accessible to Lady Mary at nearby Twickenham. Because of her intimacy with the girl she was linked to the Minister herself, and a few years later thought to be one of his favourites, and credited with having great influence over him.[4] Her friendship with the girl had led to this strange turn of fortune. 'I remember my contracting an intimacy with a girl in a village', she later wrote, 'as the most distant thing on earth from power and politics. Fortune tosses her up (in a double sense), and I am embroiled in a thousand affairs that I had resolved to avoid as long as I lived.'[5] But power and politics still lay ahead of her.

During these same years she began a new phase of her literary career—that of a patroness. Besides patronizing several writers with presents of money, she assisted them with advice. Edward Young, an indefatigable place-hunter and patron-seeker, who wrote odes to the Whigs or Tories, depending on which party was in power, won a pension from the Duke of Wharton, through whom he probably came to Lady Mary's attention. He had turned to writing verse tragedies, and in 1724 submitted to her *The Brothers*, based on a classical theme. When she suggested some changes in the last act, he acknowledged her wisdom: 'The more I think of your criticisms, the more I feel the just force of them.'[6] Her most important change was to allow the heroine to descend to the hero's dungeon, instead of

---

[1] Spence, 'Anecdotes', Huntington Libr. MS, f. 380.
[2] 'Anecdotes', *Corr.* xiv. 245.
[3] *Memoirs*, 86, 832.
[4] Pope to Fortescue, 13 Sept. [1729?], *Corr.* iii. 53; James Erskine (Lord Grange), 5–6 Aug. 1733, *Miscellany of the Spalding Club* (1846), iii. 31–32.
[5] To Lady Pomfret, 1740, ii. 61.
[6] M's letters, ii. 13–14.

passively awaiting news of his fate—a device which adds dramatic force. While the play was in rehearsal, Young entered Holy Orders, where he expected more rapid preferment, and so it was withdrawn.[1] Clerical dignity did not prevent him from continuing his series of verse satires begun in 1725. In the fifth, 'On Women', he portrayed the general 'character' of a literary patroness:

> O'er the *Belle-lettre* lovely *Daphne* reigns;
> Again the God *Apollo* wears her chains.
> With legs tost high on her Sophee she sits,
> Vouchsafing audience to contending Wits;
> Of each performance she's the final test;
> One Act read o'er, she prophesies the rest;
> And then pronouncing with decisive air,
> Fully convinces all the town—*she's fair.*
> Had lovely *Daphne Hecatessa*'s face,
> How would her elegance of taste decrease?
> Some Ladies *judgment*, in their *features*, lyes,
> And all their *Genius* sparkles from their *eyes.*[2]

In his preface to the collected edition he disclaimed any malice toward particular persons, but Daphne displayed several similarities to a lady who had recently patronized him.

The most curious episode of Lady Mary's sitting in literary judgement, hitherto unknown, occurred in her meeting with Voltaire in 1727, when he was in England. After zealously studying English, he had written an *Essay on Epic Poetry*, and showed it to various literary people for their comments and corrections.[3] When Young tried to explain the errors to him, he burst out laughing in the startled Englishman's face.[4] He showed Lady Mary the section on Milton, and asked for her opinion. After reading three or four pages of his manuscript she told him that she simply did not believe he had written it: the English was too good to be by him and too poor to be by a distinguished person.[5] He bore her no ill will for her blunt

---

[1] W. Thomas, *Le Poète Edward Young* (1901), 305.

[2] *Love of Fame* (3rd ed., 1730), 91–92.

[3] *Œuvres Complètes*, ed. L. Moland (1883–5), viii. 302–4, 352–60.

[4] Spence, 374–5.

[5] James Caldwell to Montesquieu (related by M), 26 May 1746, Bagshawe MS, B 3/7/1, f. 24.

opinion, and later expressed great admiration for her intellect, verse, and letters.[1]

As a form of patronage the custom of dedicating printed works was the most debased. 'He wins this Patron, who can tickle best', Pope wrote. The patron who was thus honoured rewarded the author with a present of twenty guineas. Young, who had befriended the unfortunate Richard Savage, arranged for him to dedicate his 1726 miscellany to Lady Mary.[2] Confessing that he did not know her, Savage lavished the most exalted hyperbole on her mind and person. In Dr. Johnson's opinion, he flattered 'without reserve, and, to confess the truth, with very little art'.[3] The miscellany contained Aaron Hill's poem from *The Plain Dealer* on Lady Mary's 'bringing with Her, out of Turkey, the Art of Inoculating the Small Pox', a tribute to her most significant patronage.

In July 1726 there was published Curll's two-volume *Miscellanea*, containing among other things verse and letters by Pope and a long anonymous piece entitled 'An Essay on the Mischief of Giving Fortunes with Women in Marriage'. This essay puts forward a radical proposal: that since the practice of giving dowries leads to personal and social misfortunes, it should be abolished. After elaborate arguments and precedents from the Ancients and Sir William Temple, the author concludes with a plea that Parliament should outlaw the use of dowries. Fourteen years later, when Spence met Lady Mary in Rome, he made a note of one of their conversations: 'The ease of divorce in Turkey has made her think of the septennial bill for married persons; and of wives having no portions: two ideas for which she is very strong, and [she] wishes seriously that the legislature would new regulate it.'[4] In his collection of anecdotes, Spence repeated the note, and then added:

The little treatise she has written upon this subject, in prose, is very pretty, and has very uncommon argument in it. She is very strong for both those tenets: that married people should have the liberty of declaring every seventh year whether they choose to continue their state together or not; and that if women had nothing

---

[1] *Lettres Philosophiques* (1734), ed. G. Lanson (1909), i. 133–4; *Œuvres Complètes*, xxxiv. 36–37; xxv. 163.
[2] Young to M, 1 Mar. 1726, ii. 13.
[3] 'Savage', *Lives of the Poets*, ed. G. B. Hill (1905), ii. 343.
[4] 5 Dec. 1740, MS owned by Mr. James M. Osborn.

to recommend them but their own good qualities and merit, that it would make them more virtuous and the men more happy; and [she] seems to wish most heartily that our legislature would regulate that affair, according to her system.[1]

The treatise which Spence saw is not preserved among Lady Mary's manuscripts. But the printed 'Essay on Marriage' conforms closely to half of his synopsis. The other half—advocating a septennial act of universal divorce—seems incongruous if marriages without dowries result in perfect unions. Once, however, Lady Mary had recommended 'a general act of divorcing all the people of England' as a way of saving the reputations of unfaithful wives.[2] On the basis of internal evidence, the printed essay seems Lady Mary's; its general ideas on marriage and feminism, its structure, and its style (including metaphors) all have clear parallels in her other writings in prose and verse. A year before the essay appeared in print, when the topic of marriage was prominent in her thoughts, she had been working 'like an angel'.[3] How Curll obtained the essay, which is wretchedly edited and printed, is as mysterious as many other episodes of his devious career.

Although she often took a jaundiced view of marriage, Lady Mary conceived of it as a rare and ideal state of felicity. Her idealism disgusted her with its frequent failure through misalliance, infidelity, or the refusal of husbands and wives to believe in connubial happiness. 'To speak plainly,' she complained to her sister, 'I am very sorry for the forlorn state of matrimony, which is as much ridiculed by our young ladies as it used to be by young fellows.' When she saw a friend's betrothed daughter 'in the paradisal state of receiving visits every day from a passionate lover, who is her first love', she laughed and sighed with envy.[4] She enunciated her moral orthodoxy toward marriage in a long French essay refuting La Rochefoucauld's maxim that marriages are convenient (*commodes*) but not delightful (*délicieux*). 'On ne peut goûter les douceurs d'un amour parfait que dans un mariage bien assorti' is her formula for achieving the most precious happiness. 'Cette félicité ne se trouve que dans l'amitié fondée sur

---

[1] Huntington Libr. MS, ff. 378–80; expanded in letter to his mother, 11 Mar. 1741, MS Eg. 2234, ff. 251–2.
[2] To Lady Mar, i. 487.   [3] Ibid. 486.   [4] i. 474, 465.

une estime parfaite fixée par la reconnoissance, soutenue par l'inclination, et éveillée par la tendresse de l'amour. . . .'[1] But such a union, she concludes, is very rare.

The notion that except for initial pleasures marriage was rarely happy had animated her epitaph on Pope's country lovers killed by lightning, and she frequently repeated it after that—most eloquently in December 1724 on the death of the newly married Eleanor Bowes.

> Hail, happy bride, for thou art truly blest!
> Three months of rapture, crown'd with endless rest.
> Merit like yours was Heav'n's peculiar care,
> You lov'd—yet tasted happiness sincere.
> To you the sweets of love were only shown,
> The sure succeeding bitter dregs unknown;
> You had not yet the fatal change deplor'd,
> The tender lover for th'imperious lord:
> Nor felt the pain that jealous fondness brings:
> Nor felt, that coldness from possession springs. . . .[2]

It seems fairly evident that she based this view on her own marriage, which had turned out to be *commode* rather than *délicieux*.

As Wortley grew older he became more methodical and humourless, devoting himself entirely to business and Parliamentary affairs. His father's death (in 1727) brought him more wealth, which he assiduously cultivated to become an enormously rich man. On his frequent trips to the north of England, where his coal properties lay, he sometimes sent Lady Mary a laconic, businesslike note.[3] He, too, had notions about marriage, and put them in writing when he amused himself at Tunbridge Wells with imitations of La Rochefoucauld's maxims. 'We are apt to fall in love with those whose professions, we are persuaded, will make us secure of their affections; but when we think we have the desired security we are apt to lose the passion.' A man may write a maxim without believing it, but Wortley did not have such empathy; and he wrote these maxims only for himself. In another he observed that so few

---

[1] 'Sur la Maxime de M. de Rochefoucault', ii. 421-2.
[2] 14 Dec. 1724, ii. 485. The poem was frequently copied, printed, and answered—once as early as 30 Jan. 1725 in the *London Journal*.
[3] 24 Aug. 1725, 27 July 1729, W MS, i. 106-9.

marriages among persons of distinction have 'the appearance of being delicious' that one is justified in doubting that any are. The kind of marriage he desired is implied by his maxim: 'The world is like a ship in which a man finds his own cabin too little and seldom agrees till the end of a long voyage with the person lodged near him.'[1]

The failure of their marriage seems to have been confirmed in the 1720's. It was foreshadowed in their long bickering courtship, and in their early years as husband and wife, when she had asked in vain for an attentive affection from a callous and unimaginative man. 'But when are people matched!' she had philosophized (in 1721)—'I suppose we shall all come right in Heaven; as in a country dance, though hands are strangely given and taken, while they are in motion, at last all meet their partners when the jig is done.'[2] As her disappointment in a blissful marriage hardened, she looked elsewhere for emotional satisfactions. Because of her active intellect and wide-ranging curiosity she could to some extent overcome her disappointment, but it remained a chink in her tough armour.

Deprived of this satisfaction in marriage, she still carried out her domestic duties in an orderly manner. Her own summary of household expenses in Twickenham and Covent Garden shows that in the years 1724 to 1727 she laid out £1,038, £849, £1,076, and £1,140. Each of these years she spent about £100 on her own clothes, and about £60 as 'pocket' money. For her country pastimes she made expenditures for her garden and for a new saddle (in 1726).[3] The effete Lord Hervey scolded her for her manner of living at Twickenham: 'Nature never designed you to perform the offices of a groom and a nursery-maid.'[4] Her maternal love allowed her some pleasure in her daughter, who though a plain child was discreet and modest; but her handsome son now began his fantastic, disorderly career.

While the thirteen-year-old boy was at Westminster School in 1726, he ran off to Oxford—'being in his own opinion thoroughly qualified for the University', Lady Mary told her sister. 'After a good deal of search we found and reduced him,

---

[1] 7 July 1729, W MS, vii. 137-8.
[2] To Lady Mar, i. 459 ('though' from MS).   [3] Wharncliffe MS 508.
[4] 28 Oct. [1727], M's letters, ii. 16 (date corrected).

much against his will, to the humble condition of a schoolboy.'
He remained 'the most ungovernable little rake that ever played
truant'.[1] A year later, when he again ran away, she did not
regard his escapade so light-heartedly. After a month's unsuccessful search she put an advertisement in two newspapers
offering a reward of twenty pounds to anyone who discovered
his whereabouts so that he could be secured. He was described
as 'low for his Age, fresh coloured, with grey Eyes, lightish
brown Hair, and two Marks' on his arms—the remains of his
inoculation. Why he had fled was apparent in the final sentence:
'If the Boy will return of himself, he shall be kindly received,
and put to Sea, if he desires it.'[2] As the weeks passed with no
news of him, she felt the anguish of his loss. 'I run about, though
I have five thousand pins and needles running into my heart',
she told her sister. Lady Stafford, then in Paris, tried to console
and reassure her.[3] At the beginning of September she fell
dangerously ill. Then the advertisement for his return was
repeated in two other newspapers.[4] But the boy was already at
sea, sailing toward Gibraltar. He had changed clothes with a
poor boy in Whitechapel, and on the London docks signed up
as cabin boy for a Quaker captain, Joseph Kemp. Although he
had at first pretended that his mother was a poor widow with
ten children, he soon boasted to the crew of his noble connexions; and then, unable to endure their jeers, he confessed his
true identity to the captain, displaying his inoculation scars as
proof. At Gibraltar the admiral of the station heard the story;
and when he saw it confirmed in the newspapers arranged for
the boy's return. In January he was restored to his family.[5]

Lady Mary, whose relations with her father had once been
so strained, was by now completely reconciled. At their meetings she treated him with ceremonious respect. Once, as her
daughter observed, she was sitting at her dressing-table when

[1] To Lady Mar, i. 501, 508. Partially fictitious accounts of his early adventures as link-boy, chimney-sweep, and fishmonger are given in Jonathan
Curling's *Edward Wortley Montagu* (1954), 38–41.

[2] *Daily Journal*, 18 Aug.; *Daily Post*, 19 Aug. 1727.

[3] i. 513; 7 Sept. o.s., W MS, iv. 244.

[4] *Daily Journal*, 5 Sept.; *London Journal*, *Mist's Weekly Journal*, 9 Sept.
1727.

[5] About 1838 the captain's grandson James Wright told this to Lord Wharncliffe (Wharncliffe MS 439); 6 Jan. 1728, *London Journal* and other newspapers.

the Duke entered unannounced; she instantly arose, and then
on her knees asked his blessing.[1] At the beginning of March
1726 he was suddenly stricken with an attack of the colic, and
his family were summoned—the young Duchess, his sister Lady
Cheyne, and his two grown daughters. (By his Duchess he also
had two young daughters, Lady Anne and Lady Caroline.) For
the benefit of her absent sister, Lady Mary described the death-
bed scene: 'My Father really expressed a great deal of kindness
to me at last, and even a desire of talking to me, which my Lady
Duchess would not permit; nor my aunt and sister shew any
thing but a servile complaisance to her.' The ladies around his
death-bed argued over the terms of his will; 'I could not get my
sister Gower to join to act with me,' Lady Mary reported, 'and
mamma and I were in an actual scold when my poor father
expired.' Some of her childhood resentment against him remained: '*au bout du compte*, I don't know why filial piety
should exceed fatherly fondness. So much by way of consolation.' The Duchess showed herself implacably mercenary, for
contrary to the Duke's will she tried to gain the guardianship
of his two grandchildren; but the young Duke confirmed his
appointed trustees, and Lady Frances went to live with Lady
Cheyne. The girl's allowance of £400 a year had awakened the
conscience of her relations, Lady Mary explained, and caused
innumerable 'lies, twattles, and contrivances'.[2] By the terms of
the will, drawn up the year before, Lady Mary was left £6,000
in trust, to go to her daughter after her death, and £200 for
mourning clothes.[3]

A year later she had to use the mourning clothes again, when
her sister Gower died after an illness of four days. Now only
Lady Mar remained of her immediate family, and she tried to
soothe her: 'I desire you would not continue grieving yourself.
Of all sorrows, those we pay to the dead are most vain; and, as
I have no good opinion of sorrow in general, I think no sort
of it worth cherishing.' In her letters to Lady Mar she constantly tried to cheer her up. She even hoped to visit Paris to
pull her out of her melancholies; meanwhile she continued to

[1] Stuart, 79.

[2] To Lady Mar, i. 497–8 (confirmed by Lady Gower to Lady Mar, HMC
5th Report [1886], 620), 495, 500.

[3] Copy of will in Somerset House, London; details of payment in Manvers
MS 4349.

ply her with advice, recipes, and philosophical pills. Some of them were simple enough: 'galloping all day, and a moderate glass of champagne at night in good company'.[1] But the spirited advice did her little good. 'I fear a time will come', she wrote to Lady Mary, 'when I shall neither write nor see anybody . . . my solitude comes from causes that you are too happy to have experienced, and gives me no other inclination but to doze upon a couch, or exclaim against my fortune, and wish . . . forgetfulness could steal upon me, to soften and assuage the pain of thinking.'[2] In the fall of 1727 she received from Lady Mary a most brilliant and amusing description of George II's Coronation. But it was wasted on her, for she was then suffering from severe mental illness.[3]

In these letters Lady Mary also revealed much of her own state of mind. The pose of detachment was her favourite remedy against life: 'I insensibly dwindle into a spectatress.' Politics did not interest her: 'we go on cheerfully with our bells at our ears, ornamented with ribands, and highly contented with our present condition.' She often regarded herself cynically, taking care 'to improve as much as possible that stock of vanity and credulity that Heaven in its mercy has furnished me with; being sensible that to these two qualities, simple as they appear, all the pleasures of life are owing'. Her pose could be shaken by specific events like the deaths of her father and sister, and more strongly by her son's disappearance. Then she hoped that life was a period of purgatory, and that 'after whining and grunting a certain number of years, I shall be translated to some more happy sphere, where virtue will be natural, and custom reasonable; that is, in short, where common sense will reign'. Once, for a cause she did not mention, she suffered a severe emotional crisis affecting her head as well as her heart, which made her uncertain whether to laugh or cry, and left her glad and sorry, smiling and sad. In general, though, she depended on her reason and common sense to enjoy 'this golden now'.[4]

Growing old was one discontent she could neither avoid nor rationalize, though she tried. 'It was formerly a terrifying view

---

[1] i. 507, 500, 506.   [2] 23 Nov., Paston, 327.
[3] Atterbury to Mrs. Morice, 28/17 Nov. 1727, *Epist. Corr.* iv (1787), 89.
[4] To Lady Mar, i. 485, 499, 480, 512, 487, 498.

to me, that I should one day be an old woman', she confessed
many years later.[1] It began to terrify her as early as the winter
of 1724, when she was only thirty-five. She could amuse herself
very pleasantly, she admitted, 'but for the damn'd damn'd quality
of growing older and older every day, and my present joys are
made imperfect by fears of the future'.[2] On this theme she
played variations to raise her sister's low spirits, and her own
as well. During a gay season in London she wished she were ten
years younger: 'I love flattery so well, I would fain have some
circumstances of probability added to it, that I might swallow
it with comfort.' When her health and vivacity improved, she
boasted of feeling like a fifteen-year-old, and tried to retain
that gaiety: 'For my part I pretend to be as young as ever, and
really am as young as needs to be, to all intents and purposes.'[3]
Perhaps she would not have been so fearful of growing old if
her marriage had brought her more happiness and serenity.

She had not, in the meantime, relinquished her literary roles.
Henry Fielding, a second cousin on her mother's side, became
the object of her patronage. His branch of the family was so
poor, he told her, that he had no choice but to be a hackney
writer or a hackney coachman.[4] In 1727, at the age of twenty,
he came to London to make his fortune as a playwright. He
showed Lady Mary a comedy he had written, *Love in Several
Masks*, with an old-fashioned plot of witty intrigue and a sentimental ending. She encouraged him to complete and polish
it; and it was then, through her influence, accepted by the
managers of the Drury Lane Theatre, and produced on 16
February 1728. During the first week of its short run Lady
Mary went twice to see it, as the grateful author acknowledged
in his printed dedication to the 'Lady, whose accurate Judgment
has long been the Glory of her own Sex, and the Wonder of
ours'. In his further praise, he repeated the feminist flattery of
her intellect: 'You are capable of instructing the Pedant, and
are at once a living Confutation of those morose Schoolmen
who wou'd confine Knowledge to the Male Part of the Species,
and a shining Instance of all those Perfections and softer Graces
which Nature has confin'd to the Female.' But the theatre

---

[1] To Lady Bute, 2 Mar. 1751, ii. 203.
[2] To Lady Mar, i. 479 (missing words from MS).
[3] i. 483, 489, 506.   [4] To Lady Bute, 23 July 1755, ii. 280.

PLATE 6

Frances Countess of Mar and her Daughter

From a painting by Francesco Trevisani

public refused to patronize the play. Exactly one month after
it was produced, the discouraged young playwright was regis-
tered as a student at the University of Leyden.[1]

Among Lady Mary's circle of friends there circulated epi-
grams, squibs, lampoons, ballads, and songs, frequently so
libellous that their writers had to disguise or deny their authorship. Once Lady Mary somehow got hold of a ballad by Pope,
at a time they no longer met. Having returned to Twickenham
after a long stay in London, she wrote to her sister the next day:
'Doctor Swift and Johnny Gay are at Pope's, and their conjunction has produced a ballad, which, if nobody else has sent
you, I will.' Ordinarily the authorship could not be so readily
assigned. A few years earlier a delightful political ballad had
been attributed first to Pope and secondly to her, she said,
'when God knows we have neither of us wit enough to make
it'.[2] Her modest disclaimer implied that like Pope she did have
enough wit, and that a ballad by one could easily pass as the
other's. This had apparently happened frequently enough to
irritate Pope, and he said so in a ballad called 'The Capon's
Tale'. It tells of a hen in Wales who hatches more chicks than
she can raise; and so a capon is duped into raising her brood,
which he thinks are his own. In the final lines Pope scolds her
(on behalf of Swift and himself):

> Such, Lady Mary, are your tricks,
> To make us capons own your chicks.
> Hatch on, fair lady! make dispatch,
> Our tails may smart for what you hatch.
> The simile yet one thing shocks,
> We're not two capons but two cocks.[3]

Since his draft remained among her papers he must have sent
it to her; it was hardly more than a brisk, good-natured warning. But in March 1728, when he issued the third volume of his
Miscellanies he included the poem, inscribed 'To a Lady *who
father'd her Lampoons upon her Acquaintance*', and made two
changes: he moved the barnyard from Wales to Yorkshire

---

[1] F. Homes Dudden, *Henry Fielding His Life, Works, and Times* (1952),
22, 24.
[2] To Lady Mar, i. 506, 466.
[3] Morgan Libr. MS; printed in Norman Ault, *New Light on Pope* (1949),
244. The 'Epigram Papal', published as Pope's in Curll's 1726 *Miscellanea*, may
also show his irritation.

(where Wharncliffe Lodge lay), and he reinforced his final warning with an obscene allusion:

> Such, Lady *Mary*, are your Tricks;
> But since you hatch, pray own your Chicks:
> You should be better skill'd in Nocks,
> Nor like your Capons, serve your Cocks.

What had been a playful tap to a friend in private became here a public slap.

Few readers could have failed to identify 'Lady Mary', that name having become familiar in print since her return from Turkey. A pamphlet issued to defend those libelled in the *Miscellanies* identified her by her full name, and added: 'Renown'd for Wit, Beauty, and Politeness, long admir'd at Court; author of many pretty Poems scatter'd abroad in Manuscript; a Patroness of Men of Wit and Genius'—which fairly sums up her current reputation in print. The anonymous defender also recognized the equivocal nature of the ballad, for he did not know whether it was intended to affront her, but he was sure she had been used with unbecoming familiarity by the two poets whose 'odd whims and unnatural Fancies are not apt to stop at any Indecency'.[1]

Pope was then preparing to launch the *Dunciad*, his epic attack on Grub Street. He had at first intended to attack Lady Mary as a literary slattern with the lines:

> See Pix and slip-shod W—— traipse along,
> With heads unpinned and meditating song.[2]

He discarded the couplet, however, and in the version published in May 1728 he dealt with her in another section of the poem; and instead of her literary activities he alluded to her private life. The Goddess of Dulness addresses Edmund Curll:

> Son! thy grief lay down,
> And turn this whole illusion on the town.
> As the sage dame, experienc'd in her trade,
> By names of Toasts retails each batter'd jade,

---

[1] *Characters of the Times* (29 Aug. 1728), 12. She is also identified by her initials in the *Compleat Collection of All the Verses, Essays, Letters and Advertisements* (12 June 1728), 52. Unless otherwise indicated, the publication dates of the pamphlets about Pope come from Appendix E of Robert W. Rogers, *The Major Satires of Alexander Pope* (1955).

[2] Elwin and Courthope, iv. 294 n.

> (Whence hapless Monsieur much complains at Paris
> Of wrongs from Duchesses and Lady Mary's)
> Be thine, my stationer! this magic gift. . . .

His allusion to the Rémond scandal, which had been played out
five years earlier, was no doubt recognized by many of Lady
Mary's friends; and the lines also implied in general terms that
like a 'battered jade' she had rewarded a French lover with a
venereal disease.[1] 'I beleive Lady *Mary W—y M—gue*, does
not think herself obliged by Mr. *Pope* for this honourable
Mention', Curll wrote in his 'key' to the *Dunciad*. In relation
to the whole satire Pope's brief dishonourable mention of her
was neither important nor conspicuous, but to her and to those
who knew her, it must have loomed large. To the reading
public, who had often seen 'Lady Mary' praised as a traveller
and a wit, and only a few months before as an intellectual
feminist (in Fielding's dedication), it was the first step in the
degradation of her reputation.

That Pope and Lady Mary quarrelled in print is a fact; why
they did, as Walter Bagehot wrote (in 1862) is 'a question on
which much discussion has been expended, and on which a
judicious German professor might even now compose an interesting and exhaustive monograph'. His own theory was dis-
armingly simple (but not true): that since they quarrelled with
everybody else why should they not have quarrelled with each
other!'[2] The causes which have been suggested cover a wide
range—from dirty linen to spurned love. When Lady Mary
once returned unexpectedly to Twickenham, according to one
anecdote, she borrowed a pair of bedsheets from Pope, and
after two weeks returned them unwashed.[3] If true it may
account for some of his later insults, but not for so deep an
antagonism. Their own explanations seem closest to the actual
cause.

Pope was the more consistent. After the quarrel had begun
he wrote to William Fortescue, who was Walpole's friend:

I have seen Sir R. W. but once since you left. I made him then my

---

[1] Twickenham, v. 112. In this passage 'Duchesses' probably meant ladies of
the evening (A. L. Williams in the *Rev. of Eng. Stud.* iv [1953], 359–61).
[2] *Literary Studies* (1895), ii. 247.
[3] Sherburn, 'Walpole's Marginalia in *Additions to Pope* (1776)', *Huntington
Libr. Quart.* i (1938), 485.

confidant in a complaint against a lady, of his, and once of my, acquaintance, who is libelling me, as she certainly one day will him, if she has not already. You'll easily guess I am speaking of Lady Mary. I should be sorry if she had any credit or influence with him, for she would infallibly use it to bely me; though my only fault towards her was, leaving off her conversation when I found it dangerous.[1]

Subsequently, in a printed but suppressed satire, Pope explained that he had terminated his friendship with Lady Mary and Lord Hervey because they had 'too much wit' for him: 'Had I ever the honour to join with either of you in one ballad, satire, pamphlet, or epigram on any person living or dead?[2] Did I ever do you so great an injury as to put off my own verses for yours, especially on those persons whom they might most offend?'[3] And he gave the same reason privately to Arbuthnot, whom Lady Mary had sent to ask why he had stopped visiting her.[4] As the one who ended the friendship he must have considered himself the aggrieved party. His complaints may seem plausible, but he never substantiated them.

The reason for his enmity seems to have puzzled her, since she sent Arbuthnot to ask what it was; and she later told Spence that she did not know why he had turned against her. But then, apparently, she recalled their friendship in Twickenham in 1722 when he had been jealous of her intimacy with the Duke of Wharton and when she had repulsed his amorous declaration with laughter. In her opinion it seemed the most reasonable way of explaining the vast change in his attitude, from adoring admiration to insulting contempt.

[1] 13 Sept. [1729 ?], *Corr.* iii. 53.
[2] He forgot the *Court Poems* of 1716.
[3] *Letter to a Noble Lord*, Elwin and Courthope, v. 427.
[4] Spence, 235.

IX. *Family Matters*

(1728–36)

In March 1728 Lady Mar, seriously ill and accompanied by her daughter, returned to England, and was put in Lady Mary's care. Then began the legal intrigue for her custody, between Lady Mary and Lord Mar's brother, the Hon. James Erskine of Grange, called Lord Grange by virtue of his having been Lord Justice Clerk of Scotland. Lord Grange had been allowed to purchase the confiscated Mar estates in 1724; and in exchange he had to pay an annual rent of £1,000 to Lady Mar, who in her own right still owned the lease of her house in Whitehall.[1] Her custody was thus a valuable financial asset. Less than a month after her return, her stepson Lord Erskine wrote to Lord Grange in Edinburgh urging him to hasten to London:

Lady Mary Wortley (who has behaved in the oddest and most unexpected manner since poor Lady Mar's misfortune) is working with all her might, and makes no scruple of speaking of it publicly that my mother's jointure should be put in some friend's hands, whom I suppose she intends to be herself, for her sister's security and use *only*. As it was a free gift of the King's, this procedure it is thought must be stopped by his influence. Lady Mary has already begun to tamper with lawyers; you see what must be the consequence of this. I must conjure you, my dear lord, as you have once already saved the family, come and ward this blow that I think would go near to make an end of us all considering all circumstances at present.[2]

At the beginning of June Lord Grange reached London, and tried to consult Lady Mar's relations, but could gain admittance only to Lady Mary. She treated him so rudely—he testified—that he assumed she did not wish to be troubled by him; and

---

[1] Thoresby Park Papers, MS Eg. 3531, ff. 102–5; Chancery Inquisitions, PRO C 211, E 16.   [2] 4 Apr. 1728, Mar and Kellie MS.

so without consulting her, he arranged for Lady Mar to be
moved to Alloa House, the Mar seat in Scotland. He travelled
separately, while she was accompanied by his agent, her daughter, her stepson, and Mrs. Murray and her mother. They left
on the 20th, and spent the first night of their journey at Barnet,
in the house of Mrs. Murray's father, and then continued on
their way. But at Stevenage, about thirty-two miles from
London, Lady Mary came riding up with an officer and a
warrant from the Chief Justice ordering the kidnapped Lady
Mar to be brought back to London in *statu quo*. She returned
first to Lady Mary's house; but on Lord Grange's insistence
that the warrant be carried out to the letter, she went to her
own lodgings. All this he set forth, insisting also that the projected journey to Scotland was not a kidnapping.[1] Still, as
he admitted in his letters, his motive was to secure control of
his sister-in-law and her money.

If Lady Mary 'tampered with lawyers', it was for the purpose of putting her sister's custody and support in legal order.
Accordingly, on 12 July 1728 a lunacy inquisition of three
commissioners and a jury of seventeen men found Lady Mar
of unsound mind, a lunatic for about four months. As to how
she had become insane, they did not know—unless 'by the
visitation of God'.[2] Then at a hearing before the Court of
Chancery, her custody was awarded to Lady Mary.[3] Lord
Grange attributed the decision to the friendship between the
Lord Chancellor (Sir Peter King) and Wortley, but it was
logical for Lady Mar to be in the care of her nearest relation;
and besides, her trustees were subject to Lord Grange's appro-
val.[4] He then tried to manipulate the case to secure from
Walpole a pardon for his brother. At first Walpole accused
Lord Mar of embarrassing him in Paris with gossip about the
influence of Lady Mary and a certain lady her companion
[Maria Skerrett]; then a tentative agreement was reached that
Lady Mar's custody would earn her husband's pardon. But

---

[1] 'Affidavit Ja: Erskine' [23–30 June 1728], Mar and Kellie MS 574. Lady
Mar's journey and return also in *London Eve. Post*, 25–27, 27–29 June 1728.
Grange's letters to Thomas Erskine of Pittodry (*Misc. of the Spalding Club*
[1846], iii. 3–67) give a garbled version of the controversy.
[2] PRO C 211, E 16.
[3] *Daily Post*, 23 July 1728, and other newspapers.
[4] Lord Monson to M, 14 July, W MS iv. 202–3.

despite petitions and applications, Lord Mar remained un-
pardoned and in exile.

The amount of money to be paid to Lady Mary for her
sister's support was the next controversial issue, and it dragged
on into the following year. In February (1729) Lady Mary
appealed to Lord Islay, Lord Justice General, that Lord Grange
had misrepresented her terms, and that she was still content to
ask no more than £500 yearly.[1] By June the solicitors, lawyers,
and both families came to terms, and articles of agreement were
signed by Lady Mary and Wortley on one side and Lord
Grange on the other that she should receive £500 to pay for
her sister's maintenance.[2] Lady Mar lived in her own lodgings
in Knightsbridge, attended by servants, and able to entertain
friends like Lady Hervey and Mrs. Murray, who were enemies
of Lady Mary. The physician chosen to attend her was Dr.
Richard Hale, an eminent specialist in treating insanity, and one
of the first to use moral means and sedatives instead of cruelty
and restraint.[3]

After the publication of the *Dunciad*, the presses of Grub
Street spewed forth angry replies. One of them (on 2 June
1728) was a prose piece *A Popp upon Pope*, subtitled: 'a True
and Faithful Account of a late horrid and barbarous Whipping
committed on the Body of Sawney Pope, a Poet, as he was innocently walking in Ham-Walks, near the River of Thames,
meditating Verses for the Good of the Public. Supposed to have
been done by two evil-disposed Persons, out of Spite and
Revenge for a harmless Lampoon, which the said Poet had
wrote upon them.' It is fairly certain that Pope was never
beaten, and that the pamphlet is only a robust literary joke.
Lady Mary's only connexion with it was that two years later
the *Grub Street Journal*, a paper favouring Pope, said that she
had 'confidently reported He once was whipt'.[4] If such a report
came from her, it was more likely a spoken one. At the outbreak
of her quarrel with Pope, according to Horace Walpole, 'he
sent her word, he would set her down in black and white; to
which she replied, if he did, she would have him set down in

[1] M to Islay, 20 Feb., Mar and Kellie MS 632.
[2] 9 June 1729, ibid. 636.
[3] Mar to M, 19 Nov. 1728, ibid. 614 (copy); MS Roll in Royal College of
Physicians, London.
[4] 21 May 1730.

black and blue'.[1] As an aristocrat she felt that in an earlier, less egalitarian age he would not have escaped the whipping-post.[2]

Since the *Dunciad* was directed at Grub Street writers, the aristocratic Lady Mary was conspicuous among them. She was, in contrast, put on a pedestal in January 1729 by Savage in his self-pitying poem *The Wanderer*, when he described the Muse of Poetry:

> Thus in the dame each nobler grace we find,
> Fair Wortley's angel-accent, eyes, and mind.[3]

If Pope had wished to remove his slur in the *Dunciad* he could have done so in April, when he added to his poem introductions, testimonials, notes, and indexes. But the insulting lines remained, and her irritation increased. For Pope was the leading poet of his day, and his satires were eagerly bought by readers who found pleasure in identifying his victims. However much she might pretend disdain, Lady Mary must have been acutely embarrassed.

Her husband went his own stolid way. When she retired to Twickenham in the summer of 1729 he went to Tunbridge Wells, where he drank the waters and wrote his bitter maxims on marriage; he then travelled north to Newcastle to look after his coal business. From there he complained to her that his two partners neglected business for gaiety.[4] He carefully avoided that fault himself. In Parliament he chided a witty speaker because he wholly disliked turning serious things into ridicule. Politically he continued his implacable opposition to Walpole; and besides voting against his measures, attacked him personally for using the King's name 'to influence our debates, and appealed to the House if it was orderly'.[5] In her friendship with Maria Skerrett and admiration of the Minister, Lady Mary showed her divergence. She wrote a poem in praise of his cheerful smile, open honest look, and neighbourliness (perhaps at

---

[1] *Corr.* xiv. 243, n. 7. Echoed in letter from Hervey to Stephen Fox, 21 Dec. 1731, *Lord Hervey and His Friends*, ed. Lord Ilchester (1950), 125.

[2] 'An Epistle from Pope to Bolingbroke', first printed 1803 ed., v. 166–70.

[3] *Works* (1777), ii. 61.

[4] W to M, 27 July 1729, W MS, i. 108–9. For his activity in the coal trade, see Edward Hughes, *North Country Life in the Eighteenth Century* (1952), ch. v.

[5] 23 Feb. 1731, 24 Feb. 1730, HMC Egmont, *Diary* (1920–3), i. 148, 58.

Richmond).[1] She wondered why his opponents judged him so harshly; her own husband was one of those who did.

Nor could Wortley have looked with favour on her entanglement in literary controversy. In the spring of 1730 a manuscript lampoon on Pope was circulated in London; and when he got hold of it he accused her of writing it. Their friend the peaceable Arbuthnot had the unenviable job of telling her so, only to be assured that she had no connexion with the villainous piece.[2] Finally published on 28 April 1730, *One Epistle to Mr. A. Pope* charged Pope with being the aggressor in the literary war. One specific accusation, that he did not let Beauty escape base detraction, is footnoted by Lady Mary's initials. Although the *Grub Street Journal* suggested that a lady was 'suppos'd to have some hand in this piece', Pope later did not mention her name when he guessed at the authorship.[3] Like other anonymous lampoons its circulation in manuscript and print aroused suspicion and rancour.

In September, soon after she returned from Twickenham to her Covent Garden house, Lady Mary fell dangerously ill.[4] Lord Bathurst, at his seat in the country, read of it, and wrote to Pope: 'the newspapers say Lady Mary is very ill pray inquire after her in your own name and mine; we have both been her humble Admirers at different times. I am not so changeable as you, I think of her now as I allways did.' Unless Lord Bathurst was joking, it was odd that he should think Pope would call on her. Instead, Pope sent him compliments from another lady but 'not Lady Mary (who wishd you and all of us at the devil last week, because she thought of going to him herself, but is now recover'd and cares not a pin for you, or any Man of honour in Christendom').[5] These words were apparently her own, repeated to him by Dr. Arbuthnot. For she had summoned the good Doctor to attend her; 'Sitting by her bed, he began to say, he hoped he had provided for his Children, tho moderately, yet honestly. She cried out, "God damn your Children and mine, mind my illness".'[6] Her quick temper could easily have made her scold her garrulous and inattentive physician.

[1] 'On Seeing a Portrait of Sir Robert Walpole', ii. 483–4.
[2] 17 Oct. [1729], Pope, *Corr.* iii. 59–60.
[3] To Bethel, 9 June 1730, ibid. iii. 114.   [4] *Grub Street Journal*, 17 Sept. 1730.
[5] 19 Sept., 1 Oct. 1730, *Corr.* iii. 134, 137.
[6] Sherburn, 'Walpole's Marginalia', *Huntington Libr. Quart.* i (1938), 487.

The case of her sister's custody, which had seemed settled, erupted once again in the following spring (1731).[1] Lord Grange in Edinburgh had heard that Lady Mar, though recovered, refused to apply to the Lord Chancellor for her liberty; and he assumed that in order to retain the yearly allowance, Lady Mary would retard her recovery. His information came from Lady Hervey and Lady (formerly Mrs.) Murray, who sided with him. When he set out for London at the end of March 1731 he had another motive. The previous year he had formally separated from his wife, who planned to join Lady Mary in London; he hoped to prevent their meeting. But his main purpose, he admitted, was to gain control of Lady Mar if she should be set free, lest she abrogate the financial arrangements made during her illness and thus cause great losses to his family.[2] In London, after calling on her ten or twelve times, he decided that in spite of moodiness and depression she possessed a sound judgement and memory. Wishing to have his opinion confirmed, he asked Lady Hervey and Lady Murray to call on her. They sat with her a long time, and then bustled off to Court where they said publicly that she was quite well, and should not be kept by her sister, who was less wise than herself. When Lady Mary discovered this, Lord Grange reported, she became alarmed, and accused the two ladies of being his confederates— as indeed they were. He finally decided to give up his attempt to gain Lady Mar's custody. When he saw her for the last time, 'fancies which now perplext her brain were, like the clouds, fleeting, inconstant, and sometimes in monstrous shapes'. And so she remained in her sister's custody, while Lord Mar remained in Aix-la-Chapelle with their sixteen-year-old daughter, Lady Frances. At the end of 1731 they asked Lady Mary to send her across to them, but she answered that her 'unhappy sister', though improved, was 'very far from being in a condition to undertake a journey, of which she herself is so sensible that I believe nothing but downright force could prevail upon her to begin one. Quiet and regularity is all that can be done for her in her present state of health, and (however I may have been misrepresented) I am conscious to myself, that it is

[1] Reconstructed from Grange's letters, cited above on p. 134, n. 1.
[2] His financial motive is corroborated by his friend Robert Wodrow in *Analecta* (1842–3), iv. 227–8.

my utmost endeavour to contribute what I can to make her easy.'[1]

Her more distant relation, young Fielding, had by now re-appeared to ask her help. He had decided, after his interlude of study in Holland, to resume his career as a playwright. In September 1730 he sent her his new play, *The Modern Hus-band*, a serious social comedy about vice in fashionable society, and explained that since it was his first attempt in that genre, he was 'exceedingly anxious' for her to like it as much as his lighter things. It was not put on until 14 February 1732; and although the audience was shocked by its depiction of a vicious husband engaged in a sordid scheme, it survived to become a moderate success. Fielding later acknowledged that Lady Mary had approved of his characterization of Lady Charlotte Gaywit, a young giddy lady of fashion, who is one of his most credible characters. When the play was printed soon afterwards, he dedicated it to Walpole, who probably accepted it out of friendship for Lady Mary, and rewarded the author.[2] Of all the men of letters whom Lady Mary patronized in one way or another Fielding repaid her with most appreciation. The next year he dedicated to her his anonymous adaptation of a Molière comedy, with praise of her taste, judgement, genius, and good nature; for—he wrote—she could pardon the faults of others with the same facility that she wrote fine things herself.[3]

In his first poem since the 1729 *Dunciad* Pope issued the *Epistle to Burlington* (December 1731), a satire on false and ostentatious taste. His enemies seized on the description of Timon as a lampoon on his friend the Duke of Chandos, and thus initiated a new phase in the literary controversy. In an attempt to profit by it, on 5 April 1732 a Grub Street pub-lisher issued a shabby anonymous play, *Mr. Taste, the Poetical Fop: or, The Modes of the Court, A Comedy*.[4] It deals not with

[1] 11 De[c.] '31, MS owned by the Rev. P. B. G. Binnall.

[2] Dudden, *Fielding*, 99–107. Among the W MS (Harrowby, vol. 255) is Lady Mary's autograph of two comedy scenes entitled 'Some People', very much in the style of Fielding's comedy, and perhaps written by her at this time.

[3] Molière, *Select Comedies* (1732), vi. He praised her wit twice in his 1743 *Miscellanies*. *Works*, ed. L. Stephens [1882], vii. 374, 377).

[4] The author may have been Mrs. Eliza Heywood, as hinted in the dedica-tion (27 May 1733) to Lady Mary of *The Neuter: or, A Modest Satire on the Poets of the Age*.

taste but with scandal and abuse. Mr. Alex. Taste is a 'poet, deformed, imagines every woman in love with him, imprudently makes love to Lady Airy'. The heroine (Lady Mary with the initial letter omitted) is a 'young widow of fortune, wit, and merit, but strangely whimsical'. Although the abuse of Pope is unoriginal, the plot is striking. Through a succession of jerky scenes with coarse or inane dialogue Mr. Taste declares his love for Lady Airy, and when he finally proposes is dismissed with contempt. This first mention in print of Pope's rejection by Lady Mary probably came from town gossip. Her unfortunate sister is also depicted—as Lady Addle, 'drove to extremities' by her husband's 'barbarous treatment'. Without any redeeming virtue, *Mr. Taste* was only a grotesque lampoon by a scandalmongering hack. In his own attacks Pope had at least one advantage over his opponents—poetic genius.

The intricate care with which he composed, emended, published, revised, and annotated his attacks on Lady Mary makes it possible to chart his satiric pursuit of her. In his draft of the epistle addressed to Lord Bathurst, *Of the Use of Riches*, he intended to jibe at her for refusing to save the life of her dying stingy husband 'Worldly'.[1] But the published version calls the husband Shylock, making the designation general. In another passage of the draft he touched on Wortley's stinginess and on Lady Mary's alleged lewdness:

> Why starves the Peer his son? the cause is found:
> He thinks a loaf will rise to fifty pound.
> Why heaps lewd Lesbia that enormous sum?
> Alas! she fears a man may cost a plum.[2]

In the published poem, finally, he coupled Lesbia with Phryne, who can buy a whole auction because of a future general excise.[3] Here he pointed to Lady Mary's friendship with Maria Skerrett and to Walpole's intention of introducing an excise bill. How many readers of the epistle recognized Lesbia as Lady Mary? Although Pope meant it for her, as he proved by his later revisions, when the poem was issued Lesbia could have been taken by uninformed readers as a generalized name. Those in Court and upper-class circles, however, who knew of Lady

---

[1] Elwin and Courthope, iii. 138.
[2] Huntington Libr. MS. Plumb was slang for £100,000.
[3] 15 Jan. 1733, Twickenham, iii. ii. 99.

Mary's intimate friendship with Miss Skerrett easily recognized
the pseudonym.

Only a month later Pope hurled his sharpest dart at her. At
his friend Lord Bolingbroke's suggestion he had tried his hand
at imitating one of Horace's satires; the result, as described by
Dr. Johnson, was 'a kind of middle composition between translation and original design which pleases when the thoughts are
unexpectedly applicable and the parallels lucky'.[1] Since the
imitation in print was matched by the Latin original on facing
pages, readers saw at a glance what Pope had added. He usually
created a place for Lady Mary. In his first imitation he toyed
with several insults, as his discarded manuscript readings show.
'Slander or lies expect from W——y's rage', echoed his old,
familiar complaint. He also tried, and discarded, the Rémond
scandal. Next he put together three vices for her—stinginess,
venereal disease, and slander:

> Alas, my friend! your days can ne'er be long.
> In flow'r of youth you perish for a song!
> How oft from Sappho have I fear'd that fate:
> P—x'd by her love or poison'd by her hate.
> Plums and directors, Shylock and his wife
> Will whip their testers now to take your life.[2]

This may have seemed too diffuse. He revised it; and in the
Imitation, published in February 1733, only two lines dealt
with Lady Mary in a passage where she was coupled with Delia
(probably the Countess of Deloraine):

> Slander or Poyson, dread from *Delia*'s Rage,
> Hard Words or Hanging, if your Judge be *Page*,
> From furious *Sappho* scarce a milder Fate,
> P—x'd by her Love, or libell'd by her Hate.[3]

The Latin text had a poisoning Candida, a harsh judge, and an
angry, threatening Cervius—for whom Pope substituted the
furious Sappho.

Lady Mary assumed that the couplet referred to her, not
because of its unproved assertions about disease and libels, but

---

[1] *Lives of the Poets* (1905), iii. 176.
[2] Elwin and Courthope, iii. 295 n., 296 n.; MS now in Berg Collection, N.Y.
Public Library. 'Tester' is a sixpenny piece.
[3] Twickenham, iv. 13.

probably because Pope's notorious antipathy to her would logically cast suspicion on his freshly created Sappho, a woman of dangerous wit. If that identification had not through some means been publicized, how can one explain why she tried to counteract it, and very unwisely embarrassed herself? She called on Pope's intimate friend Lord Peterborough to complain of the insult, but he protested that it was none of his affair. After she left him, he wrote, Pope had happened to call:

He said to me what I had taken the Liberty to say to you, that he wonderd how the Town could apply those Lines to any but some noted common woeman, that he should yett be more surprised if you should take them to your Self, He named to me fower remarkable poetesses and scribblers . . . Ladies famous indeed in their generation, and some of them Esteemed to have given very unfortunate favours to their Friends, assuring me that such only were the objects of his satire.[1]

This private and probably ironic assurance was far from placating her for the public insult.

Lord Hervey also considered himself lampooned in Pope's *Imitation* as the Lord Fanny who daily spins out thousands of weak lines of verse. Revenge was not long in appearing. Less than three weeks later a newspaper advertisement on 8 March 1733 announced the publication by A. Dodd of *Verses Address'd to the Imitator of the First Satire of the Second Book of Horace. By a Lady*. On the very next day J. Roberts advertised *To the Imitator of the Satire of the Second Book of Horace*. In repeating the first advertisement, Dodd added: by 'a Lady of Quality'; and for the rest of the month warned readers to beware of the spurious edition, and that only the one 'By a Lady' was authentic.[2] Yet except for one couplet omitted by Roberts the texts are identical. Their almost simultaneous publication may have been intended to confuse, but their contents were clear enough. It is as crude and bludgeoning a lampoon as appeared in the pamphlet wars of the time. It had very little original abuse of Pope, for even by 1725 (before the *Dunciad* campaign) he had been attacked as a papist, a cripple, a Tory, an incompetent translator and editor, a writer of

---

[1] Twickenham, IV. xvii.

[2] *Daily Post*, 8, 9 Mar.; *Daily Journal*, 9 Mar.; *Daily Post*, 10, 12, 13, 22, 31 Mar. 1733. R. W. Rogers calls the Roberts pamphlet a piracy (op. cit., 142).

blasphemy and obscenity, and an ungrateful, dishonest traitor.[1]
But his new literary experiment allowed the satire to open with:

> In two large Columns, on thy motley Page,
> Where *Roman* Wit is stripe'd with *English* Rage;
> Where Ribaldry to Satire makes pretence,
> And modern Scandal rolls with ancient Sense:
> Whilst on one side we see how *Horace* thought;
> And on the other, how he never wrote: ...

Literary gossips assumed that Lady Mary was the author.[2]
But her own statement, in a letter to Arbuthnot which she
asked to be shown to Pope, was that 'they were wrote (without
my knowledge) by a Gentleman of great merit, whom I very
much esteem, who he will never guess, and who, if he did know
he durst not attack; but I own the design was so well meant,
and so excellently executed that I cannot be sorry they were
written'.[3] Pope at first told Swift that it was by her or by Lord
Hervey: 'they are certainly the Top wits of the Court, and you
may judge by that single piece what can be done against me;
for it was labour'd, corrected, præcommended and post-dis-
approv'd, so far as to be dis-own'd by themselves, after each
had highly cry'd it up for the others'. But later that year he
apparently altered his opinion (in the printed but suppressed
Letter to a Noble Lord): 'indeed I think both sexes had a share
in it, but which was uppermost, I know not. I pretend not to
determine the exact method of this witty fornication; and if I
call it yours, my Lord, it is only because, whoever *got* it, you
brought it forth.'[4] In fact no documentary evidence survives
to prove Lady Mary's authorship of the *Verses to the Imitator*,
though she obviously did not object to seeing it advertised as
being 'By a Lady'. Lord Hervey, probably not much later,
prepared in his own hand a revised version of the poem, intending it for a second edition. He also composed a preface beginning: 'So hasty and incorrect a Copy of these Verses was first
sent into the World, and one so much more imperfect is since

---

[1] Twickenham, v. x.
[2] Theobald to Warburton, 10 Mar., R. F. Jones, *Lewis Theobald* (1919), 313;
Swift to Pope, 31 Mar. 1733, Pope's *Corr.* iii. 362.
[3] M to Arbuthnot, 3 Jan. [1735], in Pope's *Corr.* iii. 448.
[4] 20 Apr. 1733, ibid. 366; Elwin and Courthope, v. 430. For his slightly
different guess in 1736, Twickenham, v. 212.

printed,[1] that I can not help indulging my Vanity so far, since
they are to appear in Publick, as to set them forth in their best
Dress.'[2]

The controversy had a political side too. As Vice Chamber-
lain, confidant of the Queen, and colleague of Walpole, Lord
Hervey was a person of consequence at Court; and Lady Mary
was a friend of the Minister and his mistress. Pope may have
feared that his literary enmity would affect Walpole's attitude
toward him and his friends. Through Fortescue, he had apparently been asked by Walpole to alter the offensive couplet
attacking Lady Mary in his *Imitation*. On the first day the
Verses to the Imitator was published, he told Fortescue that it
was too late to make any alteration because the lady had 'taken
her own Satisfaction in an avowed Libell'. Ten days later he
piously assured his friend: 'You may be certain I shall never
reply to such a Libel as Lady Mary's. . . . I wish you would take
an opportunity to represent to the Person who spoke to you
about that Lady, that Her Conduct no way deserves *Encouragement* from him, or any other Great persons.'[3] Despite his protest that he would not answer, within a year he circulated a
squib attacking Lady Mary and Lord Hervey for the *Verses*.[4]

Two anonymous pamphleteers had sprung forth immediately
to defend him. One brutally assailed Lady Mary as Sappho; the
other scolded her to become reconciled to Pope.[5] There is
nothing edifying or amusing in these or the later scurrilous
pamphlets, but they show Lady Mary as a casualty in the
lampoon war. Even pamphlets not dealing directly with the
controversy made a symbol of her name. One of them satirically
advises the 'woman of taste' on her proper conduct:

> With city dames observe your nuptial vows,
> And with good lady M—y love your spouse;
> With your own husband seldom pleas'd or gay,
> Whom you both kiss, and cuckold in a day.[6]

[1] Referring to Dodd's and Roberts's publications.
[2] Bristol MS. A copy of the verses with Hervey's alterations was among
Robert Walpole's papers (now Add. MS 35335, ff. 53–54). Wharncliffe's
statement (1837 ed., iii. 381 n.) that the *Verses* exist in M's autograph album
[Harrowby, vol. 256] is simply not true.
[3] 8, 18 Mar. 1733, *Corr.* iii. 354, 357.
[4] Feb. 1734, *Hervey and His Friends*, 191–2.
[5] *A Proper Reply to a Lady* (3 Apr.); *Advice to Sappho* (13 Apr. 1733).
[6] *Woman of Taste* (2nd edn., 1733), 10.

PLATE 8

Alexander Pope

From a pencil drawing by Jonathan Richardson [*1733*]

There is as little demonstrable truth in this libel as in her being poxed. What is certain is that her reputation had become a coin of public currency. Some pamphleteers attempted to defend her simply to denigrate Pope. One attack on his Homer translation was inscribed to her by name; and soon a champion in the *Gentleman's Magazine* tried to protect her from the poisoned arrows of 'Dan Papa'.[1] Then a pamphlet 'By a Lady', although directed against Pope's enemies, bestowed on Lady Mary a flattering dedication and praised her for her wit and learning.[2]

More pleasant and characteristic than her part in this Grub Street controversy was her private social versifying; occasionally she wrote on behalf of friends. About January 1733 Lord William Hamilton was embarrassed to receive from the matronly Countess of Hertford a song coyly asking him to judge by her blushes and glances how much her heart was tormented for love of him. Desperately he appealed to a friend, who in turn showed the song to Lady Mary and begged her to write an answer. Lady Mary's lines enable the man to dodge the lady, and to dismiss her neatly:

> But the fruit that can fall without shaking,
> Indeed is too mellow for me.[3]

Lady Mary lent her talent to another friend in 1733, when Catherine Dashwood, a Lady of the Bedchamber to the Queen, found herself courted by James Hammond, an impecunious and poetical young man. 'He was unextinguishably amorous, and his mistress inexorably cruel', Dr. Johnson described the pair.[4] To plead his cause (in 1732) Hammond had written a series of elegies about his fruitless love for Delia (the name used by his Roman model Tibullus). Given one of the elegies in manuscript—probably by Miss Dashwood—Lady Mary answered with a long serious poem of considerable weight. The lover who offers only 'Passion founded on Esteem' is turned away with forthright practical advice: his hopes can lead either to ruin through marriage or dishonour through gallantry; and so Delia tells him:

[1] *On the English Translations of Homer, A Satire* (23 Mar. [*Daily Journal*] 1733); iii (Apr. 1733), 206.
[2] *The Neuter* (29 May 1733).
[3] To Lady Bute, 8 Nov. 1758, ii. 345-6 The poem (ii. 477) is discussed below, p. 272.   [4] *Lives of the Poets* (1905), ii. 312.

Hear then the safe, the firm Resolve I make,
Ne'er to encourage one I must forsake.
Whilst other Maids a shameless Path pursue,
Neither to Honour, nor to Int'rest true;
And proud to swell the Triumphs of their Eyes,
Exult in Love from Lovers they despise;
Their Maxims all revers'd, I mean to prove,
And tho' I like the Lover quit the Love.

The elegy and its answer were published together on 29 March
1733 in a dignified handsome pamphlet, 'By a Lady, Author of
the Verses to the Imitator of Horace'.[1] Hammond died a decade
later, and his Kitty Dashwood lived (a maiden) until 1779. His
courtship had at least stimulated Lady Mary to write one of her
finest poems on marriage, characterized by the paradox and
common sense which made her such a skilful poet of answers.

A similar marriage problem soon arose in her own family,
that of her niece Lady Frances Pierrepont. The girl's relations
had hoped for an ambitious marriage with the Hon. John
Spencer, the Duchess of Marlborough's favourite grandson, but
by August 1733 the match had fallen through. Lord Gower, in
telling a friend of it, added: 'The censorious part of the town
says she has declared she will never marry any man but Phil
Meadows, but we that are relations know nothing of it.'[2] Later
that month Lady Mary visited the young Duke of Kingston
for the purpose of putting an end to the friendship between her
niece and an ineligible suitor. To distract the girl, she took her
to the season's festivities at Lichfield, but at a ball the girl was
seized with a fit of hysterics, and fell down in the midst of the
company. She was unable to attend the races, and remained
under the care of a physician.[3] In the autumn, before the Duke
started off on his travels in France he wished to settle his affairs,
and wrote to Wortley about the girl: 'She is desirous I find to
continue with Lady Mary and her Ladyship willing she should,
provided you approve of it. This therefore is to beg the favour
of you to let me know whether it will not be disagreeable or
inconvenient to you to have my sister in your house, for in case

---

[1] Publication date in *Daily Post*, 28 Mar. Dodsley later reprinted it as
Hervey's, but it is assigned to Lady Mary in the *Annual Register*, xxii (1779),
171.   [2] To Earl of Essex, 7 Aug. 1733, Add. MS 27732, f. 218.
[3] Lady Strafford to Lady Huntingdon, 26 Aug.; unknown corr. to Lady
Huntingdon, 23 Sept. 1733, HMC *Hastings MSS*, iii (1934), 17, 18.

it should I must lose no time in looking out for another place to settle her in.' Wortley consented, and the girl stayed under Lady Mary's care—an arrangement strongly endorsed by the Gower family.[1] The day after the girl came of age (in the following spring) she accompanied Lady Mary's daughter to the opera at Lincoln's Inn Fields. In another box some distance away sat Meadows. At the end of the first act Lady Frances pretended to be ill, and went out with her cousin, who returned alone after fifteen minutes. Meadows stayed a while longer, and then left. All of London talked of the elopement. A lady who had been at the theatre thought that Lady Frances was right to marry him 'if she could not live without a husband, for nobody else would have cared for her notwithstanding her twenty thousand pounds'.[2] The girl had succeeded in doing very neatly what her guardian aunt had once done.

The pamphlet war had by now taken a new turn. Lord Hervey stepped forward more prominently as Pope's antagonist when he published further abuse in his *Epistle to a Doctor of Divinity* in November 1733. Now Pope told his friends of 'a poetical war begun upon me by Lord Hervey' and of 'a Woman's war declar'd against me by a certain Lord . . .'.[3] Perhaps he had decided that Lord Hervey more than Lady Mary was responsible for beginning and waging the war against him. She was not forgotten by other pamphleteers, who either attacked or defended her.[4] Nor did Pope overlook her in his new imitation, published in July 1734, where he expanded Horace's mention of the miser:

> Avidien, or his wife (no matter which,
> For him you'll call a dog, and her a bitch). . . .

This miserly couple consider themselves lucky when they find a lost banknote or hear that their son was drowned.[5] A pamphleteer noted that Pope's invention of the wife came from his

---

[1] Kingston to W, 30 Oct. 1733, MS in my possession; Lady Gertrude Leveson Gower to M, 1 Nov. [1733], W MS, iv. 176–7.

[2] Mrs. Pendarves to Mrs. Granville, 27 Apr. 1734, *Autobiog. and Corr. of Mary Granville, Mrs. Delany*, ed. Lady Llanover (1861), i. 461–2.

[3] To Caryll, 1 Jan.; to Swift, 6 Jan. 1734, *Corr.* iii. 400, 401.

[4] *Tryal of Skill* (17 Jan. 1734), 21; *Tit for Tat* (4 Dec. 1733), 5; Gerard, *An Epistle to the Egregious Mr. Pope* (Feb. 1734), 4; *An Epistle from a Gentleman at Twickenham* [Mar. 1734], 6.

[5] Twickenham, iv. 56–59.

hatred of a certain lady of wit and learning.[1] By his reference
to a drowned son he probably meant the truancy of Lady
Mary's son, widely publicized in the newspapers five years
earlier.

After young Wortley's return from Gibraltar he had been
sent to the West Indies under a tutor, John Forster, and he
remained there for several years busy with studies.[2] He then
moved to France, where he lived at Troyes with a different
tutor, John Anderson, who in the summer of 1732 sent Lady
Mary a report of her son's progress and behaviour. Anderson
suggested that his charge be moved elsewhere because his 'old
intriguing disposition' was taking his mind from his studies.[3]
That disposition had already led him to marry a woman of 'very
low degree' much older than himself, whom he forsook in a few
weeks, and never tried to see again, though she lived almost as
long as he did.[4] Heeding his tutor's advice, his parents sent him
to Holland, but in the autumn of 1734 he returned to England
without their permission. His visit was gossiped about by Mrs.
Eleanor Verney, who lived at Whitton near Twickenham. 'Mr.
Wortley's son is come over, came to Twickenham,' she wrote
to her son-in-law, 'but his mother would not see him, says she
is forbid to let him come into her house. . . . Lady Mary went to
town that evening, and is not returned since. The young gentleman lays claim to his grandfather's legacy and an estate that
came to his father's mother, both which they say he is entitled
to now he is of age. Lady Mary now owns her son is married.
Is Mr. Wortley still in the north?' In his absence Lady Mary
had to deal with her son, as Mrs. Verney reported a week later:
'Lady Mary W. has given her son fifty pound and persuaded
him to go back to Holland, but they say he has left orders with
his lawyer to get the estate in dispute.'[5] It was only a temporary
reprieve in family dissension.

In December (1734) Lady Mary fell seriously ill. Lord

---

[1] *A Letter to Mr. Pope, Occasioned by Sober Advice from Horace* (4 Mar.
1735), 6–7. By Thomas Bentley (Twickenham, v. 429).
[2] Nichols, *Lit. Anecdotes of the 18th Cent.* (1812–15), iv. 628–9.
[3] 18 Aug. 1732 o.s., W MS, iv. 152–3.   [4] Stuart, 111.
[5] 7, 14 Nov. 1734; from transcripts sent by Sir C. Sharp to Lord Wharncliffe
in 1836 (Wharncliffe MS 439). In assessing Mrs. Verney's letters, one must
remember that she was the mother of Mrs. Bowes, whose death Lady Mary
had used as an occasion for some verse, and that her correspondent George
Bowes was a fellow colliery owner of Wortley's in the north.

Hervey told his friend Henry Fox about it: 'Poor Lady M.
Wortley is dying. I am very sorry; I shall hear her talk no more,
but I shall see her posthumous works.'[1] He could have been
referring to her Embassy Letters and poetry albums, which she
allowed friends to read; and as her confederate he must have
known of her 'Epistle from Pope to Lord Bolingbroke', written
that autumn but not printed until the next century. While she
lay ill Pope's *Sober Advice from Horace* appeared with another
instalment of his vilification. Once again he created a place for
her in the poem (as Fulfidia), and condemned her for being
poxed, lascivious, and—more emphatically—stingy, as shown
in her profiting by her son's truancy and her sister's custody.
With this last personal attack, he added a new, unjustified
accusation. He also repeated the stale scandal of the 'wretched
Monsieur' who, in fleeing to save his throat, quit 'his Mistress,
Money, Ring, and Note!'[2] The last phase of his campaign
began on 2 January 1735 when he published his *Epistle to Dr.
Arbuthnot*. In this general *apologia* of his life and career he
defended himself against all his enemies, from Grub Street to
St. James's. But its factuality should not be confused with its
artfulness. Rhetorically pitching his defence in the tone and
form of a conversation with his benign friend, he shrugged off
bothersome poets, protested with manly indignation against the
vices of the age, and ended with calculated pathos.[3] Besides
borrowing a Biblical metaphor from the *Verses to the Imitator*,
he gave particular attention to its authors, lashing Lord Hervey
(as Sporus) in a full-length portrait. He treated Lady Mary
almost gently, with only a couplet about his having been duped
by Sappho's wit. At least he returned to his original, perhaps
legitimate, source of anger.

Mild though his latest mention was, the next day Lady Mary
was moved to protest, politely (and fittingly) to Arbuthnot.
'I have perus'd the last Lampoon of your ingenious Freind', she
began; and then, after pointing out that the town supposed
Sappho referred to her, and that she was not the author of the
Verses to the Imitator, she continued: 'I wish you would advise

---

[1] 9 Dec. 1734, *Hervey and His Friends*, 213–14.
[2] Twickenham, iv. 75–77, 79.
[3] This crucial aspect of Pope's satire is treated in Elder Olson's 'Rhetoric
and the Appreciation of Pope', *Mod. Philology*, xxxvii (1939), 13–35; and in
Maynard Mack's 'The Muse of Satire', *Yale Rev.* xli (1951), 80–92.

poor Pope to turn to some other more honest livlihood than
libelling, I know he will alledge in his excuse, that he must write
to eat, and he is now grown sensible that nobody will buy his
verses, except their curiosity is pique'd to it, by what is said of
their Acquaintance. . . .'[1] A few weeks later another form of
protest, far less effective, appeared in the anonymous *Epistle to
Alexander Pope, Esq.* which blamed him for drawing her in a
'gay Idiot's Dress' instead of in her beauty and air. On her copy
of the pamphlet Lady Mary wrote: 'not by me except a Correc-
tion or two. M.'[2] She also saw herself revenged in Dodd's re-
issue of the *Verses to the Imitator*, called the fifth edition—a
tribute not to its own popularity but to that of Pope's *Epistle
to Arbuthnot*, which had encouraged the bookseller.[3]

In February Pope unveiled a dirty and bejewelled Flavia in
his moral epistle *Of the Characters of Women*. It was at least
true that when Lady Mary had called on Lady Strafford one
morning, 'her dress was a sack and all her jewells'.[4] A reader's
suspicion that Flavia was still another view of Lady Mary was
soon confirmed in the second volume of Pope's collected works
(in April 1735) where he consolidated his vituperation, with a
few additions. The slatternly Flavia became Sappho; and in a
new poem paraphrasing Donne's satire he added to the original
a simile: 'who knows Sappho, smiles at other whores.' Worst of
all, he cushioned his *Dunciad* passage with a footnote: 'a famous
Lady who cheated a French wit of 5000 pounds in the South-
Sea year. But the Author meant it in general of all bragging
Travellers, and of all Whores and Cheats under the names of
Ladies.'[5] She apparently made no attempt to answer such brutal
name-calling. But in June Curll came to her rescue with an
unsavoury defence; he seized on the scandal of Pope's declaration of love to her, and gave it a new obscene twist.[6]

[1] 3 Jan. [1735], Pope's *Corr.* iii. 448–9.
[2] Pub. 4 Feb. 1735; M's copy in Yale Univ. Library. In June 1733 Giles
Jacob had asked her to contribute a 'letter or composition' for the second
edition of his anti-Pope *The Mirrour* (Paston, 349–50). In 1737 she wrote a
brief, apparently unpublished piece attacking the preface to his letters (Paston,
351–2 [W MS, v. 8]).
[3] The text was reset for this 'sham' new edition (Lord Oxford's annotated
copy now in the Bodleian).
[4] To Lord Strafford, 10 Jan. 1734, *Wentworth Papers* (1883), 501.
[5] Twickenham, III. ii. 50–51; IV. 133; V. 112.
[6] *The Poet finish'd in Prose* (26 June 1735), 17.

The quarrel between Pope and Lady Mary, besides provok-
ing insult and scandal, may have affected her social and family
life—or at least she suspected so. When her friend Lord Corn-
bury stopped calling on her because he thought she had declaimed against his verse, she was sure Pope had been the
mischief-maker. Of more serious consequence, she suspected
him of having encouraged her son in his arrogance and disobedience toward her husband and herself.[1] Altogether his
attacks did not make any easier these difficult years of her life.

Her dutiful and plain daughter now became the cause of
concern to her when the Viscount Perceval, only son of the
Irish Earl of Egmont, began to court the seventeen-year-old
girl. In his diary Lord Egmont clearly outlined Lady Mary's
part in the negotiations.[2] Lord Perceval visited her early in July
to tell her that his family's lawyers would call on her and
Wortley with proposals. She assured him that she was convinced of the goodness of the match, but that she was only one
of three whose consent had to be won. Most difficult would be
her daughter, who had refused two other suitors, and had asked
instead to remain unmarried. Two weeks later, when Lord
Perceval again approached Lady Mary, she told him that her
husband 'had the foible of loving money', and was considering
another, richer suitor. At the end of the month, when financial
terms were again discussed Lady Mary promised the young man
she would do what she could to advance his suit. The negotiations then ceased, but she continued on cordial terms with the
Egmont family. In January 1736, when the Duke of Buckinghamshire's lavish funeral procession was to pass through Pall
Mall, where Lord Egmont lived, she was among the few relations and friends invited to see it and take a cold dinner.[3] By
April the young suitor became discouraged. As his father
noted: 'My son Percival told me this night that seeing Mr.
Montague persisted in neglecting to hearken to any proposal
for his daughter, he had acquainted Lady Mary that he must
for his honour sake and for preserving the reputation of a man
of sense quit thought of pursuing that affair, to which she

---

[1] About 1736, to Lady Bute, 23 July 1753, ii. 237–8; to W, 8 Sept., 22 Oct.
1741, Paston, 397, 400.
[2] 12 July 1735, et sqq., HMC Egmont, *Diary*, ii. 185–90, 257.
[3] Ibid. 228.

replied he acted by her like a man of honour and she could not take it amiss.' In this delicate business, Lord Egmont implies, she herself had acted like a woman of honour.

The contrast between the Lady Mary in Lord Egmont's sober diary and the Sappho in Pope's coruscating satires evokes a double image. Can Pope's portrait be accepted as the accurate one? In the entire gamut of his allusions to her, he began (in 'The Capon's Tale') by scolding her for passing off her lampoons as his, and he ended (in the *Epistle to Arbuthnot*) by recalling that he had been duped by her wit. These related accusations are at least plausible, though not proven. But what of the other, recurring attacks over the span of seven years? His insult is the only evidence of her having the pox; and if he meant it only as the insult of hyperbole, later commentators have not understood it as such. In accusing her of profligacy, he pointed only to Rémond, yet the Frenchman's own letters prove that she never became his lover but only—to their misfortune—his financial adviser. If she were profligate, it would surely have been mentioned somewhere in the letters, diaries, or memoirs of the time. As to her relations with her sister and her son, Pope's taunts cannot be sustained by the surviving evidence. In other words, the rhetorically effective details of his satire on Lady Mary cannot be accepted as fact.

X. The Leap for Another World

(1736-9)

IN the spring of 1736, when Lady Mary met a young Italian on his first visit to England, she entered on the most sensational friendship of her life, one which has remained virtually unknown. Francesco Algarotti, born in 1712, was about half her age at the time. He was the second son of a Venetian merchant, and at the University of Bologna had made a brilliant record in natural science and in French and English *belles-lettres*.[1] He grew to be a handsome man of great charm and androgynous tastes, capable of love affairs with either sex. In 1734 he moved to Rome to take advantage of his family connexions and the cosmopolitan milieu. There he was befriended by Martin Folkes, a prominent member of the Royal Society, who encouraged his enthusiasm for England and especially for Isaac Newton. The following year he moved on to Paris, where he devoted himself to other pleasures besides intellectual ones. He soon exhausted the allowance supplied by his brother, head of their fatherless family; and so when Voltaire and the Marquise du Châtelet, whom he had met, invited him to the Château de Cirey in Lorraine, he joined them. Like them he was studying Newtonian physics and had devised a scheme reducing Newton's *Optics* to a set of dialogues like Fontenelle's *Entretiens sur la pluralité des mondes*. At Cirey he easily impressed Voltaire with his facility in writing verse and his knowledge of Locke and Newton.[2] On his departure Madame du Châtelet gave him her portrait as an encouragement for him to dedicate his book to her.

In March 1736 he reached London, and soon made the most

---

[1] Unless other sources are cited, the facts about Algarotti come from Ida F. Treat, *Un Cosmopolite Italien du XVIIIᵉ Siècle Francesco Algarotti* (1913).
[2] To Thieriot, 3 Nov. [1735], *Œuvres Complètes*, xxxiii. 546.

of his social and scientific friendships. On 1 April he attended
a meeting of the Royal Society, and a week later was nominated
for membership as 'A Gentleman of great knowledge in all
parts of Philosophical and Mathematical Learning'. In May he
was elected to the Society of Antiquaries.[1] Through Voltaire
he was introduced to Lord Hervey who in turn presented
him to influential friends, particularly Walpole and the Queen.
There could not have been much sympathy between the elegant
young Italian and the hearty Minister, but the Queen found
him sympathetic and enjoyed conversing with him on scientific
and philosophical topics. Through Lord Hervey he also met
Lady Mary; and he read to them his Italian dialogues on Newton, and they helped him to improve his command of English.
This slight information is all that Algarotti's biographer knew
of his relationship with 'la spirituelle Lady Mary Wortley
Montagu'.[2]

Her friendship was at first light and debonair. In one of her
hasty notes, undated like most of those she sent him, she wrote:
'My Lady Stafford and my self waited for you three hours.
Three hours of expectation is no small trial of patience, and I
believe some of your martyrs have been canonized for suffering
less. If you have repentance enough to be inclined to ask
pardon, you may obtain it by coming here tomorrow at seven
o'clock. Let me have a line of answer.' He usually called on her
in the evening, for in another note she told him she would
expect him at seven unless she heard to the contrary.[3] In less
than fifteen days, she later recalled, he won her heart.[4] His
rapid conquest was due to his attractiveness as well as to her
susceptibility at that time.

While he remained in London Madame du Châtelet asked
him to hurry back.[5] But he was in no haste to leave England,
where—he boasted to his brother—he knew many people of
wealth and high position. Lord Hervey, who became his most
active patron, had a definitely homosexual strain; and instead
of concealing his tendency he was apt to underline it.[6] His

---

[1] Royal Society, Certificates 1731–50, f. 116; Journal Book, xv (elected a
fellow on 8 July); Society of Antiquaries, Minutes, ii. 182, 186.
[2] Treat, *Algarotti*, 70.   [3] Bod. MS Don., c. 56, ff. 17, 19.
[4] To Algarotti, 19 Feb. 1757, ibid. f. 40.
[5] 20 May 1736, *Lettres*, ed. Eugène Asse (1882), 90.
[6] Peter Quennell, *The Singular Preference* (1952), 47.

PLATE 9

Count Francesco Algarotti

From a pastel by J. E. Liotard [*1745*]

friendship with Algarotti opened when he had come to the end of his romantic alliance with Stephen Fox, his friend for about ten years—whom he had addressed as 'mon bien aimé' and 'mea vera et sola voluptas'.[1] Since Lord Hervey lived in polite estrangement from his wife, he could easily spend much of his time with Algarotti; and as he soon revealed, he was deeply moved by him.

During the summer, while Lady Mary enjoyed her new friendship, she again had to deal with the problem of her daughter's suitors. The girl had fallen in love with John Stuart, the young and handsome Earl of Bute, nephew of the Duke of Argyll and of Lord Islay. But he had very little fortune, and Lady Mary warned her daughter of the disadvantages of poverty.[2] The girl stubbornly refused to end her attachment to him. As gossip reported, her father tried to prevent the marriage by withholding her dowry of £20,000; this in turn led to the Duke's trying to persuade his nephew to break off the match, but Lord Bute said he loved the lady, and if she would be content to live in Scotland he would marry her. She agreed, and on 13 August 1736 the young pair were married. Although Wortley gave away the bride, he did not stay to give a dinner. Two weeks later the Butes and Lady Mary dined at Lord Islay's and then went to Twickenham to drink coffee with Wortley.[3] Lady Mary had written to Lord Gower about her daughter's disobedience, and he tried to console her: 'I hope by her future conduct she will atone for her past, and that her choice will prove more happy than you and Mr. Wortley expect.'[4]

During the summer Algarotti took stock of his situation. Although he was enchanted by England, he decided to return to Italy for the publication of his dialogues, which had been as highly praised in London as in Paris. His decision perturbed at least two of his English friends. Lady Mary, in a note probably sent at this time, did not conceal her distress.

[1] Hervey, *Memoirs* (1931), xxii–xxiii.
[2] To Lady Bute, 3 Mar. 1746, Paston, 436.
[3] Eleanor Verney's letters (transcripts), 3, 31 Aug. 1736, Wharncliffe MS 439. The last part also in Walpole's 'Anecdotes', *Corr.* xiv. 244.
[4] 11 Sept. 1736, Paston, 359. His daughter, a partisan of the Mar family, blamed Lady Mary's actions on her stinginess (to Lady Frances Erskine, 13 Sept. 1736, Mar and Kellie MS).

Je ne sais plus de quel façon vous écrire. Mes sentiments sont trop vif; je ne saurais les expliquer, ni les cacher. Il faut être touché d'un enthousiasme pareil au mien pour souffrir mes lettres. J'en vois toute la folie sans la possibilité de me corriger. La seul idée de vous revoir m'a donnée un saississement en lisant votre lettre, qui m'a quasi fait évanouir. Qu'est devenu cet indifférence philosophe qui a fait la gloire et la tranquillité de mes jours passées? Je l'ai perdu pour le retrouver jamais, et si cette passion est guéri, je prévois rien qu'un ennui mortel. Pardonnez l'extravagance que vous avez fait naître, et venez me voir.[1]

When Lord Hervey in the country heard the news he immediately assured Algarotti of his friendship and affection; more than anything else in the world he desired to keep him in England for the rest of his life.[2]

On 19 August Algarotti found time to sit for a pair of ink portraits by Jonathan Richardson, senior.[3] They depict his high forehead above large, round, dark eyes, and full, pouting, sensual lips. His entire expression is pensive, almost melancholy; it is the face of a lover who is passive, accustomed to being pursued and wooed. From the country Lord Hervey pursued him with fulsome flattery of his *esprit*, his dialogues, and his ability as poet and scientist.[4] Like Lady Mary, Lord Hervey preferred to write in French, despite Algarotti's particular request for English; and the two men usually conversed in French. Now that pleasure was to be lost, as Lord Hervey told Henry Fox, brother of Stephen. 'Algarotti goes away on Monday, which I am extremely sorry for, for he amuses me exceedingly.'[5] To celebrate his friend's last evening in London, Lord Hervey invited him to supper, but he declined with the excuse that he had to sup with his old friend Martin Folkes. The next day, Monday, 6 September 1736, he left for Paris *en route* to Italy.

But he had lied; he actually supped that evening with Lord Hervey's rival Lady Mary. She apparently boasted of her favour to Lord Hervey, who could be her sympathetic friend and colleague but not in this intrigue. Stung by her victory he

[1] Bod. MS, f. 63. In her French letters I am not correcting the frequently faulty grammar and syntax.   [2] 14 Aug. 1736, Murray MS.
[3] Victoria and Albert Museum.   [4] 16 Aug. 1736, Murray MS.
[5] To Algarotti, 20/9 Sept.; to Fox, 4 Sept. 1736, *Hervey and His Friends*, 249.

revealed his irritation in his first letter to the absent Algarotti. He hoped that his ridicule would convince Algarotti how little she deserved his favour—and how much he himself did.

En verité, c'est faire trop d'honneur à l'endroit où vous avez soupé d'en faire un mystère—si c'était pour ménager *sa* reputation; si c'était pour la vôtre, je vous le pardons. Mais l'ingrate s'en est vantée, et ne s'est pas contentée de la victoire et du pillage; elle voulait un triomphe publique ... elle traverse la ville de Londres, se vante de sa conquête, et après vous avoir fait servir aux emplois les plus bas, insulte votre mémoire en les déclarant au publique: veni, vidi, vici—est la devise qu'elle a prise.

He reinforced his malicious purpose with a 'faithful portrait' of Lady Mary, in doggerel verse ending:

> To make her lover pleased, as well as kind,
> She should be never mute, you always blind.

But he ended his long letter on a note of sincerity, assuring Algarotti: '. . . je vous aime de tout mon cœur, et . . . je vous supplie de n'oublier jamais l'amitié que je vous porte, de ne laisser affaiblir celle que vous m'avez temoignée.'[1]

If Lady Mary boasted of having conquered him, she did so only out of pride. She assumed a quite different attitude in a note to him, probably the first after his departure, where she timidly declared her love, perhaps emboldened by his granting her the favour of his last evening in London.

Qu'on est timide quand on aime! J'ai peur de vous offenser en vous envoyant ce billet, quoique mon intention est de vous faire plaisir. Enfin je suis si folle en tout ce que vous regarde que je ne suis pas sûre de mes propres pensées. Ma raison murmure tout bas des sottises de mon cœur sans avoir la force de les détruire. Je suis déchiré de mille mouvements différents que vous importe très peu, et je ne sais pourquoi je vous en fais la confidence. Tout ce qui est certain, c'est que je vous aimerai toute ma vie malgré vos caprices et ma raison.[2]

'How timid one is when one loves! . . . I shall love you all my life. . . .' The reader rubs his eyes in disbelief. Can this be the forty-seven-year-old Lady Mary, battered by family troubles and disappointments, the hard-mouthed social gossip and heartless versifier? The conflict between head and heart was decidedly

---

[1] 20/9 Sept. 1736, Murray MS.   [2] Add. to Paris, Bod. MS, f. 27.

an ingrained part of her personality. What at first seems an enormous contradiction, her tumbling into love with the abandon of a romantic schoolgirl, is credible if one sees her love for Algarotti as the outlet for her bitterly repressed emotions. She had long wanted a 'swain'—as she wrote in some verse—to engrave his name on her 'marble breast'.[1] In Algarotti she had found that swain. When writing to him she usually used French, with quick fluency and erratic grammar, for she found greater freedom in its graceful extravagances. Her style in writing to him owed something to the tradition of epistolary gallantry, particularly since she often assumed a masculine aggressiveness. If the reader today is startled by her fervour, Algarotti was not, for he was aware of his talent for inspiring love in the hearts of both women and men. His personal letters to her and Lord Hervey do not survive, but their letters to him show the design of his opportunism. Passion played an inferior part to ambition in his friendship for the two rich, prominent English aristocrats.

Her timid letter drew no answer from him. As the empty days passed she saw herself as Dido deserted by the Roman hero to whom she had given her love. In her second letter she told him of her grief. 'Past midnight', she headed it—perhaps like the 'soul-racked' queen she could not sleep—and after transcribing from the *Aeneid* the passage about Dido's sorrow, she gave her own thoughts:

Je suis mille fois plus à plaindre que la triste Didon, et j'ai mille fois plus des raisons de me donner la mort. . . . Je me suis jetté à la tête d'un étranger comme elle, mais au lieu de crier parjure et perfide quand mon petit Aenée témoigne qu'il a envie de me quitter, j'y donne les mains par un sentiment de génerosité dont Virgile n'a pas cru les femmes capable. . . . C'est peut-être du mauvais français que j'écrive, mais comme mes lettres sont entre vos mains de brûler le moment qu'elles vous ennuyent j'écris tout ce que me vient à la tête. Je n'ai pas la vanité d'oser espérer vous plaire; je n'ai nulle but que de me satisfaire en te disant que je t'aime. . . . Ma raison me fait voir tout l'extravagance, et mon cœur me fait sentir toute l'importance. Faible raison! qui choque ma passion et ne le détruit pas, et qui me fait voir inutilement toute la folie d'aimer au point que j'aime sans espérance de retour. Vous étiez pourtant faché de partir. Je l'ai vu dans vos yeux, et il n'avait point d'affectation dans le chagrin qui a

---

[1] 'An Epistle to Lord Bathurst', ii. 464 (mistitled).

paru en votre air. Je me flatte pas sur l'impossible; ce n'était pas moi que vous étiez faché de quitter, mais sûrement vous étiez faché de quitter Londres. J'aurais donc pu vous retenir, et c'était une fausse délicatesse qui m'a empêché de vous faire la proposition, et j'ai donc perdu, par mauvaise honte, crainte, et générosité mal placé toute le plaisir de ma vie. Je ne sais si vous comprenez rien à ce galimatias, mais croyez que vous possédez en moi l'ami le plus parfait et l'amante la plus passioné. . . .[1]

Her extravagant sentiments were as ineffectual as her timid declaration in drawing a reply from Algarotti.

Writing to him may have quieted her unhappiness, but his failure to answer compounded it. She sent a third letter, but still he did not answer although he had promised to write from Calais. Her rival had been favoured, or at least said he had been, when she asked him. 'The body you speak of', Lord Hervey assured her, 'has not mentioned you in his letters to me; he knows I have seen you by the first of mine to him. . . .'[2] Unable to quiet her impatience, she sent Algarotti a fourth letter on 20 September (two weeks after his departure). 'Est-il possible que je n'ai pas de vos nouvelles?' she began, and then in a curious mixture of banter and misery asked why, if he was willing to spend hours talking to her, he could not send her three or four lines. She would apply to Lord Hervey, who should have news. Then after bemoaning her misfortune—a bolt of lightning would be a stroke of mercy to her—she concluded wittily: 'Vous devez être bien ennuyé des mes plaintes, mais suis-je en droit de ménager votre repos quand vous avez si peu du soin du mien?'[3]

Lord Hervey also felt the loss of his friend; as he confessed moodily to Henry Fox: 'I saw him often, and was always amused when I saw him, either by conversing with him or reading to him. I am now generally in this house (triste séjour), and generally seeing or thinking of the same thing. Adieu. I write like a fool, think like a fool, talk like a fool, act like a fool; and have everything of a fool but the content of one.'[4] He was soon rewarded; on 24 September he received a letter from Paris. In

---

[1] MS owned by Mr. Donald F. Hyde. Among Algarotti's papers was a long verse epistle describing Lady Mary as Sappho and Dido about to lose her Phaon and Aeneas. Although not in her autograph, it could easily have been by her (MS Eg. 23, f. 239).   [2] Bristol MS.
[3] MS Eg. 23, ff. 233–4.   [4] 16 Sept. 1736, *Hervey and His Friends*, 250–1.

his long reply he proved again how much his rivalry out-
weighed his friendship. Lady Mary had pursued him for a
meeting, he related, but he had successfully evaded her until
one evening when she called at his house with a companion, and
stayed six hours.

Elle m'a tourné de milles différentes façons pour me faire parler
de vous, et jamais je n'ai voulu vous nommer. Elle m'a dit en même
temps milles menteries express, et milles vérités par hazard; et au
lieu de prendre plusieurs choses sans rien dire, comme elle a proposé; elle m'a tout dit sans avoir rien appris. Enfin, monsieur, vous
l'avez laissée plus folle que vous ne l'avez trouvé; c'est tout dire.
Elle était aussi ivre auparavant que le vin peut rendre ivre, et vous
y avez ajouté du *gin.* La scène était charmante. . . .

As before, he ended with effusive expressions of love and
devotion.[1]

His malicious letter exhibits both his jealousy and Lady
Mary's distraught love. It also lifts Algarotti to some extent
from the shadow cast by his missing letters. Would Lord
Hervey have exposed Lady Mary so contemptuously if he had
not been certain of Algarotti's appreciation? The Italian's attitude toward her at this time must be gathered from the letters
of the two rival lovers. Evidently Lord Hervey set the more
objective focus; Lady Mary could not consistently see herself
as these two sharp-eyed effeminate men did. Except to the
heroine of such a love affair there was something ridiculous—
or so the world would judge—in the spectacle of a lady past
middle age and physical charms hurling herself at a handsome
young stranger. Fortunately for her, as her impulses alternated
between head and heart, she herself could see, even in the midst
of her passion, how ridiculous it would seem to the world.

What followed in this three-character drama might seem
contrived, it was so neat. The very next day after Lady Mary's
fruitless and humiliating scene with Lord Hervey, she received
a letter from Algarotti. In her reply she proved herself the more
generous of the rival lovers.

Your letter came in very good time to save the small remains of
my understanding. Your silence had so far disturbed it, that not
able to bear the perplexity of my own imaginations I sent Lord
H[ervey] word I should be glad to speak to him. You may believe

[1] 9 Oct./28 Sept. 1736, Murray MS.

PLATE 10

LADY MARY WORTLEY MONTAGUE.

Lady Mary Wortley Montagu

From a painting by Carolus De Rusca [1739]

(with his politeness) I saw him soon after, and then I was in almost as much difficulty to draw from him what I had a mind to know, that is, whether you were arrived safe at Paris. The question was very short, but the way to make it very hard; and in short I said nothing of what I had a mind to know, and all he could collect from my conversation was that I was very near, if not quite distracted. . . . I shall go tomorrow (late as it is in the year) to my country house, where I intend to bury my self for at least three months. . . . You have taken from me not only the taste, but the sufferance of those I see; but in recompense you have made me very entertaining to my self, and there are some moments when I am happy enough to think over the past, till I totally forget the present.[1]

Since she sent her grateful letter to Venice, some time passed before Algarotti received it.

He was hastening to that city to prepare his dialogues for publication; and although he did not loiter in Paris for long—six days, he wrote Lord Hervey—he stopped to pay another visit to Cirey. Voltaire assessed him this time as 'un jeune homme en tout au-dessus de son âge, et qui sera tout ce qu'il voudra'.[2] Algarotti's ambition could impress those not blinded by his charm. In his letter to Lady Mary from Paris he had promised to write from Lyons, but she waited in vain. On 21 October she could no longer restrain her anxiety, and sent him still another token of her 'tenderest wishes and . . . softest remembrance', one which ended:

I am now in the country, where I choose to see nothing but trees since I cannot see the only object dear to my heart and lovely to my eyes. 'Tis with difficulty that I restrain my pen from falling into the extravagancies of poetry, which indeed are only fit to attempt the expressing my thoughts of you or to you. . . . Only believe this serious protestation—you may believe it since there is no appearance of deceit in it—that the impression you have made on my heart can never leave it, while I have life enough to feel a warmth in it.[3]

At Twickenham in the fall of 1736 she was harried by another kind of unhappiness. Her niece Lady Frances Erskine had come of age that year, and since she sided with her father's family—she married Lord Grange's son a few years later—she

---

[1] MS Eg. 23, ff. 235–6.
[2] To Berger, 10 Oct. 1736, du Châtelet, *Lettres*, 104 n.
[3] MS Eg. 23, ff. 237–8.

naturally opposed Lady Mary, and demanded the custody of her mother.[1] It had been bothersome for Lady Mary and Wortley, involving them in legal and financial business. In November, while in the north, Wortley ordered her to relinquish custody of her sister and to 'be prepared to get out of this affair soon after I am come to London'. He pointed out that trustees and other members of the family could control the daughter's management.[2]

Lady Mary's daughter lived in Scotland, and her errant son in Holland under the care of a tutor; and now she was relieved of caring for her sister. Possibly that is why she sent Algarotti her most astonishing proposal at this time:

> I have sent you so many verses, this shall wait on you in the form of plain prose. My picture went last, wrapped up in poetry without fiction. I could be angry at your haste in restoring a trifle that if you ever intend to see me again might have been time enough delivered to my own hand. If you seriously wish to see me, it will certainly happen. If your affairs do not permit your return to England, mine shall be arranged in such a manner as I may come to Italy. This sounds extraordinary, and yet is not so when you consider the impression you have made on a heart that is capable of receiving no other. My thoughts of you are such as exceed the strongest panegyric that the vainest man upon earth ever wished to hear made of himself; and all conversations since I lost yours are so insipid to me that I prefer my closet meditations to all the amusements of a populous town or crowded court. . . . Let me know when you receive my picture. Write to me, and believe whenever you do it you are bestowing the only happiness I can be sensible of in your absence.[3]

It did indeed sound extraordinary, as she realized, to propose an idyll abroad with him. In her long letter echoing Dido's lament she had only hinted at a proposal; now she clearly stated it.

In Venice Algarotti busied himself preparing his book for the press; and in taking the advice of his friends and teachers in Bologna spent almost a whole year revising it. His friends in England did not forget him, although he wrote to them very rarely. At Hampton Court, Lord Hervey repeatedly asked for a reply. 'Am I never to hear from you again?' he asked on

---

[1] Gower to M, 11 Sept. 1736, Paston, 359.
[2] 6 Nov. 1736, W MS, i. 146–7 (frag. in Paston, 359–60).
[3] Bod. MS, ff. 54–55.

18 July (in a third letter). 'I enquire often of Lady Mary what she knows of you. Sometimes she says she hears from you, sometimes that she does not; which is true I know not.'[1] It seems certain that he occasionally answered her frequent and impassioned letters. In September, when Lord Hervey received an answer to his July letter, he replied at great length. Like Lady Mary he still felt a great tenderness for the young Italian; his closing sentiment was: 'Adio, Carissimo.'[2]

Lord Hervey and Lady Mary could agree more comfortably in their political allegiance. He had many duties as Walpole's supporter in the House of Lords and emissary to the Queen. Lady Mary's activity was limited, of course, by the handicap of her being a woman. If it were not for that, George Saintsbury has conjectured, she might have rivalled Lord Chesterfield in his achievements.[3] But unknown to most of her contemporaries, as well as to later readers and scholars, she did transcend her limitation to become a political journalist.[4] That career was to some degree congenial to her talent. She had shown an active interest in her husband's early Parliamentary career and embassy; but then his animosity to Walpole cut him off from further government activity, while her friendship with Maria Skerrett and Lord Hervey drew her closer to the Minister.

She had begun her defence of Walpole after his victory in the Parliamentary election of 1734. The Opposition denounced him for political bribery and corruption, which (they said) would put an end to English liberty. That alarm had long been a rallying cry for writers in search of a theme and politicians in search of an office. Poets (including Pope), dramatists (including Fielding), and journalists subsidized by the Opposition took it up. Among some company once, when the topic arose whether to reform or close the playhouses, Lady Mary's witty comment was recorded: 'Lady Mary Wortley declares aloud for a reformation, but then she says the Parliament should have first began with Westminster Hall and the Church, for truly what they are now about is of no more use than the saving an

---

[1] 29/18 July 1737, Murray MS.
[2] 28/17 Sept. 1737, *Hervey and His Friends*, 271-3.
[3] *The Peace of the Augustans* (repr. 1946), 220-1.
[4] Unless otherwise specified, the material on Lady Mary's career as journalist is drawn from my edition of *The Nonsense of Common-Sense, 1737-1738* (1947).

old pair of bellows when a house is on fire.'[1] She went much further to express a similar opinion in an essay 'An Expedient to Put a Stop to the Spreading Vice of Corruption'.[2] Yes, she admits, there is a vast amount of that vice, which has infected Parliament as well as England's national and social life. 'I have sufficiently set forth the evil of corruption, and it has been often most pompously performed by abler pens, but how can we prevent this contagion after it has gained so strong a head that it passes among foreigners for a part of our constitution?' She then set forth her scheme—as immodest a proposal in its way as Swift's famous one: that since it is easier to remove the source of corruption than corruption itself, the English should abolish Parliament, and be safely governed by their virtuous King and their just and honest Minister. At the end she reinforced her thesis:

I am so well convinced of the universal benefit that would arise from this proposal, I heartily pray God could open the eyes of the people to see it as plain as I do, and instead [of] bellowing about the excise and mobbing the Minister, the whole city would rise, and with a great deal of good manners, surround the Parliament House the first day of their meeting, and telling them plainly they are a pernicious set of people who assume to themselves a power of defrauding poor tradesmen of just debts, turn them all out of doors, distinguishing some few by some gentle kicks, and assure them they should meet there no more to cant liberty and promote slavery, talk pertly of the King and sell the subject.

The audacious 'Expedient' was apparently never printed. Its seditious proposal would certainly have put its printer (and author, if known) in danger of arrest and imprisonment. As an exercise it at least prepared Lady Mary for her activity on the field of journalistic combat.

When she acted, in 1737, Walpole faced an increasingly strong Opposition made up of Tories, disgruntled Whigs, and urban radicals. In newspapers, pamphlets, stage farces, ballads, and prints he saw his person and his politics attacked. 'No Government ever punished so few libels,' he boasted in Parliament, 'and no Government ever had provocation to punish so

---

[1] Lady Elizabeth Finch to Lady Burlington [May or June 1735], Chatsworth MS 230.8, owned by the Duke of Devonshire.
[2] Printed for the first time in 1947.

many.' He tried to protect his administration by hiring hack writers, but their papers—as described by Lord Hervey— 'being only written for hire, gave the readers as little pleasure, as they did service to their paymasters'.[1] The most important and long-lived one was *The Daily Gazetteer*, so mild that it easily persuaded its readers to slumber.[2]

The leading Opposition paper in 1737 was *Common Sense*, whose popularity the Ministerial writers ineffectually tried to challenge. Without warning, a new adversary appeared on Friday, 16 December 1737. Its title *The Nonsense of Common-Sense* clearly advertised its function: to refute the Opposition paper; and its first paragraph attacked *Common Sense* as 'a certain Paper with many Flights and small Reason, that is handed about at Coffee-Houses and Tea-Tables, for the Amusement of the Idle, the Entertainment of the Malicious, and the Astonishment of the Ignorant, who are very numerous in this Part of the World'. That rabidly partisan paper had pretended to be unaffiliated with any party; and the author of *The Nonsense of Common-Sense* insisted throughout the paper's run that its only purpose was to expose social evils and defend moral virtue without favouring either Ministry or Opposition. In its first issue, the author emphatically stated: 'I will positively praise whatever I think right; *tho' I foresee I shall be supported in this Design by no Party whatever.*' Yet in that issue, the scolding administered to Peers who refused to put their equipages in mourning for the recently deceased Queen was aimed only at the Peers in the Opposition, who had resented her as Walpole's close ally. The Ministerial bias of the new paper was insinuated in this way.

Who was the author of the new paper? Under the title in all its issues appeared the flippant statement: 'To be continued as long as the Author thinks fit, and the Publick likes it.' The Author, whose identity remained shielded, was Lady Mary. For among her private papers are preserved her autograph drafts of six essays which she sent to the printer. On the top of the essay that appeared as Number I she wrote the full title of the paper, and under it a Biblical motto; and on the back of the sheet she addressed a note to the printer naming the day for

[1] *Memoirs*, 263.
[2] Johnson, *London* (1738), l. 72.

the paper to be issued, and cautioning him to be sure the author would remain anonymous. Then after asking for the original to be returned to her, she ordered half a dozen printed copies.

Ten days later, on Tuesday—its regular day of publication —the second number of her paper appeared. It advocated that the rate of interest on the national sinking-fund be reduced from 4 to 3 per cent. In the previous April Wortley had helped to draw up a bill for the reduction, but it had been defeated— with Walpole against it for reasons of policy, not conviction. Lady Mary's support half a year after the bill's defeat could serve a useful purpose: a great deal of propaganda was put out in the months before a parliamentary campaign, when members came up to London; and since a new session was about to begin, this essay could be regarded as preparatory ammunition if the topic—a very popular one—should be raised again. Lady Mary tied her political theme to feminism, chiding the ladies for their selfish and frivolous influence. 'I have always been an humble Admirer of the Fair Sex. Nay, I believe, I think of them with more Tenderness, than any Man in the World.' In this opening sentence she forgot that the Author was supposed to be a man; she then continued:

I do not look upon them as Objects of Pleasure, but I compassion-ate the many Hardships both Nature and Custom has subjected them to.—I never expose the Foibles to which Education has inclined them; but, contrary to all other Authors, I see, with a favourable Eye, the little Vanities with which they amuse themselves; and am glad they can find, in the imaginary Empire of Beauty, a Consola-tion for being excluded every Part of Government in the State.— But with all this Fondness for them, I am shock'd when I see their Influence prevail, in Opposition to Reason, Justice, and the common Welfare of the Nation.

A beneficial measure, like the one they oppose, must be forced on people against their wishes: 'Like a tender Mother who forces necessary Physick down the Throat of a beloved Infant, tho' it squawls and struggles with all its Strength.' When the printer put her essay through the press, he saw an opportunity for innuendo, and so added: 'or like a Lover that, &c.'. The printer's excuse, the Author explained in the fifth essay, was that bawdy might increase the paper's popularity.

For the third issue, on 3 January 1738, Lady Mary used a

journalistic trick to give some zest to her essay. It is a letter to the Author from one 'Balducci', beginning:

SIR, I fancy your Paper is not so much designed either to support the Measures of the Court, or to justify the Complaints of the Patriots, as to expose common Prejudices and vulgar Errors wherever you meet with them. It is on this Account I apply myself to you; for as I intend to get Money from both, I would not offend either; and we Foreigners are seldom, you know, great Zealots either in Politicks or Religion, our chief Principle of Action being, to serve those by whom we get most Money, which is the only End most of us have in sojourning amongst you.

He then announces that since the English spend such vast sums on Italian opera singers, he can provide mechanical substitutes at a fraction of the cost. Although mostly a pleasant satire on the rage for opera and other foreign luxuries, the essay gently adds some propaganda for the Ministerial party when Balducci promises to replace the famous Farinelli, then performing in Spain, and thus remove one of the principal causes of war with that country. Here Lady Mary ridiculed the Opposition's clamour for a Spanish war.

A mild, dull essay on the etiquette of levees—perhaps a defence of Walpole's—made up her next paper, but for her fifth, a week later, she wrote one of her most amusing pieces. It is the narrative, mostly fictitious, of the Author's difficulty in having his innocent paper printed. The first printer insists that to be successful it must be anti-Ministerial or full of old jokes, and actually inserts some bawdy himself:

You may imagine how much I was provoked; I blotted it out of the few Copies I sent to my Friends, and immediately sent for the Fellow to expostulate with him, but found him as much out of Humour as my self. I'll assure you, Sir, said he, in a Heat, I have done all I could for the Service of your Paper; but it is a damn'd ministerial Thing, and the Hawkers refuse to sell it, and the Coffee-houses will not take it in, and if you will rail at no Body, nor put in no feign'd Names that every Body may understand, all the Bawdy in the *Dunciad* will not carry it off.

When the Author takes his next paper to a 'declared Printer on the Court side', he is more courteously treated, but looked upon as mad because he intends neither a political nor a profitable paper, but only a moral one. In this way Lady Mary subtly defends Walpole, whom the Opposition accused of destroying the freedom of the press. The Author concludes, after attacking *Common Sense*, that 'the Liberty of the Press is as much block'd up by the Combination of the Printers, Pamphletsellers, Authors, *&c.* or perhaps more, than it would be by an Act of Parliament'.

With her sixth paper, on 24 January 1738, Lady Mary defended something closer to her heart—feminism.[1] Since *Common Sense* a week earlier had treated women condescendingly, she stepped forward to defend them as worthy of respect and sympathy. The intensity of her arguments, which range through scorn, sarcasm, sentimentality, and wit, makes it one of the best essays of all her writings. 'If I was a Divine', goes one of her arguments, 'I would remember, that in their first Creation they were designed a Help for the other Sex, and nothing was ever made incapable of the End of its Creation. 'Tis true, the first Lady had so little Experience that she hearkened to the Persuasions of an impertinent Dangler; and if you mind, he succeeded by persuading her that she was not so wise as she should be.' (The printer eliminated the rest of her sentence: 'and I own I suspect something like this device under the raillerys that are so freely apply'd to the Fair sex.') As another demonstration of her view, the Author states: 'I have some Thoughts of exhibiting a Set of Pictures of such meritorious Ladies, where I shall say nothing of the Fire of their Eyes, or the Pureness of their Complexions; but give them such Praises as befits a rational sensible Being: Virtues of Choice, and not Beauties of Accident.' Although inflamed by her feminist theme, Lady Mary did not forget her journalistic mission: 'Begin then Ladies', she concluded, 'by paying those Authors with Scorn and Contempt, who, with a Sneer of affected Admiration, would throw you below the Dignity of the human Species.' The essay was considered lively enough to be reprinted in the January issue of *The London Magazine*.

Then, for some reason, no issue of *The Nonsense of Common-Sense* appeared until three weeks later. The delay may have been caused by Lady Mary's indecision whether to continue it or by family affairs. The previous autumn her daughter had

---

[1] This essay, the only one known to previous editors and biographers, is reprinted with her letters (ii. 414–18).

returned to London with Lord Bute for her lying-in, and stayed at her parents' house in Cavendish Square until her husband could find one.[1] In January she gave birth to a daughter, and the following month Lady Mary and Wortley stood as god-parents, along with the Duke and Duchess of Argyll.[2]

In her seventh periodical essay, on 14 February 1738, Lady Mary resumed her attack on indecency—especially as pub-lished in *Common Sense*—and on moral cynicism in English life. Her opening sentence, though a typical journalistic pose, had a special aptness to her identity: the Author claims to be indifferent to censures passed on the moral essays, 'neither my Fame nor Fortune being any way affected by their Success'. When she sent the printer her eighth essay—on public virtue and private vice—she jotted a message on the back, asking him to call on her the following evening 'having many matters to communicate'. Almost certainly she wished to discuss the con-tinuation of the paper, which had not caught on with the public.

In Milan Algarotti had finally seen his dialogues printed in December 1737 as *Il Newtonianismo per le dame*, with a dedication not to Madame du Châtelet, but to the venerable Fontenelle. In it he complimented the ladies as 'that half of our World, which always commands the votes of the other'.[3] (By a coincidence, at that moment Lady Mary—in the second number of her paper—scolded the ladies for exerting their influence.) Although his book was now published, Algarotti found a new reason to remain in Milan—a young man named Firmaçon, whose company completely enchanted him. In Jan-uary (1738) Madame du Châtelet teased him for his absence: 'Je ne veux point demander ce que vous faites, car je sais que ce sont de ces choses qu'on ne dit point. Vous avez abandonné la philosophie.'[4] She could treat him lightheartedly; Lady Mary's involvement was far deeper and more complicated.

A few days after she had written the essay on morality for the eighth issue of her paper, she sent him a letter revealing not only her emotions but also her activity.

[1] The Wortley Montagus had moved from Covent Garden shortly before Sept. 1731.
[2] *General Eve. Post*, 24–26 Nov. 1737; 19–21 Jan., 18–21 Feb. 1738.
[3] *Sir Isaac Newton's Philosophy Explain'd For the Use of the Ladies*, transl. Elizabeth Carter (1739), iii.
[4] 10 Jan. 1738, *Lettres*, 176.

There needs only your absence to make any place disagreeable to me, but at present we have a complication of every thing in London that is contrary to my inclination—noise, crowd, division, and almost an impossibility of keeping entirely clear of the infection. Though my mind is too well filled with soft remembrances to be penetrable to the rough impressions of faction and nonsense, yet my ears are daily wounded with epidemic madness and my person exposed to the rheumes and disorders incident to this watery climate. I am forced to remember this by a cursed toothache that endeavours to torment me at this very moment, but your idea shall give me stoicism enough to resist it. This is doing a great deal, but you cannot expect me to carry it so far as to be entertaining in my present situation. 'Tis enough that you can make me insensible either to pain or politics, but I must necessarily be dull when the sun and you are both so distant from me. May the spring bring a return of both!

> You, lovely youth, shall my Apollo prove,
> Adorn my verse, and tune my soul to love.[1]

Her tormenting toothache or merely her indecision may have caused the three-week pause before Number IX of *The Non-sense of Common-Sense* succeeded Number VIII; and it too attacked the immorality, cynicism, and depravity in English life. That spirit was especially prevalent in published libels, the Author complains.

I forbear speaking of the Injuries which such Writings may do occasionally to private Families; but they have one very pernicious Effect on the Publick, I mean lessening the Value People ought to set on *Reputation*, which was once a very great Restraint on Vice, even to those whose ill Dispositions inclined them to the Practice of it.—We see now frequently Heaps of miserable Verses sold by the Help of initial Letters, which are sometimes ingeniously contrived to serve for several Names, that the Reader may apply as best suits his own ill Nature, and the Author perhaps escape beating, by throwing the Application from one to another; and this Propagation of Scandal takes off the Fear of it.

In this complaint the Author was relying on Lady Mary's unfortunate experience in pamphlet controversy. Like all the previous numbers of the periodical, the ninth bore the tag that it would be continued as long as the Author thought fit and the public liked it. Neither of these conditions was now met, and

---

[1] 24 Feb. o.s. [1738], Bod. MS, f. 33.

so on 14 March 1738 *The Nonsense of Common-Sense* ceased publication.

Lady Mary's authorship of the series was her only excursion of the kind, although she had written a newspaper letter on inoculation and a *Spectator* essay. She was especially proud of the sixth, on feminism, since she kept the printed essay, and put on the top of it: 'Wrote by me. M.W.M.' Then, on a batch of printed issues she noted: 'All these wrote by me M.W.M. to serve an unhappy worthy man.'[1] Perhaps the unhappy worthy man was an editor, who was paid to see her essays through the press and gather the remaining columns of news items, statistics, and stock reports. Or, it is even remotely possible that she meant Walpole, whom she thus tried to serve; she believed he was worthy, and if she wrote her inscription after June 1738, he was very unhappy over the death of Maria Skerrett, whom he had married less than a year before.

Lady Mary's friendship with her *amie choisie* may explain the mystery of her entrance into political journalism. It was commonly supposed that Miss Skerrett influenced Walpole's policies; Lord Hervey thought so, and anonymous satirists repeated it.[2] Lady Mary later remembered that because of this friendship, which seemed remote from 'power and politics', she had been 'embroiled in a thousand affairs'; she may have had in mind *The Nonsense of Common-Sense*.[3] The paper's effect in the political war was negligible. It was too mild in tone, perhaps too derivative from the *Spectator*, to have much impact. Its circulation was apparently very slight, since it carried no advertising in its columns; and only two incomplete runs survive today to tell of its short existence. But it is important as a phase of Lady Mary's career. Her most forceful argument for feminism she could not divulge to her readers—that the essays came from a woman's pen. As a political and moral reformer she insisted that it was nonsensical to be rabidly partisan or hypocritically noble—that, in short, plain common sense is the best guide for belief and conduct. As a woman, however, in her

[1] The batch (in Yale Univ. Library) contains five, and these are preserved in her autograph drafts along with a sixth; the remaining three are clearly cognate with the others.

[2] *Memoirs*, 748; *The Rival Wives* (1738); *The Rival Wives Answer'd* (1738).

[3] To Lady Pomfret, 1740, ii. 61. Discussed above, p. 119.

friendship with Algarotti, she allowed herself to be guided by her heart.

He had finally left Milan, taking Firmaçon with him, ostensibly bound for Paris; instead he started on a leisurely tour of southern France. As he had instructed her to, Lady Mary addressed her letter to Paris, telling him of her pleasure in recalling their meetings, and of her 'sweet illusion' that he sometimes thought of her.

... J'ai un cœur fait pour entretenir un sylphe [she continued], et si vous étiez un de ces intelligences qui lise dans le fonds de l'âme, vous seriez charmé de voir le mien si rempli de tendresse délicate et désinteressé. Sérieusement, si vos affaires mettaient de l'impossibilité dans votre dessein de venir en Angleterre, et que j'étais bien persuadé que je vous ferais un vrai plaisir de me retirer à Venise, je ne balancerai pas de m'établir dans les états de la Seignorie pour le reste de ma vie, je vous l'assure de bonne foi. C'est assez vous dire que je suis tout à vous.[1]

More than a year had elapsed since her first proposal to retire with him to Italy; and in one of his subsequent letters, as she later reminded him, 'vous m'assurais que en quelque ville que je m'établirais, vous ne manquerez pas de vous rendre, et j'ai choisi Venise comme celle que vous convenait le plus'.[2] But what suited him most in the summer of 1738 was quite different; he preferred to remain in the south of France with his friend.

In London Lady Mary had acquired a new friend, Henrietta, Countess of Pomfret, a pleasantly mediocre person, sympathetic and considerate. Until the Queen's death she had been Lady of the Bedchamber, and her husband Master of the Horse. Since their small income was inadequate for their large family in England, they decided to move to the Continent with two of their daughters. When they left on 8 July 1738, Lady Pomfret wrote a short farewell note to Lady Mary; and four days later, after sending another letter, made an entry in her diary: 'Her wit and charming conversation joined to the most obliging friendship she has in a great many instances showed to me at a time when she could not propose even the return of my passing some hours with her has engaged me extremely to her.' When she received Lady Mary's letters (filled with polite apologies

[1] 15 June o.s. [1738], Bod. MS, ff. 30–31.
[2] 12 Mar. N.S. [1740], Bod. MS, f. 71.

and incisive London gossip) she was charmed, finding them indescribably witty and tender.[1]

Only a few days before her friend departed, Lady Mary received the first letter from Algarotti since he had left Milan; and in it he accused her of not having replied to his previous one. How could he believe she would let his most amiable letter go unanswered? she asked. No, it was only an artifice to excuse his silence, but she forgave him, for her memory of him was the only pleasure in her life. 'The enthusiasm you have infected me with is as violent as ever', she confessed; and she fully displayed it in a mixture of French, English, and verse. 'J'ai été la Penelope de votre absence', she told him, seeing herself as another classical prototype.[2] Her gallery of self-identifications —Sappho, Dido, and now Penelope—were all women deserted by their lovers. Her gallery also reveals that in her extravagant love she was to some extent indulging her imagination in the same kind of language which her own admirers had once lavished on her.

When she finally received the pleasure of a letter, it contained his accusation that since her love had begun so precipitously it could not last. Her denial had a desperate urgency.

Votre indifférence, votre oubli même (tout cruel qu'il est) m'est plus supportable que votre injustice. Je ne saurais souffrir un moment que vous me croyiez capable de n'être pas toute ma vie occupé de vous. Non, vous ne me connaissez point; j'ai une constance et une probité qui doivent tenir lieu des charmes et d'agréments, et malgré la promptitude avec laquelle vous m'avez plu, je suis assez difficile à plaire, et par conséquence incapable de changer l'objet de mon attachement.[3]

If only she had treated him as casually as his other admirers sometimes did! Lord Hervey playfully scolded him for not writing.[4] Madame du Châtelet was delighted to hear of his being in France, and hoped that in Paris he would receive the applause his charming book deserved. In her candid opinion, confided to their friend Maupertuis, his book was a trifling imitation of Fontenelle with some elegances, and would succeed with the

[1] Finch MS D3, ff. 1, 9; 20/9 Sept. 1738, D4 i.
[2] 11 July o.s. [1738], Bod. MS, ff. 22–23.
[3] 24 July o.s. [1738], Bod. MS, ff. 24–25.
[4] 24 July o.s. 1738, Murray MS.

frivolous and not the wise. (Her opinion was coloured by her resentment that his book should be set up as a rival to Voltaire's *Élements de Newton*.)[1] Since Lady Mary assumed that Algarotti had reached Paris, she was puzzled and irritated by his failure to reply to some of her letters sent there. In August she told him so in a brief note ending: 'Je n'ose entrer en détail de mes sentiments. Imaginez ce que j'ai à vous dire, accablée comme je suis de votre silence.'[2] When her unhappy complaint reached Paris, he was still in the south of France with his companion.

At the same time as Lady Mary wrote these *cris du cœur*, she sent Lady Pomfret the stiff aristocratic letters suitable to a lady of her age and rank. 'We are as much blinded in England by politics and views of interest as we are by mists and fogs', she remarked at the end of July 1738, 'and 'tis necessary to have a very uncommon constitution not to be tainted with the distempers of our climate.' Only a few months had passed since she herself had written essays for a political weekly; yet she continued to strike the pose of retirement. 'I moralise in my own dressing-room on the events I behold,' she said in September, 'and pity those who are more concerned in them than myself.' Her retirement from the world of affairs led quite naturally to her mentioning retirement from England altogether, and in October she told Lady Pomfret: 'The delightful description of your retirement makes me wish to partake it with you; but I have been so much accustomed to wish in vain, that I dare not flatter myself with so pleasing an idea.'[3] This polite, conventional remark may have been a shrewd social preparation for an unconventional retirement.

Algarotti finally arrived in Paris in the autumn, and found her letters there. One of them offended him, and he told her so. Her reply was as abject as he could wish:

Je suis trop touché par vos manières d'agir avec moi. Qu'avez vous vu de si désobligeante dans ma dernière lettre? Plût au dieu que je reçevrai des pareilles marques de votre attachement pour moi. Mais je ne suis pas fait pour inspirer la tendresse que je suis capable de sentir, et j'ai tort de m'offenser. . . . j'ai si peu d'idée de trouver rien autre agréable, je voudrais de tout mon cœur, si je perds l'espérance de vous voir, perdre la vie dans le même instant.[4]

---

[1] 27 Aug., 1 Sept. 1738, *Lettres*, 227, 229.   [2] 20 Aug. N.S. [1738], Murray MS.
[3] ii. 24–25, 27, 28.   [4] Add. to Paris, Murray MS.

Her extreme adulation invited his pitilessness. With the new year (1739) there was still no letter from him, and she appealed to him in a brief one of her own: 'J'ai juré de ne plus vous écrire jusqu'à j'entends de vos nouvelles. On a beau jurer quand l'inclination entraine. . . .' The homage that would make her happiness, she told him, he perhaps squandered on a painted and gilded Parisienne; and she begged for a little amiable letter.[1]

The next month, probably, she received a letter of a different kind: he told her that he believed she loved him, but that he had no money with which to go to England and stay there; more bluntly, that if she were sincere, she would give him the money he required. This can be conjectured from her reply, in which she assured him of her sincerity and good faith. 'Vous pouvez croire que je suis beaucoup plus content de faciliter votre retour que votre départ, quoique j'avoue que je tremble et ma philoso-phie m'abandonne quand je songe que je vous verrai peut-être cherchant d'autres attachements;—mais laissons ces réflections; je veux m'aveugler là-dessus.' She did not know how to send him a money-note, she continued, and thought it better for him to draw the sum agreed from Tribble, her jeweller near Soho Square, of whose discretion she had a good opinion, though she had never put it to any test. He replied ungraciously, offended that she should offer him such a note—perhaps because it was not easily negotiable. That is implied by her apology and ex-planation. 'Que vous êtes injuste, et que vous me connaissez mal! Mais êtes vous obligé de me connaitre? Vous m'avez trop peu vu, mais pourtant il me semble qu'une tendresse à l'épreuve de l'absence et de la silence doit produire plus de confiance.' She now sent him a bill of exchange as he wanted it, and added that she could reproach herself for nothing except her weakness in loving him.[2]

She could still cast a cold eye on the amorous absurdities of other women. Lady Henrietta Herbert, the young widowed daughter of the Earl of Waldegrave, had insisted on marrying John Beard the singer, which 'furnished the tea-tables . . . with fresh tattle' for a fortnight. Lady Mary's comment to Lady

---

[1] 8 Jan. o.s. [1739], Bod. MS, f. 61.
[2] Murray MS; 12 Mar. o.s. [1739], Bod. MS, f. 60. Dating her letters is particularly problematic; I have assumed that these two belong together because both refer to a *billet de change*.

Pomfret was that since the young lady was capable of such low amours 'I really saw no method of saving *her* from ruin, and her *family* from dishonour, but by poisoning her; and offered to be at the expense of the arsenic, and even to administer it with my own hands' if she were invited to tea that evening. Lady Herbert's disgrace led her to reflect on one of her favourite subjects: 'Such examples are very detrimental to our whole sex; and are apt to influence the other into a belief that we are unfit to manage either liberty or money.'[1] How did she reconcile her own behaviour with her moral pronouncement? If her friendship with Algarotti went beyond the bounds of convention, she could rationalize it by the fact that as a wife and mother she had paid her debt to morality. Besides, she proposed to conduct her life *à deux* without openly breaking out of those bounds.

Her fervent desire that the spring would bring Algarotti back to her was at last granted—with the aid of a bill of exchange. Some time in March 1739 he reached London to renew his friendships and pursue his advancement. At first he stayed with Andrew Mitchell, a young barrister (later diplomat); then, that friend not offering sufficient scope for his ambition, he moved on to Lord Hervey's lodgings in St. James's Palace. He saw his book on Newton published in an English translation; and Lord Hervey solicitously sent copies to influential friends, and his own copy to Lord Carteret.[2] But the influence he could command had waned since the death of the Queen and the weakening of Walpole's Ministry. When Algarotti realized that no substantial favours could come from his old friendship, he moved on again—this time to the Earl of Burlington, wealthy patron of the arts and a friend of Pope. At Lord Burlington's Palladian villa on the Thames at Chiswick, not far from Lady Mary's Twickenham house, he enjoyed living in lavish elegance and shining in a varied circle of friends.

During these weeks Lady Mary must have seen him as often as he would permit. When her impetuous emotion overflowed, she expressed it in verse which she sent to him, probably at this time:

> Prepared to rail, and quite resolved to part,
> What magic is it awes my trembling heart?

---

[1] ii. 34–35.   [2] To Algarotti, 8 Mar. 1739, Murray MS.

PLATE II

Letter from Lady M. W. Montagu to Algarotti, 16 July 1739

From Bodleian Library, MS Don, c. 56, f. 52

At that fair vision all resentments fly,
And on my tongue half-formed reproaches die;
My beating heart one tender glance disarms,
I faint—and find all Heaven within his arms.[1]

In their conversations together, she later reminded him, he agreed to retire with her to the Venetian States, and he swore to her that he would bring her a happiness beyond imagining.[2] By the beginning of May they had agreed on their plan. In a letter to Lady Pomfret she again mentioned it, now more pointedly, among the dull compliments. 'Nothing can be more agreeable or more obliging than your letter. I can give you no greater proof of the impression it made on me than letting you know that you have given me so great an inclination to see Italy once more, that I have serious thoughts of setting out the latter end of this summer.'[3] Her 'inclination to see Italy' was the road she hoped would lead her to 'happiness beyond imagining'.

When Algarotti saw no solid advantages in Lord Burlington's friendship, he shifted to a new active patron. Lord Baltimore, an officer in the Prince of Wales's household, had been appointed emissary to the Russian Court for the marriage of the Princess of Mecklenburg, heiress to the throne; and Algarotti accepted his invitation to accompany him there on his yacht. They sailed 10 May on the mission, which was to last several months. Lady Mary made preparations for her own journey to Italy. Unable to repress her ardour, she wrote to him in St. Petersburg after the middle of July to tell him: 'Je pars pour vous chercher. Ce n'est pas nécessaire d'accompagner une belle preuve d'un attachement éternelle d'une broderie de parolles. Je vous donne rendezvous à Venise.' She had intended to meet him *en route*, but it was more discreet and certain to meet him at the end of her pilgrimage. Then she instructed him not to write to her any more in London; a letter found there would have very unfortunate consequences.[4]

She did not take much baggage with her, having arranged with her husband for most of it to be sent to Italy later by boat. During her final weeks in London she made farewell visits to

[1] MS in Municipal Library, Treviso, Italy.
[2] 24 Dec. n.s. 1739, 12 Mar. n.s. [1740], [24 July 1739], Bod. MS, ff. 69, 71, 66.   [3] 2 May 1739, ii. 39–40.
[4] 16 July o.s. [1739], Bod. MS, ff. 51–52.

old friends like Lady Irwin and the Dowager Duchess of Marlborough.[1] The day before she departed, she sent Algarotti her
last note from England:

Enfin je pars demain avec la résolution d'un homme bien persuadé
de sa religion, et contente de sa conscience, rempli de foi et d'espérance. Je laisse mes amis pleurant ma perte et franche le pas hardi-
ment pour un autre monde. Si je vous trouve tel que vous m'avez
juré, je trouve les champs élysée, et la félicité au delà de l'imagination; si—mais je ne veux plus douter; et du moins je veux jouir de
mes espérances. Si vous voulez me recompenser tout ce que je
sacrifie, hâtez vous me trouver à Venise, où je presserai mon arrivé
autant qu'il m'est possible.[2]

In spite of her inflated style—'friends weeping for my loss' is
surely an exaggeration—she seemed sincerely touching. In her
fifty years she had endured much disappointment and pain;
now she 'took a leap bravely for another world', even though
she wished to doubt Algarotti no more but only to revel in her
hopes.

On 25 July she left London early in the morning, accompanied by two servants, a man and a maid. By noon she reached
Dartford, after having stopped for an hour to visit the Duchess
of Montagu. She sent a brief businesslike note to Wortley, asking him to write to her at Dover, where she arrived the following day. Instead of waiting for the packet, which sailed at night,
she hired a boat for five guineas. 'The wind is fair,' she told her
husband, 'and I hope to be in Calais to-morrow. I cannot say I
am well, but I think not worse for my journey.'[3] So far as he
knew, she journeyed abroad for the purpose of mending her
health; but in her own mind, or at least to that side of it which a
handsome, sympathetic young Italian had aroused, she travelled
toward Elysium.

---

[1] To W, 17 July 1748, ii. 168; to Lady Bute, 29 July 1758, ii. 329.
[2] [24 July 1739], Bod. MS, f. 66.
[3] ii. 40, 41.

XI. *Venetian Civilities*

(1739–40)

LADY MARY's letters to Algarotti clearly set forth one reason
why she went abroad, but it was not the only one. She had once
told her sister (in 1727): 'I have a mind to cross the water, to
try what effect a new heaven and a new earth will have upon
my spirit.'[1] During the intervening decade her spirit had encountered a variety of ordeals. Why then, when her family
burdens had been lifted (though unhappily) and her marriage
had long since lost its savour, should she not have decided to
cross the water? The journey would also improve her health,
as Wortley solicitously agreed. All these reasons help to explain,
negatively, why she left England; her rendezvous with Algarotti gave her a positive impetus.

She guarded that secret so well that, except for Lord Hervey,
none of her friends or family knew of it. When inquisitive
people inquired she offered evasive explanations: to Spence that
she travelled 'because she could not bear to see the distresses of
her country', and to others that 'people were grown so stupid
she could not endure their company, all England was infected
with dullness'. The unendurable dullness, conjectured Elizabeth Robinson, was Lady Mary's husband.[2] To explain the
oddness of leaving him, Lady Mary told Lady Pomfret that
although she had persuaded him to travel, she was so much
afraid he would change his mind that she hastened before him;
and then his business and (in October) England's war with
Spain forced him to remain.[3] Yet in their letters she and Wortley
never mentioned his joining her at any time; nor did they try

---

[1] i. 511–12.
[2] 'Anecdotes', Huntington Libr. MS, f. 374; Walpole's 'Anecdotes', *Corr.*
xiv. 245; Eliz. Montagu, *Corr. 1720–61*, ed. E. J. Climenson (1906), i. 50–51.
[3] Dec. 1739, ii. 51.

to meet in later years when he went abroad three times. In her letters to him she consistently stated that her purpose in travelling and living abroad was to improve her poor health. He soberly acknowledged it, assuring her that he was not at all surprised that travelling mended her health, that he had found it a remedy for every disorder of the head or stomach.[1]

Certainly he agreed that she should stay abroad a long time. For the sake of economy and convenience they had arranged to send her baggage after her by boat to the city where she settled. As described in the bill of lading prepared by Wortley, the thirteen parcels contained a bureau of papers, room furnishings of a table, chairs, carpet, and hangings, a box of china, a book case, a box of dressing plate (formerly stored at her banker's), Turkish cloth, a scarlet Turkish costume, riding costumes, a saddle, bridle, and whip, a box of snuff (its dimensions 23 by 16 by 12 inches), and three boxes of books.[2] This library contained about five hundred titles, many of them in two to ten volumes each, and encompassed an astonishing variety: English, French, and Italian plays, romances, fairy tales, novels, biographies, poetry, collections of letters, the Latin classics in the original as well as in English and French translation, Greek writers in translation, dictionaries and grammars in English, Latin, French, Italian, and German, English local histories, collections of periodical essays, 51 volumes of plays, 9 single plays, 137 pamphlets, and 34 volumes of manuscripts. She had also included a copy of Pope's poems and of the Italian and English editions of Algarotti's book on Newton.[3] Her sojourn in Elysium was not to be devoid of intellectual and literary pleasures.

On 26 July 1739, as the shores of England receded, a high wind drove her boat toward France; and after a voyage of less than three hours she arrived at Calais. The customs officers confiscated her snuff, but did not open her jewel boxes. Then she bought a chaise for fourteen guineas, and started south by the most direct route to Italy, one which by-passed Paris. At St. Omers she met and supped with the young Lady Peterborough, who warned her that she would not receive full value

[1] 16 Aug. 1739, ii. 43.
[2] W MS, i. 117–18. It is less specifically described in M to W, 31 Sept. 1739, Paston, 370.
[3] Wharncliffe MS 135 (3). Some of the books may have been W's, according to another list he endorsed (ibid.).

for English guineas, and Lady Mary therefore allowed her money to be converted into a note drawn on a Paris banker. After going through Arras and Péronne to Laon, she found her health and spirits much mended, she informed Wortley; and she would continue southward seeking 'a fine climate' in Burgundy.[1]

Going through Reims and Châlons-sur-Marne she arrived at Dijon, a journey of four to five days. Among the many English living in the town—no fewer than sixteen 'families of fashion' —a daughter of her old friend Lord Bathurst entertained her. In the house where she lodged she met Lord Mansel, who was on the Grand Tour; and he put himself out to be particularly obliging to her. When she offered the landlord her bank-note he refused to accept it until he could have it verified in Paris, which would take more than a week. Without telling her, Lord Mansel went to the landlord and pledged his word for her credit. Grateful for his courtesy but unwilling to make use of it, she waited several days until her bill was accepted. This was the first of many times that English people whom she met abroad treated her with great courtesy and deference. Altogether she remained in Dijon two weeks, finding it so pleasant—she pointed out to Wortley—that she would pass the winter there were it not that the prices were excessive for her allowance. Elsewhere in France, she said, the crowds of English people would keep her from enjoying the quiet retired life she wished: 'I think now of moving very soon, but am yet undetermined as to my place of residence.'[2]

Although she persisted in her conventional reasons to her husband, she had told the secret one to Lord Hervey. Her first letter to him was festive, he commented, 'to show you thought you had left nothing behind you worth lamenting'. From Dijon she sent him her third letter, in which she proposed that he follow her abroad, but he refused; 'unless you could give me the same motive that you have for jolting in post-chaises and lying in dirty inns, I do not see I should get much by taking your advice, . . . for you . . . are to enjoy his [Mahomet's] Paradise upon earth. You are in the right to take the pilgrim's

[1] To W, 27 July, ii. 41; 27 Aug. 1739, *Cat. of Morrison Coll.* iv. 286; also in *Rev. of Eng. Stud.* iv (1928), 327–30.
[2] To W, 27 Aug. 1739.

staff in your hand.'¹ For both love and health, her pilgrimage lay to the south.

From Dijon, at the beginning of September, she sailed down the Saône to Lyons, a disagreeable but cheap trip. In Lyons she met Lady Pomfret's son, Lord Lempster, who attended an academy there. He visited her several times, and took her to the opera. 'The most beautiful and the best-behaved young man I ever saw', she described him to his mother, by then settled in Siena. Lyons was agreeable as a place of residence, but it, too, was overrun by English people, she told Wortley, and so she was resolved on Turin, where she hoped 'to be unknown, and live at as little expense' as she pleased.²

She left Lyons on 13 September 1739, and travelled over safe roads to Pont-de-Beauvoisin, the last French frontier town. At the inn where she lodged she met Lady Irwin's brother, Lord Carlisle of Castle Howard, and he offered her all the civilities he could. Since he had already supped, he lent her his cook, for ordinarily she refused to eat at the public table in inns; as she explained to Wortley: 'the decency of my sex confines me to eat in my chamber'—for which she paid double.³ Lord Carlisle, who was returning home after a sojourn in Italy, advised her on where to settle. His first choice was Rome, his second Venice. But Rome, he warned, could be unpleasant because the Pretender lived there and caused political intrigue. Lady Mary would therefore try the second city, she told Wortley: 'if I find Venice too cold or moist (which I am more afraid of), I can remove very easily.'⁴

She now had ahead of her the dangerous Alpine pass of Mount Cenis. Before starting she notified Wortley: 'I hasten to cross the Alps, being told that the rains very often fall in this month, which will make the passage more disagreeable.'⁵ At the same time, she sent Algarotti a passionate affirmation of her pilgrimage.

Me voici aux pieds des Alpes, et demain je franche le pas qui doit me conduire en Italie. Je me recommande à vous dans tous les périls comme Don Quichotte à sa Dulcinée, et je n'ai pas l'imagination

---

¹ 28/17 Aug. 1739, Bristol MS.
² To W, Paston, 372; to Lady Pomfret, 11 Sept., ii. 45; to W, 1 Sept. 1739, Paston, 368.   ³ 23 May 1742, ii. 111.   ⁴ 10 Sept. o.s. 1739, ii. 44.
⁵ Paston, 368 (corrected from MS).

moins échauffée que lui. Rien m'effraye, rien me dissipe un moment; receuilli en moi-même ni les fatigues de la poste, ni les plaisirs qu'on m'a proposé dans les villes, m'ont distrait un instant de la douce contemplation où je suis plongé—

> Such soft ideas all my pains beguile,
> The Alps are levelled, and the deserts smile;
> These pendant rocks and ever 'during snow,
> These rolling torrents that eternal flow,
> Amidst this chaos that around me lies,
> I only hear your voice, and see your eyes.[1]

Her inflamed imagination had now put her in a new literary role, that of Don Quixote who for a passive Dulcinea faced the frightful dangers of a mountain pass. She had quite uneventfully traversed it twenty years earlier with the Ambassador returning to England.

At Turin, where she stopped for a few days, the English Resident Arthur Villettes called on her; and though she avoided being presented at court because she had no court dress, she could not avoid visits from her countrymen. In Milan, her next stop, she climbed to the top of the great church as proof (to Wortley) that she had recovered her health.[2] About 20 September she left for Venice. Her fairly leisurely journey from England had so far taken about two months, for she knew she would have to wait for Algarotti.

On his journey back to England he and Lord Baltimore had disembarked at Danzig, and travelled overland to Berlin and Potsdam. They called on the Prussian Frederick William I, famous for his stinginess and his regiment of giant soldiers. Then, at the end of September, they visited the court of the Crown Prince Frederick at Rheinsberg. The Prince, twenty-seven at the time, was the antithesis of his Spartan father; he wrote French verse, played the flute, and amused himself with philosophical speculation. As described by a recent biographer: 'He was a very nice, smiling, young man, a little fat, a little feminine, with quick movements and a habit of carrying his head bent over a trifle to his left.'[3] His wife, whom he had married six years before at his father's command, lived also at Rheinsberg, but he spent very little time with her. Solomon, he

---

[1] Bod. MS. f. 67. [2] 10, 25 Sept. 1739, ii. 45, 47.
[3] Pierre Gaxotte, *Fred. the Great*, transl. R. A. Bell (1942), 176.

remarked, found a seraglio of women not enough: 'I have one, and that is too much for me.'[1] Although historians disagree, according to some contemporary opinion Frederick's 'unnatural tastes' made him live apart from his wife.[2] In any case he and Algarotti found each other extremely sympathetic. Since Lord Baltimore spoke French too badly and English too quickly (Frederick complained), Algarotti could shine freely. He and the Prince spoke of everything possible: philosophy, science, poetry, trifles; and the versatile Algarotti composed the libretto for a cantata which the Prince planned to set to music. A few days after Algarotti departed, Frederick wrote to him—dubbing him the Swan of Padua—to assure him that he would never forget the eight-day visit; and to Voltaire, his literary mentor since 1736, he described how enormously the young Algarotti had pleased him. 'Il a beaucoup de feu, de vivacité et de douceur, ce qui m'accommode on ne saurait mieux.'[3]

Algarotti, who had promised that he would return, broke into raptures; he had been in third heaven, he exclaimed to Voltaire. 'Mon Dieu! quel prince est-ce là?'[4] He announced to Lord Hervey that the Prince was 'the lover and favourite of the Muses' and 'the most intelligent and most amiable of men'.[5] Both men told Madame du Châtelet of their mutual delight; and she tossed back to Frederick a well-turned compliment: 'M. Algarotti m'a mandé avec quelle surprise il avait vu V. A. R., la mienne est qu'il ait pu vous quitter.'[6] He had returned to England at the end of September for his third and last visit there.

By then Lady Mary had reached Venice. 'I am at length happily arrived here, I thank God', she piously informed Wortley; and then, continuing her pretence: 'I wish it had been my original plan, which would have saved me some money and fatigue . . . since I am convinced it has greatly contributed to the restoration of my health.' She immediately engaged lodgings on the Grand Canal; and she would stay until the

---

[1] G. P. Gooch, *Fred. the Great The Ruler, the Writer, the Man* (1947), 120.
[2] Earl of Ilchester and Mrs. Langford-Brooke, *Life of Charles Hanbury-Williams* (1928), 216–17. Cf. Gooch, 149.
[3] Fred. to Voltaire, 10 Oct. 1739, Fred.'s *Œuvres* (1850), xxi. 327; to Algarotti, xviii. 4. All letters by or to Fred. come from this edition, unless otherwise cited.   [4] Quoted in Treat, *Algarotti*, 101.
[5] [Sept. 1739], *Letters from Algarotti to Hervey and to Maffei* [on the] *Russian Empire* (1769), ii. 33.   [6] To Fred., 29 Dec. 1739, *Lettres*, 376.

spring carnival, she told Wortley, to see if the air agreed with her and to await the promised visit of Lady Pomfret.[1] After two weeks she had formed a definite impression of the city. The many foreign ambassadors and the Venetian nobility gave it a cosmopolitan air, yet it was still the cheapest place in Europe, particularly with its laws and customs contrived to avoid expense. Amusements like the opera and the comedy, held every night, were very cheap, and since ladies attended them in domino—as they did all public functions—they had no expense of dressing or equipage. The custom of going about in masks, she pointed out to Lady Pomfret, led to another of the felicities of Venice: 'a universal liberty that is certainly one of the greatest *agrémens* in life . . . it is so much the established fashion for everybody to live their own way, that nothing is more ridiculous than censuring the actions of another. This would be terrible in London, where we have little other diversion.'[2] To her husband she emphasized instead the cheapness of living there, which she could manage 'very genteelly' on her allowance, and the great courtesy shown to her by foreign dignitaries and noble Venetians.

For a curious turn of fortune had overtaken her on the Continent, and more clearly in Venice. At home she had outlived many of her friends and friendships; on the Continent she met Europeans, even many of her countrymen, whom she impressed with her charm and vivacity. She was to some extent liberated from her unfortunate past of literary notoriety and family feuds. Her new life in Italy enabled her to enjoy the characteristic hospitality of the country. She had contemplated a solitary pilgrimage to Venice and private bliss in the company of a young Italian. Instead she had suffered too much company on the road, and had been entertained wherever she stopped. As she described her popularity: 'I find (contrary to the rest of the world) I did not think myself so considerable as I am; for I verily believe, if one of the pyramids of Egypt had travelled, it could not have been more followed.'[3]

Two of the important Venetians who honoured her were friends of former days. The Abbé Conti called to offer what civilities he could. Her other old friend, Pietro Grimani, had

---

[1] ii. 46, 47.   [2] 10 Oct., 6 Nov. 1739, ii. 47-48, 50.
[3] To W, ii. 49, 46.

been Venetian ambassador in London, and was now Procurator of St. Mark's—and soon to be elected Doge of Venice. He had always retained his great partiality for the English.[1] He put himself out to oblige her, brought his niece to invite her to stay at their palace (an invitation she graciously declined), and introduced her to the leading Venetian families. 'As he takes pains to appear my friend,' she told Wortley, 'his relations and allies, of both sexes (which are the most considerable people here), endeavour to oblige me in all sort of ways.' He joined her for her literary evenings too. Throughout her life she never gave up her literary interests, and in Venice, after she had been there for a short time, she boasted to Wortley: 'My house is properly a meeting of Literati; the Procurator Grimani seldom fails coming when I am at home, and the Abbé Conti never.'[2] At Grimani's death (twelve years later) she recalled receiving 'every good office from him I could have expected from a tender father, or a kind brother'.[3] As an intellectual Englishwoman she was doubly favoured by this eminent Venetian.

In the diplomatic corps the Spanish Ambassador, Prince Campoflorido, and his wife accorded her great hospitality, and entertained her at a dinner where they could not have shown her more honours if she had been an ambassadress. Even after England's declaration of war against Spain, in October 1739, the Spanish ambassadress remained one of her best friends. She was, in Lady Mary's opinion, 'one of the best sort of women I ever knew'. The Papal Nuncio also paid her particular courtesies; he visited her house and offered her the use of his box at the opera.[4]

While pleased by her honours and dignities, she wanted to utilize her exalted friendships. She believed that government officials in general did not guard themselves against a woman's observations as they might a man's.[5] Her possible usefulness as a political informer arose from the fact that England did not maintain full diplomatic relations with the Republic. (The Resident had been recalled because the Young Pretender on a tour of Italy in 1737 had been received in Venice with royal

---

[1] James Gray to Holderness, 8 Mar. 1752, SP 99/65.
[2] ii. 49; 11 Dec. 1739, ii. 52; 21 Jan. 1740, Paston, 375.
[3] To Lady Bute, 16 Mar. 1753, ii. 232.
[4] To W, ii. 48; 20 Nov. 1739, W MS, i. 332; 25 Jan. 1740, ii. 54; ii. 49.
[5] To W, 12 Oct. 1741, ii. 97.

honours.) An English consul was maintained, however, with commercial duties; at this time Niel Browne, a man of eighty, and in Lady Mary's opinion a thoroughly ineffectual agent.[1] At the beginning of November 1739, when she told Wortley of her new friendships, she put forth her proposal: 'If you would have me, I will inform you of all I hear amongst the Foreign Ministers.' In reply, Wortley outlined his strategy: to send him news in a disguised hand or written by her maid, and to address it to him under another name at an inn in Holborn. 'If I could have any good intelligence from abroad,' he concluded, 'it might be of use to me in many respects.'[2] But instead of following his instructions, she waited until she could send him a letter privately by a friend returning to England. Such an opportunity did not arise until some months later; and she then informed him: 'I have sent you a letter by Lord Mansel, in which you will find a full answer to yours of January 1, and something that will much surprise you.'[3] All her honours and opportunities had come as an accompaniment to the primary purpose of her sojourn in Venice. That purpose was still unfulfilled.

Algarotti had reached London by the end of September 1739. Lord Hervey at Bath welcomed him with great cordiality, offering to do anything to make his stay in England pleasant.[4] The young Italian's thoughts were not on Lady Mary, whose letters he did not answer, but undoubtedly on his host at Rheinsberg. Frederick was delighted that he still cherished the memory of the place, and assured him: 'Souvenez-vous toujours des amis que vous vous êtes faits içi en vous montrant simplement, et jugez de ce que ce serait, si nous avions le plaisir de vous posséder toujours.'[5] Of the three people who wished to possess the irresistible young Italian, Lady Mary had gone farthest, literally and figuratively. She wrote to Lord Hervey in October to tell him of her satisfaction with Venice and of her friendship with the ambassadors, but said nothing of her anxiety about Algarotti. In his garrulous reply, Lord Hervey offered chatter and compliments before treating what he knew

[1] To W, 28 June [1740], W MS, i. 359-60.
[2] 1 Nov. 1739, 1 Jan. [o.s. 1740], W MS, i. 330-1, 158-9.
[3] 28 June [1740].   [4] 29 Sept. 1739, Murray MS.
[5] 29 Oct. 1739, xviii. 6-7.

she wanted to know. 'Our friend is in London. He dined with me today. I did not say I had heard from you because you gave me no directions to do so; and whenever I am afraid to err whatever I do, I generally prefer tacit to loquacious errors, as they are easier corrected, and their consequences not so dangerous. Whatever instructions you send I will execute, but do not let them be too delicate or too refined. . . .'[1] He needed no instructions, for Algarotti himself wrote to Lady Mary a few weeks later.

He accused her of too eagerly pursuing the pleasurable social life of Venice, and suggested that they might instead settle in Paris. She was angered by his accusations; and sustained by her new dignity among the Venetians, she mustered courage to answer him with unusual firmness.

J'ai de la peine à croire que tous mes lettres, que j'ai envoyé par différents routes, vous ont manqué, mais même quand cela aurait arrivé, il me semble encore plus extraordinaire que vous pouviez imaginer que je coure le monde pour voir des carnivals et des fêtes. Vous devez vous souvenir que vous êtes convenu avec moi de vivre dans les états de Venise, et je ne peux pas deviner aucune nouvelle raison pour vous détourner de ce dessein. J'ai rangé tous mes affaires sur cet plan, et il n'est pas possible que je va à Paris quand même j'aurais un envie, que je suis très éloigné d'avoir. J'ai assez fait pour prouver le désir de passer ma vie avec vous. Il est sûr que si je ne suis pas capable de faire votre bonheur, vous ne pouvez pas faire le mien. Je ne prétends pas vous gener. J'ai reçu içi beaucoup plus des civilités et même honneurs que je ne mérite; et je menerai une vie assez douce si elle n'était troublé par le souvenir d'un ingrat qui m'a oublié dans un exile qu'il a causé.[2]

Her pride did not allow her to tell Lord Hervey of her disappointment and indignation; she only emphasized the honours she received in Venice. He knew well enough the purpose of her 'pilgrimage' there. At the end of December, he interrupted a long letter to her: 'I had written thus far when our friend came into the room. I did not tell [him] to whom I was writing, and as you decline giving me any directions for my conduct, am at a loss to know what sort of conduct I should hold . . . and shall not tell [him] what I really believe, which is that as [a Venetian] when you was at London made you forget every

[1] 2 Nov. 1739, Bristol MS.   [2] 24 Dec. [1739], Bod. MS, f. 69.

Englishman, so a Piedmontese at Venice will make you forget every Venetian.'[1] It was a cruelly ironic joke. Perhaps Algarotti joined him in laughing.

On the same day that Lady Mary sent the Venetian in London her angry letter she sent one of her customary reports to Wortley, telling him of the young Lord Granby's visit to Venice, of Lady Pomfret's delay in visiting, of compliments from Grimani, who—she did not fail to add—treated her with great amiability. As to her remaining in Venice, she would if the weather remained favourable.[2] After writing these contrasting letters, she went off to enjoy one of the honours she could boast of in both. It was Christmas Eve; and the Doge of Venice, who celebrated High Mass in the Cathedral of St. Mark, invited her and the Prince of Wolfenbuttel (nephew of the Austrian Empress) to his private gallery. When she arrived, the Doge's niece met her at the palace gate and conducted her through to the cathedral. Although she had no sympathy and often great contempt for Catholic ritual, she curiously watched the ceremony, and was happily 'not obliged to any act of adoration'.[3] She could tell her husband such thoughts and events with complete candour.

On his side Wortley was a methodical husband and manager. He regularly remitted her allowance of £245 a quarter, which with £150 a year from her father's bequest brought her yearly income up to £1,130.[4] He could not ship her baggage immediately because the war between England and Spain made an unescorted ship subject to seizure by the enemy. He waited until he could ship it to Leghorn escorted by a convoy.[5] She disliked being deprived of her possessions; and although she posed to Lady Pomfret as being 'wrapt up among my books with antiquarians and virtuosi', she had to borrow a copy of Horace to quote a passage to Wortley. She then reminded him how impatient she was to receive her own books.[6]

A more important matter she discussed with him was their children. By obeying his request to correspond with them, she clearly regarded her exile as no exemption from family respon-

---

[1] 31 Dec. 1739, Bristol MS. (Words struck out are here inserted.)
[2] 24 Dec. [1739], W MS, i. 335.   [3] 25 Dec. 1739 o.s., ii. 53.
[4] M to W, 19, 25 June 1740, W MS, i. 361-2, 363-4.
[5] W's memo., W MS, i. 115; M to W, 29 Mar. 1740, ii. 58.   [6] ii. 51, 52.

sibilities. On his side, by his reliance on her opinion of their son, he put some faith in her judgement. Her son's unfortunate marriage could not be set aside, for his wife virtuously refused to provide grounds for divorce. In Lady Mary's view, she was not young enough to attract gallants, and not rich enough to buy them.[1] In England young Wortley—more often known under his last name, Montagu—had taken advantage of his position as presumptive heir to his wealthy father and borrowed heavily from money-lenders. Since his father refused to pay the debts, he had to remain on the Continent to avoid the debtors' prison. In Italy, before Lady Mary's arrival, he had tried to impose on the Procurator Grimani, and then in Florence had been received by Horace Mann, who recognized his authentic if disreputable identity.[2] By the time Lady Mary settled in Venice she was embittered almost beyond hope by her son's indiscretions and moral instability. As she confessed to her husband: "'tis long since that I have looked upon the hopes of continuing a family as one of the vainest of mortal prospects.'[3] In spite of her cynicism Wortley relied on her to serve as a buffer and referee.

As her sojourn in Venice lengthened, she found it increasingly delightful and dignifying. With the approach of the carnival season, throngs of visitors arrived from all over Europe. They ranked from sovereign royalty to private gentlemen on the Grand Tour. Frederick Christian, the Electoral Prince of Saxony, eldest son of the King of Poland, arrived about Christmas, and took a house next to hers. Since she had been 'particularly well acquainted' with his mother in Vienna, she looked forward to attending his receptions. His governor, Count Wackerbarth, was the son of a lady whom she had known intimately in Vienna, and so he specially favoured her, and obliged the Prince to do the same.[4] As the festival season advanced, the Prince graciously continued to favour her. He was badly crippled and of poor intellect, but a civil and well-tempered young man.[5] He invited her into his box at the opera; and when the Senate tendered him a great ball on Shrove Tuesday

---

[1] To W, 25 Apr. 1742, ii. 108–9.   [2] M to W, 17 June 1740, Paston, 385.
[3] 25 Dec. 1739 o.s., ii. 53.
[4] To Lady Pomfret, to W, ii. 51, 53. The 'Heads' of her letters from Turkey lists the 'Countess of Wackerbarth' (i. 17).
[5] Hanbury-Williams, *Works* (1822), ii. 216.

(1 March), she was led in by the Procurator Grimani, and at the Prince's request placed at his side.[1] In spite of the loss of Algarotti's company, she found other satisfying pleasures in the city of their rendezvous.

In London Algarotti had maintained a busy correspondence with Crown Prince Frederick, mostly about literary matters. When he did not answer promptly enough, the Prince gently prodded him, 'car vous pouvez être persuadé que je vous aime et vous estimerai toujours'.[2] At about the same time that Algarotti received this assurance of continued royal favour, Lady Mary received a letter from him—probably a belated reply to her indignant one in December. He now proposed a new scheme for their retirement: instead of Italy, which he thought unsuitable, he would prefer France or Geneva or Holland. 'Pourquoi si peu de sincerité?' she began her firm reply. He had not, as he claimed, remonstrated against Italy; and she had chosen Venice as the city most agreeable to him. As he knew, the least of his desires would have sent her even to Japan! Geneva and Holland, since they were always filled with English people, were not suitable. Then, to emphasize how great a sacrifice she would make for his sake, she told him how in Venice she had found amenities and honours.

Enfin je me trouve miraculeusement beaucoup plus à mon aise qu'à Londres. Il est sûr que je quitterais une seconde fois toutes les commodités de ma vie pour faire le bonheur de la vôtre si j'étais persuadé que j'y étais nécessaire. Soyez assez honnête homme pour penser sérieusement là dessus. Consultez votre cœur. S'il vous dit que vous seriez heureux auprès de moi, je sacrifie tout pour cela. Ce n'est plus un sacrifice; votre amitié et votre conversation feront les délices de ma vie. Il n'est pas possible que nous vivons dans la même maison, mais vous pourriez loger près de chez moi, et me voir tous les jours si vous voudriez. Dit moi naïvement vos pensées. S'il est vrai que le goût vous détermine à choisir ce plan, je retournerais en France, et m'établirais en quelque ville de province, où nous pourrions vivre en tranquillité.[3]

Her new existence in Venice had moderated the expression of her passion; and now, in the absence of poetical flights of amorous imagination, a clearer design emerges. In sober prose, she wished to live with him in tranquillity; she would stay in a

---

[1] M to W, 15 Feb., 16 Mar. 1740, Paston, 376, 378.
[2] 26 Feb. 1740, xviii. 8–10.   [3] 12 Mar. N.S. [1740], Bod. MS, ff. 71–72.

separate house and would enjoy his friendship and conversation. Whether there was any element of sexual passion in her love is doubtful; although she was touched deeply by him, she was too well aware of his limitations. Algarotti's tastes were predominantly if not entirely homosexual; his soft graces and tender sympathies had in fact strongly attracted her. Conversely, she frequently assumed a masculine aggressiveness in her correspondence with him. In her early letter echoing Dido's lament, when she had extolled herself as 'l'ami le plus parfait et l'amante la plus passioné', she had continued: 'J'aurais été ravi que la nature m'avait permis de me borner à cet premier titre; j'enrage d'avoir été fait pour porter des juppes.

> Why was my haughty soul to woman joined?
> Why this soft sex imposed upon my mind?
> Even this extravagance which now I send
> Were meritorious in the name of friend.
> Thee I might follow, thee my lovely guide,
> Charmed with thy voice, and ever by thy side,
> Nor land nor sea our common way divide.
>   How much these golden wishes are in vain!
> I dream to pleasure, but I awake to pain.'

At the foot of the Alps she had seen herself as Don Quixote on a quest for Dulcinea. In Venice, however, the pleasure of her dreams and the pain of her awakening were both moderated. If she hoped that her tactful pliancy would encourage him to act, she was disappointed; he remained in England.

She made the best of her 'exile'. On 4 May, for the first time in thirty years, a great regatta was held to honour the Prince of Saxony. Although she could have watched the spectacle from her rooms on the Grand Canal, she did not refuse the Procurator's invitation to watch it from his palace, where at a great reception she was 'nobly entertained'. She was still startled by all the exalted honours paid to her, and could hardly believe it was herself 'dressed up at balls, and stalking about at assemblies'. She was amazed that after travelling a thousand miles to establish herself 'in the bosom of a republic, with a design to lose all memory of kings and courts', she should find herself seated next to a sovereign prince, and herself courted by all as though she were a 'sovereign princess'.[1] Taking advantage of her exalta-

[1] To W, 19 Apr., 1 June 1740, ii. 59, 64–66; to Lady Pomfret, ii. 61, 53.

tion, she had already proposed to send political intelligence to her husband, but after the arrival of the Prince of Saxony, she applied to a more important recipient. At the beginning of May (1740) she wrote a letter to Walpole desiring to know 'in what manner I could send intelligence, if anything happened to my knowledge that could be of use to England'. She transmitted her letter through Lord Hervey; and he replied that Sir Robert

has desired me to thank you for your remembrance of him, and the offer you make of opening a farther correspondence; but as the subject of that correspondence must depend on the Prince of ––––
[Saxony] remaining where you are, and on a more secure canal [channel] than the common post being found out for this negotiation, the difficulties of adjusting the last point, and the design of soon removing the Prince of –––– to another place, has induced Sir R. W. to confine his answer to you, to the thanks I have already mentioned, and to ordering me to let you know he thinks himself obliged to you for the trouble you have taken, and for that you are ready to give yourself, and is sorry things are so circumstanced as not to allow him the pleasure of continuing a commerce which if it had not been for the obstacles I have mentioned would in every light have been so agreeable to him.

Behind these verbal convolutions lay a simple refusal. As Lady Mary interpreted it, Walpole 'imagined that I wanted some gratification, and only sent me cold thanks'.[1]

Young Englishmen on the Grand Tour, when they stopped in Venice, did not fail to call on her. She suffered 'inundations of them', she complained, as they took over her apartment for their refuge.[2] Lady Pomfret, who had taken lodgings in Florence in December 1739, gave a letter of introduction to the Prince de Beauvau, son of the head of the Tuscan Regency; and in return Lady Mary thanked her for sending 'the most agreeable young man I have seen in my travels'.[3] She informed Wortley that he had arrived with Lord Shrewsbury, and added: 'they came to see me as soon as they arrived, as all strangers do'.[4] Among her young visitors was Jan Teding van Berkhout, heir of a patrician Dutch family, who had been

---

[1] 21/10 June 1740, Bristol MS; M to W, 17 Feb. 1744, ii. 128. She also told Horace Mann of her offer (Mann to Walpole, 30 July 1741, *Corr.* xvii. 98).
[2] To Lady Pomfret, 17 Feb., to W, 19 Apr. 1740, ii. 56, 59.
[3] 21 Jan., Finch MS D 4 ii; 17 Feb. 1740, ii. 55.
[4] 15 Mar. 1740, Paston, 378.

travelling through France and Italy since the year before. He dutifully kept a full diary of his observations and impressions.[1] On the evening of 18 May he was conducted to the house of the Spanish Ambassador, and—as he wrote in his diary—'le Prince Ajaci me présenta à l'ambassadeur et l'ambassadrice, qui me reçurent très poliment et gracieusement. Il y avait de compagnie le nonce du Pape, deux dames vénitiennes, et une dame anglaise Mylady Montagú. On y causa jusqu'à minuit lorsqu'on se retirait....' The young Dutchman thus observed Lady Mary among the notable company she boasted about in her letters. Two days later, when he went sightseeing with Lord Mansel, who had been in Venice for several weeks, they met another young Englishman, Sir Henry Englefield, with whom Lady Mary had spoken several days before.[2] Led by Lord Mansel, they all called on her at her own house. That night van Berkhout dutifully set down his fresh, perhaps ingenuous, impression of her. 'Elle est une dame déjà d'un certain age. Elle passe pour une femme d'esprit et même savante. Son mari était en angleterre, et avait été ambassadeur à Constantinople, où depuis elle avait pris tant de goût pour voyager qu'elle s'était brouillé avec son mari, et pris ce prétexte pour aller voir l'Italie. Il était six mois qu'elle se trouvait à Venise. Elle avait sa maison, femme et valet de chambre. [Nous] restâmes une bonne heure à causer avec elle....' Later that day he made other calls, one to the Prince of Saxony, who graciously entertained him.

The young Dutchman soon decided to adopt the local custom of *cicisbeism,* and attached himself to the pretty Signora Marina Buonvicini. On 25 May he wrote in his diary:

Vers le soir j'allais au café où j'avais été la veille avec ma belle Excellence. Je sus qu'elle y devait venir, aussi elle y vint accompagné de Mylady Montagú et Mylord Mansel. Comme elle n'était pas masquée, elle ne sortait pas de la gondole, mais me fit appeler et me proposa d'aller avec à l'opera. C'était 9 heures du soir qu'il commençait et finissait à 1 heure après minuit. Il était plein comme un œuf. La musique me parut belle, mais le bruit que le parterre faisait et le caquet dans les loges fait qu'il est difficile d'en juger.

The culmination of the season came on the following Day of Ascension (26 May), when in the traditional marriage ceremony

---

[1] Diary in possession of Jonkherr Frans Teding van Berkhout, Haarlem.
[2] M to Lady Pomfret, 17 May 1740, ii. 63.

PLATE 12

The Bucentaur at the Piazzetta, Venice

From a painting by Antonio Canaletto

between the Republic and the Adriatic the Doge sailed out in the *Bucentaur* to the entrance of the sea and dropped into it a ring as a sign of espousal. Lady Mary had already seen the boat launched, and had sailed in it during its preliminary trials.[1] But in none of her surviving letters is the ceremony described. Since she observed it in the company of van Berkhout (and several other friends) his full diary-entry traces her exact activities on the holiday. 'J'allais le matin de bonne heure avec du Canges chez Mylady Montagú. Madame Buonvicini y venait de même avec un jeune noble homme nommé Victor Moro. [Nous] étions à nous six, et partîmes en deux gondoles. J'avais dans la mienne Madame Buonvicini et du Canges; dans l'autre était Mylady, Mylord Mansel et le jeune noble.' They first rowed to St. Mark's Square, and took a short walk while waiting for the *Bucentaur* to sail. Since the Doge was ill, the Vice-Doge and the whole Seignory emerged from the palace in great pomp and embarked. Lady Mary and her friends re-entered their gondolas, and followed the *Bucentaur* on its half-hour journey to the Lido, where the nuptials took place, and observed the elaborate ceremonial. After following the boat back to the Square, they went into the palace to behold the dessert which was to be served at the Doge's banquet for the ambassadors and Seignory.

A few days later, on 1 June, van Berkhout spent the morning with Lord Hartington, and in the afternoon they called on Lady Mary and spent an hour with her.[2] Then they all put on their masks and went through the customary evening activities: a stroll in St. Mark's Square and attendance at the opera. When he and du Canges called on Lady Mary again, on 5 June, he met two other visitors there: 'le Procurator Grimani et le Chevalier Vesnier, qui passent pour deux bonnes têtes de la République.' With the end of the festivities, travelling foreigners moved on to other centres. On 9 June van Berkhout made his farewells— to Madame Buonvicini, Lady Mary, the French ambassador, and the Prince of Saxony; and two days later left for Padua. The record of his friendship with Lady Mary, as set down in his personal diary, is an authentic, extremely valuable picture

---

[1] To W, 29 Mar. 1740, ii. 58.
[2] M later wrote she was 'well acquainted' with Lord Hartington (to Lady Bute, 3 Feb. 1748, ii. 160).

of her life in Venice. Since he was accustomed to the highest social circles, and had entrée to the houses of the nobility and ambassadors, he could objectively assess her importance; and he confirms her own estimate.

While Venice emptied for the summer, she remained. Several of her friends among the nobility invited her to their summer palaces, but she politely declined. Lady Pomfret, who had found Florence so agreeable that she had rented a palace there in March, began to urge Lady Mary to visit her.[1] At first the Prince of Saxony and the festivities kept her, she said; but at the beginning of June she gave a different reason: 'Here is a new, unforseen, impertinent impediment rose up; in vulgar English called a big belly. I hope you won't think it my own; but my dear chambermaid, the only English female belonging to me, was pleased to honour me last night with the confidence that she expects to lie in every day.' Her servants Mary and William then confessed that they had been married before leaving England, but the inconvenience and expense of their 'foolish accident' still vexed her.[2] When Lady Pomfret scolded her for postponing her visit she replied: 'You can't possibly suspect I have got my chambermaid with child myself for a pretence to stay here. This is a crime of which all mankind will acquit me.' Lady Pomfret's invitation was reinforced by Lord Lempster's personal appeal, but she still refused to leave Venice, this time hinting at an important reason. Although she had at last achieved complete liberty—'I have most philosophically thrown off all the chains of custom and subjection'—she could not set a definite date for her visit because 'certain atoms of attraction and repulsion' kept her in suspense.[3] What the 'atoms' were she did not say. But since a few months earlier she had submitted to Algarotti that she would wait in Venice until he chose the place for their retirement, he was almost surely the main atom. Her suspense was very soon resolved.

For in his letter about Walpole's disinclination to use her services, Lord Hervey added a postscript, with deliberate casualness: 'I am at present in great affliction for the loss of my friend Algarotti, who left England last Friday [6 June] for the

[1] She moved on 19 Mar. 1740 (Finch MS D 4 ii).
[2] 4 June, ii. 66; to W, 17 June 1740, W MS, i. 357-8 (frag. in Paston, 385).
[3] 29 June 1740, ii. 69, 68.

Court of Berlin on a summons he received from the new King of Prussia, and a very kind one under his own hand, before he had been five days on the throne.' On 31 May the fifty-one-year-old king had died. Officially the new King began his reign with a set of liberal edicts freeing the country from his father's tyrannies; unofficially he sent charming notes to his distant friends summoning them to Berlin. 'Mon cher Algarotti', he wrote to one, 'mon sort a changé. Je vous attends avec impatience. Ne me faites point languir.' The Baron Keyserling, generally regarded as his prime favourite, added his own appeal in verse.[1] Algarotti was struck by the intimate tone of Frederick's summons, and made no secret of it to those around him. He wasted no time in obeying it. Since he did not have enough money for the journey to Berlin, he borrowed some from Lady Hervey, and left his belongings in her care to be shipped to him later.[2] For some reason Lord Hervey could not bid him farewell in person, but he sent him a letter of introduction (probably to the English ambassador) along with an affectionate message: 'I do not know whether I am sorry or glad not to have seen you. It is unnecessary to say why I could not, and too late for particulars. . . . I wish you all sort of good, and beg you not only not to forget me, but often to let me know you remember me; and to relate every particular of your reception, continuation, and occupation where you are going. Adieu.'[3]

The day after Algarotti hurried off to Berlin, Lord Baltimore sent him a farewell note full of warm remembrances of the past and rosy hopes for the future. After sending his compliments to the King, he added: 'as you are now in the land of Canaan, nothing can be wanting to make you the happiest of men.'[4] In diplomatic circles, Frederick's summons to Algarotti aroused great interest and speculation; for the new King was an unknown factor in European politics, and his choice of intimates might point to his orientation. The French Ambassador in London, in reporting that Algarotti had been called, was even able to quote the King's summons.[5] When Algarotti arrived in

---

[1] 3 June 1740, xviii. 15. At the same time and in his own hand he sent an almost identical summons to his old French tutor Duhan, exiled by his father (xvii. 283).   [2] Hervey to Algarotti, 7 Oct 1740, Murray MS.
[3] Thursday night [16/5 June 1740], ibid.   [4] 7 June 1740, ibid.
[5] F. Baldensperger in *Rev. de Lit. Comp.* x (1930), 233.

Berlin in the third week of June, Frederick was in Charlotten-berg, and wrote to his 'Swan of Padua' of his regret in not being able to see him immediately. Then he proudly informed Voltaire that he had laid the foundation of his new academy in Berlin. 'J'ai fait acquisition de Wolff, de Maupertuis, d'Alga-rotti'; and he still waited to hear from three other men.[1] In the opinion of de Valori, the French ambassador in Berlin, the young Italian, though very frivolous, was more important than a mere academy member; but he could not discover what role he was to play in the new court.[2] During the coronation ceremonies the King kept Algarotti close to his side, and imme-diately afterwards when he set out on a month's journey to receive the homage of his subjects, Algarotti accompanied him, along with Baron Keyserling and another friend.[3] As Frederick described his pastimes to his favourite sister, 'Nous raisonnons en chemin de philosophie, Algarotti et moi, et nous badinons avec Keyserlingk'.[4]

The young man who chatted philosophy with a king did not answer Lord Hervey's or Lord Baltimore's letters; nor, surely, did he favour Lady Mary. Lord Hervey was kept busy for-warding the letters she sent from Venice. For himself, he wished to hear that Algarotti's expectations were confirmed, and that —he added tactfully—the King would be skilled enough to distinguish his uncommon merit. Again he pleaded for some news: to 'write to me and ever remember one who can never forget you'. When his affectionate appeal failed, he turned peevish: 'I am astonished I have yet received no letter from you from Berlin, and wait for one with an impatience which, if you could guess, I am sure you would be more ready to satisfy; unless the words *ne me faites point longtemps languir* make an impression upon you only when stamped by a royal hand.'[5] But Algarotti was not content with adoration from distant friends or his royal patron; he wanted a lucrative diplomatic post.

Before July Lady Mary knew of his pilgrimage to Berlin. How did she regard this new stroke of his fortune—and of her misfortune? The answer lies in the fragment of a letter she

---

[1] To Algarotti, 21 June; to Voltaire, 27 June 1740; xviii. 16; xxii. 12. Maupertuis was the mathematician, and Wolff the philosopher-mathematician.
[2] Baldensperger, 236.   [3] Gaxotte, *Fred. the Great*, 180.
[4] To the Margravine of Bayreuth, 14 July 1740, xxvii. 87.
[5] 28/17 June, 2 July [N.S.], 13/2 July 1740, Murray MS.

probably sent him at this time (along with some literary pro-
ducts of her leisure). '. . . Voilà l'amusement que je me suis
donné dans votre absence. J'ai peur que votre grande visite est
destiné à une grande sotte [sottise]. En ce cas là, je vous verrai
tard. Mais j'attendrais avec tant de patience et de soumission,
que doivent mériter des récompenses extraordinaire.'[1]

While she waited during the hot summer, patiently and sub-
missively, she also endured the unpleasantness of trying to
straighten out her son's affairs. On 1 August he had written to
thank her for approving an increase in his allowance (to £300);
and he added a characteristic promise of reformation: 'I shall
always search all means of testifying to you my gratitude for
this your great tenderness, and of rendering myself more and
more worthy of your affection; and as I am persuaded nothing
can acquire me that so soon as a strict course of a sober and
prudent conduct, I am absolutely determined never to follow
any but the strictest rules of Virtue and Honour, as I am very
sensible how much my former conduct must render me suspect.' To prove his reformation, he requested to be allowed the
honour of accompanying her while she stayed abroad.[2] It was
an absurd request, which she did not consider seriously for a
moment; and she suspected that he wished to win her over so
that she would persuade Wortley to make him sole heir.[3] These
remote negotiations with her son and husband made up the
dreary subplot in the mixed comedy of her unhappiness over
Algarotti's faithlessness and her satisfaction in Venetian life.

[1] Murray MS.   [2] Paston, 384.
[3] M to W, 6 Oct. 1740, Paston, 391.

XII. *Wanderer in Italy*

(1740-1)

INSTEAD of waiting in Venice through the entire summer for
an answer from Algarotti, Lady Mary set out for Florence on
13 August 1740 to visit Lady Pomfret for 'one month's happiness'. When she arrived at Bologna, after an easy three-day
journey, she sent ahead her bulky baggage, and a note beginning: 'I am thus far arrived towards the promised land.' Two
days later she started 'the dreadful passage' over the Apennines.[1]

Her arrival was eagerly awaited by Lady Pomfret, who had
put off visiting the Duke's gallery of paintings and sculpture
until she could conduct her visitor there.[2] Her arrival was also
awaited by Horace Walpole. Accompanied by his Eton school-
fellow Thomas Gray, he had been on the Grand Tour since
March 1739, and was passing the summer with Horace Mann,
and enjoying the abundant social life of Florence. Prominent
among the English people living there was Lady Walpole,
married to his eldest brother but estranged from him and on
bad terms with his family. When Walpole heard of Lady Mary's
imminent arrival he wrote to his Eton friend Richard West:

On Wednesday we expect a third she-meteor. Those learned
luminaries the Ladies Pomfret and Walpole are to be joined by the
Lady Mary Wortley Montagu. You have not been witness to the
rhapsody of mystic nonsense which these two fair ones debate incessantly, and consequently cannot figure what must be the issue
of this triple alliance: we have some idea of it. Only figure the
coalition of prudery, debauchery, sentiment, history, Greek, Latin,
French, Italian, and metaphysics; all, except the second, understood
by halves, by quarters, or not at all. You shall have the journals of
this notable academy.[3]

---

[1] To Lady Pomfret, 12, 16 Aug., ii. 70.
[2] Lady Pomfret to Lady Hertford, 11 Sept. 1740, *Corr. 1738–1741* (1805),
ii. 93.   [3] 31 July 1740, *Corr.* xiii. 227–8.

He had clearly cast Lady Mary in a grotesque role for his chronicle. Yet he could hardly have known her; he was only twenty-one at the time, and there is no record that he had ever been in her company. But she had been the intimate friend and protectress of Miss Skerrett, whom he hated as his mother's rival; and he hinted that his father's second marriage had driven him out of England.[1] His bitterness against Lady Mary may have come from this deep, subconscious feeling. Besides, he generally regarded those he met in a spirit of mockery and ridicule.

On Monday, 22 August, Lady Mary arrived at the Palazzo Ridolfi, which Lord Pomfret had rented for a year. It was a great square house on the outskirts of the city, and still contained the elaborately decorated ceilings and the pictures and furniture of its original builder, a Medici cardinal. In its large garden, which was planted with orange and lemon trees, the main promenade was lined with marble statues, and in the centre a fountain spouted water at the base of a colossal sculptured figure of a mountain goatherd.[2] To Walpole it seemed 'a vast palace and a vast garden, which is vastly commode, especially to the cicisbeo-part of mankind, who have free indulgence to wander in pairs about the arbours'.[3] The palace, in typical fashion, was divided into separate apartments. Lady Mary with her servants was installed in one of them, and so could either join the Pomfret family or conduct her own social life apart from them. They were certainly pleased by her visit. A week after her arrival Lady Pomfret told her friend Lady Hertford that her guest would remain until her belongings arrived by boat at Leghorn, and that in the meantime she was 'endeavouring to make Florence as agreeable to her' as she could. At the same time, her daughter Lady Sophia Fermor wrote to a friend in London: 'All the news I can tell . . . is that we are so happy as to enjoy my Lady Mary Wortley's conversation at present. She arrived here from Venice a week past, and does us the honour to accept of an apartment in our

[1] Stuart, 73; Walpole to Ashton, 28 May 1740, *Corr.* xiii. 221 and n. 19. In later years he got his information from Lord Mar's grandson, an obviously biased source (Malone's notes in Prior's *Life of Malone*, 151).

[2] Lady Pomfret to Lady Hertford, 29 May 1740, *Corr.* i. 227–30. At present 85 via della Scala.

[3] To Conway, 9 July 1740, *Letters*, ed. Mrs. P. Toynbee (1903), i. 76.

house.'[1] Instead of a visit of one month, Lady Mary remained for two months, spending much of her time with her hostess.

Lady Pomfret's careful diary of her social life records many of her guest's activities.[2] The day after her arrival she was driven to the Cascine, one of the famous pleasure spots of Florence, a large park on the bank of the Arno not far from the Palazzo Ridolfi. The Pomfret family drove there almost every evening to enjoy the cool air of its lawns and groves, so poetical a setting that it reminded Lady Pomfret of Arcadia.[3] The following day (24 August) Walpole, Gray, and Mann called on Lady Pomfret, and were undoubtedly introduced to her house guest. Lady Walpole also called, accompanied by her lover Samuel Sturgis, with whom she had left England to live abroad. On 25 August Lady Pomfret jotted in her diary: 'We all dined at Mr. Mann's.' As England's representative in Tuscany, Mann often entertained important compatriots who visited or lived in Florence. At this dinner he and Walpole had the opportunity to scrutinize their countrywoman whose reputation, through gossip and Pope's satires, had preceded her appearance. After dinner the Pomfrets and Lady Mary called at the Marchesa Riccardi's, and at night attended a ball.

Lady Pomfret customarily held her *conversazione* on Friday; and so on 26 August Lady Mary met many more callers. She held her own *conversazione* in her own apartment the following Thursday (1 September). When she informed her husband: 'I am lodged with Lady Pomfret', she added that she was visited by all the quality. One of the important sights of the city was the Duke's great art collection in the Uffizi Gallery. Lady Mary was taken by her hostess to see it on Monday, 29 August, and was particularly struck by the famous Venus de Milo.[4] They visited the gallery again at least twice, on 15 September going through all of its six rooms. But formal sightseeing was only a minor pastime; everybody busily paid visits, either informally or at the *conversazione*. On the day when Lady Mary had inspected the entire gallery, she went alone to spend the evening

---

[1] 28 Aug. 1740, *Corr.* ii. 82; to Lady Noel Somerset, 28 Aug. 1740, Finch MS. Walpole's inaccurate version in 'Anecdotes', *Corr.* xiv. 246.

[2] Finch MS D 4 ii. She kept another, briefer diary (D 1), probably an abstract of this one.

[3] To Lady Hertford, 7 Aug. 1740, *Corr.* ii. 42–43.

[4] To W, 5 Sept. 1740, W MS, i. 366–7.

with the Princesse de Craon. As the wife of the head of the
Regency in Florence, the Princess was the most considerable
social figure. (Lady Mary had already entertained her son
Prince de Beauvau in Venice.) On her first visit to the gallery
she had met Lady Walpole, and at her invitation spent an evening at her house. In Lady Mary's later opinion, Lady Walpole
had 'parts, and a very engaging manner', but her free-thinking
(rather than her notorious gallantries) made her a person whose
company was to be avoided. Since a 'collection of free-thinkers'
met at her house every week, Lady Mary discovered, she civilly
refused to go there when invited.[1] But Lady Walpole herself
frequently called at the Palazzo Ridolfi.

The social visits and calls were varied with more formal functions. On 4 September Lady Mary accompanied the Pomfret
family to the comic opera. At the end of the month, on the 29th,
they attended 'the public conversation on the wedding in the
Casa Giraldi'. Walpole, one of the other guests, described it to
West: ''twas a charming feast: a large palace finely illuminated;
there were all the beauties, all the jewels, and all the sugar-plums
of Florence. Servants loaded with great chargers full of comfits
heap the tables with them, the women fall on with both hands,
and stuff their pockets and every creek and corner about them.'
With its generous hospitality and its close-knit, pleasure-loving
society, Florence offered an abundance of the *agréments* of life.
'An excellent place to employ all one's animal sensations in',
thought the pensive Gray, 'but utterly contrary to one's rational
powers.' Walpole agreed at least with the first part of his friend's
remark: 'one rises at eleven in the morning, goes to the opera at
nine at night, to supper at one, and to bed at three! But literally
here the evenings and nights are so charming and so warm, one
can't avoid 'em.'[2]

He frequently attended the same social functions as the ladies
from the Palazzo Ridolfi, and visited them there as well. His
impression of Lady Mary in person was consistent with his
anticipation. 'Did I tell you Lady Mary Wortley is here?' he
asked Henry Conway, a cousin on his mother's side; and then
he set down his spirited sketch. 'She laughs at my Lady Wal-

---

[1] M to W, 20 June 1751, ii. 207.
[2] Walpole and Gray to West, 2 Oct., 31 July, *Corr.* xiii. 230, 228; Walpole
to Conway, 25 Sept. 1740, *Letters*, i. 84.

pole, scolds my Lady Pomfret, and is laughed at by the whole town. Her dress, her avarice, and her impudence must amaze any one that never heard her name. She wears a foul mob [cap], that does not cover her greasy black locks, that hang loose, never combed or curled; an old mazarine blue wrapper, that gapes open and discovers a canvas petticoat. Her face [is] swelled violently on one side with the remains of a —, partly covered with a plaister, and partly with white paint, which for cheapness she has bought so coarse, that you would not use it to wash a chimney.'[1] How accurate, one wonders, is this portrait? In a mobcap and loose house-gown Lady Mary was attired to receive guests in her own apartment; Italian custom allowed a lady to receive at home with easy informality. The swelling was the 'swelled face' she had mentioned to Lady Pomfret before leaving Venice, and not—as Walpole suggested—a suspicious sore.[2] Her appearance as he recalled it many years later is more credible: 'She was not handsome, had a wild, staring eye, was much marked with the smallpox, which she endeavoured to conceal by filling up the depressions with white paint.'[3] But in 1740, when he saw her at close quarters, he tried to send a sparkling high-lighted chronicle to his friends. In his personal acquaintance with her he did not show the ridicule which animates his letters about her; actually he was 'particularly civil' to her, she later recalled.[4]

Since the nobility were preparing for the *villegiatura*—retirement to their country villas until Christmas—Lady Pomfret held her last *conversazione* on 30 September. For the occasion she had music in the great hall, and the dancing continued until two in the morning.[5] A few days later Walpole, who had attended, fulfilled his promise to send West the journals of the notable academy of three ladies. 'But for the Academy, I am not of it, but frequently in company with it: 'tis all disjointed. Madam [Pomfret], who, though a learned lady, has not lost her modesty and character, is extremely scandalized with the other two dames, especially Moll Worthless, who knows no bounds.' Then, after explaining that the 'two dames' were rivals for a young man: 'Lady Mary is so far gone, that to get him

[1] *Letters,* i. 84–85.   [2] 12 Aug., ii. 70.   [3] Prior, *Life of Malone,* 149–50.
[4] To Lady Bute, 31 Oct. 1758, ii. 344.
[5] Lady Pomfret to Lady Hertford, 2 Oct. 1740, *Corr.* ii. 115.

from the mouth of her antagonist, she literally took him out to dance country dances last night at a formal ball, where there was no measure kept in laughter at her old, foul, tawdry, painted, plastered personage.'[1] The formal ball must have been Lady Pomfret's; and Lady Mary's energy in country dances was in the mode of the Italians, who—Walpole said elsewhere —were very fond of them.[2] He also reported in his 'journals' that she played cards with the Princesse de Craon, and cheated 'horse and foot'.

'She is really entertaining', he conceded at the end: 'I have been reading her works, which she lends out in manuscript, but they are too womanish; I like few of her performances.' She had never been modest in displaying her writings to her friends; and she handed him the manuscript album of her poems, identified the persons in them, and even allowed him to copy out the poems he wished.[3] And Lady Pomfret, when she read the French essay about La Rochefoucauld's maxim on marriage, was so pleased that she sent a copy of it to Lady Hertford, who vowed that she had never read anything with more truth, wit, and delicacy, that its author had more wit than La Rochefoucauld himself.[4] In Venice the essay had already been flattered by the Abbé Conti, who translated it into Italian verse.[5]

After Lady Pomfret's last *conversazione* and dance, the social activity still continued. During her final week in Florence Lady Mary did not lessen her festive routine: on Tuesday, 11 October, a last visit to the gallery and to a *conversazione* at Madame Suares; the next day to the opera; the next another *conversazione*; on Friday a ball; and on Saturday, the day before her departure, her hostess had an unusually large number of visitors, who probably came to bid her farewell. Prince de Craon called, as did the triumvirate of Walpole, Mann, and Gray, and Lord Shrewsbury and Mr. Dashwood. On Sunday the 16th, exactly eight weeks after her arrival, she left for Rome. A week later she sent Lady Pomfret a proper letter of thanks for her 'many civilities'.[6] The two ladies then resumed their correspondence with undiminished intimacy.

During her last weeks in Florence Lady Mary had impa-

---

[1] 2 Oct. 1740, *Corr.* xiii. 233–4.   [2] To West, 27 Feb. 1740, ibid. 201.
[3] *Corr.* xiv. 38, n. 40.   [4] 8 Oct. 1740, *Corr.* ii. 153–4.
[5] Printed in his *Prose e Poesie*, ii. 309 ff.   [6] 22 Oct. 1740, ii. 77–78.

tiently awaited word from Algarotti. She sent a constant stream of letters to Lord Hervey to be forwarded to Berlin. 'I send you enclosed another letter from Sappho', he advised Algarotti. 'They seem to me like Sancho's geese and Banquo's kings, as if there was no end of them.'[1] A few days before she left for Rome she sent Algarotti another letter, containing her plain, blunt offer. 'Je vous écrirai peu de choses parce que je crains que vous ne reçevrai pas ma lettre. Je ne veux pas croire que vous ne vouliez pas y répondre. Faites-moi le plaisir de savoir vos résolutions. J'ai quitté Venise et suis prête d'aller où vous voudrez. J'attends vos ordres pour régler ma vie. Songez y qu'il y a longtemps que je suis indécis, et qu'il est assurément temps de me déterminer.' In a postscript she asked him to address her in care of the English Resident in Florence since she was leaving there to go on a short tour while awaiting his answer.[2] In the same spirit of sober decision she had shown in Venice, she would regulate her life by his decision. She was apparently unaware of his own ambitious suspense at the Prussian court.

He had told his brother of his bitter discouragement, and in return was cautioned that the most lovable of sovereigns who had already bestowed on him kindnesses, honours, and caresses would not leave his cash-box empty.[3] At the beginning of August he set out for Paris with the King, who at Wesel fell ill of a fever. When Voltaire met them there, he found the feverish King at supper surrounded by his favourites, Algarotti, Maupertuis, and Keyserling, discoursing on the immortality of the soul, liberty, and the hermaphrodites in Plato. In order to convalesce, Frederick returned to Rheinsberg, while Algarotti went to Berlin in the expectation that his absence would persuade his patron to be more generous. In Voltaire's opinion, he stayed in Berlin for two reasons, to make love and to write the life of Caesar.[4] Before returning home, Voltaire himself stopped at Berlin, and at the French Ambassador's observed a scene which he later described to Frederick in a verse epistle. As he had predicted, Berlin was now an Athens in its pleasures and its spirit:

[1] 22 Sept. 1740, Murray MS.
[2] 11 Oct., Bod. MS, f. 64.
[3] 6, 17 Aug. 1740, quoted in Treat, *Algarotti*, 104–5.
[4] *Mémoires* (1784), 37; to Thieriot, 24 Nov. 1740, *Œuvres*, xxxv. 548.

Mais quand, chez le gros Valori,
Je vois le tendre Algarotti
Presser d'une vive embrassade
Le beau Lugeac, son jeune ami,
Je crois voir Socrate affermi
Sur la croupe d'Alcibiade. . . .[1]

The Venetian Socrates (whom he described as having large eyes and an aquiline nose) coyly negotiated with the King: he wished a diplomatic post in England, but Frederick offered only a travelling allowance and a title. Like Lady Mary, he asked Algarotti to be 'open and sincere'. In November, the King sent his wishes for the return of Algarotti's health and powers; his meaning was made clearer in a later letter: 'Adieu, illustre invalide de l'empire de l'Amour. Guérissez-vous des blessures de Cythère, et faites du moins que nous profitons à Berlin de votre esprit, tandis que les p . . . ne pourront profiter de votre corps.'[2] In this uncomfortable situation, Algarotti could hardly be in a mood to answer Lady Mary's importunate letters.

She reached Rome on 19 October, three days after leaving Florence, and rented an apartment for a month.[3] Although it had a ceiling painted by Zuccaro, it was very small—merely a hovel compared to the Palazzo Ridolfi, she told Lady Pomfret; and then she philosophized: 'but my whole life has been in the Pindaric style'.[4] During these weeks in Rome she lived very quietly, studiously viewing the antiquities and avoiding acquaintances. The ceremony of the new Pope's investiture had drawn many English travellers there; one of them, John Cotton, gossiped to Lady Pomfret's daughter that the English shunned Lady Mary and that the Roman princes neither sent for her nor came to see her.[5] But she pursued a solitary way by her own choice. 'The life I now lead is very different from what you fancy', she explained to Lady Pomfret. 'I go to bed every night at ten, run about all the morning among the antiquities, and walk every evening in a different beautiful villa.' Then, almost involuntarily, she confessed the reason: 'if amongst the foun-

[1] 15 Dec. 1740, Fred.'s Œuvres, xxii. 56.
[2] Fred. to Algarotti, [Oct.], 2, 21 Nov. 1740, xviii. 18–19, 21, 26.
[3] To W, 22 Oct. 1740, ii. 76.   [4] 22 Oct. 1740, ii. 77.
[5] Lady Sophia Fermor to Lady Anne [?], Sunday Capo d'Anno [1 Jan. 1741], Finch MS.

tains I could find the waters of Lethe, I should be completely happy.

> Like a deer that is wounded I bleed and run on,
> And fain I my torment would hide.
> But alas! 'tis in vain, for wherever I run
> The bloody dart sticks in my side,

and I carry the serpent that poisons the paradise I am in.'[1] These emotional tremors probably arose from her frustrated love for Algarotti and his refusal to settle their rendezvous.

In the meantime Wortley had suggested that she should visit Naples; she might find it agreeable as a place of residence, and she could see the newly excavated city of Herculaneum, 'the greatest curiosity in the whole world'.[2] Following his advice, she left Rome at the end of her four-week stay. After a journey marred by the breakdown of her chaise, she arrived in Naples on 22 November. It was a gay, flourishing city, she reported, but so crowded she had to be content with a 'very sorry lodging'. The opera, which was the finest in Europe, the cordial nobility, and especially the mild climate led her to consider settling there. Even her health was completely recovered, she assured Wortley—though that did not at all suggest her returning to England. She applied to the King of Naples for permission to visit the ruins of Herculaneum, and enlisted the aid of Prince Campoflorido's son, but without success.[3] She had to gather what information she could at second hand, and was particularly shocked by the King's action in melting down a beautiful copper statue to make medallions for a christening; 'more barbarous than any of the ancient Goths', she indignantly complained.[4] For all its felicities, living in Naples required an elaborate and expensive equipage, since the Spanish court made much of ceremonials. On 5 December she found out that her baggage had arrived at Leghorn, and that instead of Venice, to which it had been consigned in March, it would be sent wherever she directed.[5] She left Naples, then, after staying six weeks, and returned to Rome.

---

[1] 11 Nov. 1740, ii. 79. Her verse is very similar to lines she had once copied as Pope's expression of his unhappy love for her (to Lady Mar, 1722, i. 462).

[2] W to M, 23 Oct. 1740, Paston, 392.

[3] M to W, 23 Nov.; to Lady Pomfret, 25 Nov., to W, 6, 12, 27 Dec. 1740, 13 Jan. 1741, ii. 80–85.

[4] To W, 13 Jan. 1741, ii. 85.   [5] To W, 6 Dec. 1740, ii. 83.

The cunning Algarotti at last secured his rewards. On 20 December 1740 he was raised to the Prussian peerage with the title of count for himself and his heirs. His royal patron could not bestow the honour in person, for he was marching at the head of his army to invade Silesia. With his title Algarotti was given a secret diplomatic mission to Turin, and he left for Italy at the end of December. 'Vous négocierez, tandis que nous combattons', Frederick wrote him. 'Adieu; voyagez en paix et négociez avec succès, et soyez aussi heureux que vous êtes aimable. . . .'[1] In his military campaign Frederick planned to seize Silesia, in violation of the Pragmatic Sanction (contrived to keep Maria Theresa's possessions intact); and in his parallel diplomatic campaign Algarotti was to persuade the Duke of Savoy to turn against Milan, one of Maria Theresa's possessions, and thus help to reduce her forces. The English Ambassador to Berlin correctly surmised the mission of Algarotti, 'who is well known in England'.[2] Algarotti was finally bound for the country where, as he had originally agreed, Lady Mary waited for him; but he went on a different errand for a different patron.

On her second visit to Rome, where she arrived on 12 January 1741, she did not resume her solitary existence, but mixed with the other English visitors. News of her popularity reached Florence, where Lady Pomfret's daughter heard that she 'sups and dines with the English, and I hear diverts them very well, adapting her conversation and humour to their taste'.[3] Among them she again met Samuel Sturgis, whom Lady Walpole had discarded as her lover in favour of Count Richecourt, the Emperor's representative to the Regency council in Florence. The mild Sturgis won Lady Mary's sympathy. When Lady Pomfret accused her of being in love with him, she objected: 'Because I tell you another woman has a very agreeable lover, you conclude I am in love with him myself.' All the men she met were as indifferent to her, she insisted, as though they were carved in marble.[4] But she lavished a kind of maternal solicitude on the young travelling Englishmen she met. She thought Lord Strafford possessed modesty and genteelness without pertness,

[1] 20 Dec. 1740, xviii. 27.
[2] M. Guy Dickens to Harrington, 31 Dec. 1740, SP 90/48.
[3] Lady Sophia Fermor to Mrs. Wallop, 10 Feb. 1740 [/41 o.s.], Finch MS.
[4] 15 Feb. 1741, ii. 88.

and Lord Lincoln spirit and understanding. The travellers were exceedingly obliging to her, she told Wortley; they 'really paid a regular court to me, as if I had been their queen, and their governors told me, that the desire of my approbation had a very great influence on their conduct. While I stayed there was neither gaming nor any sort of extravagance. I used to preach to them very freely, and they all thanked me for it.' She retained for many years a pleasant recollection of how she had encouraged their good conduct in Rome.[1]

Lord Lincoln, whom she regarded so benignly, was astonished by her; as he wrote to his uncle the Duke of Newcastle:

Well! My Lord, we have at last Lady Mary Wortley at Rome, who is as extraordinary as my imagination had fancied her (which by the by is not saying a little). I am so happy as to be mightily in my kinswoman's good graces, for you must know she claims a relation, which I own I did not in the least suspect. She takes a sure way to be well with me, for she flatters me so much as to tell me that I am extremely like your Grace, not only in person but in my ways.[2]

Through his mother, the young earl was related to Lady Mary; and she pointed out their common taste: 'Ay, my lord, we had both of us our love of reading from the same source.'[3]

Joseph Spence, Lord Lincoln's governor, also found her an extraordinarily vivid personality. He confided to his mother that one of the greatest advantages that travelling offered to a 'little man' like himself was the great ease of acquaintance and familiarity with those of higher rank. 'I have had an instance of this here at Rome', he continued. 'I always desired to be acquainted with Lady Mary Wortley, and could never bring it about, though so often together in London; soon after we came here her Ladyship came to this place, and in five days' time I was as well acquainted with her as a modest man could be.' His impression of her is couched in terms that tell only how much she dazzled him: 'Lady Mary is one of the most extraordinary shining characters in the world; but she shines

---

[1] To W, 13 Jan.; to Lady Pomfret, 20 Jan.; to W, 25 Feb. 1741, ii. 86–90; to Lady Bute, 3 Jan. 1753, ii. 235.   [2] 21 Jan. 1741, Add. MS 33065, f. 392.
[3] Spence, 'Anecdotes', Huntington Libr. MS, f. 380. (Their common ancestor was William Pierrepont.) Walpole's ambiguous anecdote about them in Hanbury-Williams, *Works*, ii. 35 (cf. letter to George Montagu, 8 Nov. 1759, *Corr.* ix. 255).

His grand mother Lucy Pelham +1736 Lady Lincoln was an aunt of the Dukes. his wife Catherine Pelham was niece of the Dukes.

like a comet; she is all irregular and always wandering. She is the most wise, most imprudent; loveliest, disagreeablest; best natured, cruellest woman in the world.' Dazzled though he was, he wrote down what she told him, and used it in letters to his mother and in his collection of anecdotes. She spoke to him of her education, the London wits she had known as a girl, and her opinion of Pope as a poet, admirer, and enemy. When she related her fantastic adventure in Saint Sophia, her power of invention may have been stimulated by his wide-eyed, open-eared receptivity. She remembered her literary accomplishments too, allowing him to read her French essay refuting La Rochefoucauld, as well as her treatise on the abolition of dowries and the septennial bill for divorce.[1] Since Spence met Lady Mary during the same period as Walpole, his observations —like van Berkhout's—help balance her portrait.

By now Lady Mary had been in Italy for a year and a half, and her baggage had arrived; yet she had not decided where to settle. On 20 January 1741 she admitted to Lady Pomfret that she was still undetermined, though she could hardly resist the importunities of friends in Venice who pressed her to settle there. Then she enigmatically added that their friend the Abbé Niccolini, a Florentine ecclesiastic in Rome, was very obliging to her, 'but I fear his interest is not sufficient to do the service to my friend, that I endeavour with all my heart; though I've little hopes of success from what the Venetian ambassador told me last night'.[2] Who was the unnamed friend, and what was the unspecified service? In his diplomatic mission Algarotti had won no success, for the Duke of Savoy saw little use in allying his military fortunes with so distant a court as Berlin. When Algarotti realized his failure, he reverted to an earlier ambition —to be appointed Prussian envoy to the Venetian Republic. On 11 February he hinted it to his brother, but his royal master named another to the post.[3] Perhaps, then, Lady Mary's attempt to do a service for a 'friend' had some connexion with his fluent ambition and with her own desire to settle in Venice. This may also explain why she so freely cultivated the young travelling noblemen; they had important political connexions—particularly her kinsman Lord Lincoln, whose uncle was Secretary of

---

[1] 25 Feb., 11 Mar. 1741, MS Eg. 2234, ff. 247-52; *Anecdotes*, 230-7.
[2] ii. 87. [3] Treat, *Algarotti*, 115.

State for the Southern Department. She had, in any case, not given up her plans for a tranquil retirement with her 'friend'.

On 19 February 1741, after five weeks in Rome, she set out for Leghorn, and arrived there after a five-day journey speedily made through moonlit nights. She found her enormous baggage of clothes, furniture, and books in order. 'She designed to set up her standard in Italy when she first came abroad,' Lady Pomfret's daughter gossiped, 'if things went to her mind; but as I fancy they have not, and that though her ship has brought fine goods enough to adorn any Italian house, the principal piece of furniture would be wanting, I'm of opinion she will lay aside the thoughts of settling abroad and return to England to spend the rest of her days with old and odd Mr. Wortley.' In Lady Pomfret's more accurate opinion, Lady Mary was 'wandering about Italy and for aught I know out of it, to find some place where she may have six friends to pass the evenings with her. As her merit is uncommon perhaps she may find in bundles what most people, long before they arrive at her years, give over the hopes of finding single.'[1] Lady Pomfret, who was rarely sarcastic, believed that Lady Mary's uncommon merit had set her on a difficult quest.

She remained in Leghorn several weeks. According to an anecdote Walpole heard many years later, she 'begged a passage' to or from Genoa from Commodore Barnard [*sic*] and during a frightful storm at sea wrote a couplet:

> Mistaken seaman, mark my dauntless mind,
> Who, wrecked on shore, am fearless of the wind.

Safe on land, she presented the commodore with an emerald ring, which he later found to be glass.[2] This episode may very well be true, for on 3 March in her letter to Lady Pomfret she made the puzzling remark that she expected 'every hour to be summoned on board'.[3] And on 5 March the *Dragon*, a sixty-gun ship of the Mediterranean fleet, under Captain Curtis Barnet, set sail from Leghorn, and before reaching Genoa ran into gales and rains.[4] From there Lady Mary travelled by road to Turin,

---

[1] To Mrs. Wallop; to Lady Evelyn, 29 Apr. 1741, Finch MS, D 5, p. 140.
[2] Told to Walpole by Admiral Forbes, to Mann, 27 Jan. 1761, *Letters*, v. 22–23. If true, then she herself wore the imitation emerald ring.
[3] ii. 90.
[4] Captain's log, Ad 51/274; J. Charnock, *Biographia Navalis* (1795), iv. 212.

arriving there with all her baggage on 16 March.[1] She surely
knew that there she would find the single friend with whom she
hoped to pass her time in happiness and tranquillity.

What were Algarotti's feelings when he again saw the lady,
after having been pursued by her letters for almost two years?
'Milady Montaigu se trouve içi depuis quelques semaines', he
wrote to his brother; 'et sa rencontre n'est pas une des moins
curieuses époques de ma vie, du reste assez singulière'.[2] His
comment seems to mask his amused, perhaps startled observation of the vivacious Englishwoman whose individuality and
energy startled most people she met. For almost two months
both she and Algarotti lived in Turin, but almost nothing of
their activities can be discovered. Immediately on her arrival
she had written to Lord Hervey a letter which, he said, 'gave
me the double pleasure of finding you desire to contribute to
mine, and are in a way of promoting your own'. He knew she
tried to promote her pleasure by being with Algarotti; and in
writing to her he sent messages to her 'Friend' who had inserted
a paragraph in two of her letters. And in a letter to Algarotti, he
concluded with: 'Adieu, my best respects and wishes attend
your delightful companion.'[3] Apparently, then, they were frequently together.

But her projected idyll with Algarotti was not achieved;
with her inflamed imagination and his amused detachment, it is
difficult to imagine how it could be. One of her undated letters
to him was perhaps sent to him at this time (in April) when her
vision of their rendezvous was rudely shocked into what Lord
Hervey soon called a 'very disagreeable epoch' of her life.

Oui, je passerais le matin à vous écrire quand vous devriez enrager.
Je me suis mis à mépriser votre mépris, et sur ce pied là je ne veux
plus me contraindre. Dans le temps (de sotte mémoire) que j'ai eu
un goût effrené pour vous, l'envie de vous plaire (quoique je com-
pris toute l'impossibilité) et la peur de vous ennuyer m'éttoufait
quasi la voix quand je vous parlai et par plus forte raison m'arrêtait
la main cinq cents fois par jour quand j'ai pris la plume pour vous
écrire. A l'heure qu'il est ce n'est plus cela; je vous a étudié, et si bien
étudié que le Chevalier Newton n'a pas dissecté les raions du soleil

[1] To W, 17 Mar. 1741, Paston, 395.
[2] 25 Mar. 1741, quoted in Treat, *Algarotti*, 118.
[3] Hervey to M, 20 Mar., 2 May 1741, Bristol MS; to Algarotti, 29/18 May
1741, Murray MS.

avec plus d'exactitude que j'ai déchiffré les sentiments de votre âme. . . . On vous trouverait toujours du goût, de la délicatesse, et de la vivacité. Pourquoi donc est-ce que je ne trouve que de la grossièreté et de l'indifférence? Ce que je suis assez épais pour n'exciter rien de mieux, et je vois si clairement la nature de votre âme que j'ai tout autant de désespoir de la toucher que Mr. Newton avait d'augmenter ses découvertes par des telescopes, que par leur propres qualités dissipent et changent les raions de la lumière.[1]

During her unhappy weeks in Turin, she thus forced herself to recognize that her romantic scheme had been an impossible self-induced, perhaps self-indulgent, vision.

She still pursued her usual expatriate mode of life in Turin, which had 'the most agreeable court in Europe, where the English are extremely caressed'.[2] She particularly frequented the house of the Marquis Scipio Maffei, the writer and savant, whom she had known in London in 1736. Elected to the Royal Society and to the Society of Antiquarians in that year, he had visited her house to inspect an inscribed stone brought back from her Mediterranean voyage.[3] At his house in Turin she received Lady Pomfret's letters.[4] Young Englishmen on the Grand Tour still called on her, among them Lord Hervey's son to show her the gifts he had bought for his mother and father.[5] When Lord Lempster called—as he informed his mother—he told her that Lady Walpole had gone to Venice.

But sure, says she, poor Sturgis can't be fool enough to go after her. This kind speech was accompanied with such a compassionate tone of voice that I did not know whether it was compassion or if my Lady was not a little in love with him. When I broke her silence in saying that I believed he was too much in love to let her go out of Italy without following of her, she then contained herself no longer, and said in a passion that I had no discernment, for that Sturgis was too sensible a man to love a woman who treated him so ill.[6]

Like his mother, Lord Lempster suspected that Lady Mary's feeling for Sturgis was warmer than pity.

At the beginning of May, Algarotti—who had received his letters of recall the month before—left Turin to rejoin

---

[1] Bod. MS, ff. 57-58.   [2] To W, 1 June 1743, ii. 120.
[3] To Lady Bute, 24 July 1755, ii. 277.
[4] Lempster to Lady Pomfret, 19 Apr. 1741, Finch MS, D 5, pp. 133-4.
[5] M to W, 10 June 1742, ii. 115.   [6] 19 Apr. 1741, Finch MS, D 5, p. 134.

Frederick. In what manner he parted from Lady Mary can only be conjectured; but clearly it was a definite rift accompanied by disagreeable circumstances. With his departure, their friendship, which had run its unsteady course for five years, seemed to be ended, and neither her letters nor her vain hopes pursued him. Toward the end of May she retraced her route to Genoa, arriving before the 31st with all her baggage.[1] There she meditated on her future, and awaited Lord Hervey's advice. For when it was clear that her rendezvous had failed, she sent him a letter which he described as 'dated from Turin near a very disagreeable epoch of your life'. His cryptic advice, and especially the scraps of Latin he quoted, clearly imply the disaster and her questions.

As to your present situation on which you say you would ask my advice if I was nearer and follow it, it is impossible on [?] subject you mean that Solomon and Socrates together coul[dn't] g[ive] you any so good as what you may give yourself; in [truth?] where people's pleasure and interest clash foreign counsel may be of great use, but on the present occasion as you have nothing but your pleasure to consider, your own breast must be your best cabinet council, your passions, affections, and inclinations must compose it, and your heart be the president of it. But as for its not being material because late in your life, I am so far from saying what you suppose I would say, that I think it the more material. The less one has left the more industrious one should be to manage and improve it; and if I knew I was to die at eight o'clock and lay uneasy, I would get up and have my bed made at half an hour seven! Adieu, and for your *Oh where is now the soft etc.*, I answer from Ovid:
Intrat amor mentes usu; dediscitur usu.
Successore novo vincitur omnis amor.
Probatus est. . . .[2]

His two lines of Latin come from Ovid's poem prescribing remedies for love: 'By practice love comes into the mind, by practice love is unlearnt'; and 'All love is vanquished by a succeeding love'. In other words, Lord Hervey advised her to banish the fear that she is too old to enjoy love again, and to cure her unhappy past love by choosing a new object. If there were a candidate to replace Algarotti, the most likely would be

[1] To W, 31 May 1741, W MS, ii. 12–13.
[2] 22/11 June 1741, Bristol MS; *Remedia Amoris*, ll. 503, 462.

poor Sturgis; but he remained attached to the impervious Lady Walpole until his melancholy death two years later.[1]

Even if the primary motive of her journey abroad had been dissipated, Lady Mary did not consider returning to England. The many *douceurs* and *agréments* of living on the Continent had no equivalents in England; and the unpleasantness and disappointments there still existed. Wortley, to whom it did not occur that she might return home, was puzzled by her frequent erratic journeys. Genoa, she explained to him, was an independent republic, and unlike Naples would not be involved in the wars of the great powers. It was, besides, a pleasant place to spend the summer. By the middle of June (1741) she had rented a house by the sea.[2] Except for the absurdly cheap rent, living in Genoa proved expensive—even though Wortley had generously increased her allowance because of her constant travelling.[3] As in all the cities where she had lived, the local nobility paid her marked civilities, and she enjoyed the dignity of her position.[4] She could pass her leisure time reading in her own considerable library; and she asked Lord Hervey to send her new books being published in England. He sent Middleton's life of Cicero (to which she had subscribed) and the immensely popular *Pamela*.[5] She also wrote some verse almost surely addressed to Lord Hervey, who at this time struggled to remain in Walpole's faltering ministry. Instead of pursuing ambition, she counselled him, he should 'enjoy the remnant of declining light'.[6] Yet she herself was unwilling to follow a course of inaction.

England was at war with Spain, and maintained a strict naval blockade of Spanish possessions in Italy. On 5 June (1741) while Captain Richard Hughes of the galley *Dursley* lay anchored in Genoa harbour, a bark flying the Genoese flag passed; and since she came from Sardinia without a pass, he seized her and her crew of fourteen. The Genoese, indignant at the breach of their neutrality, imprisoned an English officer and some of the crew

---

[1] Mann to Walpole, 2 Apr. 1743, *Corr.* xviii. 197–8.

[2] M to W, 31 May, 17 June 1741, W MS, ii. 12–13, 14.

[3] W to M, 19 Mar. 1741, Paston, 395. The addition was probably £150 a year.

[4] To W, 25 Aug.; to Lady Pomfret, 2 Oct. 1741, ii. 94, 95.

[5] Hervey to M, 16 July 1741, Bristol MS.

[6] 'Conclusion of a Letter to a Friend. Sent from Italy, 1741', ii. 502.

when they went ashore, and prepared to seize the *Dursley*. But the captain cut his anchor cable, and sailed off to Leghorn with the captured boat and crew to await the outcome.[1] The Doge and Senate protested to the English consul, John Birtles, a young, inexperienced diplomat, and demanded the bark's release and satisfaction for the affront.[2] In this diplomatic muddle, Lady Mary was convinced that the Genoese were in the right and the captain and consul in the wrong. She appealed to Lord Hervey, her most strategically placed friend in the government. 'There is no resolution yet taken in the Genoese affair', he informed her at the end of June. A few weeks later he sent her a longer though still evasive report: 'The Genoese Affair has been under our consideration, and very proper directions in my opinion have been given for the termination of it, which I make no doubt will be complied with, and prevent your being any way inconvenienced by a farther dispute between our Court and that Republic.'[3] She had evidently written twice, to the annoyance of Birtles, urging that the captain should be broken.[4] On 1 August both sides released their prisoners, and the *Dursley* returned to Genoa harbour.

While this hubbub went on, Horace Walpole arrived in the middle of July from Venice with Lord Lincoln and Joseph Spence. 'Who do you imagine we found here?' he exclaimed to Mann. 'Lady Mary Wortley; of three months' standing, full of abuse on Turin, where, I suppose, she was found out as well as at Florence, Rome, Naples, Venice, etc. etc. etc. . . .'[5] Why she exerted herself on behalf of the Genoese is not clear. Walpole, with his customary contempt for her, assumed that she wanted thus to court the nobility, but Mann thought she had an affection for republics. Perhaps she merely wanted to see justice done. When the case was put before the Lord Justices in London, it was decided in favour of the Genoese.[6] Lady Mary's sympathy for them was thus justified.

When she heard that Walpole and Lord Lincoln were in

[1] Log of Master, Ad 52/374; log of Lieutenant, 51/4176; Hughes to Corbett, 6 June, 1 Aug. 1741, Ad 1/1882.
[2] Birtles to Newcastle, 17, 21, 24 June, 12 Aug. 1741, SP 79/19.
[3] 25 June, 16 July 1741, Bristol MS.
[4] Mann to Walpole, 30 July, 12 Aug. 1741, *Corr.* xvii. 98, 103–4.
[5] 19 July 1741, ibid. 91–92.
[6] *Daily Advertiser*, 31 Aug. 1741, cited in Walpole, ibid. 92, n. 5.

Genoa she had immediately invited them to call on her.[1] During
this new encounter with Lady Mary, Walpole did not receive
a sweeter impression. A short time later, while in Toulon on his
way home, he 'imitated' some lines from an ode of Horace, and
addressed them not to a boat (as the Latin poet had) but to the
postchaise that carried Lady Mary. The last lines of his imitation are the most remarkable:

> O chaise, who art condemn'd to carry
> The rotten hide of Lady Mary,
> To Italy's last corner drive;
> And prithee set her down alive;
> Nor jumble off with jolts and blows,
> The half she yet retains of nose![2]

If accurate, the last line would indicate that she suffered from
an advanced case of syphilis, cancer, leprosy, or tuberculosis.
Since no other person who met her—either before this time or
during the remaining years of her life—ever mentioned such
an injury, it must be considered the embellishment of Walpole's
poetic imagination.[3]

After remaining in Genoa about four months, she became
alarmed by the rumours of approaching Spanish troops, and so
on 25 September (1741) she resumed her wanderings, bound
this time for Geneva. A week later she passed through Turin,
where Lord Lempster again visited her.[4] From there she crossed
Mount Cenis, and, continuing northwards, on 11 October
reached the Swiss city. The mode of living there, she observed,
was exactly the reverse of that in Italy: without outward forms
of show 'this little republic has an air of the simplicity of old
Rome in its earliest age'. But everything cost a great deal,
especially for a stranger. The main drawback was the sharpness
of the air, which so disagreed with her that she feared a return
of her poor health.[5]

During this time Wortley discussed with her the character
and fate of their troublesome son. In the summer of 1741
Montagu had proposed that if his marriage were dissolved he
could marry someone more suitable to his rank and his father's

---

[1] M to W, 29 July 1741, ii. 92.   [2] *Corr.* xiv. 247.
[3] It may be derived from the phrase 'pox'd by her love' by Pope, whose
satires Walpole greatly admired.
[4] To W, 22 Sept., W MS, ii. 28-29; to Lady Pomfret, 2 Oct. 1741, ii. 95.
[5] To W, 12 Oct., 5 Nov. 1741, ii. 97-98.

expectations—a proposal Lady Mary thought absurd. She was annoyed because he had written to her at Genoa in care of Birtles, who then dunned her for one of his debts. 'I expect nothing from him but going from one species of folly to another', she told Wortley, quoting La Rochefoucauld's maxim that folly was the only incorrigible fault. Wortley's own fault, she told him, was excessive lenity.[1] Fortunately Montagu was content to remain in Holland, where on 6 September (1741) he enrolled as a student of oriental languages at the University of Leyden.[2]

After staying in Geneva for a month Lady Mary moved south (by 15 November) to Chambéry. She thought it a small, ill-built place, but its inhabitants, poor Savoyard nobles, were at least well-bred and 'extremely caressing to strangers'. In its congenial society: 'Many of us have travelled, and 'tis the fashion to love reading. We eat together perpetually, and have assemblies every night for conversation.' She could live there in 'the most profound peace and unbounded plenty that is to be found in any corner of the universe'.[3] During this quiet period her affection revived for her 'old and odd' husband. From Chambéry her first letter had ended with: 'I beg you would write soon. When you are long silent I am so uneasy on the account of your health that it affects mine.' Aware of his loneliness she was glad that their daughter sometimes stayed with him.[4] When the next spring she heard that their daughter was again with him, she uttered a revealing sentiment: 'I hope her obedience and affection for you will make your life agreeable to you. She cannot have more than I have had; I wish the success may be greater.'[5] Her affection was mild compared to her feelings during their early married life; still it revealed a heart capable of some affection toward him. She and Wortley, from their far-separated domiciles, continued to share their family problems with mutual trust and sincerity, if not always with complete agreement. Their daughter pleased them by her respectability as Lord Bute's wife and the mother of a rapidly

[1] To W, 15 Aug., ii. 92–93; 8 Sept. 1741, Paston, 397–8.
[2] *DNB*.
[3] To W, 15 Nov., W MS, ii. 36–37; 30 Nov., 22 Dec. 1741; to Lady Pomfret, 3 Dec. 1741, 4 Mar. 1742, ii. 98–102.
[4] To W, 15 Nov. 1741, 21 Jan., 9 Feb. 1742, W MS, ii. 36–37, 43, 44.
[5] 6 Apr. 1742, W MS, ii. 46 (frag. in i. 45).

increasing family. She pointed up the moral instability of their son.

In accordance with Wortley's plan, Montagu visited England at the end of 1741, and after three months was only with difficulty persuaded to return to Holland (in March 1742) accompanied by John Gibson, employed as his companion and governor. He was to spend about a week near Lady Mary, so that she could decide whether he deserved his father's favour and permission to live in England. 'I cannot imagine any one is so likely as yourself', Wortley told her, 'to give an impartial account of him.' She agreed to interview him only because Wortley insisted, and promised to judge him in 'the most sincere and unprejudiced manner'.

In the spring of 1742 she found Chambéry uncomfortable because of reports that the French planned to invade it. In the middle of April, after a two-week pause in Lyons, she went on to Avignon, where she established her residence. For her meeting with her son she laid down several conditions: it was to take place in the town of Valence, where they were less likely to meet any English people; and he was to go there under a feigned name and without a servant. Before the interview actually took place she continued her elaborate and slow negotiations with her husband and son to establish its exact conditions. She did not approach it in an optimistic mood. Perhaps aware of this, Wortley cautioned her to converse with their son in 'the most calm and gentle way possible' to encourage him to be open and sincere with her. But she had so often seen his 'falsehood and weakness' that she now prepared to guard herself from his charms, for 'his figure . . . was very agreeable and his manner insinuating'. As to his expectations: when she had once suggested that if he would enlist in the Emperor's army he could retrieve his character, he had answered that he supposed she wished him killed and out of the way.[1] Mother and son did not have much faith in each other.

[1] W to M, 22 Mar.; M to W, 23, 25 Apr. 1742, ii. 102–8.

XIII. *Avignon*

(1742–6)

AT the beginning of May 1742 Lady Mary settled in Avignon, a place with many advantages. The cost of living was low, and good bread, mutton, and wine plentiful; in general, it was 'what the French call *Un pays de bonne chère*'.[1] Far more important, as a possession of the Papal State it was secure from the wars in northern Italy. Its great medieval palace and stone walls did not appeal to her taste, as did its government, 'a sort of imitation of the old Roman'—with two consuls elected yearly to govern in conjunction with the Papal Vice-Legate. This brought the decorous splendour of official functions for visiting royalty and church dignitaries.[2] Although the city was the refuge of many Jacobites, at first they did not disturb her. It was 'perhaps the town in the whole world where politics are the least talked of'. She could even attend the assemblies of the attainted Duke of Ormonde, who lived in great magnificence. Several English ladies who had settled there behaved with decency; and the French she met were 'polite and obliging to strangers'. At night she could attend assemblies, which concluded with supper, or go to the theatre to see comedies tolerably well acted. She described these social felicities to Lady Pomfret, who had returned to live in England in the fall of 1741. 'In short,' she concluded, 'I think one may while away an idle life with great tranquillity: which has long since been the utmost of my ambition.'[3] But, as she knew, before her stood one threat to her tranquillity: her meeting with her son.

On 8 June 1742 in the town of Orange near Avignon she met a Dutch officer called Monsieur du Durand, the name her son had agreed to assume, and spent two days in his company. She

---

[1] M to W, 8 Jan. 1743, Paston, 407–8. [2] M to W, 12 June 1744, ii. 132.
[3] To W, 19 July; to Lady Pomfret, 1 June 1742, ii. 117, 112–13.

found him greatly altered in his appearance since she had last seen him four years before; no longer handsome, he had grown fat and looked more than his twenty-nine years. Still, he had an air of gentility and politeness, and conversed gaily on a great variety of subjects. They talked mostly about his allowance and about Wortley's estate and will, and she preached high moral sentiments to him. After promising to retain his pseudonym he left for Flanders to await his father's orders; and she returned to Avignon, and immediately wrote to Wortley a full account of her interview.[1] A few weeks later she was more confident of the good effect of their meeting: 'we parted very good friends, he protesting to follow my advice in all things'. But in spite of his promise to write to her as soon as he reached Paris, no letter came.[2] She soon discovered that his other promises were as lightly given. He had called on a lady in Montelimar whom he had met, revealed his identity and told a long story about himself and his family. When Lady Mary discovered this she berated him: 'I wish you would consider there is nothing meaner or more unworthy a gentleman than breach of promise, and that tattling and lying are qualities not to be forgiven even in a chambermaid.' Her scolding, she insisted, was the best way she could prove that she was his 'affectionate Mother'.[3] For the rest of the year he continued to arouse her worry and anger, though she continued to write to him in an attempt to make him reform.

In one of her letters to Lord Hervey, Lady Mary apparently related how a workman in her Avignon house had fallen and been killed quickly and painlessly. The remote tragedy seemed especially poignant to him. Disappointed in his political ambitions and suffering ill health, he wrote to her from Ickworth Park, his family seat in Suffolk: 'The last stages of an infirm life are filthy roads, and like all other roads I find the farther one goes from the capital the more tedious the miles grow, and the more rough and disagreeable the ways.' At the end, he pronounced a benediction on his old comrade: ' "May all your ways (as Solomon says of wisdom) be ways of pleasantness, and all your paths peace"; and when your dissolution must come,

[1] 10 June 1742, ii. 114–16. The interview was later gossiped about by Walpole, who gave it an incestuous interpretation (to Mann, 14 Jan. 1745, *Corr.* xviii. 567).   [2] To W, 27 June 1742, W MS, ii. 62.
[3] To W, 20 Nov. 1743, ii. 121–2; 29 Dec. 1744, Paston, 416–17.

may it be like that of your lucky workman. Adieu.'[1] Less than two months later he himself was dead. He had outlived his last inch of character, Horace Walpole wrote—because he had deserted Sir Robert shortly before the fall of the ministry. His old enemy Pope was more charitable; 'Requiescat in pace!' was his only comment.[2] His death removed still another of Lady Mary's old and intimate friends.

In England she had been a friend of Henrietta, Countess of Oxford, who had not shared Lord Oxford's friendship for Pope. She was an estimable but dull woman. Once after she had called on Lady Mary, little Miss Wortley exclaimed, 'Dear mamma! how can you be so fond of that stupid woman?' Whereupon Lady Mary reprimanded her daughter with a lecture on rash judgements, ending with: 'Lady Oxford is not shining, but she has much more in her than such giddy things as you and your companions can discern.'[3] Before Lady Mary left England their friendship had been very cordial. She had presented Lady Oxford with her miniature, painted by Zincke in 1738, and in the following year with a large portrait of herself 'done from life by Carolus De Rusca'.[4] They corresponded afterwards, though the letters preserved today do not begin until 1743, and continue their dry, sedate progress for more than ten years.[5]

Lord Hervey's will was the chief topic of gossip in London, Lady Oxford wrote in September, for he had left money to all his younger children born in wedlock, and some to 'Lady Hervey because I can not help it'. No one knew why he had treated his wife so rudely, and had refused to see her for many weeks before his death.[6] Lady Mary, however, knew that he had lived with Lady Hervey 'as well bred as if not married at all'. He had kept the many letters he had received from Lady Mary, and his eldest son sealed them up to return to her, with the assurance that he had not read them. She thanked him for

[1] 18 June 1743, Bristol MS.
[2] Walpole to Mann, 14 Aug. 1743, *Corr.* xviii. 294; Pope to Orrery, 12 Aug. 1743, *Corr.* iv. 466.   [3] Stuart, 94.
[4] The miniature, now owned by the Duke of Portland, was engraved by Vertue in 1739; the Rusca portrait is now owned by Lord Wharncliffe.
[5] Drafts of Lady Oxford's letters to M, owned by the Duke of Portland, are deposited in the BM as the Harley MS, Misc. 13 a, b, c, d, e.
[6] 17 Sept., 22 Oct. 1743, Harley MS.

his honourable conduct, adding that had he glanced at them he would have been surprised to see that a long and steady friendship could exist between two persons of different sexes without any mixture of love.[1] The letters, which unfortunately do not survive, must have been brilliant, and revealing of the interests they had in common: politics, literature, and love. During the summer she often strolled in the evening to the hill behind the Palace of the Popes. From its crown, the Rocherdes-Doms, she could enjoy the fresh breezes and the magnificent panorama of the Rhône and the Durance, the landscape of Languedoc and Provence, and in the far distance the mountains of Auvergne. It was the most beautiful land prospect she had ever seen, she wrote to Lady Pomfret; to her husband she tactfully added 'except Wharncliffe'. On the top of the hill stood the remains of some fortifications, including an ancient round tower. She was so charmed with it that in the presence of a town consul she remarked that she would fit up the tower as a belvedere if it were hers.[2] The result of her request can be read in the minutes of the town council for Friday, 18 October 1743:

... a été exposé par Mons. Le Premier Consul que Milady Montaigu lui a fait connaître qu'elle serait bien aise d'avoir à sa disposition une des tours que la ville a sur la Roche pour en pouvoir jouir de la beauté de la vue et se reposer quand elle y va, et que Le Conseil lui ferait plaisir s'il lui en accordait la jouissance sa vie durant, ce qu'entendu par Le Conseil celui a unaniment agrée la demande de la d[ite] Dame, et lui a accordé la jouissance d'une des dites tours pour tout le temps qu'elle restera dans cette ville, sans préjudice de la propriétée de la ville sur celle.[3]

She proudly told her correspondents about it. At the cost of only £26, as she informed her husband, she had a domed roof built over the shell of the tower, and then a little pavilion around the outside. Within the belvedere, where she kept her books, she usually spent her evenings. Her hill-top retreat pleased that side of her nature that craved quiet and contemplation. Like her Turkish kiosk it provided an appropriate décor.

[1] Stuart, 95–96.
[2] To W, 20 Dec. 1743; to Lady Pomfret, 12 July 1744, ii. 122–3, 134–5.
[3] Archives in Palais des Papes, Avignon, xxxxi. 446.

With the coming of winter she could not pass her evenings in her solitary retreat, and so she entered more into the social life of the town. When she saw an opportunity to turn a social occasion to more important use she exerted herself with characteristic energy. In the town of Nîmes, forty miles away, the Freemasons were to give a magnificent entertainment in January 1744 in honour of the Duc de Richelieu, Governor of Languedoc, a grand-nephew of the Cardinal, and famous in affairs of war and gallantry. Lady Mary allowed herself to be persuaded by the Duchesse de Crillon and some other ladies to attend the function. A few hours after she arrived in Nîmes she was solicited by the two leading Huguenots of the town to intercede with the Duke on behalf of a minister and a dozen of his congregation who had been imprisoned. (Louis XIV's edict to stamp out protestantism was still in force.) She promised to try to serve the unfortunate Huguenots, though she had little hope of success. Instead of dressing formally, she went to the ball in a mask to converse with the Duke more freely. Several ladies easily arranged an introduction, and after an exchange of compliments she asked him to liberate the Huguenots. Actually the Duke had successfully carried out a policy of tolerance. As he wrote in his memoirs: 'Je ne me montrai pas tolérant en amour seulement.' His tolerance had a political motive; it encouraged the provincial legislature to make liberal contributions of men and money to the King. At the moment Lady Mary came to Nîmes, the Duke had to decide the fate of several imprisoned ministers and zealous laymen condemned to be hanged. 'Je m'y transportai', he later recalled, 'affectant la plus grande colère et la résolution de sévir contre ces malheureux; je les interrogeai moi-même; je vis plus d'égarement et de fanatisme que de crime, et j'engageai les femmes les plus distinguées de la ville à me demander leur grâce.' But he answered Lady Mary by saying he was powerless to order the prisoners' release but would solicit it at court. When they promised to abide by the law, he pardoned and freed them—an act of humanity which, he claimed, he could exercise only because of his favour with the King.[1]

As he continued conversing with Lady Mary, he turned to a political topic closer to her interests. He asked how strong a

[1] Richelieu, *Mémoires historiques et anecdotiques* (1829), v. 71–72, 289–91.

party the Pretender had in England. When she assured him that they were a very small group, the Duke's reply, casual though it was, contained a hint of the greatest importance. 'We are told otherwise at Paris; however, a bustle at this time may serve to facilitate our other projects, and we intend to attempt a descent; at least it will cause the troops to be recalled, and perhaps Admiral Mathews will be obliged to leave the passage open for Don Philip.' In other words, a Jacobite invasion and uprising would force England to recall her troops from Flanders and her fleet from the Mediterranean. As an ally of Austria her withdrawal on land and sea would be to the advantage of France and Spain. The revelation astounded Lady Mary. But to whom could she convey it and by what means? Her letters had to travel through Paris, where they were opened; and Walpole, even if she could reach him, had by now resigned from office. On 5 February 1744 she told her husband that she had learned a secret of great importance, but did not dare send it by post. Three weeks later she sent a letter by her servant William Turner, who was returning to England.[1] When Horace Walpole met Madame d'Aiguillon, wife of Richelieu's nephew, in Paris twenty years later, she told him 'that a great masquerade being made at Marseilles [*sic*] for Duc de Richelieu, Lady Mary Wortley set out from Avignon, went to it in a dirty domino, talked to him for 3 hours, and then said she had satisfied her curiosity and returned without unmasking.'[2] In her long conversation Lady Mary had learned more from the indiscreet Duke than she had expected.

Her servant William had been struck with palsy during their first winter in Avignon; and his wife had borne a second child, which was an additional bother in the household. Still Lady Mary wanted them to stay, for they were honest and faithful. But William insisted on returning home with his family, vowing that he had rather be a chimney-sweep in England than a lord in France. She bore the couple no ill-will, and asked Wortley to present his wife with five guineas and to help them re-establish themselves. Since English servants were generally difficult to

---

[1] W MS, ii. 101; 25 Mar. 1744, ii. 126–8.
[2] 'Paris Journals for Dec. 1765', *Corr.* v. 281. When the Duke was later put in command of an expedition to invade England, he publicized it so much that it was abandoned (H. Noel Williams, *The Fascinating Duc de Richelieu* [1910], 193).

keep abroad, she thenceforth hired foreign ones, and found them satisfactory.[1] But the departure of her servants further alienated her from life in England. Avignon no longer seemed a peaceful haven. Even before France's declaration of war (in March 1744) the military preparations had created an animosity toward English people there. After war was declared the Jacobites became much bolder, and the reputed mistress of the Pretender, the wife of Colonel Hay, spread gossip that Lady Mary was an English spy and should be carefully watched. Avignon became so unpleasant that she would gladly have moved elsewhere, but France was forbidden, and a journey to Italy impracticable.[2] She complained to Lady Pomfret: 'I endeavour to amuse myself here with all sorts of monastic employments, the conversation not being at all agreeable to me, and friendship in France as impossible to be attained as orange-trees on the mountains of Scotland ... and I try to content myself with reading, working, walking, and ... building.'[3] She still had these defences against social friction and personal ennui.

However remote England became, Lady Mary tried to keep in touch with family affairs. When Wortley forwarded a letter from Lady Mar, she was pleased because it seemed the most rational one since her illness.[4] In her answer, Lady Mary commented on the unfortunate marriage of their niece: 'I am sorry for Miss F. Leveson's distress. I am afraid she will find more uneasiness in a narrow fortune than she yet apprehends. If I was in England I would use all my endeavours to serve her. Perhaps her marriage may turn out better than is expected.'[5] In Lady Oxford's opinion, the young lady should have divulged her marriage before giving birth to her child. Lady Mary expended some compassion on the indiscreet newly-weds, and hoped their relations would not treat them too harshly.[6]

At this time she was able to congratulate another young lady on a far more prudent match. Lady Sophia Fermor, whom

---

[1] To W, 26 Mar. 1744, Paston, 412; 25 Aug. 1745, W MS, ii. 139–40.
[2] M to W, 1 Mar., W MS, ii. 128; 15 May 1744, Paston, 415.
[3] 12 July 1744, ii. 134.
[4] W to M, 25 July, W MS, i. 133; M to W, 19 Aug. 1743, W MS, ii. 88.
[5] 14 Apr. 1744, MS in Princeton Univ. Library.
[6] Lady Oxford to M, 7 May, Harley MS; M to Lady Oxford, 1 June 1744, ii. 131.

Lady Mary remembered at the Palazzo Ridolfi as having 'few
equals in beauty, or graces', had become a conspicuous London
beauty.[1] In Italy she had been courted by Lord Lincoln, the
Duke of Newcastle's heir, but the infatuated young man was
ordered home by his uncle lest he make an unsuitable match
with her.[2] Lady Mary, however, was irrepressibly romantic
about the young pair, and in the summer of 1742 told Lady
Pomfret: '*A propos* of angels, I am astonished Lady Sophia does
not condescend to leave some copies of her face for the benefit
of posterity; 'tis quite impossible she should not command what
matches she pleases . . . and I am still of opinion that it depended
on her to be my relation.'[3] It depended more on the young
man's uncle. In London Horace Walpole at first had nothing to
say about the Pomfret family because (he told Mann) the city
was so full of absurd people that Lady Pomfret was scarcely
outstanding. But in the spring of 1744 he had very much to say:
'Who do you think is going to marry Lady Sophia Fermor?—
only my Lord Carteret. This very week! A drawing-room
conquest. Do but imagine how many passions will be gratified
in that family! Her own ambition, vanity and resentment—
Love she never had any. . . . Lincoln is quite indifferent, and
laughs. My Lord Chesterfield says, "It is only another of Carteret's *vigorous* measures".'[4] Lady Sophia's marriage to the
Secretary of State, a widower thirty years older, elevated her
to power and influence. While Lady Mary congratulated her
mother, she did not expect to be favoured by the daughter, she
told Wortley, having 'so often seen prosperity cause an entire
oblivion'.[5] But there was very little time to see, for the next year
Lady Carteret died in childbirth.

In May 1744, when Pope died, neither Wortley nor Lady
Oxford mentioned it in their letters to Lady Mary, perhaps to
spare her the memory of a past unpleasantness. 'I hear that Pope
is dead,' she wrote to Lady Oxford, 'but suppose it is a mistake,
since your ladyship has never mentioned it.' She was particularly curious about his will and the disposal of his house at
Twickenham. 'It is true Pope is dead', Lady Oxford then told

[1] To W, 6 May 1744, ii. 130.
[2] Lincoln to Newcastle, 8 Apr. 1741, Add. MS 33065, ff. 405-7.
[3] 1 June 1742, ii. 113.
[4] 14 Apr. 1743, 22 Mar. 1744, *Corr.* xviii. 210, 424.
[5] To Lady Pomfret, 12 July, ii. 134; to W, 15 May 1744, Paston, 414.

her. 'I did not mention it, knowing the contempt you have for worthless people.'[1] Lady Mary was relieved by his death; a year later, while discussing with Wortley some satiric verse missing from Lord Oxford's collection, she remarked: 'Wherever this is, I think you need be in no pain about it. The verses are too bad to be printed, excepting from malice, and since the death of Pope I know nobody that is an enemy to either of us.'[2]

Her son's erratic career had taken a new turn when he had gone to Belgium (in July 1743) to join the English army preparing to fight as Austria's ally against France and Spain. She allowed herself a grain of optimism: 'Perhaps the same rashness which has ruined him in other affairs, may be lucky to him there.'[3] On 20 September he began his formal army career when he was commissioned a cornet in the 7th Hussar Dragoons commanded by Sir John Cope. He energetically pursued advancement through his relations, and was appointed aide-de-camp to General James Sinclair, Quartermaster General.[4] This was his post when, at the beginning of May 1745, the army of the Austrian allies was severely beaten in the Battle of Fontenoy by a French army twice its size. The English in particular suffered many dead and wounded. Cut off from English news, Lady Mary relied on the local paper *Le Courier d'Avignon*. 'It is reported here that the English have extremely suffered in a late action', she wrote to Wortley. 'I cannot so far forget I am a mother as not to be under concern for my son, notwithstanding all the reasons he has given me to be indifferent about him; I am impatient for a true account.' A month later she was still uneasy because she had not seen a list of the casualties.[5] Her son had survived unhurt, and both he and General Sinclair informed Wortley of his creditable behaviour. The proud father then raised his allowance; he also sent Lady Mary extracts from the commendations of their son's actions, and advised her to hasten his reformation with moral precepts. She then administered a sensible letter to the prodigal son, encouraging him to choose the best company and to win the

[1] 10 Aug. 1744, ii. 136; 18 Aug. 1744, Harley MS.
[2] 8 June 1745, ii. 141.
[3] To W, 28 July 1743, W MS, ii. 87.
[4] Material on his army career in C. T. Atkinson's article in *Journ. of the Soc. for Army Hist. Research*, xxvii (1949), 160–70.
[5] 20 May, 16 June 1745, W MS, ii. 130, 133–4.

approbation of his colonel.[1] In the meantime he had been transferred (on 29 May) to General Sinclair's Royal Scots Regiment
with the rank of captain-lieutenant. For the first time since his
boyhood it seemed as though he could redeem himself and win
his parents' respect.

In June 1745 Lady Mary received other, less pleasant family
news from England: that Thoresby had burned to the ground.
It had been occupied by the young Duke of Kingston and
his mistress, whom he had brought from France in 1736. Its
destruction, Lady Mary told Wortley, was 'a piece of news
that furnished me with many reflections'. One of them she
expressed to Lady Oxford: 'I cannot help feeling some concern, and at the same time making many reflections on the
vanity of all worldly possessions: I thank God my heart is so
entirely detached from them, that I never desire more than the
small portion I enjoy.'[2] Lady Oxford, who lived at Welbeck
Abbey, about five miles from Thoresby, sent reliable news of
the fire: that the Duke's loss was great, although he had saved
all his papers and plate, and most of the good furniture.[3] To
Lady Mary the destruction of her family home must have
widened her exile from her native country. That summer (1745)
Wortley spent several months at Pyrmont, a spa in northern
Germany. 'I hope your journey has been rather for pleasure
than necessity of health', she told him afterwards.[4] That they
might have met was not even mentioned.

At the beginning of 1746 her isolation and discomfort in
Avignon became more acute. War with France interfered with
the trickle of letters from England; as a result (she told
Wortley): 'I am as totally ignorant of all English affairs as if I
was the inhabitant of another planet.' She soon felt the effect
of the Pretender's unsuccessful invasion of England; a new
influx of Jacobites sought the protection of the Papal city, and
intensified its unpleasant political atmosphere. Another disadvantage was that under the *droit d'aubaine* the French King
could seize foreigners' effects when they died; and she wanted
her jewels and plate to go to her daughter. The Duc de Richelieu

[1] W's drafts, 14 May, 18 June 1745, W MS, v. 63–64, i. 134; M to W, 7, 19
July 1745, Paston, 422, 426–7.
[2] 16 June, W MS, ii. 133–4; to Lady Oxford, 1 June 1745, ii. 140.
[3] 12 June 1745, Harley MS.
[4] M to W, 10 Jan., ii. 143; W to M, 4 Mar. 1746, Paston, 433.

had promised to obtain a special dispensation for her, but she did not trust his 'court promises'.[1] She also felt insecure because she could not trust her foreign servants as she had her faithful English ones. But they suffered from a similar human frailty. 'I am fallen into the same distress that gave me so much trouble in Italy', she told Wortley. 'The man and maid servant who I had taken in place of William and Mary have followed their example. They are married and she big with child. I find it impossible to have a family small enough to consist of reasonable creatures.'[2]

But at least she was not plagued by her own children. At the beginning of 1746, while in charge of a garrison, Montagu was captured by the French, and sent to Liége a prisoner. He did not relax his efforts for advancement in the army and in his father's favour. Lady Mary sent him a very kind letter to encourage him since his behaviour deserved it.[3] She had by now been completely reconciled to her daughter, and tried to mediate with Wortley when, against his wishes, Lady Bute left Scotland with her husband and rented a house in Twickenham. Assisted by her mother's advice, she soon ingratiated herself with him.[4]

Lady Mary's frequent complaints do not tell the whole story of her life in Avignon. Many years afterwards, one of the town's lawyers wrote to her about a servant's pension, and reminded her of his own high regard for her:

Il est vrai que dans le séjour que vous fîtes, Myledis, dans notre ville, tout ce qu'il y a de personnes distinguées par leur naissance ou par leur mérite personnel ont conservé une vénération particulière pour vous qui tenez un si haut rang dans le monde et dans la république des lettres. J'eus l'honneur de vous voir et de vous admirer tant chez feue Madame la Marquise de Fortia que dans d'autres des meilleures maisons de cette ville.[5]

His eulogy, even with its element of professional politeness, is impressive.

Lady Mary had never given up her activity in 'the republic of letters'; and to avoid boredom retired to the solitude of her

[1] M to W, 11 Feb. 1746, W MS, ii. 141–2; 10 Jan. 1746, ii. 143.
[2] 20 Mar. 1746, W MS, ii. 144.   [3] M to W, 20 Mar. 1746, Paston, 437.
[4] W to M, 4 Mar., Paston, 433; M to W, 2 Apr., 20 July 1746, W MS, ii. 145–6, 147.   [5] Rigaud-avocat to M, 30 Apr. 1762, W MS, iv. 233–4.

belvedere where she could write. In one piece, she pretended
to be answering a letter received from Margaret of Navarre, the
sixteenth-century Queen and writer. It begins: 'Vous me faites
bien de l'honneur, Mademoiselle, de penser à moi dans une
situation aussi heureuse que la vôtre et parmi des illustres qui
doivent vous donner beaucoup de mépris pour nous autres
misérables vivants.' She went on, after a brief criticism of her
correspondent's literary style, to defend her favourite enthusiasm, feminism, urging that women should be educated in the
sciences as well as the arts. She ended her defence on a personal
note:

Plaignez-moi, Mademoiselle; il n'y a point ici d'académie de
cavaliers ou de dames. Je n'ai pas de relais des yeux; quand ils sont
fatigués je suis forcée d'écouter et de parler des pertes et des gains,
qui sont les seuls sujets intéressants pour l'Avignon moderne. Si
j'avais l'honneur d'avoir une compagnie comme la vôtre je renon-
cerais avec plaisir à tous mes barbares, et m'appliquerais à cultiver
la bonté que vous m'avez témoigné avec toute la reconnaissance et
respect que vous méritez de la part de, Mademoiselle, &c. [Post-
script] Je suis si charmée de votre coterie que si vous me donnez
parole de m'y admettre immédiatement; j'irai me jeter dans la
Rhône pour vous trouver, moitié par désire de vous voir, et moitié
d'ennui de tous ceux que je vois.[1]

The essay is a witty *jeu d'esprit*, which she could hardly have
shown to her friends in Avignon, the friends whom she sometimes found so dreadfully boring.

She had other ways of escaping ennui. In the spring of 1746
the ruins of a Roman temple to Diana were discovered and
excavated in Nîmes. Lady Mary may have visited them; at least
her interest was aroused, and she purchased a medallion with
sculptured figures from a peasant, and promised to send it to
Wortley.[2] Later that spring she actually travelled through
Provence and Languedoc on a tour unknown to her previous
biographers. Unattended by any servant, she left Avignon in
April and returned there at the beginning of June. She then
sent Wortley a résumé: 'I have made a little journey (on the
account of exercise) into the high Languedoc, and find my

---

[1] W MS, viii. She used the same literary device in 'A Letter from the Other
World', ii. 413–14.
[2] To W, 20 Mar. 1746, Paston, 437.

health much mended by it. I have seen Toulouse, Montpellier, and several other towns in my way, and met with great civilities everywhere. The Archbishops of Narbonne and Toulouse invited me to supper the first night of my arrival. It is impossible to travel unknown in France, there is such strict enquiry in every town of passage.'[1] Her colourless summary was a sort of façade; but in Toulouse she met a young Irish gentleman whose testimony reveals far more of her flamboyant and intensely fascinating personality.

Sir James Caldwell, then about twenty-six years old, had attended Trinity College, Dublin, and in 1743 had gone abroad to further his education and fortunes.[2] He had won the friendship of Montesquieu, who lived in Bordeaux, and was soon to issue *L'Esprit des Lois*. On 25 May 1746 Caldwell met Lady Mary, and spent an hour talking to her. The next day he sent his full observations to Montesquieu.[3]

Il y a quelques jours que my Lady Mary Wortley Montagu est arrivée ici de Montpellier sans domestique en bateau de poste. C'est la dame la plus riche et la plus particulière de chez nous, et c'est la dame de l'Europe (comme tout le monde convient) qui a le génie le plus universel et le plus cultivé. Elle a donné au public plusieurs ouvrages très goûtés mais en particulier le Progrès de la Poésie, qui est un chef-d'œuvre. Elle sait le grec et le latin, et parle toutes les langues modernes. Elle a resté un mois dans le Sérail du Grand Seigneur lorsque son mari y était ambassadeur.

One wonders whether Caldwell was repeating gossip he had picked up about the embassy and about her non-existent chef d'œuvre or whether she had imposed on a gullible listener. She did show him her album of verse, and let him copy two poems.[4] They spoke of Montesquieu too; and Caldwell repeated her remarks:

Elle a l'honneur de vous connaître, non seulement par réputation comme tout le monde, mais encore personnellement. Elle m'a prié de vous faire mille compliments de sa part. Elle a grand envie d'aller à Bordeaux (peut-être à pied) exprès pour vous voir. Elle m'a dit que vous n'avez pas seulement fait honneur à votre langue et à votre

---

[1] 3 June [1746], Morgan Libr. MS.
[2] F. Taylor in *Bull. of Rylands Lib.* xxxv (1952), 213–14.
[3] 26 May 1746, Bagshawe MS, B 3/7/1, f. 24.
[4] Now among Bagshawe MS: 'Addressed to . . . 1736' (ii. 504) and 'Lines Written under General Churchill's Picture' (ii. 498), actually by David Mallet.

nation mais aussi à genre humain. J'ai été charmé de rencontre[r] cette dame la plus éclairée de l'Europe du même sentiment que moi.

When Montesquieu had been in London in 1731 he had indeed written to Lady Mary, asking her to attend a benefit performance by the dancer Marie Sallé, whom he was sponsoring at Fontenelle's request.[1]

At their first meeting, Lady Mary conversed with Caldwell for only an hour since she was engaged to sup with the Archbishop of Toulouse. During her subsequent meetings with him she confided more personal matters. Her residence in Avignon had become intolerable because of 'the Jacobites, priests, and gamesters'; and, as she also told Wortley, she could neither settle in France because of the war nor go to Italy alone because of the dangerous journey.[2] The young Irish baronet was himself bound for Italy; and as he then informed an English acquaintance: 'I am now determined to go to Italy, having made the party with Lady Mary Wortley Montagu.'[3] At about the same time as he contemplated this journey, he met an Irish lady with her physician on their way to the baths of Barèges in the Pyrenees, and they persuaded him to accompany them. When he returned to Toulouse, he found that Lady Mary had already returned to Avignon. On her tour of the province, he reported to Montesquieu, she tried to find a town or village where she could remain for eight days without being overcome by ennui. 'C'est que aux grands esprits comme aux vainqueurs', he concluded, 'Unus non sufficet [*sic*] orbis.'[4]

Disappointed to find that she had left Toulouse before his return, Caldwell sent her a gay letter about his Pyrenean tour and about his future plans. 'I am off my intended schedule of going to Italy this autumn. As there is a likelihood that the peace will continue, and as I intend studying the language this winter, and lastly as I have lost a great part of the money intended for that journey at play, I should like retiring into a

---

[1] Montesquieu to M, 11 Mar. 1731, W MS, vi. 282-3; Émile Dacier, *Une Danseuse . . . Mlle Sallé* (1909), 61-71.

[2] Draft, Caldwell to M [July 1746], Bagshawe MS, B 3/15/104; M to W, 23 Aug. 1746, ii. 148.

[3] Letters of introduction from Montesquieu and Count de Marans, Feb. 1746, Bagshawe MS, B 3/6/1; Caldwell to Henry Belasys [n.d.]; also to Lady Clifford [n.d.], ibid. B 3/7/1.

[4] [*c.* June 1746], ibid. B 3/6/1, f. 19.

small town for part of this winter, and should choose none so soon as that where I might have the honour and pleasure of your Ladyship's company and conversation.' He also told her that he had written to Montesquieu inquiring for 'a person that would be proper to live in the house with as a companion'. Crossing out that phrase, he substituted: 'such a person as you spoke to me of at Toulouse', and continued: 'and find by his answer that he knows of none, Abbé Venuti that I mentioned to your Ladyship having got a benefice at Bordeaux.[1] If I have the good fortune to be in the town with your Ladyship this winter I shall do all in my power to be as agreeable and as useful to your Ladyship as I can. I must beg leave to copy that part of President Montesquieu's letter that regards you as I think it very pretty and very just *que vous êtes* etc.'[2] From Caldwell's letter it would seem that after his brief but warm acquaintance with her, he had planned to accompany her into Italy, paying his own way. As an alternate plan, he had suggested that they settle in a French town, for which she would require a suitable companion like the Abbé. (Had she perhaps contemplated a tranquil retirement like the one she had proposed to Algarotti?) But she carried out neither plan; she merely remained in Avignon through most of the summer.

[1] The Abbé Venuti, Italian savant and poet, was a friend of Montesquieu, who also tried to find employment for him (Montesquieu, *Corr.*, ed. F. Gebelin and A. Morize [1914], i. 363–4).

[2] Draft, Caldwell to M [July 1746]. He passed into Italy the following January (Bagshawe MS, B 3/7/1 [29 Jan. 1747]).

XIV. *Retirement in Brescia*

(1746–56)

TOWARD the end of July there came to Avignon Count
Ugolino Palazzi, the thirty-year-old heir of an impoverished
Brescian family.[1] He had been gentleman of the bedchamber to
the Prince of Saxony, and was now returning to his home in
northern Italy. He called on Lady Mary with a letter of introduction from the Prince's governor, whom she had known in
Venice. During her conversations with the Italian she lamented
the impossibility of travelling into Italy alone; whereupon he
offered her his protection. If she would travel in the guise of a
Venetian lady returning home, she could pass safely through
northern Italy, where Spanish and French troops were retreating before the victorious Austrians. Two weeks later, about
9 August, they set out. Taking her French Huguenot servant
girl, and leaving most of her baggage and furniture in the care
of the Vice-Legate, they probably travelled by coach to Marseilles and then by felucca directly across the Gulf of Genoa.

During their few days in Genoa Lady Mary stayed in seclusion because she had no passport. They left on 16 August in
hired carriages, and as they made their way through the narrow
mountain road they met coming from the opposite direction
part of the Spanish army. The Count ordered the drivers to say
that they served Don Philip, the Spanish commander, and they
were allowed to pass; but their progress was so slow that by
nightfall they had only reached Serravalle, about twenty miles
away. As they entered the town they met the Spanish troops
commanded by Don Philip retreating in such confusion that
they were not questioned. After a night without beds or supper
they encountered the Austrians entering the town. As an officer

[1] Poliza d'estimo del Catasto Censuario di Brescia anno 1723, n. 321 (Citta-
della Vecchia), Archivio di Stato, Brescia.

at the Court of Saxony the Count showed his credentials and introduced Lady Mary to the generals, who treated them with great civility. But they were forced to remain in the town for two days because the Spaniards had seized all the horses; they then resumed their journey with an escort of hussars provided by the Austrian generals. Without telling Lady Mary, the Count had written to his mother, who greeted them on their arrival in Brescia on 20 August, and insisted that Lady Mary should stay at her house until suitable lodgings could be found. Five days later, while still there, Lady Mary fell ill, so seriously that she was confined to her bed for two months. The Count's mother took as much care of her as though she were a sister, omitting no expense or trouble. By November she was well enough to write of her journey and illness.

She sent a full account of this to her husband.[1] In general she seems never to have lied to him or to her daughter; instead she omitted from her letters whatever she did not wish them to know. She told them of the Count's courtesy and helpfulness on the journey to Brescia, but she never again mentioned him in her surviving letters, though during the next ten years, while she lived in that province, she was involved in a somewhat puzzling friendship with him. At the end of that time she planned to take legal action against him for the swindles he had perpetrated on her; and so she wrote her memoirs of their transactions and friendship.[2] In this Italian memoir—which exists only in a fair transcript in another hand—she explained that she had been slightly acquainted with him in Venice (in 1740). When he had appeared again in Avignon and volunteered to escort her, he insisted that she should stay at his mother's house in Brescia, and then showed her a letter inviting her. Their journey, Lady Mary agreed, was to be entirely at her own expense. Then, as her memoir continues:

The evening before my departure the Count told me that he was really mortified, but that since all his property was in his mother's hands and he had only a small allowance, he had been forced to incur debts, and could not leave Avignon without 300 sequins [about £150]; and that he would give me a note for it which his

---

[1] 23 Aug., 24 Nov. 1746, ii. 148–51.
[2] Wharncliffe MS 510. Briefly summarized in Earl Stanhope, *Miscellanies. Second Series* (1872), 3–7.

mother could certainly not refuse to pay upon our arrival. I hesitated to make such a loan, and saw he put too high a price on the
escort he wished to perform for me; still, having strong reasons for
leaving Avignon, I counted out 300 sequins for him and took his
note. In truth I found his escort very necessary. We had to pass the
Spanish army, and certainly if I had not travelled as a Venetian lady
favoured by his company, I would surely have been in great danger.
I was received by the Countess Palazzi with the greatest politeness.
She spoke to me in confidence, telling me that her son had ruined
his fortunes by extravagances in Saxony; and from this I realized
that she would not be in any humour to pay his debts. And so I
thought it useless to present her with the note from Avignon.[1]

One important clue to their friendship appears in the record
kept by a local historian: 'Anno 1746; capito Sua Eccellenze la
Marchesa di Montagu inglese servita da Ugolino Palazzi.'[2] In
other words, it was thought that he served her as *cicisbeo*, an
office whose duties were extremely flexible; and in her case
probably confined to formal escort and general assistance.[3]
After her two-month illness, the doctors advised her to benefit
by the country air, and—as she related in her memoir—the
Count invited her to use one of his country houses in the village
of Gottolengo, about eighteen miles south of Brescia. Still so
weak that she had to be carried in a litter, she went there accompanied by his mother. Soon, however, the Countess left with her
son for her own home in Brescia. A few days later the Count
returned and assured Lady Mary she was mistress of his house
and everything connected with it. Then—she continued—

I told the Count how mortified I was that Madame Palazzi had
been so incommoded by me, and that I was embarrassed for the
nuisance and expense she had suffered for my sake; and I begged
him to tell me with absolute candour what present would please
her. He hesitated for some time, and after many ceremonies told
me that his mother was the most sympathetic person in the world
as well as very ambitious, and that if she received a present from
me, she would think herself obliged to give me one in return, for
which she would be deeply embarrassed; but that if I was absolutely
set on making a payment, she would not mind receiving as much

---

[1] 'Italian Memoir', ff. 1–3 (all quotations transl. from Italian). A sequin was
worth approximately 10 shillings.
[2] Conti's 'Cronologia di Lovere', quoted in C. L. P. Marinoni, *Lady Montagu
Wortley* [*sic*] *e la sua decennale dimora alle rive del Lago d'Iseo* (1904), 11.
[3] Ibid., 10.

money as she had quietly paid out already, and that he would see to it that she received it. So I gave him 200 sequins for this purpose, and in the morning he left (so he said) to take it to her.

If she had any suspicion that the Count was dishonest, she should have been convinced by one of his most flagrant tricks, which he played out like a grotesque comedy. In November, soon after she had arrived in Brescia, he persuaded her to go to the feast of San Martino at an aunt's house about two miles away. Not yet having completely recovered from her illness, she went in a closed carriage. Although she wished to leave her maidservant in her apartment, he insisted that she should take both her maid and her manservant. His own serving man, he assured her, would remain in charge of the house. At his aunt's house, where she was entertained at a magnificent dinner, she fell ill, and by the doctor's advice was put to bed, while the Count left with his brother, an abbé. When she returned to her rooms the next day, she found that her jewel-cases were missing. She notified the Count, and (as her memoir continues): 'He pretended to be unable to believe it, but when convinced he came and threw himself at my feet, dissolving in tears, inconsolable—as he said—for the dishonour to his house. I replied that it was only necessary to find them. I was again seized by fever, and returned to bed.' In the morning the Count told her he had searched the house in vain, and would make inquiries in the neighbourhood. She gave him forty sequins for 'these pretended searches'; and after staying away for three days he returned crying and sobbing that he had found no trace of the jewels, and that he was ruined and disgraced. Then he told her that he suspected his brother the abbé, but she cautioned him not to accuse his own brother, a churchman, without proof. 'Oh God,' he replied, weeping bitterly, 'I am mad. I don't know what I am saying. Have pity on a poor man who knows himself dishonoured by this cruel accident.' In spite of all his demonstrations, she could not rid herself of a secret suspicion that he was the thief, but she was afraid to show it without a valid reason. In her limitless tolerance for his scheming, she bought from him a very worn upholstered chair at a very high price; had locks put on the doors, and glass panes in the windows of his house; and at his suggestion bought a large quantity of wall tapestries from a friend of his. Since her furniture was still in

Avignon she had to lay out a large amount of money to make the borrowed house habitable.[1]

In Gottolengo, as she recorded in a private memorandum, she 'sought houses all winter'.[2] But she apparently rented the Count's house, and later bought it. To her correspondents she described it as the shell of an unfinished palace which had been empty for many years. It stood on a hill in the middle of the village, and she greatly improved it by fitting up the interior and levelling the neglected courtyard.[3] She now settled down to an easy retirement. Every day she rode in the fresh morning air, and by March (1747) could boast of her complete and miraculous recovery from her long illness.[4] In Brescia, the most important town of the province, she found a stimulating intellectual circle; and according to an historian of the region, she maintained an apartment there, and became well acquainted with several members of its flourishing Academy of Natural Sciences.[5]

While she had been ill, her son had been released by the French in an exchange of prisoners, and he had then gone to Breda (in September 1746) to join his cousin Lord Sandwich, who was plenipotentiary in the peace negotiations. When Wortley sent her news of their son's favour with his relation, she commented: 'I wish good company may reform my son, as bad debauched him.'[6] Montagu had been urging his father to secure a Parliamentary seat for him, mainly because it would enable him to live in England protected from his creditors.[7] Through Lord Sandwich's favour, he was elected for Huntingdon on 18 July 1747.[8] His proud father promptly informed Lady Mary; she replied that she was glad to hear of his good fortune, and hoped he would make up for his past follies.[9]

Because she feared a recurrence of her fever, and found bark ineffectual as a remedy, Lady Mary was advised by her doctor to take the water cure at Lovere, on the western shore of Lago

[1] 'Italian Memoir', ff. 3–4, 5–10.   [2] CB MS, f. 22.
[3] To Lady Oxford, 29 Nov. 1747 (date corrected), ii. 172; to Lady Bute, 10 May 1748, ii. 164; to W, 24 Apr. 1749, ii. 178.
[4] To Lady Oxford, 1 Mar. 1747, ii. 151.
[5] Marinoni, *Lady M e Lago d'Iseo*, 10, 18, 26.
[6] To W, 17 Mar. 1747, Paston, 445.
[7] Montagu to Gibson, 1 Sept., Paston, 442; 12 Oct. 1746, W MS, v. 79.
[8] Walpole, *Corr.* xix. 450, n. 14.
[9] 25 July, Paston, 446–7; 10 Sept. 1747, W MS, ii. 162–3.

PLATE 13

View of Lago di Garda, Brescia
From a lithograph [1834]

d'Iseo. Its mineral water was a specific against fevers. She made the uncomfortable forty-mile journey, and arrived in the middle of July (1747) at 'the most beautifully romantic' spot she had ever seen in her life. From the shores of the long glassy lake rose high hills covered with a great profusion of rocks, vineyards, orchards, and natural waterfalls. It was a place full of 'all the delightful ideas of romance'. In contrast to the sleepy quiet of Gottolengo, Lovere raged with social festivities: operas, balls, puppet shows, a gaming room, and every evening an instrumental concert before the townspeople assembled on the lake. But she did not take part in any of the gay activities, she told her husband and daughter, preferring a placid existence: she drank the mineral waters, played whist for an hour or two in the afternoon, and in the evening sailed on the lake and landed at various places on the shore to walk about.[1] After enjoying this pleasant cure for about six weeks, she returned to her 'very convenient' house in Gottolengo.[2]

Although she had intended to leave it in April 1747, when she had fully recovered her strength, the Count prevailed on her to remain by means of his tantrums over the jewel robbery. He became desperate, telling her that she had 'cost him his honour and left an eternal smirch on his family'. His conduct seemed so crazy in all ways that she lost her suspicion of his plotting, and instead considered him an object of pity. When she pointed out that his house lacked a garden, he countered with a new scheme: an old priest near by, who owned a large garden, would sell it to her if she would allow him to occupy the house on it for the rest of his life. She looked at the property, bought it for 800 sequins, and spent 200 more improving it. She did this, she admits in her memoir, even though she had decided not to stay in Gottolengo. But since she had allowed herself to be 'induced' to repair the old shell of a house, she wished to send for her furniture, books, and other possessions still in the care of the Vice-Legate in Avignon. The ever-obliging Count arranged to have it brought by a reputable merchant he knew, for which she paid the Count 200 sequins. When her goods came, many pieces of furniture and china, and four snuffboxes, one of them jewelled, were missing. The Count

---

[1] To Lady Bute, 24 July 1747, ii. 153–4; 5 Sept. 1749, Paston, 468.
[2] To Lady Oxford, 1 Sept. 1747, ii. 156.

put on a great spectacle of anger, cursed all merchants as thieves, and threatened to shoot the one he had hired; but Lady Mary charitably assumed that the merchant's agent had been negligent. Since all her books had come in good condition, she was consoled for her losses. Then, with a deed signed in the presence of witnesses, the Count sold her the house, which she repaired more thoroughly and fitted with her own furniture.[1] In November (1747) she told Lady Oxford that she had purchased at a very cheap price the house she had fixed up.[2]

Neither to Lady Oxford nor to her husband and daughter did she hint of the plot in which she had allowed herself to become entangled. She told them instead about her sweet retirement. Since her weakened eyes did not allow her to read after dark, she played at whist every evening (for absurdly low stakes) with some old priests from a neighbouring monastery to whom she had taught the game. Without any regret she admitted: 'I am entirely given up to rural amusements, and have forgot there are any such things as wits or fine ladies in the world.'[3] At about this time, London's literary world was reminded of her. For on 14 November Dodsley published in a quarto pamphlet *Six Town Eclogues. With some other Poems. By the Rt. Hon. L. M. W. M.* It had been arranged by Walpole, who had copied the poems in Florence, and disliked them as too 'womanish'; in print they still did not please him, though he considered them 'excessively good'.[4] Dodsley reprinted them several months later in the first volumes of his popular *Collection of Poems*, and thus spread Lady Mary's literary reputation among a new reading public. The characters and scandals of the thirty-year-old poems—when she had moved among wits and fine ladies—had lost their sting as personal satire, but still glittered as *vers de société.*

As her health returned she took a greater part in the local pastimes. At the beginning of 1748 she planned to attend the carnival and opera in Brescia, but was prevented by cold weather and bad roads. Then she unexpectedly found a substitute opera. Before she had moved into her 'castle' the villagers had been accustomed to erect a theatre in the stables. Since

[1] 'Italian Memoir', f. 10.   [2] 29 Nov. 1747, ii. 172.
[3] To Lady Bute, 17 Dec. 1747, ii. 157.
[4] To Mann, 24 Nov. 1747, *Corr.* xix. 449–50.

these were now occupied by her horses, they petitioned her to let them erect a theatre in her main salon. When she agreed, they put up their scenery (so beautiful that she let it stand), and for three days put on delightful performances with music, costumes, and lighting. It cost her only a barrel of cheap wine, this amusement 'in low life'.[1] Occasionally she had high-life amusements too. It was the fashion for groups of ladies and gentlemen to visit about at castles, hunting and dancing. Once thirty of them (with their servants) descended on her with the intention of staying a fortnight, though she had never met them before. She managed to provide them with supper and with fiddles for their dancing; and when she retired at one in the morning they continued their ball undisturbed and unoffended. Another time some ladies in the neighbourhood favoured her with a visit in masquerade. Dressed in white like vestal virgins and with garlands in their hands they came at night with violins and flambeaux, stayed for one dance, and then moved on to another house some miles away. A more stately visitor, once, was the Duchess of Guastalla, who rode up with a great suite of attendants, stayed for supper, and when the moon rose, an hour after midnight, galloped off to return home.[2] Although she complained of the expense, Lady Mary undoubtedly enjoyed these visits which flattered her dignity and varied her pleasures.

Through the letters from her daughter she remained conversant with events in England. Lady Bute could now provide her with more gossip about London activities, for she and Lord Bute, through their intimacy with the Prince and Princess of Wales, went about in public. Lady Mary strongly approved of her son-in-law's ambition, and seems to have fastened on to him some of her hopes thwarted in Wortley's career. And when she heard of the young couple's continued devotion to each other —another failure in her own life—she thought it extraordinary that Lord Bute should have remained in love after marriage.[3]

In the eyes of the world her son's career had also taken a favourable turn. He had succeeded in leaving the army without

[1] To Lady Bute, 3 Feb., 10 May 1748, ii. 161, 163-4.
[2] To Lady Bute, 5 Jan. 1747, 3 Feb. 1748, ii. 158, 161; to W, 25 Dec. 1748, ii. 172-3.
[3] To W, 24 Apr., 17 July; to Lady Bute, 26 July 1748, ii. 162, 168, 169.

prejudice to his career, and on 7 January 1748 was placed on the retired list.[1] Although he remained in Lord Sandwich's good graces, much to his father's satisfaction, Lady Mary remarked dryly that she would be pleased if she could depend on Lord Sandwich's opinion.[2] In July 1748 he was appointed a secretary at the Congress at Aix-la-Chapelle called to draft terms of the treaty.[3] Proud of the honour, he sent Lady Mary a letter, which she thought 'very long and childish', asking her to persuade Wortley to increase his allowance further. She replied with a sermon on how 'a modest behaviour and a frugal expense are necessary to persuade the world you are convinced of the folly of your former conduct'.[4] In his duties at the Congress he proved useless because his handwriting was 'villainous' and he could not be trusted with secrets.[5] When the treaty was finally signed on 18 October 1748 his job was finished. In spite of her pious advice Lady Mary scarcely believed he would ever amount to anything.

As the summer of 1748 drew on, instead of returning to Lovere to drink the waters, she moved to her garden and farm on the outskirts of Gottolengo. Here she could indulge her taste for planting and landscaping, diversions which filled the time she could no longer give to writing and needlework, for her eyesight was poor and she could not have spectacles fitted there. The farm was about a mile from her 'castle' and on the banks of the Oglio River. It contained terraces covered with vineyards and fruit trees, and a little wood 'carpeted, in their succeeding seasons, with violets and strawberries, inhabited by a nation of nightingales, and filled with game of all kinds'. In the gardens she raised flowers and a variety of produce for her table. She even succeeded in raising tea, though not so strong as India tea.[6] To avoid travelling back and forth from her house to her gardens she fitted up a room in the farmhouse with simple furniture and decorated it with earthenware basins filled with

---

[1] Curling, *Montagu*, 114.
[2] Draft of letter, W to Sandwich, 22 Mar. 1748, MS in my possession; to W, 24 Apr. 1748, ii. 162.
[3] Commission 22/11 July 1748, Add. MS 36121, f. 194.
[4] M to W, 10 Sept. 1748, W MS, ii. 173-4 (frag. in Paston, 461-2).
[5] Chesterfield, *Letters*, ed. B. Dobrée (1932), 890 n.; Richard Lodge, *Stud. in 18th Cent. Diplomacy* (1930), 325.
[6] To Lady Bute, 10, 26 July; to W, 17 July 1748, ii. 166-9.

flowers. Her activities, as she listed them to Lady Oxford, seemed casually genteel—walking, riding, amusing herself with a little garden. But they were as regular as in a convent: she rose at six, weeded her garden for several hours at the head of her weeding women, and inspected her dairy and poultry (two hundred chickens, besides turkeys, geese, ducks, and peacocks). At eleven she retired to her books for not more than an hour, dined at twelve, then slept until three. In the afternoon she sent for the old priests to play whist until it was cool enough to go out—when she either walked in her wood, rode her horse, or set out on the river in her little boat rowed by her fisherman and his son. Her 'castle' and garden delighted her so much, she vowed that if they were not so far apart she would not exchange them for the noblest estate in England.[1]

But despite her country amusements and her pretence of feeling 'more and more weaned' from the world, she hungrily looked forward to letters from England.[2] She continually complained that her letters did not reach their destinations. At Lovere her mail was secure, for a regular courier passed between there and Brescia, the main post town; but at Gottolengo she had to send and receive her letters by private messengers, who could put the franking money in their pockets and throw the letters away. Even letters in the regular post were delivered open or carelessly resealed. Still another interruption came from the quarantine imposed by the Venetian government in fear (real or pretended) of some contagious disease. Or her innocent tattle about family affairs was suspected of being deep political intelligence in code.[3] At the end of 1748 she became so annoyed at the irregularity of the post that she thought of moving in spite of the winter weather.[4]

Her intention of moving came from another cause which she did not mention in her letters, Count Palazzi's imposition on her patience and her pocket with his fantastic schemes. In one, as described in her memoir, the Count arrived from Brescia one day with a joyful countenance. 'God be praised!' he said to her. 'I have found a way to repair, although only in part, the loss

---

[1] 2 Feb. 1749, ii. 174; to Lady Bute, 10 July 1748, 27 May 1749, ii. 166–7, 182.
[2] To Lady Oxford, 27 Apr. 1748, ii. 163.
[3] To W, 8 Sept. 1749, Paston, 468; 18 Dec. 1747, W MS, ii. 164; 3 Sept. 1750, 14 July 1749, 10 Oct. 1753, ii. 196, 183, 244.
[4] To W, 23 Oct. 1748, W MS, ii. 175–80 (3 letters sent by different routes).

which you have suffered in my house, and which always fills me with horror. There is an old epileptic man at Trenzano, a few miles from Brescia, who has no sons. He has offered to sell me all his holdings for an annuity of 1600 sequins a year. He is ninety years old, as shall be verified by his baptismal record ... ; his lands are worth at least 70,000 ducats. I have had them examined and valued by professional appraisers. I have seen them, and fallen in love with them. This poor decrepit man cannot live more than six months, and whatever remains will be yours.' In her sensible answer she pointed out that although she was not without assets, she did not want to encumber herself with lands in a foreign country. The Count then exploded into a hysterical outburst: that she would not allow him to restore his honour—for which he was willing to die—and that since he had planned to bring the deed for her to sign the next morning, he would be disgraced before his mother and all who knew them. Accordingly an old white-haired man appeared, bent and trembling, carrying an inventory of his possessions and the deed. Lady Mary signed it in the presence of a notary and two witnesses, and handed over the first payment. After this (she wrote): 'I continued in solitude, entertaining myself with my books and my garden. The Count came only rarely, which pleased me, for he ruined my horses and broke my chairs.'[1]

In the summer of 1749 she returned to Lovere to drink the waters and enjoy the pleasant cure. The medicine she took was so salubrious that she projected a scheme to transport it to England, but Lady Bute apparently did not encourage her enterprise.[2] Wortley went abroad that summer for about four months, this time travelling and taking the waters in France. They corresponded—she dutifully, he neglectfully—but as before nothing was said of their possible meeting.[3]

As her eyesight improved she began to read new books from England with a passionate curiosity. In her exile they were a bridge to her native country. One evening in the autumn (1749), after riding with a party on horseback, she returned home at ten and found a box of books newly arrived from England. She

[1] 1749, 'Italian Memoir', f. 13.
[2] To Lady Bute, 11, 22 Aug. 1749, Paston, 466.
[3] M to W, 25 Dec. 1749, W MS, ii. 195–8 (2 letters).

then wrote to her daughter: 'I could not deny myself the pleasure of opening it; and, falling upon Fielding's works, was fool enough to sit up all night reading.'[1] Although she preferred *Joseph Andrews*, her opinion of *Tom Jones*, jotted in the last volume, was 'agreeable'.[2] When her obliging daughter sent her a list of new books to choose from, she asked for all of them except the ones she had already read. 'I thank God my taste still continues for the gay part of reading,' she wrote. 'Wiser people may think it trifling, but it serves to sweeten life to me, and is at worst better than the generality of conversation.'[3]

Her leisure also allowed her to lavish on her daughter long intimate letters; and since her daughter praised the letters as agreeable and entertaining, she was grateful for the encouragement.[4] When Lady Bute asked her advice on the education of her four small daughters, she complied, with apparent satisfaction in being consulted. Her ideas were clear and without cant. The girls should be bred free of prejudice, and always treated with honesty. Their qualities, even good ones, should be frankly appraised—especially beauty, riches, greatness, and so on, which were usually regarded with contempt by conventional moralists. But the girls should be taught to confine their desires to their future possibilities, and to practice sincerity, pity, and generosity in moderation, since a virtue in excess becomes a vice.[5] In these long affectionate letters she relaxed with her pen—'thinking upon paper', she called it. After retailing some local news, she apologized: 'I am afraid you are tired with this insignificant letter; we old women love tattling; you must forgive the infirmities of your most affectionate mother.'[6] One understands, then, why her correspondence assumed such importance to her; for it assured her not only of affection and friendship, but also of a continued existence in England—in the minds of her daughter, her husband, and even of the colourless Lady Oxford.

In the spring of 1750, while at her house in Gottolengo, she suffered the severest illness of her life, so dangerous that she

[1] 1 Oct. 1749, ii. 186.
[2] Lady Mary's personal library, now owned by Lord Harrowby, listed in Sotheby Cat., 1 Aug. 1928, 85.   [3] 24 Dec. 1750, ii. 201.
[4] 30 Nov. 1749, 22 June 1750, ii. 187, 194.
[5] Jan. 1750, 19 Feb. 1750 (misdated 1749), ii. 214–15, 174–6.
[6] ii. 194, 182.

'heard sentence of death' pronounced against her. She explained the harrowing details to Lady Oxford (though not to her daughter or husband): a 'defluxion' had fallen on her mouth, tongue, and gums, which had become so deeply infected that the local physician diagnosed her case as hopeless. One of her neighbours summoned the most noted surgeon from Cremona, and he successfully operated by applying red-hot irons to her gums. She recovered with amazing speed.[1]

Before she had completely convalesced (in the early summer) Count Palazzi called on an unusual mission, she noted in her memoir. He had received a message from his mother that the Magistrate of Brescia, Angelo Contarini, had heard that Lady Mary was held prisoner in his castle in Gottolengo. The Count asserted that the report had been spread by enemies, and would bring disgrace to his family; and he tearfully begged her to save them. Nothing could be more just, she assured him, and promised to testify that she stayed there voluntarily and had never been treated disrespectfully. A few hours later the magistrate's officer arrived with orders to conduct her to him, but she insisted that she had received only politenesses from the Palazzi family; and she then wrote to the magistrate thanking him and repeating her testimony. But that did not satisfy the Palazzi family. Two days later the Count returned with a letter from his mother entreating Lady Mary to be gracious enough to visit her in Brescia and thus silence the false rumours. In her weak condition, though with the doctor's permission, she made the journey. At the Countess's house other members of the family waited on her; and she received visits from a great number of ladies and gentlemen. 'I laughed at the idea of being restrained by violence at Gottolengo'—she wrote—'and it seemed very natural to me that a lady of my age should seek retirement, and I said so to all those I saw.' At the family's request she remained until the magistrate arrived from the north, and repeated the same denials to him.

Having satisfied the pride of the Palazzi family, she prepared to leave for Lovere. The evening before her departure the Count warned her that since she would have to pass through a dangerous wood, she had best leave her money in the hands of

---

[1] To Lady Oxford, 24 May, ii. 193; 23 June [1750], Wharncliffe MS 507; 'Italian Memoir', f. 14.

a banker. When she asked to see the banker, the Count replied that the man had the gout—but she could leave the money with him, and he would give her a receipt. In her inexhaustible gullibility she gave him about 200 sequins, and set out to pass the summer at Lovere.[1] Suddenly, at the end of September she moved to Salo, about twenty-five miles to the east, a resort town at the foot of Lago di Garda. She saw there a vast palace and magnificent gardens so enchanting that only fairy tales could convey its real charm. Count Martinenghi, the owner, who was too poor to maintain it, was willing to rent it for a trifle.[2] This time she apparently resisted the temptation to add still another piece of property to her holdings. After passing about a month in Salo, by November (1750) she had returned to her own house and garden in Gottolengo.[3]

In her advice to her daughter, Lady Mary had cautioned her to moderate her fondness for her children as the best preparation for disappointments and other misfortunes. She herself had arrived at that state of mind with regard to her son. No news of him had reached her in more than a year. 'I can no longer resist the desire I have to know what is become of my son', she appealed to Wortley in May 1751. 'I have long suppressed it, from a belief that if there was anything of good to be told, you would not fail to give me the pleasure of hearing it. . . . I beg to be informed, and prepare myself for the worst, with all the philosophy I have.'[4] Her son's behaviour that year would have challenged the philosophy of a saint. As secretary at Aix-la-Chapelle and a silent Member of Parliament he had at least been inconspicuous. Then without warning, in January 1751 he burst on London as a dazzling sensation when he arrived from Paris with a vast supply of rare and elegant furnishings, including the entire contents of a shop. On his shoes he wore diamond buckles, and on his head a wig made entirely of wire.[5] That summer he went about in London with Miss Elizabeth Ashe, a

---

[1] 'Italian Memoir', ff. 14–16. The magistrate's inquiry was gossiped about by Walpole (31 Aug. 1751, *Letters*, iii. 68) and Mann (8 Oct. 1751, J. Doran, *'Mann' and Manners at the Court of Florence* [1876], i. 328).
[2] To Lady Bute, 17 Oct. 1750, ii. 197.
[3] To W, 20 Nov. 1750, ii. 200.
[4] 24 May 1751, ii. 204. On 8 Mar. 1751 she had volunteered to write to him (to W, W MS, ii. 229–30).
[5] T. Bowlby to P. Gell, 19 Jan. 1751, HMC *9th Report*, ii (1884), 402.

lady of bad reputation who moved about in good society; and he was bigamously married to her by an unfrocked parson. A short time later he went off to Paris with her and two friends, became involved in an affair of gambling and robbery, which ended in November with his imprisonment in the Châtelet. He remained in prison for eleven days before the English ambassador could arrange for his release on bail. Lawsuits and counter-lawsuits dragged on into the following year at great expense to his father.[1] Lady Mary did not hear of his escapades until later, when she stoically advised Wortley not to be disturbed by their son's follies.[2]

For the summer of 1751 she had been reluctant to go to Lovere on account of the disagreeable journey and the noisy diversions there, but at the end of July was 'dragged' there by her doctor's orders. The journey at least improved her health.[3] She remained for several months, taking the regular cure, and did not return to Gottolengo until after November. During these months Wortley was on the Continent, having left England in June to travel in Hungary, Germany, and Lorraine, and returned home in November. They had been living apart for twelve years. She once judged his character well (about another matter) when she said that she knew no other man 'capable of such strength of resolution'.[4]

Her affection for her daughter continued to grow. As she told Wortley, 'Time and distance have increased, and not diminished, my tenderness for her'.[5] Lady Bute dutifully dispatched boxes of books, and as they arrived Lady Mary seized on them. She particularly relished memoirs of all kinds, for they revived the memory of people and places she had known. *Pompey the Little*, the adventures of a London lapdog, delighted her with its picture of social manners. Lady Vane's memoirs aroused her to reminisce about that persistently amorous lady and to add a crisp sermon on morality.[6] But the anonymous *Memoirs of a Coxcomb* must have startled her, though she did not tell Lady Bute. For as one of his adventures, the coxcomb

---

[1] These adventures are treated in detail in Curling, *Montagu*, 127–45.
[2] 22 Mar. 1753, W MS, ii. 237–8.
[3] To Lady Bute, 1 Nov., ii. 209; to W, 1 Aug. 1751, W MS, ii. 217–18.
[4] ii. 209 n.; M to W, 10 Sept. 1751, W MS, ii. 219–20; 29 Jan. 1752, ii. 216.
[5] 20 June 1751, ii. 208.
[6] To Lady Bute, 1 Mar., 16 Feb. 1752, ii. 220, 217–18.

tells about his affair with a lascivious woman of fashion named
Lady Bell Travers.[1] She had eloped to marry, thus saving her
father the expense of a dowry; and her rich suitor, having won
her, had become an indifferent husband. The coxcomb calls her
a 'seraglio of beauties', and is struck by her travelled air and by
her house at Twickenham furnished with ottomans and sofas;
and one of her friends is a caricature of Lord Hervey called
Lord Tersillion. The similarities between Lady Travers and
Lady Mary are unmistakable. The inventor of these memoirs
was John Cleland, who later won great fame with his porno-
graphic *Fanny Hill*. He may have met Lady Mary somewhere
in his wandering career, or he may have gathered the facts and
scandal from contemporary gossip to put together his *roman à
clef*. More surprising than anything in the book is that when
Lady Mary finished reading it she wrote on the flyleaf of her
copy her initial and one word: '*Instructif*'.[2]

When she read Richardson's *Clarissa Harlowe*, she was 'such
an old fool as to weep' over it like any milkmaid of sixteen over
a sad ballad. In her sober judgement she thought that it was
'miserable stuff' with a low style and absurd incidents; and that
together with *Pamela* it would do more general mischief than
the Earl of Rochester's works. Her simultaneous susceptibility
to the sentimental and disapproval of it was a frequent pattern
of her thought. She was aware of her inability to change it: 'All
that reflection and experience can do is to mitigate, we can
never extinguish, our passions. I call by that name every sentiment that is not founded upon reason.'[3]

The same attitude of reasonableness permeated her advice on
the education of her grandchildren. In January 1753 when Lady
Bute mentioned her eldest daughter's proficiency in arithmetic,
Lady Mary set about discussing education and feminism—as
she had three years before. Let the girl be educated in languages
('vehicles of learning'), in history, geography, and philosophy;
let her read English poetry; but let her conceal her learning
with as much care as she might hide crookedness or lameness.
The most peculiar part of her advice was that since matrimony
at best is hazardous, the girl should be prepared for spinster-

[1] (1751), pp. 281–324.
[2] Sotheby Cat. (1928), 84.
[3] To Lady Bute, 1 Mar. 1752, 24 May 1751, ii. 222, 204.

hood.[1] This time her prescriptions displeased Lady Bute, who answered sharply, pointing out as one objection the high expense of such a learned education. Lady Mary conceded that 'every one has a right to educate their children after their own way, and I shall speak no more on that subject'. A year later, when Lady Bute revealed her anxiety over her daughter's education, Lady Mary merely repeated that she still believed learning necessary to women's happiness, and ignorance the basis of bad morals and conduct. Her later remarks on education were pitched to the girls' being older: that they should gain their knowledge of people through going about in company instead of through reading silly novels; and that the maxim 'civility costs nothing and buys everything' should be engraved in their hearts.[2]

Except for her brief journeys to Lovere, she told Lady Bute, she lived 'in solitude not unlike that of Robinson Crusoe', and the people around her were as much companions to her as Crusoe's goats and kids were to him.[3] Yet her retirement was also an exile. When a box of china arrived from Lord Bute, she confessed that everything from England was precious to her, even the straw used in the packing. It was a severe destiny that denied her the happiness of seeing her daughter and her grandchildren. 'A mother only knows a mother's fondness', she said; and although she no longer mentioned her son, she occasionally thought of him because she could not overcome her tenderness in spite of her 'melancholy experience'.[4]

Late in the spring of 1754 she again became violently ill of a fever, and again her physician at Gottolengo diagnosed her certain death. But her neighbours sent for her physician at Lovere, and he ordered her to be carried there immediately. When her local physician warned her that she would not survive the journey, she declared it a matter of the utmost indifference where she expired. Carefully tended by servants and physicians, she reached Lovere alive, drank the curative waters, and in three days again enjoyed perfect health. She was so grateful to the 'miraculous' physician that in addition to his

---

[1] To Lady Bute, 28 Jan. 1753, ii. 224–8.
[2] To Lady Bute, 3 June 1753, 15 Apr. 1755, 19, 30 May 1756, ii. 234, 276, 298, 299.   [3] 3 June 1753, 28 Apr. 1754, ii. 235, 247.
[4] To Lady Bute, 22 Mar. 1756, 22 July, 28 Apr. 1754, ii. 293, 261–2, 248.

fees she later presented him with a Pinchbeck watch sent from England. Unwilling to stay as before in a public lodging-house, she purchased for the price of only £100 a ruined and tattered old palace with terraced gardens down to the lake. Instead of trying to restore the entire building, she had the walls and windows repaired in the rooms she needed—six for herself (including a great salon) and lodgings for her servants. She thus became a citizen of the town.[1] She liked it so well that instead of leaving at the end of the season she remained through 1755. An historian of the region described her house as having a staff of five servants and two extra maids, and costly horses in the stables. She entertained very hospitably when in good spirits and not retired to her inaccessible solitude.[2]

In August Count Palazzi, who also suffered from ill health, came to Lovere and took an apartment in a house near hers. As his neighbour, she observed that he led 'the most ridiculous life in the world'. This time he persuaded her into still another financial scheme: as a service to the Duchess of Guastalla, who wished to purchase furniture and china in England, Lady Mary gave him bills of exchange worth 2,000 sequins, payable to her in Venice or wherever she would spend the winter. In the following spring (1755) he moved to another resort where he hoped to restore his health.[3]

As in Avignon, she retired to her 'inaccessible solitude' in order to write. She again addressed an imaginary letter to Margaret of Navarre, this time in English:

> You will be surprised, my dear Mademoiselle, after so long having taken leave of follies of this nature, that I return to the little amusements of my childhood. But I am alone, 'tis [such] ill weather that I can find no diversion abroad, and 'tis necessary for me to make some to myself, or my melancholy, which you know to be too reasonable, would not fail to throw me into an ill state of health, which must always be an addition to any misfortune. I find these little works of fancy employ my thoughts more than any trifling book, and I would not indulge myself in being too attentive on a serious one. I choose to dedicate my follies to you, since I know you have that goodness not to expose them.

[1] To Lady Bute, 23 June 1754, 22 Sept. 1755, ii. 248–52, 284. Further details in 'Italian Memoir', ff. 17, 19–20.
[2] Marinoni, *Lady M e Lago d'Iseo*, 39.
[3] 'Italian Memoir', ff. 19–21.

She then launched abruptly into an elaborate pseudo-historical cycle of romantic tales of the Court of Louis XIV.[1] One tale recounts a tragic and thoroughly fictitious love affair between Mademoiselle de Condé and Fontenelle; and then neatly leads into the next tale, about the love of Mademoiselle's brother for a young ward of Madame de Maintenon.

During this period, probably, Lady Mary also wrote a long untitled fairy tale in French. It begins in witty fashion: 'Il y avait une reine de je ne sais quel royaume, très favorisée d'une vieille fée sans trop de raison; car c'était peut-être la personne du monde qui la méritait le moins, mais il est assez ordinaire de voir le caprice ou le hasard décider de la faveur des grands. . . .' As it continues it uses traditional devices of the genre, long digressive tales of intrigue, love, and adventure. In one of them a sea captain who has already voiced his cynicism with the remark: 'au vrai, je trouve le vieux honneur d'aussi mauvais goût que la vieille cuisine', reveals the great secret of life: 'c'est de [ne] s'ennuyer jamais!'[2] Never to be bored was the guiding principle of Lady Mary's own life, and in Lovere she succeeded through these literary exercises in seventeenth-century fictional modes.

All these private writings, along with her verse, were intended only to overcome loneliness and boredom. Remote from publishers in England and without any literary friends there, she could not write for publication. Besides, her aristocratic rank would not allow her to submit to the vulgarity of publication. At least she professed such an attitude. In Brescia she knew the rich and respected Cardinal Querini, who had founded a college for one hundred scholars, and installed a handsome library next to it. He sent one of his chaplains to her (in 1753) to ask whether she would present her works for his English collection. Surprised at the request, she told the chaplain that she had never published anything in her life. But he refused to believe her, and departed as though offended—as she knew his master would be. 'I really could cry for vexation,' she exclaimed to her daughter—and then revealed more than she intended: 'Sure nobody ever had such various provocations to print as myself. I have seen things I have wrote, so mangled and falsified,

---

[1] W MS, v. 11–12; ibid. vii. 379–87; ibid. Harrowby, vol. 257.
[2] W MS, vii. 310–78. Her interest in the *conte de fée* is discussed in my article in *Comp. Lit.* iii (1951), 174, 177.

I have scarce known them. I have seen poems I never read, published with my name at length; and others, that were truly and singly wrote by me, printed under the names of others. I have made myself easy under all these mortifications, by the reflection [that] I did not deserve them, having never aimed at the vanity of popular applause . . . I confess I have often been complimented, since I have been in Italy, on the books I have given the public.'[1] The unauthorized publication of her poems in 1747 had helped to keep her literary reputation alive. In 1754 a pamphleteer, riding the wave of moral reform in England, put her among Vice's friends and Virtue's foes, the 'nobly born' poetess who had disgraced her modest sex and illustrious race. But this same year she was extravagantly eulogized in an inoculation pamphlet for 'bringing into her own country a practice, of which ages to come will enjoy the benefit'.[2]

Her insistence that she had never published anything under her name was an expression of her aristocratic code that a person of quality should never turn author.[3] This was allied to another class standard, that writing for money made it a 'trade'. She enunciated the lofty belief that one of 'the most distinguishing prerogatives of mankind, writing, when duly executed' did honour to human nature, and that it was contemptible if done for the purpose of making money.[4] As she grew older, her other aristocratic principles ossified. She especially condemned the 'levelling principle' which exalted the lower classes. 'I wish to God I had always thought in the same manner,' she exclaimed; 'yet the silly prejudices of my education had taught me to believe I was to treat nobody as an inferior, and that poverty was a degree of merit: this imaginary humility has made me admit many familiar acquaintances, of which I have heartily repented every one, and the greatest examples I have known of honour and integrity have been among those of the highest birth and fortunes.' Her views were so reactionary, she realized, that if they were known she would be called an arrogant enemy of the poor. She particularly condemned Swift and Pope who

---

[1] 10 Oct. 1753, ii. 240–2.

[2] John Duncombe, *The Feminiad* (1754), 14; James Burges, *Account of the Preparation and Management Necessary to Inoculation*, 3.

[3] To Lady Bute, 23 July 1753, ii. 238. See pp. 50–51 above.

[4] To Lady Bute, 23 July 1753, 23 July 1755, ii. 236, 281; also *The Nonsense of Common-Sense* (ed. 1947), 25, 32, 40.

'by their birth and hereditary fortune' deserved to be only a couple of footmen.[1]

She championed the aristocracy at this time, in the 1750's, because she considered it maligned in the new English novels. She directed her sharpest criticism against Richardson, whose *Pamela* ('foolish stuff') had made him the rage of Europe. When her daughter sent her *Sir Charles Grandison*, she read it and then—as with his other novels—revealed her contradictory attitude: 'This Richardson is a strange fellow. I heartily despise him, and eagerly read him, nay, sob over his works in a most scandalous manner.' Yet she wrote on her copy: 'mean sentiments meanly expressed'. Then in a spirited analysis she explained to her daughter how he had distorted the morality and manners of his heroines to present a grossly inaccurate picture of upper-class life.[2] Richardson himself was aware of Lady Mary and her ideas. For in the first volume of *Grandison* he caricatured her as Miss Barnevelt: 'a lady of masculine features, and whose mind belied not those features; for she has the character of being loud, bold, free, even fierce when oppos'd; and affects at all times such airs of contempt of her own sex, that one almost wonders at her condescending to wear petticoats.... One reason, indeed, she everywhere gives, for being satisfied with being a woman; which is, *that she cannot be married to a* WOMAN.' Lady Mary assured her daughter that she was not 'angry with him for repeating a saying of mine, accompanied with a description of my person, which resembles me as much as one of the giants in Guildhall, and plainly shows he never saw me in his life'.[3] But Miss Barnevelt's mannerisms do resemble Lady Mary's, and as early as 1723 she had uttered her impatient remark about women.[4]

Reading English novels not only sweetened her solitude but also encouraged her to relate the human dramas around her— as part of her 'maternal privilege of being tiresome'. She saw

---

[1] To Lady Bute, 23 July 1753, 23 June 1754, ii. 237, 254.

[2] To Lady Bute, 8 Dec. 1754, 22 Sept., 20 Oct. 1755, ii. 262, 285, 285-91; Sotheby Cat. (1928), 95.

[3] Vol. i, Letter x; M to Lady Bute, ii. 289. The passage has never before been identified.

[4] To the Hon. Mrs. Calthorpe, 7 Dec. 1723, ii. 10. A variant among a group of her maxims, *c.* 1715-25: 'I am never pleased to think I am not a man but when I think I can never be married to a woman' (CB MS, f. 4).

nature imitate *Pamela* when a poor but virtuous and talented servant girl succeeded in marrying a wealthy nobleman who had first tried to seduce her. Her own servant Chechina was like Fanny in *Joseph Andrews*; and in another domestic comedy she observed a shrew as virtuous as a Richardson heroine accuse her husband of trying to poison her. Once Lady Mary even played the heroine of 'a small history' when she persuaded an irate husband not to kill his wife whom he discovered offering extreme hospitality to a young tenant.[1] In her little histories she often commented on the morality of Italian life. Yet at the same time she herself was heroine and victim in one stranger than those which she related to her daughter with so much gusto.

Her friendship with Count Palazzi was approaching its denouement. As she stated in her memoir, he had returned to Lovere in the fall of 1755, and although she wished to depart for Venice he persuaded her to return to Gottolengo to collect her belongings. When they arrived there, at the end of October, the Count pretended to be ill, and took to a bed in her house where he remained behind closed doors. At his suggestion she entrusted to a friend of his her last remaining jewel, a ring, consigned to one of her granddaughters.[2] Then, when he heard that her friend Lady Oxford had died, he had himself carried to her antechamber to tell her that his merchant-friend needed certain sums of money in London, which would be returned to her in Gottolengo, and that she should consign to him the legacy left to her, amounting to 400 sequins. At first she refused, but he nagged her so incessantly that after a month she gave in, and made out a note to the Duke of Portland (Lady Oxford's son-in-law) to pay the sum to the bearer. This was the last straw, as she related: 'Spring [1756] was advanced, and I was preparing to make the trip to Venice; and it was then I realized that I was a prisoner.' The Count had not imprisoned her in the ordinary sense of the word but rather through trickery and stratagems. Perhaps she realized it then and took action because she was visited by Lord Bute's relation General William Graeme, who had been asked by her worried daughter to look for her.

Now that she was resolved to move to Venice, somehow her carriages were broken, her horses lamed, her servants ill, the

---

[1] To Lady Bute, ii. 284, 262-7, 186, 294-6, 187-91.
[2] To Lady Bute, 2 Nov. 1755, ii. 293.

rivers reported swollen and roads impassable; and the doctors warned her that the journey would certainly cause her death. When the Count saw that she was determined to leave, he enacted a new, more dramatic scene. He had her summoned to his bedroom where he lay pale and disfigured, and whispered to her that he thought he could find her jewels; they had been pawned to a relation of the Pope's, and could be redeemed for 1,200 sequins. She greeted his story with laughter, and left. That afternoon he had himself carried into her room, and in another tearful scene begged her help in removing the blot from his family escutcheon: the thief had confessed before dying, and now the jewels were in the house. Whereupon a monk entered carrying one of the Count's valises, and took out of it some of her belongings sent from Avignon (including a diamond and ruby snuff-box) and her jewels broken as though for dispersal. She reclaimed them, but refused to pay anything to the Count. In the morning, while the postilion and horses waited, at his request she wrote a letter stating that she was satisfied with his conduct. As a favour he begged her to visit his aunt Madame Roncadelli, and he extracted from her a note for 400 sequins drawn on her Italian banker. She then set off for Venice.

In her party were her maid, her old *valet de chambre*, and Dr. Bartolomeo Moro, originally the Count's secretary, whom she had engaged the year before because she thought him a man of spirit, erudition, and honesty.[1] When she reached Madame Roncadelli's house, where she was cordially received, she drew from her suitcase the little bag where she kept her notes and deeds. They had all been transformed into blank paper. When the Count arrived the following day she refused to listen to him except in his aunt's presence, and Madame Roncadelli agreed. Then, Lady Mary's memoir continues: 'She wept, and took my hand and kissed it, and led me into the room where he was. He wanted to make a long discourse with sobs. I cut his sermon short, and said to him that I had not come to hear his excuses, but to demand the return of my papers. "They are burned," he replied weeping, "but if they hadn't been they would be of no further use to you, for they were all false." His aunt seemed to

---

[1] Her will in 1762 states that Dr. Moro had been in her employ for seven years (1887 ed., i. lxviii, n.). His name was sometimes spelled Mora.

swoon, and I left the room saying, "You are an unworthy thief."' Lady Mary then locked herself in her room and reflected on her strange situation. Fearful that the Count might have her killed on the road if he thought she would prosecute him, she hid her resentment, and in the morning faced Madame Roncadelli calmly. New land deeds were drawn up, except for the house in Gottolengo, which was entailed. As a final concession the Count was to repay her last note for 400 sequins. Lady Mary agreed to all the proposals. The Count drew up an agreement, which his aunt brought in, along with a notary and witnesses.

'When I had read it,' Lady Mary continued, 'I found that in obscure terms it stated that I had lived ten years at his expense. I tore the paper into a thousand pieces, saying loudly that they wished to betray me vilely. Dr. Moro came near me, all trembling, and said in a low voice, "Madame, calm yourself. Think of your danger." I answered, raising my voice, "I would rather die than subscribe to such an infamous lie which dishonours me." The lady and all her attendants went out confused, and I returned to bed.' The next morning Madame Roncadelli apologized, saying that she had not read the agreement, and presented a new one providing for the restitution of the lands and the 400 sequins. Lady Mary signed it in order to be allowed to leave. When the Count, as a last favour, asked whether she would allow him to accompany her as far as Mantua, she consented, perhaps out of fear.[1]

At Mantua, where she stopped at an inn, she sent her daughter a letter on 22 August. In it she complained of her difficulties in obtaining Lady Oxford's legacy, and then stated: 'I am determined to go to Venice myself to try to settle our commerce in a better manner.'[2] At Vicenza she was surprised to hear that the Count had taken a room at the inn where she planned to stay. She did not ask why, but simply left for Padua in the morning without seeing him. Then—as her 'Italian Memoir' abruptly concludes:

I met him a mile from the city, and he informed me that he had prepared an apartment for me. I understood that he wished to hide from the public his evil proceedings, and I went into the apartment. I stayed two or three days, during which time I took a house in

Padua, and afterwards went to Venice. The Count had again prepared an apartment for me. I stayed in it three days, and again
returned to Padua, where I found the Count had installed himself
in the quarters of my Swiss servant near the door. I sent him word
that I did not run a lodging-house, and asked him to leave. I
demanded the deeds to my lands and the name of the merchant who
had received the Countess of Oxford's legacy. He refused the one
and the other, and left for Gottolengo. He came back a few weeks
later, but he neither returned the deeds nor did he wish to tell me
who had received the money from the Duke of Portland.[1]

Although rid of him she was still embarrassed by the scandalous reputation of their friendship. After she had arrived in
Venice on 8 September 1756 the English Minister John Murray
described her in his dispatch: 'She has been for some years past,
and still continues, in the hands of a Brescian Count, who it is
said plunders her of all her riches.'[2] During this brief visit in
Venice, she saw General Graeme again. He was also a friend of
Algarotti—then living in Bologna—and wrote to him after she
had left: 'Lady Mary is at liberty, lives at Padua, and I fancy
intends to call Count Palazzi to account. I do not know the
tenth part of her history there, but she began to hint it to me
when last here. She is more ashamed, I believe, for passing for
a dupe in the eye of the public, than she is for passing for a
woman of gallantry.'[3]

She then drew up her memoir for legal purposes, intending
to have the Count prosecuted. According to General Graeme's
report, Count Rosenberg, the Imperial ambassador, an old
acquaintance of Lady Mary's in Vienna, was 'friendly to her
in a process she had with Count Palazzi about a house in the
Mantuan [province] . . .'.[4] It is difficult to see the whole picture
from her own testimony in the memoir, with its necessarily
detailed emphasis on her financial involvements with the Count.
There is not a hint of any amorous involvement, and there is
little likelihood that there was any. She enjoyed the felicities of
her retirement in spite of the Count's financial importunities.

---

  [1] 'Italian Memoir', f. 36. The total sum which the Count extracted from her,
as added from her memoir, was at least 5,000 sequins (equivalent to about
£2,500).
  [2] To Henry Fox, 10 Sept. 1756, SP 99/66.
  [3] Quoted in *Quart. Rev.* xxiii (1820), 417.
  [4] To Lord Bute, 8 Sept. 1758, Bute MS.

Her memoir at least uncovers one important aspect of her decade in Brescia which she does not show in her ample letters where she described her country pleasures, commented on new books, and doted on her daughter and growing grandchildren.

xv. *Venice and Padua*

(1756-61)

WHEN Lady Mary, at the age of sixty-seven, moved to Venice and Padua, she anticipated a pleasant life among new and old friends. Lord Bute's relation General William Graeme was a Scottish gentleman who had entered the military service of the Dutch states and then of Venice, where he had risen to commander-in-chief.[1] The English Resident John Murray and his wife Lady Wentworth were 'worthy friendly people', the General thought; and Lady Mary passed much of her time with them and with the old Consul Joseph Smith who was married to Murray's sister. The Imperial ambassador, an old acquaintance, visited her. Of the Venetians whom she knew from her earlier visit, Madame Chiara Michieli was her most intimate friend.[2]

The most surprising of her friendships was with the ambitious and ubiquitous Algarotti. Except for the years 1742 to 1746, when he was employed by the King of Poland, he had remained at Frederick's court until 1753; he then retired on account of ill health, and settled in the villa Mirabella ten miles from Padua. His former Royal master remembered him acutely as 'a man of taste, of gentle mind, keen, shrewd, supple, but a great wheedler, and above all very selfish'.[3] By the time Lady Mary arrived in Venice he had moved from Mirabella and was staying in Bologna.[4] From there he had apparently written to her before she left Brescia, and she did not answer him for the curious reason (or joke) that she had been assured that he had died of an apoplexy a few days after writing to her. The friend who

---

[1] Louisa G. Graeme, *Or and Sable, A Book of the Graemes and Grahams* (1903), 428.   [2] Graeme to Bute, 8 Sept. 1758, Bute MS.
[3] 1758, Henry de Catt, *Fred. the Great*, transl. F. S. Flint (1916), i. 33.
[4] Treat, *Algarotti*, 195.

repeated this to Algarotti (from Padua on 30 October) continued: 'Enfin, elle vous fait les excuses et désire de vous connaître elle sera à Venise en 10 ou 12 jours. Si vous voulez faire connaissance avec elle, je vous prie d'avance de manger la soupe avec Madame Zenobio et Lady Mary. . . . Adieu, cher comte. Vale et me ama.'[1] Despite the invitation to meet Lady Mary, whom he had not seen in fifteen years, Algarotti remained in Bologna.

Their revived friendship was far different from its initial phase. Perhaps a trace of coquetry remained in Lady Mary, for in her Commonplace Book she made a memorandum: 'to wear jet bracelets when I see Al.'. But in another entry she expressed a more realistic opinion of his importance to her: 'Algarotti *hors d'œuvre*'.[2] Instead of going to Venice he sent her several of his published works, and offered her the use of his villa. 'I gratefully accept your obliging offer of your delightful Mirabella,' she answered at the end of December, 'but am resolved to see it in full beauty, which it cannot be without the presence of the Master. . . . I cannot refuse the General's solicitation, and shall pass (at least) some part of the Carnival at Venice. I propose to be the Lent in Padua, or if you are there, at Mirabella.'[3]

When Algarotti answered to say he would not go to Mirabella for Lent, he apparently bestowed some charming flattery on her. After thanking him for it, she went on:

Je n'ai pas manquée de faire vos compliments au General. Il vous embrasse de tout son cœur, dit-il, mais (entre nous) je lui crois un peu piqué d'avoir assiégé une place six mois sans qu'il peut se vanter d'avoir fait grand progrès que vous avez emporté d'assaut en moins de quinze jours. Il faut pardonner des froideurs que viennent d'une cause si legitime. Il a beau donner des fêtes, servir à l'opéra et, qui pis est, perdre son argent à pharaon. Si l'inclination ne trahit point, le chateau est invincible. Je me garde bien de lui annoncer cette triste nouvelle. La chasse est souvent agréable, quoi qu'on ne prend rien. . . . Nous nous reverrons. Que j'aurais des choses à vous dire![4]

How did Algarotti regard her giddy letter? His answer from Bologna, the only one of his letters to her that is preserved, had enough dignity to find a place in his collected works. 'Da questa

[1] Murray MS.
[2] CB MS, f. 21.
[3] 30 Dec. 1756, Murray MS.
[4] 19 Feb. 1757, Bod. MS, ff. 39–40.

dotta città in cui sono io trasmetto un breve saggio sopra gli antichi e moderni a voi, Milady, che dimorando in Padova vi avete fermate le Muse.' Continuing in the same vein of pompous compliment, he alluded to her many writings and journeys and to her mind free of all prejudices.[1] As a savant and writer, he preferred to restrict their friendship to literary matters, and to remain in the distance.

Soon after her arrival in Padua she had leased a modest, convenient house and garden on the San Massimo, a street bordering the small river on the outskirts of the city. Here she indulged in the domestic pastimes that had so delighted her in Brescia; and when guests came she served home-made bread and butter. Since Padua lay on the main road to Milan and Turin many English travellers stopped to see her. It was in general her favourite place, where she would have preferred to stay; but Venice also attracted her, though for different reasons. She lived there in lodgings until the spring of 1757, when she leased a small house with a garden large enough for her to walk in during the morning. Since both her houses were unfurnished, she had the 'pains and expense' (as well as pleasure) of furnishing them.[2] Once established in her two houses she made alterations and additions, which she explained to her daughter: 'Building is the general weakness of old people; I have had a twitch of it myself.'[3] Her way of life was, in a sense, a throwback to her residence in England, with Venice as her London, and Padua as her Twickenham. When she moved from Venice to Padua, as in April 1757, she was accompanied by her steward, her secretary Dr. Moro, and a man and woman servant.[4] She passed frequently between the two places, her activities alternating between studious retirement and social pleasures.

For her reading she still depended on her daughter to send her new books. She wanted no translations or periodicals, she told her, and no duplicates of the ephemeral books that made up the bulk of her reading: 'as well as I love nonsense, I do not desire to have it twice over in the same words'. She copied titles

[1] 3 Mar. 1757, Algarotti, *Opere* (1792–4), ix. 312–13.
[2] To W, 8 Dec. 1756, Paston, 497; to Lady Bute, 3 Apr., 9 Oct. 1757, 20 Jan. 1758, ii. 305, 312–13, 314; to W, 24 Jan. 1759, ii. 354.
[3] To Lady Bute, 22 May 1759, ii. 358.
[4] Busta 758 (Forestieri), Inquisitori di Stato, Archivio di Stato, Venice.

from booksellers' advertisements in London newspapers, and apologetically sent them to her daughter: 'I do not doubt at least the greatest part of these are trash, lumber, etc.' Yet when her daughter criticized her choice as trash, lumber, and sad stuff, she vigorously defended her favourite amusement as the pleasure of her second childhood. Frivolous reading soothed her nerves, and as a pastime was greatly superior to cards or company. As her experience had proved, it was 'capable of softening the cruelest accidents of life; even the happiest cannot be passed over without many uneasy hours; and there is no remedy so easy as books, which, if they do not give cheerfulness, at least restore quiet to the most troubled mind'.[1]

In general her life in Venice was cheerful and untroubled. Foreigners living in the city enjoyed the many cheap amusements, the gentle manners of the Venetians, and the perfect freedom in everything (except local politics).[2] Lady Mary had been struck by these felicities on her first visit; and now, seventeen years later, when she was an old lady, they were even more delightful and convenient. There were no formalities of a court or set *devoirs* to force one into public; and the custom of masking allowed her to go to the opera 'without the mortification of showing a wrinkled face'.[3] Old age had not diminished her normal share of vanity. She put the matter succinctly when she wrote to a friend of the advantages of masking: 'no toilette can fight against nature'. She even wore her jewels occasionally, though for the odd reason that if she did not it would be reported that she had pawned them.[4] (When General Graeme had seen her wearing them, he estimated their value at £2,000, though Consul Smith put the figure at £1,500.)[5] During the carnival season preceding Lent, a time of 'much pageantry and very fine Balls', the privilege of masking was not at all disagreeable to her.[6]

But before long her enjoyment of life in Venice was wrecked by her bitter hatred of John Murray and his family. Eight

[1] To Lady Bute, 3 Apr., 30 Sept. 1757, 3, 13 May 1758, ii. 305, 310–11, 317, 318.

[2] John Moore, *A View of Society and Manners in Italy* (1803), i. 206.

[3] To Lady Bute, 5 Dec. 1758, ii. 352.

[4] To Miss Tichborne, 30 May 1760 (summary), CB MS, f. 18; to Lady Bute, 5 Sept. 1758, ii. 337.   [5] Graeme to Bute, 8 Sept. 1758.

[6] To Lady Bute, 7 Mar. 1759, Paston, 509.

months after she met him, she had changed her opinion of his character: 'a scandalous fellow, in every sense of that word, he is not to be trusted to change a sequin, despised by this government for his smuggling, which was his original profession, and always surrounded with pimps and brokers, who are his privy councillors'. How unfortunate, she exclaimed, that with few exceptions England's foreign ministers were of such low birth and behaviour. As proofs of his discourtesy, she charged him (in February 1758) with neglecting to send her the English newspapers or to visit her. She blamed his enmity on politics: that he accused her of favouring William Pitt, co-leader of the new coalition government, while he zealously supported the opposition faction. At the beginning she took their feud lightly, and laughed at being mistaken for a politician, but a few months later his 'political airs' were so disagreeable that she was inclined to move away, were it not for her leased and furnished houses.[1]

Her political role may have developed from the fact that Lord Bute was Groom of the Stole and principal adviser to the Prince of Wales. The failure of her own son obscurely living in England swelled her pride in her son-in-law, so that she congratulated her husband: 'It is a satisfaction I never hoped, to have a son that does honour to his family.'[2] When Lord Bute informed her in August 1757 that Lady Bute had given birth to a daughter, she thanked him and then added: 'I wish I was as well known to you, as you are to me. Though I was only acquainted with you in your early youth, your character then appeared to me the same which is now universally allowed you.'[3] She served as godmother to the child, who was christened Louisa, and prophetically told her daughter: 'may she be as meritorious in your eyes as you are in mine!' Lady Louisa, who never married, was her mother's favourite child and constant companion, and eventually became her grandmother's memoirist. Lady Mary lavished her grandmotherly affection on all the 'little colony', though their remoteness filled her with 'melancholy joy'. In her emotion she returned to the 'milky disposition' of her infancy, she explained, and like an old fool wept

---

[1] To Lady Bute, 30 May 1757, 21 Feb., 12 Apr. (date corrected) 1758, ii. 307, 315-16, 314.
[2] 4 Jan. 1757, 16 Sept. 1758, ii. 304, 337.
[3] 24 Sept. 1757, Bute MS.

for her daughter and grandchildren who were the remote comfort of her exile.[1]

She expressed another, quite different side of her disposition in her friendship for Algarotti and in her practice as a writer. In the summer of 1758, probably, she completed a short lyrical poem entitled 'A Hymn to the Moon', written (her subtitle stated) in an arbour. In this setting she confided her grief to the 'silver deity of secret night' who is both the Lover's guardian and the Muse's aid. Then, in an obvious parallel between the 'fair queen' and herself, she pointed out that the moon, even though great, cold, and high, could draw the charms of young Endymion.[2] Perhaps the poem hinted of her friendship for Algarotti, for she sent him a copy of it with a letter invoking the memory of Lord Hervey—the equivocal witness of their early intimacy.

I received yours by General Graham with great pleasure, but as I am destined never to taste pleasure without a strong dash of mortification, I am very sorry to find my two letters miscarried and also the copy of the ode you desired. Here is another [copy] which I hope may reach you, notwithstanding the mountain between us. If we ever meet, the memory of Lord Hervey shall be celebrated; his gentle shade will be pleased in Elysium with our gratitude. I am insensible to every thing but the remembrance of those few friends that have been dear to me.[3]

Algarotti thought highly enough of her ode to print it in his works accompanied by a graceful eulogy of her literary talents. 'Tiene ella nel Parnaso inglese un onoratissimo luogo', he put in his introduction to it.[4]

His flattery encouraged her to try to deserve it, and she sent him a strenuously clever letter. '. . . Vous voyez que je donne tête baissée dans tous les désordres du Carnival. J'avoue que je ne suis plus en droit de me moquer des monarques qui dissipent leur trésors et diminuent leur sujets pour une fantôme d'ambition; moi, qui dissipe ma santé et diminue le peu de jours qui me restent pour courir après une fantôme. . . .' She then set forth a

[1] Lady Mary Coke to Lady Dalkeith, 5 Sept. 1757, Letters and Journals (1889) I. xiii, n. 1; 174, n. i; M to Lady Bute, 30 Sept. 1757, 5 Sept. 1758, ii. 310, 335. [2] ii. 487; her Italian transl. ii. 488.
[3] Murray MS. In the margin of the letter: 'Hymn to the Moon.'
[4] Opere, vii. 79–81.

paradox: pheasants and partridges are killed to serve man; and while many men killed in war deserve the noose, the poor birds are completely innocent. 'Est-il juste,' she asked, 'de regarder avec horreur un champ de bataille jonché de corps morts, et avec joie un souper pour lequel on a fait un massacre de cents espèces différents? Si j'étais d'humeur à écrire, je ferai un épître au nom de tous les animaux au plus grand guerrier du siècle pour l'encourager au carnage de ces tyrants qui s'imaginent d'être privilégié d'exerciser la cruauté le plus énorme.'[1]

'Si j'étais d'humeur à écrire. . . .' Apparently using her letter as a rough sketch, she wrote a brief, delightfully pointed fable. 'Dans une belle journée de l'automne un dindon marchait à la tête de sa troupe avec autant de fierté qu'un consul romain à la tête du Sénat.' The turkey advises his comrades to enjoy life as much as they can because the cruel tyrant man cuts their days short. As he invites them to enjoy a meal of some nearby ants, one of the insects speaks up: 'Et vous barbare, que vous plaignez de l'homme! Vous croyez qu'il vous est permis de massacrer tout un peuple pour un déjeuner! Sachez que quand nous vous voyons plumé nous regardons cette main meurtrière comme l'instrument de la juste vengeance de la désolation de notre race.'[2] When Algarotti flattered her—perhaps for her fable— she acknowledged it with effusive thanks: 'Vous me flattez, Monsieur, mais vous savez assaisonner la flatterie de tant des grâces, il est impossible de ne pas s'y plaire. . . .'[3] He could still exhibit the grace and delicacy which had once enchanted her; now, as a fellow *bel esprit*, he aroused only her intellectual and literary passion. He was, as she phrased it, *hors d'œuvre*.

In the spring of 1758 she acquired a new, warmer friend. Sir James Steuart, a brilliant Scottish lawyer, after having been exiled for his part in the 1745 Jacobite uprising, had eventually settled with his wife, Lady Frances, and their son at Tübingen, where he devoted himself to learned studies. He had written books on Newton's chronology and on German coins, and a still unpublished *magnum opus* on political economy. Then, because of poor health, he travelled with his wife through the

---

[1] Bod. MS, ff. 48–49. It probably refers to Fred. of Prussia's bloody victory of Rossbach, Nov. 1757.

[2] W MS, vii. 308–9. The same apologue had been used by John Gay for his 38th fable.

[3] 5 Mar. 1758, Bod. MS, ff. 42–43.

Tyrol and into Italy.[1] When they reached Venice at the beginning of May, John Murray reported to the Secretary of State: 'Sir James Steuart arrived here ten days ago with his family from Suabia. He has taken pains to induce me to receive him, but I could by no means comply with it. I don't find that he has any other call into Italy but on account of his health, and I am told he intends to take a house in the Venetian State.'[2] As England's representative Murray obviously could not receive a man outlawed by the government, but he was clearly aware of Sir James's non-political mission.

When Lady Mary heard of their arrival, she told her daughter, their name—the same as Lord Bute's—made her 'fly' to call on them: 'I was charmed to find a man of uncommon sense and learning, and a lady that without beauty is more amiable than the fairest of her sex. I offered them all the little good offices in my power, and invited them to supper.'[3] Many years later Lady Frances recalled to what an extraordinary degree they had experienced Lady Mary's 'humanity and benevolence', how she 'flew to them with eagerness, and, quitting all other company, made it her sole business to administer to their consolation and entertainment'. As to Lady Mary's personality: 'Sir James Steuart could not avoid being charmed with such a companion, especially as Lady Mary's judgment was accompanied with a refined taste, and her opinions of things were pronounced with a decision which rendered them very lively and forcible, if not absolutely convincing. Her temper was warm and keen, and, wherever she conceived an attachment, she carried it to the utmost height . . . her friendship for them partook of all the ardour of her disposition.'[4] Lady Mary once reminded Sir James: 'You know I am enthusiastic in my friendships.'[5] Her enthusiasm for him and his family did not flag for the rest of her life.

In Padua, where the Steuarts moved after a short time, they lived in Lady Mary's house, which (her concierge informed her in Venice) they had found clean and comfortable. She con-

[1] [Andrew Kippis] 'Memoir of Sir James Steuart Denham, Bart.', *Coltness Coll. 1608–1840*, ed. J. Dennistoun (1842), 295–309, 376.
[2] To William Pitt, 12 May 1758, SP 99/67.
[3] 13 May 1758, ii. 318.
[4] Kippis, 'Memoir' (obviously Lady Frances's recollections), 309–10.
[5] 4 Sept. 1758, ii. 331.

tinued to perform whatever 'good offices' she could. Since an accident had deprived them of their trusted woman servant— the accident was seduction—she hired a man servant who would return with them to Germany.[1] Then in order to enjoy the best company she had ever known, before the end of May she rejoined her new friends at Padua and (according to Lady Frances) 'became the kind, the generous, and the constant support of their drooping spirits, and entered deeply into all their concerns'. Sir James derived more enjoyment from some hours of her conversation, when she was in good spirits, than he could have had from the most interesting and entertaining book.[2] At the end of August the Steuarts departed for Germany, but she continued her attempts to help Sir James: through her daughter to have him pardoned and allowed to return to England; and probably through the Imperial ambassador in Venice, to recommend him as instructor to Maria Theresa's son and heir.[3] The Steuarts themselves had been of great benefit to Lady Mary by assuaging her loneliness.

At the beginning of September (1758) General Graeme, who had been on a fourteen-month tour of the Venetian dominions, returned to Venice. He called on Lady Mary, and was shocked at how much she had 'failed' in the two years since her arrival there. She had also developed a slight deafness. When he tried, as before, to persuade her to return home, she again waved the subject aside, telling him that the air of England never agreed with her health. He observed that she lived a retired life, staying at home a great deal and exchanging a few ceremonious visits with the ladies whom she had known when she first came to Venice. Her household consisted of a cook, two men and two maidservants, all directed by Dr. Moro. Although she tried to prevent their cheating her, the General noted that she suffered the disadvantages of being old and of employing Italian servants. He sent these observations to Lord Bute, and promised that when he saw Lady Mary he would remind her of her former intention of sending her jewels to England and of making him executor of her will. He would also again urge her

---

[1] To Sir J. Steuart, May 1758, ii. 320–1.
[2] Kippis, 'Memoir', 310–11.
[3] 'Anecdotes', Steuart, *Works Political, Metaphysical, and Chronological,* ed. Gen. Sir J. Steuart (1805), vi. 372.

to return to England.[1] But when he dined with her a few weeks later,[2] he failed to win her consent to any of his proposals.

Her effusive friendship for Sir James Steuart had opened a new, more intensive period of her war with Murray, who she claimed had thus discovered her to be 'in the interest of popery and slavery'. His main persecution was to keep English people from visiting her. 'Such is the behaviour of my loving countrymen!' she exclaimed to her daughter, whose sympathy she repeatedly tried to win. Although she pretended that she suffered very little in losing the visits of English boys and their governors, it diminished her opportunities for finding eligible young men to marry her numerous granddaughters.[3] Lest her daughter should think that her 'imprudent behaviour' had caused the feud, she assured her that she always treated Murray and his family with the utmost civility. At the same time, she cautioned Lady Bute: 'Do not tell your father these foolish squabbles'; she feared he would blame her for misplaced raillery or vivacity.[4] But she gently prepared him for finding out by telling him that she supposed factions in England must be high since the English Resident in Venice made such great distinctions.[5]

In one of her letters to Sir James Steuart, she apologized: 'you are bound to have indulgence for me, as for a sister of the quill'.[6] It was true that she had never relinquished her pen. She was almost seventy at this time when she began a form of writing new to her. The most amusing of her 'trifling' employments, she told her daughter, was writing a history of her own time:

It has been my fortune to have a more exact knowledge both of the persons and facts that have made the greatest figure in England in this age, than is common; and I take pleasure in putting together what I know, with an impartiality that is altogether unusual. Distance of time and place has totally blotted from my mind all traces either of resentment or prejudice; and I speak with the same indifference of the court of G[reat] B[ritain] as I should do that of Augustus Caesar. I hope you have not so ill opinion of me to think

---

[1] Graeme to Bute, 8 Sept. 1758.　　[2] M to Lady Bute, 3 Oct. 1758, ii. 340.
[3] To Lady Bute, 29 May, 14 July, 21 Aug., 4 July 1758, ii. 318, 322, 326, 329, 323–4.　　　　　　　　　　　　　　　[4] ii. 322, 327.
[5] To W [n.d.], rec'd 21 July 1758, W MS, ii. 251.
[6] 5 Sept 1758, ii. 334.

I am turning author in my old age. I can assure you I regularly burn every quire as soon as it is finished; and mean nothing more than to divert my solitary hours.[1]

Her private purpose breaks through in one of the fragments of her history when she explains: 'as I write only for myself, I shall always think I am at liberty to make what digressions I think fit, proper or improper'.[2] Two fragments escaped the flames, a very brief one on the death of Queen Anne, and a long brilliant sketch of George I's court at the time of his accession. These memoirs, which have recently been accorded historical importance, display the undiminished power of her mind and pen.[3]

Her earlier career as a writer of witty verse, as remote as the Court of George I, flared up briefly. The song which she had written as Lord William Hamilton's answer to Lady Hertford's 'passionate addresses' in 1733 had never been printed until Dodsley put it into the sixth volume of his *Collection of Poems.* When Lady Mary saw the verses, she exclaimed to her daughter that she was provoked beyond Job and Socrates: 'By what accident they have fallen into the hands of that thing Dodsley, I know not, but he has printed them as addressed, by me, to a very contemptible puppy, and my own words as his answer.' In print it is Lady Mary who makes the amorous proposal to Sir William Yonge, a politician and wit.[4] Although her friends would be aware of Dodsley's impudence, she thought, her reputation in England would suffer.[5]

At the end of 1758 she missed her new friends in Germany so keenly that she planned to spend the following summer in the Tyrol with them, but changed her mind because of the difficult journey.[6] Though distant, she still regarded Sir James with esteem and affection, and could even confide in him her opinion of Algarotti, as when she remarked: 'Algarotti is at Bologna, I believe, composing panegyrics on whoever is victor in this

---

[1] 1 Oct. 1758, ii. 338.   [2] i. 128.

[3] i. 122, 123–4. Extracts on pp. 45–47 above. They are accepted as reliable by Wolfgang Michael, *England under George I,* i. 82–101 *passim.*

[4] *Collection,* vi. 230–1. In M's album (Harrowby, vol. 255) the verses are labelled: 'Answered (Song by the Countess of Hartfort) by Me. M.W.M.' Discussed on p. 145 above.

[5] 8 Nov., 5 Dec. 1758, ii. 345–6, 351.

[6] To Sir J. Steuart, 27 Nov. 1758, ii. 350; to Lady Bute, 31 Dec. 1758, W MS, iii. 217–18; to Lady Bute [n.d.], ii. 371.

PLATE 14

Mary Countess of Bute

From a pastel by Catherine Read

uncertain war.'[1] She was now a better judge of the Italian's character. Sir James on his side had a high opinion of her judgement, and sent her a manuscript copy of his book on political economy, with a dedication addressed to her. She had never before received so much pleasure and instruction from a treatise, she replied; its 'nervous' style pleased her, and its dedication would have done honour to Lord Burleigh or even Julius Caesar![2] When her thoughts turned to old age, she found him a sympathetic recipient of her philosophy of genial stoicism.[3] This attitude was her defence against Murray's persecution, which she suffered again in the spring of 1759. A young visiting Englishman and his governor who were civil to her had been disagreeably treated by him, and General Graeme's intervention brought no relief. The General was her confidant, as she noted in a memorandum: 'to tell the General [that] M[urray] asked me to be employed in my affairs; I did not ask him'.[4] When she inquired of Murray why he did not behave civilly to her, he replied that it was not in his instructions.[5] She could defend herself from his rudeness by means of her facile versifying, a weapon she used during an encounter one evening with him and some of the English colony in Venice.[6]

As her daughter became increasingly occupied with family and social duties, and her husband with old age, Lady Mary found other recipients for her letters besides Sir James. In an old revived friendship she had begun to write to Miss Wilhelmina Tichborne in London, who had been Woman of the Bedchamber to Queen Caroline.[7] 'The world the same in all climates and generations', she summarized one letter; 'perhaps wars are all of the past; knowledge out of reach; we are condemned to stay below ever since the Tower of Babel.'[8] She occasionally expressed herself more pungently to her than to her daughter; instead of describing her retired 'college hours' amidst the social bustle, she wrote: 'I am at Padua like a mouse in a Parmesan

---

[1] 8 Aug. 1759, ii. 366 (referring to Fred. of Prussia and the Seven Years War).
[2] To Sir J. Steuart, 1 Mar. 1760, ii. 376. Published in 1767, when Lady Mary was no longer alive, the book bore no dedication.
[3] ii. 353; 8 Aug. 1759 (date corrected), ii. 362.
[4] To Lady Bute, 11 Apr. 1759, ii. 355; CB MS, f. 21.
[5] ii. 320, n. 1.   [6] 8 Aug. 1759 (date corrected), ii. 362-4.
[7] Only the summaries of Lady Mary's letters to her are preserved in the Commonplace Book; and one letter from her, 25 July 1757, in Paston, 500-2.
[8] 13 Apr. 1759, CB MS, f. 16.

cheese.'[1] In May 1759 she mentioned to her friend a desire as yet unrevealed to her daughter and her husband: 'I wish to see nothing in London but herself and the museum'—referring to the newly opened British Museum. A few months later she put it more elaborately: that she 'would part with all the palaces of Palladio for a pavilion near hers, and avoid being troublesome'. But, she added, she 'must not indulge such day-dreams'. When General Graeme had suggested it, she waved it aside. Now, when Miss Tichborne encouraged her, she stifled the plan with: 'I would be troublesome if at London'.[2]

A few months later, in February 1760, she had a sound reason for broaching the plan to her daughter. As Wortley approached his eighty-third year, he suffered failing health and imminent blindness.[3] Lady Mary feared that if he fell into the control of his servants, particularly since their son was on the scene, he would be imposed upon—probably to change his will. Her own motives, she assured her daughter, were completely unselfish: 'I have outlived the greatest part of my acquaintance, and to say truth, a return to crowd and bustle after my long retirement would be disagreeable to me; yet if I could be of use either to your Father or your Family, I would venture shortening the insignificant days of your most affectionate Mother.'[4] But apparently she received no encouragement to return. Her son had published a long, turgid study, *Reflections on the Rise and Fall of the Antient Republicks* (whose authorship was also claimed by one of his former tutors), and he sent Lady Mary a copy, and then a deeply contrite letter to confess past mischief and beg for guidance.[5] But her disgust for him was firmly set; she had 'long wept the misfortune of being mother to such an animal'.[6]

She was amply consoled by her son-in-law's spectacular rise. Lord Bute's political power, which depended on the Prince of Wales and the Dowager Princess, steadily advanced as the health of the King declined. On 25 October 1760 the Prince ascended the throne as George the Third. Two days later Lord

---

[1] To Lady Bute, 24 June, ii. 360; to Miss Tichborne, 15 June 1759, CB MS, f. 16.   [2] 20 May, 12 Aug., 17 Nov. 1759, CB MS, ff. 16–17.
[3] Drafts W to M, 15 Oct. 1757, 5 Jan., 29 Dec. 1759, W MS, i. 141–4 (frag. in Paston, 509–10).   [4] 12 Feb. 1760, Paston, 511.
[5] Curling, *Montagu*, 146–7; Paston, 512.
[6] To Lady Bute [Mar. 1760], Paston, 510–11.

Bute, retaining his post as Groom of the Stole, was appointed to the Privy Council. As soon as Lady Mary knew of her daughter's elevation, though she knew her to be 'sufficiently tormented by pretensions and petitions' she requested only that Anderson, her son's former tutor, be rewarded, and that Sir James Steuart's name be included in the act of indemnity. She also sent her good wishes: 'I bless God I have lived to see you so well established, and am ready to sing my *Nunc dimittis* with pleasure.'[1] Lord Bute's position had no effect on Murray's persecution, of which she complained to Sir James Steuart, her daughter, and James Stuart Mackenzie, Lord Bute's brother, who was Minister in Turin.[2] Murray ingeniously protected himself, she told her daughter, by spreading reports that she had forfeited her daughter's favour, and hence could not possibly share in Lord Bute's power.[3] The Venetians had already asked her to recommend that their two ambassadors appointed by the Senate to compliment the King should be received (instead of merely thanked and not permitted to come); and she passed the request on to her daughter only a week after she knew of the King's accession.[4] Still, at that distance she remained a passive, discreet witness of her son-in-law's good fortune.

Almost two years had elapsed since she sent for a pair of china jars standing in the windows of her London house. After being convinced that the shipment had been seized by a French privateer, she was delighted when the jars arrived safely in September 1760. She sent a short note of thanks to Wortley, who replied from London on 16 December.[5] She dutifully wrote again on 12 January to say that she was glad he was again well. He had always been a fussy cataloguer of correspondence, carefully endorsing every letter he received with a date and usually a summary. Her letter of 12 January 1761, however, remains with no endorsement; on 21 January Wortley had died.[6] In his long, elaborate will, drawn up in 1755, Lady Mary

---

[1] 18 Nov. 1760, ii. 379–80.

[2] To Sir J. Steuart, 22 July 1761, ii. 384; to Mackenzie, 6, 28 Mar. 1761 (summaries), CB MS, f. 13.   [3] 17 June 1761, Paston, 523 (date from MS).

[4] 26 Nov. 1760, ii. 381. The Venetians' request was granted, not necessarily through Lady Mary's advocacy (Mackenzie to Pitt, 18 Feb. 1761, SP 92/68).

[5] 5 Oct. 1760, W MS, ii. 257; draft, W MS, i. 145.

[6] W MS, ii. 258–9. Although 1 Jan. is sometimes given as the date of his death, 21 Jan. appears on the plaque erected by Lady Bute in Wortley Chapel. London newspapers reported it as 22 Jan.

was left £1,200 a year, which at her death was to be added to their son's bequest of £1,000 a year. After some specific mention of Lady Bute's children, the bulk of the great fortune went to her and then to her second son, who would take the name of Wortley.[1] In England, where the size of Wortley's estate aroused comment, Elizabeth Montagu speculated on the 'most notable sum'—£800,000 in money and £17,000 a year in land, mines, &c.—and added a moralistic wish that it might 'make his heirs as happy and illustrious as the getting it made him anxious and odious'.[2] His heiress discovered how 'anxious' he had been in building his fortune when she saw that his records of 2,200 acres of wooded land bore a mark for every tree lest he be cheated of one.[3] In his posthumous frugality, he had specified in his will that his funeral should not cost more than £150 and his monument not more than £100.

However Lady Mary felt about her husband, she behaved with the proper decorum for a widow. About six weeks after the news came to her, she had still not recovered her sleep and appetite, she told her daughter.[4] Certainly she waited anxiously for a copy of the will. At the end of February, through Mackenzie in Turin, she received a packet which probably contained her copy. In her opinion, her rascal son had been given more than he deserved, and she regretted not having been left any 'mourning' money since she had no cash for a journey to England to see that the will was duly executed.[5] A month later she was 'resigned' to her ill fortune, for her income was contingent on her giving up all her dower rights. Since the will emphasized that she might retain all her moneys and securities, she complained that Wortley seemed 'to imagine I have sums of money concealed, which I have not, nor ever had any with which I did not acquaint him'. But in general, she informed Mackenzie in Turin, she acquiesced.[6]

Mackenzie wrote to Lord Bute that the will was 'certainly a most extraordinary one, especially with respect to my poor little neighbour here, to whom the testator has indeed been most

[1] Copy of will in Somerset House. M was also allowed to keep all her paraphernalia, jewels, plate, and books.
[2] To her husband, W's cousin, 1762, *Letters*, i. 14–15.
[3] 1774, Coke, *Letters and Journals*, iv. 391–2.
[4] 11 Mar. 1761, Paston, 517.　　　　　　　[5] 5 Mar. 1761, ibid.
[6] 10 Apr. 1761, Paston, 519; to Mackenzie, 28 Mar. 1761, CB MS, f. 13.

unkind, as well as to his worthy son—*mais, patience!*' Less than
two weeks later, he sent his brother a more complete report of
Lady Mary's behaviour.

> She says nothing of what she intends to do, and by what I learn
> from those who see her frequently she does not seem to know her-
> self what she will do. She is so undetermined about everything, she
> makes fifty resolutions every day, and changes them before night.
> I once thought of imparting to her that there was a possibility of
> my being soon where she is, as I know that that would be an
> inducement to her to remain there, which I imagine is what you
> would choose she should do . . . if I learn from a correspondent of
> mine there that there is any likelihood of her moving from thence...
> I believe I shall drop her some hints, from the notion I entertain of
> your sentiments on that subject.[1]

A few years earlier Lord Bute had tried through General
Graeme to persuade Lady Mary to return to England; now he
apparently wanted her to remain in Venice. But by April she
had made up her mind to leave in September and return to
England.[2]

Her son had not stayed in London long after hearing the
disappointing terms of the will; on 19 February he re-entered
the University of Leyden as a student of Oriental languages.[3]
Although Lady Mary assured Lady Bute, 'I never will join with
your profligate brother, and hope you will not compound with
him', she took the initiative of writing to him in March—using
Anderson as intermediary—to tell him of her affliction for his
father's death, and to remind him of his past and present infamous behaviour.[4] He answered with a letter that 'frighted'
her, and she then promised Lady Bute to have nothing more to
do with him. But she again wrote to him in June, again through
Anderson, to beg him to submit to his father's will.[5]

In preparation for her long journey home, she drew up her
own will on 1 April, and told Lady Bute exactly where it was
hidden.[6] She arranged for the furniture of her two houses to be

---

[1] 25 Feb. (by a slip of the pen 'father' instead of 'son'), 7 Mar. 1761, Bute MS.
[2] To Lady Bute, 3 Apr., 20 May 1761, Paston, 518, 522.   [3] *DNB.*
[4] To Lady Bute, 5 Mar. 1761, Paston, 517; 11 Mar. 1761, W MS, iii. 221-2
(frag. in Paston, 517-18); to Anderson 'to be showed my Son', 13 Mar. 1761
(summary), CB MS, f. 13.
[5] To Lady Bute, 29 Apr., [3 May] 1761, Paston, 520, 522-3; to Anderson,
3 June 1761, CB MS, f. 14.
[6] 3 Apr., Paston, 518; 10 Apr. 1761, W MS, iii. 233-4 (frag. in Paston, 519).

sold, and her bulky baggage—including most of her clothes—to be shipped to her later.[1] At least two of her servants accompanied her, her secretary Dr. Moro and her maid. The others were dismissed; one of them, Jean François (Fribourg), she generously pensioned off in Avignon.[2]

At the beginning of September (1761) she set out. Since France was at war with England, she travelled through Germany and Holland, a safe route that also offered her the possibility of seeing Sir James Steuart, who had moved to Holland that spring. By the beginning of October she had reached Augsburg, and three weeks later Rotterdam, after having detoured to Amsterdam in the vain hope of seeing Sir James. 'I began to think we resembled two parallel lines,' she wrote him, 'destined to be always near and never to meet.' As the weeks went by she waited impatiently for an opportunity to sail, but first the wind and tide were against her, and then her maid fell ill.[3] She was impatient to reach London to see her daughter and perhaps attend the wedding of one of her granddaughters.[4] But after her maid recovered from her illness, the storms prevented her crossing. The delay had important consequences.

'I have here neither amusement nor conversation,' she complained to Sir James, 'and am so infected by the climate, that I verily believe, was I to stay long, I should take to smoking and drinking, like the natives.'[5] Fortunately she found one sympathetic person, the Reverend Benjamin Sowden, minister of the English Church in Rotterdam, in whose house she lodged. He was an enlightened and humane member of the learned society of the city, and subsequently a reviewer of foreign books for the *Monthly Review*.[6] If she let him read her Embassy Letters, he then persuaded her that they should be published—as Mary Astell had tried to do. She agreed because she felt her life drawing to an end. (She had told Miss Astell they were 'condemned to obscurity during her life'.)[7] It is a matter of fact that she handed over to him her autograph copy of the letters,

[1] Antonio Fachini to M, W MS, iv. 170–1; Moser de Ailseck to M, 9 Apr. 1762, ibid. 172–3; Walpole to Mann, 29 Jan. 1762, *Letters*, v. 168.
[2] Rigaud-avocat to M, 3 Oct. 1761, 30 Apr. 1762, W MS, iv. 231–4.
[3] To Sir J. Steuart, 1 Oct. 1761, ii. 385; 19 Nov. 1761 (date corrected), ii. 385–6.   [4] ii. 386; Paston, 526.   [5] 26 Dec. 1761, ii. 388.
[6] *Gentleman's Magazine*, lxvi (1796), 356, 385; B. C. Nangle, *The Monthly Review* (1934), 108 ff.   [7] i. 222.

and inscribed on the cover: 'These two volumes are given to
the Rev. Benjamin Sowden, minister at Rotterdam, to be disposed of as he thinks proper. This is the will and design of
M. Wortley Montagu.'[1] The disposal, evidently agreed on ver-
bally, was that the letters should be published posthumously.[2]
She must have known that her daughter and son-in-law would
not permit her to appear publicly as an author, even after her
death.

As the delay lengthened she bolstered her spirits by writing
frequently to Sir James and his wife to assure them she would
look after their affairs in London. The winter snows, her weak
eyesight, worried thoughts, and feeble strength threw her into
a deep depression.[3] Then at the end of December the ice began
to thaw; and on the 31st, with her baggage and servants, she
embarked on a small boat, but the quantities of ice in the sea
forced her to return to Rotterdam. In her impatience she went
down to the port of Helvoetsluys to get passage on any kind of
boat. Finally, on 15 January 1762, the British agent in Rotterdam, acting on orders from the ambassador at The Hague, put
a paquet boat at her disposal to sail 'at her own time'—which
must have been immediately.[4] After almost twenty-three years
in foreign lands, she described her return in a vivid phrase: 'I am
dragging my ragged remnant of life to England.'[5]

---

[1] 11 Dec. 1761, facsimile in 1803 ed., i. 30.
[2] [Rev. George Ashby] *Gentleman's Magazine*, lxxix (1809), 204; lxiv (1794),
194. One detail of his account is improbable: that Sowden's house, where Lady
Mary lodged, was at Courtrai, a town about 90 miles south of Rotterdam.
[3] To Lady F. Steuart, Dec. 1761, ii. 387.
[4] Wolters to Underwood, 1, 15 Jan. 1762, HMC *10th Report*, i (1885), 323,
325.
[5] ii. 385.

XVI. *Last Words*

(1762 ...)

In England at last, soon after the middle of January 1762, Lady Mary went with her servants and baggage to the house which her daughter had rented for her in St. George Street, off Hanover Square. After the spacious Italian houses open to air and sun, she felt confined in the small harpsichord-shaped London town-house. 'I am most handsomely lodged,' she quipped. 'I have two very decent closets and a cupboard on each floor.'[1] Lady Bute lived on South Audley Street, a short distance away, and so she could be near her mother—as much for surveillance, one suspects, as for filial affection. Her attitude toward Lady Mary was reflected in that of her children. Lady Louisa was scolded for reading books, and accused of wanting to be like her grandmother: 'It was this reproach that first informed me I had ever had a grandmother, and I am sure I heartily hated her name. Whatever I wanted to learn, everybody was up in arms to oppose it, and represent that if I indulged in it I should become such a pedant nobody would be able to bear me.'[2] Not only Lady Mary's literary interests offended her conventional daughter; her feuds and eccentricities, as well as Pope's constantly republished satires, kept alive a reputation hardly suitable to the mother-in-law of the King's first minister.

As in Florence, Horace Walpole's curiosity and prejudice had been excited by her imminent arrival in London. When he received a false report of it three months prematurely, he told Mann she had not yet performed 'quarantine for her own dirt'; and to another friend he made an obscene allusion to her alleged sexual appetite.[3] When she actually arrived, he did not delay, but called on her one night within two weeks. As he described

---

[1] Stuart, 117.   [2] *Letters to Louisa Clinton*, ii. 21.
[3] 8 Oct. 1761, *Letters*, v. 127–8; to George Montagu, *Corr.* ix. 392.

the scene, he was admitted into her miserable bedchamber, a
room dimly lighted by only two tallow candles—but he still
managed to see, and then describe in detail, her slatternly
clothes from her head (bound in an old black laced hood) to
her feet. She wore slippers instead of shoes, he reported with
disgust, forgetting that slippers were more appropriate to a
bedchamber. He found that in general her avarice, dirt, and
vivacity had increased. But her face was hardly changed in
twenty years. When he told her so, she was so flattered that she
literally boxed his ear. He had good cause for describing her
as very lively.[1]

Elizabeth Montagu's brother in Italy regretted that Lady
Mary had left Venice, for he had hoped to see 'that extraordinary Phoenomenon'. Mrs. Montagu was luckier. When she
called and was shown into the drawing-room, she was highly
entertained by Lady Mary, who 'neither thinks, speaks, acts
nor dresses like anybody else'. Like Walpole, Mrs. Montagu
observed that she looked no older than when she had left
England, and had an extraordinary vivacity and perhaps a
unique memory.[2] All the world went to do homage to her as
Queen Mother (in Walpole's phrase). Lord Hervey's son, the
Earl of Bristol, who had visited her in Turin and had written
to her after Wortley's death, now asked Lady Bute's permission
to pay his respects.[3] Sir James Caldwell, her Irish admirer from
France, also appeared on the scene to renew their friendship.

He had remained on the Continent until 1749, serving as
aide-de-camp to the King of Sardinia, and then in the army of
Maria Theresa, who created him Count of Milan in the Holy
Roman Empire.[4] But that Imperial title did not satisfy him. He
eagerly sought an Irish peerage, which he almost received in
1760, when the old King's death put an end to his hopes. Now
that his 'old acquaintance and agreeable friend' had returned to
London to be near her illustrious daughter, he travelled over
from Ireland, probably in April, to call on her. On his first visit
he found her extremely well and in good spirits, and they talked
of literary matters. As he described his visit to a friend: 'I am

---

[1] To Mann, 29 Jan., *Letters*, v. 168; to Montagu, 2 Feb. 1762, *Corr*. x. 5.
[2] 4 Sept. 1762, ed. W. Powell Jones, *Huntington Libr. Quart.* iv (1941), 349;
Mrs. Montagu, 16 Feb. 1762, quoted in Paston, 528.
[3] M to Bristol, 2 May 1761 (summary), CB MS, f. 14; Stuart, 96.
[4] *Bull. of Rylands Libr.* xxxv (1952), 213-14.

sure you must often have heard me mention her as one of the greatest geniuses of her time. I have been all this morning endeavouring to persuade her to publish something, but without effect, though I know she writes a great deal and has many excellent performances by her.'[1]

Soon afterwards, when he again visited her, she told him that of her own accord she had spoken about him very favourably to Lord Bute. Did he, she asked, have anything in particular to solicit? He soon admitted his ambition for an Irish peerage. In her estimation, as she had once told her daughter: 'Ever since I knew the world, Irish patents have been hung out to sale, like the laced and embroidered coats in Monmouth-street, and bought up by the same sort of people; I mean those who had rather wear shabby finery than no finery at all.'[2] Still, she assured Caldwell that she would help him, but he would have to keep the matter a secret. Since she was still 'almost a stranger to her family', she told him, it would be wiser if she waited a few months before exerting her influence. He was to go home to Ireland in the meantime, and return to London shortly before Lord Halifax, the Lord Lieutenant, bringing some documents to help his suit. With these instructions he confidently took his leave of her.[3]

After Walpole's first view of Lady Mary, he had pitied Lady Bute, and exclaimed: 'what will the progress be of such a commencement!' But two months later when he saw her again at a party held at her niece the Duchess of Bedford's house, he mended his opinion. She was 'dressed in yellow velvet and sables, with a decent laced head and a black hood, almost like a veil, over her face. She is much more discreet than I expected, and meddles with nothing—but she is woefully tedious in her narrations.'[4] It would seem, from outward appearances, that Lady Bute had succeeded in transforming her mother from a phenomenal curiosity to a properly dignified old lady.

The returned exile herself deserved some pity. After having been in London less than a month, she complained of her discontent, and thought of leaving—perhaps to return to Venice.

[1] To Lord Newtown, Bagshawe MS, B 3/10/595.
[2] 22 June 1750, ii. 194.
[3] [Sept. 1762], Caldwell to Lady Bute, copy in hand of John Hawkesworth, Bagshawe MS, B 3/16/127.   [4] To Mann, 22 Mar. 1762, *Letters*, v. 190.

She confided her unhappiness to her intimate Venetian friend Chiara Michieli. Far from encouraging her, Madame Michieli answered: 'Puisque vous avez eu le bonheur d'arriver saine et sauve entre les bras de votre chère et illustre famille, qui était l'objet de vos souhaits, restez-y, ma chère, croyez-moi: réfléchissant que l'humanité ne doit point aspirer à la félicité dans ce monde lequel pourtant est le meilleur que nous connaissions....'[1] Her daughter's family knew of her discontent too, and believed that had she lived much longer she probably would have gone abroad again.[2]

The members of her 'dear and illustrious family' unfortunately included her son. He had settled in Venice to study oriental languages for his intended journey to the Near East.[3] Since he found his income insufficient, he forged his mother's name to get additional money. 'You have shortened your father's days,' she reproved him, 'and will perhaps have the glory to break your Mother's heart. I will not curse you—God give you a real, not an affected repentance.' She also accused him of producing 'infamous libels' in her name; and she denied their authorship to Lord Bute with a desperate unhappiness: 'I own I am weary of fighting with one hand ty'd behind.'[4] The sentimental nostalgia with which she had anticipated returning home must have seemed absurd now, oppressed as she was between the stringency of a conventional daughter and the trickery of a rascal son.

She had not ceased in her attempt to help Sir James Steuart's family, and assured his wife that in her frequent meetings with Lady Bute she always mentioned their affairs.[5] Her activity for Caldwell, thanks to his testimony, is more clearly documented. He had followed her instructions, and come to London shortly before Lord Halifax. When he called on her, he emphasized how important it was to him and his family that his peerage be granted without delay. Whereupon she pointed out that a financial gratuity would speed up those responsible for it, and that she would gladly lay out the cost and he could reimburse her afterwards. Warmly expressing his obligations to her, he refused

---

[1] 19 Mar. 1762 (answer to M's of 15 Feb.), W MS, iv. 198–9.
[2] Stuart, 116.   [3] Curling, *Montagu*, 163–4.
[4] 3 Mar. 1762, Paston, 529 (date corrected); [n.d.], Paston, 529–30.
[5] 23 Apr. 1762, ii. 390.

to impose in that way; instead, since he had a thousand guinea
note with him, he begged her to use all or part of it for the purpose she suggested. She finally consented, though reluctantly,
and said (according to Caldwell) that 'it was the greatest proof
she could give me of her regard, as she did not know a man in
England to whom she would be an agent on the like occasion
except myself'. Then she advised him to return to Ireland to
make his regiment useful, for she had heard of civil commotions
there. If he had to write to her, he must observe the greatest
secrecy. She took two pieces of paper and wrote on both of
them several code words: 'my Brother for Peerage, Mr. Thomp-
son for Lord Bute, and the Captain for Lord Halifax.' Putting
one piece in her pocket book she gave him the other. He immediately returned to Ireland, after having stayed in London three
months.[1]

Along with this questionable negotiation, she pursued her
incessant activity as a writer. By the end of May she had somehow met one John Lane, with whom she formed a literary
friendship of some sort. When he called on her she presented
him with a sample of her verse. In his preposterously effusive
letter of thanks, he repaid her in kind; but since he ended by
lavishing some of his sycophancy on Lord Bute, one suspects
that he looked for more substantial rewards in the friendship
than verse couplets.[2]

Lady Mary still went about in society. When Mrs. Montagu
met her at Lady Bute's house in June she looked well. It was thus
all the more shocking that about the middle of the month she
could no longer conceal her illness, a breast cancer of terrible
malignancy. Nothing could be done for her, and so she was
given doses of hemlock to free her from pain. Although fully
aware that death was approaching, she remained very placid
and easy, behaving with great fortitude. She had lived long
enough, she told those around her.[3]

A new will was drawn up for her, and signed on 23 June. As
she had promised, she left Lady Bute her whole estate except
for several specific bequests: a ring to Lady Oxford's daughter,

[1] Caldwell to Lady Bute, cited.
[2] Lane to M, 1 June 1762, Paston, 530–1.
[3] Mrs. Montagu, 10 July, Oct. 1762, *Letters*, i. 25, 35; Walpole to Mann,
31 July 1762, *Letters*, v. 224.

another to Madame Michieli, a gold snuff-box to Mackenzie, £500 to Dr. Moro for seven years' faithful service. She treated her other servants liberally, leaving all her clothes and linens to her maid, and ten guineas above a year's wages to the remaining servants, with passage home added for the foreign ones. Casually inserted amidst these bequests was the most dramatic one of all: 'I give to my son Edward Wortley, *one guinea*, his father having amply provided for him.'[1] That bequest—instead of simply leaving him nothing—has usually been interpreted as a sign of her vindictiveness.[2] But she probably followed the layman's misconception that it would prevent him from contesting the will. She could not, in any case, keep from him the great benefit which his father's generosity and her death would bring: her income of £1,200 a year. And that benefit, she knew, would come to him before very long.

At the beginning of July she could still write, though with difficulty; and she sent a short note to Lady Frances Steuart to reassure her that her affairs would be attended to.[3] Lady Frances's son was then in London, and when he called at Lady Mary's house and sent up his name, he was immediately summoned to her bedroom. There he saw her surrounded by her relatives, including Lord and Lady Bute. She received him in the most affectionate manner, and ordered all the others to leave the room instantly, saying, 'My dear young friend has come to see me before I die, and I desire to be left alone with him.'[4] It was a scene of both sentimental and stoic nobility.

A comic theme was also being enacted in the drama of her death. At the end of July, while her friend at Castle Caldwell was listening to his wife read a letter from her sister in London, one bit of news made him sit up: 'that Lady Mary was given over by her physician'. He immediately took post horses, and arrived in London three days later. At her house he discovered that her physician was his friend Mr. Middleton.[5] She was very weak

---

[1] Copy in Somerset House; printed in *Notes & Queries*, 2 S. x (1860), 507; repr. in 1887 ed. 1. lxviii, n.
[2] Walpole to Mann, 26 Sept. 1762, *Letters*, v. 250; Paston, 532, n. 1.
[3] 2 July 1762, ii. 390.
[4] *Original Letters from Lady Mary Wortley Montague to Sir James and Lady Frances Steuart* (1818), iv–v.
[5] David Middleton (1703–85), Principal Surgeon and Sergeant-Surgeon to the King.

and unable to receive visitors, but Middleton spoke to her about Caldwell. She remembered him in a friendly, affectionate manner, and sent out word that she had neither forgotten nor neglected his affair. She also hoped to be able to see him in a few days. Since he had left Ireland without permission while under military orders, he had to post back the same day. Before going he told Middleton of the entire transaction, relying on his professional discretion. But Middleton carried discretion beyond Caldwell's intention. Fearful that Lady Mary's Italian secretary, of whom he had a very low opinion, might take possession of the thousand guinea note, he wrote to the banker on whom it was drawn to stop payment and detain the person presenting it. When Caldwell was informed of this safeguard, he was shocked to think that his transaction with Lady Mary would thus become known—and misinterpreted—at the expense of her reputation. He therefore informed the banker by the fastest mail to honour the note without question, for, he later declared to Lady Bute, he would have suffered infinitely less by losing a thousand guineas than by causing injury to Lady Mary's reputation.[1]

Lady Mary, of course, knew nothing of all this confusion. To one whose death-bed thoughts were that she had lived long enough, it would have made little difference. She lay quietly, drugged to an easy comfort. On 21 August 1762 she died.

The last words of many others have been recorded, and they illuminate their speakers' characters. Joseph Addison's 'See in what peace a Christian can die' and Lord Chesterfield's 'Give Dayrolles a chair' are eloquent final signatures. Algarotti, who died two years after Lady Mary, did not have her fortitude: 'Mourir, c'est bien, mais souffrir tant!'[2] What were Lady Mary's final words, one wonders? They are nowhere unequivocally recorded. She had lived long enough, Walpole reported; and she may have repeated that dry comment as she looked back at a long full life, and faced death with the equanimity of the stoic Epictetus, whom she had translated in her girlhood. Or: 'My dear young friend has come to see me before I die, and I desire to be left alone with him.' That was one of her last statements, an imperious command uttered to England's Prime Minister in order to honour the son of her affectionate friends.

---

[1] Caldwell to Lady Bute, cited. [2] Treat, *Algarotti*, 209.

But the closest to her actual dying words comes from Walpole: at her death she 'expressed great anxiety' that the two volumes of letters she had given to the clergyman in Holland should be published. Her family were in terror lest they should be.[1] It was a fitting conclusion to her whole life. For although she defied the conventions of her social class, she expressed one of the strongest, most persistent impulses of her long erratic life: her desire to win fame as a woman of letters.

On 22 Aug 1762, the day after her death, she was buried in the vault of Grosvenor Chapel, close to the fashionable square.[2] But even death had not endowed her with respectability. Within six weeks Walpole reported that Lady Bute had tried to obtain the volumes which had been given to the clergyman in Holland, but that the man at first proved inflexible.[3] When the Rev. Mr. Sowden heard of his generous friend's death, he apparently notified the family of her request, and asked if they had any objection to his publishing the letters. They most decidedly objected; and after negotiating for six months they settled the compensation he was to receive. For £500 he turned the volumes over to Lady Bute.[4] It seemed as though Lady Mary's ultimate attempt to win literary fame would be frustrated.

The affair of the Embassy Letters was not the only one of her problems bequeathed (with her estate) to her anxious daughter. Caldwell's note for the thousand guineas had not yet been turned in at his banker's; nor had he received an Irish peerage. He decided to reveal the whole transaction to Lady Bute. Distrustful of his own ability as a writer, he employed Dr. John Hawkesworth, the well-known literary journalist whom he knew, to set down his case in a long letter. 'Thus Madam,' he concluded, 'have I given you with the most scrupulous exactness and the most open sincerity an account of my whole transaction with a Lady whose friendship I always considered as an honour and whose loss at this moment I regret with undis-

---

[1] To Mann, 3 Oct. 1762, *Letters*, v. 258. One death-bed remark frequently attributed to her—'It has all been very interesting'—comes from Iris Barry's *Portrait of Lady Mary Montagu* (1928), but it is clearly fictitious.

[2] MS Register Book of Burials, St. George's, Hanover Square, p. 13.

[3] To Mann, 3 Oct. 1762, cited.

[4] [George Ashby], *Gentleman's Mag.* lxiv (1794), 195 (confirmed, ibid. 305); Stuart, 83.

sembled sorrow. Your Ladyship has seen to what lengths her
zeal to serve me carried her, and if you should in tender regard
to her memory and in disinterested generosity to me. . . .' His
letter ends there, with room no doubt for a personal flourish
before his signature. As a result of his application, the thousand-
guinea note was returned to him.[1] Lady Bute's disinterested
generosity did not go beyond that; and he remained for the rest
of his life a mere baronet.

With Caldwell's note returned, and with Sowden's manuscript volumes in her possession, Lady Bute might hope that her
mother would be decently forgotten. But what must have been
her terror when she read in *The London Chronicle* of 7–10 May
1763 that 'This Day was published' the *Letters of the Right
Honourable Lady M----y W-----y M------e*!

As Lady Bute knew if she had read the letters in the manuscript volumes, they did not contain the racy scandal and gossip
of her mother's private letters and diary. Instead they showed
Lady Mary as she wished to appear before the world, a brilliant
and graceful *bel esprit* on a tour through foreign lands. She had
succeeded, after all, in her death-bed wish. But how had the
letters been published when the two manuscript volumes lay
locked up in Lady Bute's care? The honest, naïve Rev. Mr.
Sowden explained to her that while the volumes were still in
his possession two English gentlemen called to look at them,
and contrived to have him called away. When he returned they
had disappeared with the volumes, which they brought back
the next day with many apologies. Presumably the letters had
been copied out during the night.[2]

Lady Mary's success as a letter-writer was instantaneous.[3]
The first edition was quickly sold out, and a second issued.
It was followed by further editions to meet the enthusiastic
demand. The letters were extravagantly praised in the two
leading monthly book reviews; in the *Critical Review* Smollett

[1] Diaries of William Windham, 1772, HMC *12th Report*, ix (1891), 210 (the
Irishman unidentified). In 1763 Sir James Steuart was allowed to return to
Scotland, partly through Lady Mary's efforts (Steuart, *Works*, vi. 373).

[2] Dallaway, 'Memoir', 1803 ed., i. 25–26; [Ashby], *Gentleman's Mag.* lxxix
(1809), 204. John Cleland is usually credited with 'editing' the letters (Dallaway, 24; Stuart, 84).

[3] The most recent critique: W. H. Irving, *The Providence of Wit in the
English Letter Writers* (1955), 205–15.

wrote that the letters were 'never equalled by any letter-writer
of any sex, age, or nation'.[1] Voltaire confirmed the high praise,
and spread it on the Continent through the *Gazette Littéraire
de l'Europe*; her letters, he said, were far superior to Madame
de Maintenon's and Madame de Sévigné's (whose writings
interest only their own nation) because they seemed written
for all nations wishing to be instructed.[2] Other eminent men of
letters found the letters irresistible. They were the only work
Dr. Johnson read for sheer pleasure; and Edward Gibbon,
when he finished reading them, exclaimed, 'What fire, what
ease, what knowledge of Europe and of Asia!'[3]

But Lady Bute's sense of propriety was offended. All the
public acclaim (and the private praise that she must have heard)
did not alter her belief that it was unseemly for Lady Mary to
be an author, an idea which remained in her family until the
middle of the next century. The popularity of the Embassy
Letters (in 1763) encouraged an editor, supposedly John
Cleland, to fabricate an additional volume in 1767, containing
five probably spurious letters along with an authentic and previously printed essay, letter, and some verse. As the letters continued to be printed, reprinted, and pirated, her verse also
became more popular and was collected and reprinted (in 1768,
1781, 1785). None of these publications had Lady Bute's sanction. Shortly before she died, in 1794, she burned the volu-
minous diary kept by Lady Mary from her marriage until the
end of her life.[4] There still remained in the family's possession
a large number of her private letters and poems.

Lady Bute's eldest son, who was raised to a marquess, was not
any more liberal than his mother in the matter of publishing his
grandmother's works, but he was persuaded to do so in 1803
through a strange circumstance. As he explained to his relation
John Erskine of Mar, the publisher Richard Phillips had 'purchased for a large sum nearly two hundred' letters of Wortley,
Lady Mary, and their friends, of so private a nature that to get
them out of his hands, he consented to a general authorized
edition.[5] Lord Bute explained to another friend that the barter

---

[1] xv (1763), 426.   [2] *Œuvres Complètes*, xxv. 163.
[3] Mrs. Piozzi in *Johnsonian Misc.*, ed. G. B. Hill (1897), i. 319; Gibbon,
17 Feb. 1764, *Private Letters*, ed. R. E. Prothero (1896), i. 53.
[4] Stuart, 63–64.   [5] 8 Apr. 1803, Mar and Kellie MS.

had taken place and authority granted in order to get hold of letters 'relating to private transactions of her son's, a quondam theft no doubt'.[1] Before letting the editor John Dallaway see the manuscripts, Lord Bute put aside the letters he wished to burn—to keep his descendants from letting them fall into 'the hands of a future Mr. Phillips'; and he then allowed the collection to pass the inspection of his uncle the Bishop of Armagh.[2] The edition of Lady Mary's *Works*, in five volumes, exhibited for the first time the wide range of her literary skill. 'What a fascinating Creature *'tis*!!' exclaimed Mrs. Piozzi when she read them.[3] But the edition was shockingly incompetent; Dallaway had been allowed to proceed by guesswork, according to Lady Louisa Stuart, who relinquished her plan of improving the next edition because he was such a 'decided blockhead'. More justly Byron blamed the 'proud and foolish family' for the blundering edition.[4]

The faults of that edition were corrected to some extent by Lady Mary's great-grandson Lord Wharncliffe. In 1835 the publisher Richard Bentley offered him £250 for the copyright; he hesitated until the offer was raised to £300, and then accepted.[5] Although he retained Dallaway's inaccurate memoir, he added some notes by his cousin the Rev. Stuart Corbett and the valuable 'Introductory Anecdotes' by his aunt Lady Louisa Stuart, who was well qualified by talent and knowledge, having been Lady Bute's confidant and the only one of the family allowed to read the diary later burned. Since Lord Wharncliffe hoped to rescue Lady Mary's reputation, he tried to suppress the scandals of her Italian sojourn—in particular her friendships with Count Palazzi and with Algarotti. His efforts make an intriguing story. He had found among Lady Mary's manuscripts the 'Italian Memoir', and he merely described it very briefly in his edition. Soon afterwards, when he sent the document to Lord Mahon, the historian, for his 'private and exclu-

---

[1] To the Earl of Fife, 11 June 1804, MS formerly owned by Lord Wharncliffe. The barter is mentioned by Isaac Disraeli in *Curiosities of Lit.* (1870), iii. 208.
[2] An inscription in 1803 ed., Deering Library of Northwestern University.
[3] *Thraliana*, ed. K. C. Balderston (1951), 1041.
[4] To Scott, 4 Dec. 1820, Scott's *Letters 1819–21*, 309 n.; Byron, *Letters and Journals*, ed. R. E. Prothero (1898–1901), iv. 184.
[5] 31 Dec. 1835, 18 Feb. 1836, Wharncliffe MS 439.

sive perusal', Lord Mahon urged him to publish it for its authenticity and importance.[1] But it did not appear in his second edition; and Lord Mahon was subsequently informed that it had been lost or mislaid. Today, through the enlightened generosity of the Wharncliffe family, it lies in the Sheffield Central Library.

The drama of Lady Mary's letters to Algarotti took a different turn, involving Byron, who was a great admirer of 'the charming Mary Montagu' and of her extraordinary talents.[2] In 1817, while in Venice, he tried to find out about her life there, but—as he wrote to John Murray, his publisher and friend—nothing was remembered about her, 'for the story of to-day is succeeded by the scandal of to-morrow; and the wit, and beauty, and gallantry, which might render your countrywoman notorious in her own country, must have been *here* no great distinction—because the first is in no request, and the two latter are common to all women, or at least the last of them'. Byron knew Dr. Francesco Aglietti, a Brescian physician who had edited Algarotti's works and owned his manuscripts. Since many of the letters were from English correspondents, the doctor decided to sell them in England, and sent them there in the care of an Italian dealer. Byron suggested to Murray that he should purchase the letters, which (he thought) might make up a volume if a good editor arranged them and wrote the preface and notes. He was especially struck by the six letters to Algarotti from Lady Mary—'the *French* not good, but the sentiments beautiful'.[3] A few months later he again told Murray about the Lady Mary letters: 'They are very pretty and passionate; it is a pity that a piece of one of them is lost. Algarotti seems to have treated her ill; but she was much his senior, and all women are used ill—or say so, whether they are or not.' Still acting as go-between, he proposed that Murray should pay Dr. Aglietti fifty pounds in books and money.[4] Accordingly Murray bought the collection, and placed it in the archives of his publishing house at 50 Albemarle Street. Then, almost twenty years later, when Lord Wharncliffe's edition appeared, Murray

---

[1] 22, 23 Mar. 1837, Wharncliffe MS 510.
[2] *Don Juan*, v. iii; *Lett. and Journ.*, v. 566.
[3] 3 Dec. 1817, 12 Apr. 1818, ibid. iv. 183–4, 223–4.
[4] 17 July, 26 Aug. 1818, ibid. 246–7, 251–2.

remembered the Lady Mary letters, and generously sent them to him. But Lord Wharncliffe returned them with his thanks: 'It did not appear to me . . . that they could be advantageously made use of in the 2nd edition, and I did not therefore avail myself of the kind permission which you gave me to print the whole or such parts of them as I thought proper.'[1] Obviously he did not think it proper (in another sense) to publish his ancestress's letters to a young Italian unmentioned by her editors and biographers. And so the letters, an important group in the series, remained in the Murray archives.[2]

Lord Wharncliffe's edition was the last in which a member of Lady Mary's family served her as editor. Since then W. Moy Thomas and Miss E. M. Symonds have used the Wortley Manuscripts, which had passed to the Earl of Harrowby. The unrestricted generosity and vision of the descendant-owners is proof that Lady Mary can no longer be cautiously regarded as merely a member of an aristocratic family. This extraordinary woman had gone beyond the boundaries of her time and class.

[1] 6 Dec. 1837, Murray MS.

[2] Twenty-four of the letters, formerly owned by Dr. Aglietti, turned up in Venice in 1850, and at Sotheby's in 1938, when they were bought for the Bodleian.

Index

M indicates Lady Mary Wortley Montagu; W indicates her husband, Mr. Edward Wortley Montagu, senior.

PRINTED IN
GREAT BRITAIN
AT THE
UNIVERSITY PRESS
OXFORD
BY
CHARLES BATEY
PRINTER
TO THE
UNIVERSITY